Essays on
Urban Spatial
Structure

Essays on Urban Spatial Structure

by John F. Kain

With Contributions by:

David Harrison, Jr.
Gregory K. Ingram
John R. Meyer
John H. Niedercorn
Joseph J. Persky
John M. Quigley

Ballinger Publishing Company ● Cambridge, Mass.
A Subsidiary of J.B. Lippincott Company

Copyright © 1975 by Ballinger Publishing Company. All rights reserved. No part of this publication may be reproduced, stored in a retrieval system, or transmitted in any form or by any means, electronic mechanical photocopy, recording or otherwise, without the prior written consent of the publisher.

International Standard Book Number: 0–88410–411–7

Library of Congress Catalog Card Number: 75–6871

Printed in the United States of America

Library of Congress Cataloging in Publication Data

Kain, John F
   Essays on urban spatial structure.

   1. Urban economics—Addresses, essays, lectures. I. Harrison, David, 1946–   II. Title.
HT321.K34   330.9'172'4   75–6871
ISBN 0–88410–411–7

To Bob and Mary Nick

Acknowledgments

This book contains a collection of essays written over the period of more than a decade. The obligations I have incurred to students, colleagues and several research assistants over this period are too numerous to list. I hope these many unnamed contributors will not be offended by this general acknowledgement of their assistance. In addition, a number of persons made more recent contributions to the preparation of this volume and its introductory essay. John E. Jackson, Gary R. Fauth, Robert C. Schafer, and Laura Steig made numerous suggestions that greatly improved the overall organization of the book and read and commented on one or more drafts of the introductory essay. In addition I owe a substantial debt to Pattie Beckett and Madeleine Lane, who made major and essential contributions to the preparation of both the introductory essay and to the editing of the remaining essays.

In addition to the individuals identified above, I would like to thank the editors and publishers of several professional journals, conference proceedings, and collections, who permitted me to use previously published material in this book. For example, Chapters One and Five are adapted from papers with the same titles published in Volume nine (1962) and Volume eleven (1963) of the *Regional Science Association Papers.* Similarly, Chapter Two is based on material first published as "The Commuting and Residential Decisions of Central Business District Workers," in *Transportation Economics* (New York, National Bureau of Economic Research, Copyright ©, 1965, by National Bureau of Economic Research) and Chapter Three is based on material published as "A Contribution to the Urban Transportation Debate: An Econometric Model of Urban Residential and Travel Behavior," *The Review of Economics and Statistics,* Vol. XLVI, No. 1 (February, 1964).

The first part of Chapter Four, *The Distribution and Movement of Jobs and Industry* appears in almost the same form as it was published in *The Metropolitan Enigma: Inquiries in the Nature and Dimensions of America's*

"Urban Crisis", James Q. Wilson (ed.) (Cambridge, Mass.: Harvard University Press, 1968), © Copyright 1968 by the President and Fellows of Harvard College, © Copyright 1967 by the Chamber of Commerce, U.S.A., while Chapter Six combines material from two previously published papers, "The Commuting and Residential Decisions of Central Business District Workers," cited previously, and "Effect of Housing Market Segregation on Urban Development," published in the *1969 Conference Proceedings,* United States Savings and Loan League, May 7-9, 1969.

Chapter Seven is an only slightly modified version of a paper by John Quigley and myself published in the June 1972 issue of the *American Economic Review* and the first part of Chapter Eight is a more extensively revised version of the *Quarterly Journal of Economics* titled "Housing Segregation, Negro Employment, and Metropolitan Decentralization". Chapter Nine, "Alternatives to the Gilded Ghetto," was first published in the *Public Interest*, Number 14, (Winter 1969), 74-87, Copyright ©, 1969 by National Affairs, Inc.

Chapter Ten "The NBER Urban Simulation Model as a Theory of Urban Spatial Structure," is adapted from a paper of the same title which appeared in a conference volume edited by Alan A. Brown, Joseph A. Licare, and Eugene Neuberger, of *Urban and Social Economics in Market and Planned Economies* (New York: Praeger Publishers, Inc., 1974), © Copyright 1974 by Praeger Publishers, Inc. Chapter Eleven is practically identical to a paper by the same name published in the January 1974 issue of the *Journal of Urban Economics,* Chapter Twelve is a somewhat more modified version of a paper by the same name published in the June 1970 issue of the *Journal of the American Statistical Association,* Chapter Thirteen is a somewhat condensed version of a paper bearing the same title published in the June 1973 issue of the *American Real Estate and Urban Economics Association Journal,* and Chapter Fourteen is a shortened and edited version of a paper that appeared in the May 1974 issue of *The Journal of Finance.*

Of the remaining three essays, Chapter Fifteen makes extensive use of material included in an earlier paper, "The Analysis of Metropolitan Transportation Systems" published in a conference volume edited by Thomas A. Goldman, Washington Operations Research Council, *Cost-Effectiveness Analysis: New Approaches in Decision Making* (New York: Frederick A. Praeger, 1967 © Copyright,) 1967 by Frederick A. Praeger, Inc.; Chapter Sixteen reprints a paper by the same title published in the summer 1972 issue of *Public Policy;* and Chapter Seventeen "Transportation and Poverty" was first published in *The Public Interest,* Number 18 (Winter 1970), 75-88, Copyright © 1970 by National Affairs, Inc.

Table of Contents

List of Figures   xiii

List of Tables   xvii

Introduction   1

I. Residential and Commuting Decisions   27

Chapter One
The Journey to Work as a Determinant of
Residential Location   29

Chapter Two
Commuting and Residential Decisions of
Central Business District Workers   53

Chapter Three
An Econometric Model of Urban Residential
and Travel Behavior   65

II. The Location of Jobs   77

Chapter Four
The Distribution and Movement of Jobs and
Industry   79

Chapter Five
An Econometric Model of Metropolitan Development
with John H. Niedercorn   115

ix

III. Effects of Racial Discrimination 131

Chapter Six
Theories of Residential Location and
Realities of Race 133

Chapter Seven
Housing Market Discrimination, Homeownership,
and Savings Behavior — *with John M. Quigley* 161

Chapter Eight
Housing Market Discrimination and Negro
Employment 175

Chapter Nine
Alternatives to the Gilded Ghetto
with Joseph J. Persky 199

IV. Analysis of Urban Housing Markets 211

Chapter Ten
The NBER Urban Simulation Model as a Theory
of Urban Spatial Structure
with Gregory K. Ingram 213

Chapter Eleven
Cumulative Urban Growth and Urban
Density Functions — *with David Harrison, Jr.* 233

Chapter Twelve
Measuring the Value of Housing Quality
with John M. Quigley 261

Chapter Thirteen
A Simple Model of Housing Production
with Gregory K. Ingram 277

Chapter Fourteen
What Should America's Housing Policy Be? 291

V. Urban Transportation 305

Chapter Fifteen
Comparative Costs of Alternative Urban
Transport Technologies 307

Chapter Sixteen
How to Improve Urban Transportation at
Practically No Cost   323

Chapter Seventeen
Transportation and Poverty
with John R. Meyer   341

Appendix A   353

Appendix B   357

Notes   363

Index   407

About the Authors   411

List of Figures

1–1   Total Iso-Location Rent Curves   33
1–2   Marginal Location Rent and Transportation Cost Functions   34
1–3   Proportion of the Central Business District's Low, Medium, and High Income Workers Residing in Each Residential Ring   40
1–4   Percentage of Ring 2 and Ring 6 Workers Residing in Each Ring, by Structure Type   50
2–1   Cumulative Percentage Travel Times and Distances for Chicago and Detroit Central Business District Workers   56
2–2   Percentage of Chicago and Detroit Central Business District Workers Residing in Each Structure Type   57
2–3   Percentage of Automobile Commuters in Each of Chicago's Residence Areas, by Percentage of Area's Single Family Dwelling Units   59
4–1   Construction of Public and Private Industrial Buildings in the United States, 1915–1965   82
4–2   Major Geographic Districts of the City of Chicago, by Postal Zone   95
4–3   Total Person-Trip Destinations: Chicago   98
5–1   An Econometric Model of Metropolitan Development   117
6–1   Negro Workers Residing in Each Detroit Analysis Area as a Percentage of All Workers Residing in the Analysis Area, 1953   147
6–2   Negro Workers Residing in Each Chicago Analysis Area as a Percentage of All Workers Residing in the Analysis Area, 1956   148
6–3   Percentage of White and Negro Central Business District Workers Residing in Each Two Mile Distance Ring from the Chicago and Detroit Centers   149

6–4   Percentages of Chicago White and Nonwhite Central Business
        District Workers Residing in Each Sector, 1956   150
6–5   Percentages of Chicago White and Nonwhite Sector O
        Workers Residing in Each Sector, 1956   151
8–1   Cumulative Manufacturing Employment by Distance from
        the Ghetto Centroid, 1950 and 1960   188
10–1   Block Diagram of Submodels as Encountered in NBER
        Model   216
10–2   Relation of Submodels to Demand, Supply, and Market
        Clearing Sectors   218
10–3   House Prices   221
10–4   Travel Costs   222
10–5   Gross Prices   222
10–6   House Prices and Travel Costs for Two Workplaces   223
10–7   Gross Prices for Two Workplaces   223
11–1   Percent of the Total Housing Stock in Boston and Los
        Angeles, 1960, by Time Period in Decades   236
11–2   Times Trends for Areas of 100 000 Dwelling Units: Compari-
        son of the Two Formulations   240
11–3   Scatter Diagram of Estimated Gross Density by Distance and
        Time Period: Chicago, pre-1879–1960   244
11–4   Estimated Density Functions for Denver in 1910   250
11–5   Estimated Density Functions for Denver in 1960   252
12–1   Value of Owner-Occupied Homes at Alternative Levels of
        Quality and Size   273
12–2   Monthly Rent at Alternative Levels of Quality and Size   275
13–1   Rents, Structure Services, and Neighborhood Quality   279
13–2   Production Functions for Two Output Levels and Two
        Structure Types   280
13–3   Structure Life as a Function of Operating and Maintenance
        Inputs   281
13–4   Present Value of Operating and Maintenance Costs   282
13–5   Present Value of Rent Streams Over Structure Lives   283
13–6   Maximum Present Value Obtainable by Activity and Rent
        Level   284
13–7   Structure Service Level Produced by Structure Types S_1 and
        S_2 as Rents Vary   286
13–8   Relation Between Rents and Structure Level Mix Produced
        at Times t_0 and t_1 287
13–9   Production Functions Subject to Building Code Restrictions   289
15–1   Line Haul Systems: Ten Mile Route Length With Complete
        Two Way Service   310

15–2   Low Cost Line Haul Systems: Complete Two Way Service,
        Ten Mile Route Length   311
15–3   Residential Cost Relationships Under Different Trip Origina-
        tion Densities and Volumes Per Block   318
15–4   Comparative Costs of Downtown Distribution Modes   320

List of Tables

1-1   Purpose of Trips Originating in the Dwelling Unit in 38 Cities   31
1-2   Proportion of Males and Females Residing in Each Distance Ring, by Ring of Employment   39
1-3   Ranked Residential Distributions for Occupational Groups Employed in Ring   41
1-4   Rank Order Coefficients Between Occupations Ranked by Income and Occupations Ranked by Rate of Residential Selection, for All Employment and Residence Rings: All Workers   42
1-5   Rank Order Coefficients Between Occupations Ranked by Income and Occupations Ranked by Rate of Residential Selection, for All Employment and Residence Rings: Male Workers Only   42
1-6   Cumulative Percentages of Ring 1 Workers Residing in Rings 1 Through 6, by Family Size   44
1-7   Cumulative Percentages of Ring 2 Workers Residing in Rings 1 Through 6, by Family Size   44
1-8   Cumulative Percentages of Ring 5 Workers Residing in Rings 1 Through 6, by Family Size   45
1-9   Cumulative Percentages of Ring 6 Workers Residing in Rings 1 Through 6, by Family Size   46
1-10 Percentage of Inner Employment Ring Workers Residing in Each Ring, by Structure Type   47
1-11 Percentage of Outer Employment Ring Workers Residing in Each Ring, by Structure Type   48
1-12 Percentage Residing in Each Structure Type, by Employment Ring   49

2–1   Percentage of Detroit White Workers Using Public Transit, by Workplace Ring and Residence Type   58

2–2   Percentage of Chicago Central Business District Workers Residing in Various Structure Types, by Travel Mode Combinations   60

2–3   Percentage of Chicago Business District Workers Using Each Mode at Their Residences and Workplaces   61

2–4   Percentage of Chicago Workers Employed in Sector O Using Each Mode at Their Residences and Workplaces   62

2–5   Percentage of Chicago Workers Using Each Combination of Origin and Destination Modes, by Workplace Location and Residence Type   63

3–1   Elasticities at the Sample Means for Equations (3.9a) Through (3.12)   73

4–1   Mean Yearly Value of Construction Put in Place, by Period   83

4–2   Value of New Nonresidential Construction and Number of New Nonresidential Structures During 1939–1946   85

4–3   Mean SMSA, Central City, and Ring Employment and Population in 1948 and Central City and Ring Shares   87

4–4   Estimated Mean Annual Percentage Changes in Population and Employment for the Central Cities and Suburban Rings of 40 Large SMSAs   87

4–5   Estimated Mean Annual Absolute Changes in Population and Employment for Central Cities and Suburban Rings of 40 Large SMSAs   89

4–6   Estimated Number of Central City and Suburban Rings Having Employment and Population Declines   91

4–7   Estimated Mean Annual Percentage Changes in Employment and Population for the Central Cities and Suburban Rings of 40 Large SMSAs   92

4–8   Estimated Mean Annual Absolute Changes in Employment and Population for the Central Cities and Suburban Rings of 40 Large SMSAs   93

4–9   Annual Absolute and Percentage Change in Employment by Subarea: Chicago 1958–1963   96

4–10 Suburban Ring Share of SMSA Employment and Population   97

4–11 Yearly Percentage and Absolute Changes in Central City and Suburban Employment   101

4–12 Central Office "Mover Firms" Locating in New Geographic Areas, 1950 and 1960   103

4–13 Thirty Large Metropolitan Areas: Change in Employment   106

4–14 Employment, by Industry, in the Cities of Newark and St. Louis, and in Their Metropolitan Areas   109

4–15	Job Trends and Structural Changes in Eleven Large Cities	111
4–16	Covered Employment in Newark, New Jersey	112
4–17	Private Employment Change in Eight Major Cities, 1970–1971	113
6–1	Percent of White and Negro Families Living in the Suburban Ring of the Ten Largest Urbanized Areas	136
6–2	Ghetto Housing Supply by Source and Region	139
6–3	Quartile Distance Time and of Travel for Central Business District Commuters, by Race and Residence Structure Type	152
6–4	Percentages of Chicago and Detroit White and Negro Central Business District Workers Residing in Various Structure Types	153
6–5	Change in White and Nonwhite Central City and Suburban Ring Population, 1950–1960	156
7–1	Models of Homeownership and Purchase	165
7–2	Coefficients and *t*-Ratios of Race Variable for Alternative Specifications of Income: OLS and GLS	166
7–3	Actual and Expected Ownership Rates of Negro Households by Metropolitan Area	169
7–4	Means and Standard Deviations of Variables Used in Intercity Regressions	171
8–1	Geographic Distribution of Nonwhite Employment by Occupation and Industry: Chicago	182
8–2	Coefficients of Determination and Elasticities for Distance to Major and Distance to Ghetto Centroid Models by Occupation and Industry Group	183
8–3	Estimates of Nonwhite Job Losses for Chicago and Detroit Assuming a Uniform Residential Distribution of Nonwhites	185
8–4	Total Actual and Estimated Negro Manufacturing Employment in the Chicago Metropolitan Area: 1950 and 1960	189
10–1	Transportation Cost Array	227
11–1	Cross-Section Models of Net Residential Density	241
11–2	Illustrative Computations of Density Gradients: Chicago	242
11–3	Estimated Density Functions for Selected Urban Areas, 1960	245
11–4	Comparison of Muth, Barr, Mills, and Harrison-Kain Estimated Density Functions	247
11–5	Historical Changes in Density Functions, Mills and Harrison-Kain Models: 1910, 1920, 1930, 1950, 1960	250
11–6	Denver Development 1910–1960, Mills Estimates	251
11–7	Denver Development Pre-1879–1960, Harrison-Kain Estimates	253
11–8	Historical Changes in Chicago Density Function, for Model Elaborations, 1920, 1930, 1945, 1950, and 1960	256

11–9   Percentage of Housing Units Added in Each Time Period by
        Distance from the Loop, Chicago   259
11–10   Average Population Per Dwelling Unit by Distance from the
        Loop, Chicago, 1940, 1950, and 1960   259
12–1   Factor Loadings on Individual Quality Variables   264
12–2   Regression Equations for City Renter and Owner Markets   267
12–3   Regression Equations for Rentar Model With Suburban
        Observations, School, and Crime Variables Deleted   271
12–4   Regression Equations for Owner Model with Suburban
        Observations, School, and Crime Variables Deleted   273
16–1   Vehicle Volumes at Different Performance Speeds and
        Bus-Auto Mixes   332
16–2   Passenger Volumes at Different Performance Speeds and
        Bus-Auto Mixes   333
16–3   Summary of Estimated Additional Capital Cost of Traveled
        Way and Estimated Annual Operating Cost of Surveillance
        and Control System for the Bus-Freeway System   337
16–4   Estimated Costs of the Freeway Rapid Transit System in 20
        Large Cities.   338

Introduction

This book is comprised of 17 essays which summarize more than a decade of research on various aspects of urban economic analysis and policy. Perspective on the essays is provided by an examination of the reasons for the late emergence of urban economics as a field of specialization in economics, its birth in the late 1950s, its vigorous development during the mid–1960s, and its abrupt decline or reduced growth in the first part of the decade of the 1970s.[1] In each case the explanation lies outside the economics profession, in the concerns of the larger society.

The interest among economists in explaining the physical growth and geographic arrangement of activities within large metropolitan areas that emerged during the second half of the 1960 decade was due to the widespread popular concern and interest in the problems of urban growth and development that followed World War II. After experiencing only minimal physical growth for a decade and a half, first as a result of the Great Depression and then as a result of wartime controls, America's cities literally seemed to explode after World War II.

Fed by 15 years of pent-up demand, by large stocks of wartime consumer savings, and by a variety of supportive government programs, urban areas grew at an unprecedented rate and extent. To many contemporary observers and opinion leaders, this postwar development seemed a sharp break with the past, ugly in form and wasteful. Actually, as several of the analyses presented in this book illustrate, the pattern of urban development after World War II was not nearly so much a break with the past as many contemporary observers presumed, and the evidence on the alleged inefficiency of postwar development is hardly clear-cut. In particular, the urban development that followed the war bore more than a passing similarity to the pattern of urban growth during the 1920s, which reflected long-term trends in the growth of technology and income. Given the parallels between the 1920s and the postwar period, it is not terribly surprising that the historical antecedents to modern urban economics are to be found in the writings of economists during the 1920s, rather than the intervening period.

Robert Murray Haig's work, in particular, bears a surprisingly close resemblance to modern works on urban economics.[2] And I for one can attest to the considerable influence Haig's writing had on the development of my thinking about the determinants of urban growth and residential location decisions of urban households. The similarity of Haig's concerns and theoretical approach to those of modern urban economists is clearly traceable to the similarities between the urban phenomena that he sought to explain and those occurring since the end of World War II. Haig was by no means the only economist interested in these problems during the 1920s, and, except for the Depression, urban economics would almost certainly have been solidly established as a field of study in economics decades earlier.

The onslaught of the Depression brought both popular and scholarly interest in the problems of urban growth and development to an abrupt halt. Urban growth stopped, and other more pressing problems demanded solutions. Foremost among these were problems of how to combat mass unemployment, how to feed and house a suddenly impoverished population, and how to prevent a complete collapse of the credit system. Fledgling urban economists became housing economists or housing finance economists, and urban economics ceased to exist as a distinct field of economic analysis and research.

Rapid urban growth after World War II rekindled interest in the questions that have come to define urban economics. But the response of the economics profession was slow. With a few exceptions, the development of urban economics had to await the emergence of a new cadre of urban economists, drawn from specialists in closely related areas and, more importantly, from the graduate student cohort. Indeed, the origins of a large part of modern urban economics are clearly visible in the Ph.D. dissertations begun during the 1950s. For example, William Alonso's influential book, *Location and Land Use,* is a revision of his Ph.D. dissertation completed in 1959.[3] Similarly, Richard Muth still draws heavily on his Ph.D. dissertation, "The Demand for Non-Farm Housing," for both inspiration and parameter estimates.[4] And as Chapter One of this book, which was abstracted from my Ph.D. dissertation, makes clear, a surprising portion of the insights and hypotheses that have guided my research during the past decade were previewed in that seldom read, indeed virtually unreadable manuscript.[5]

All of the studies referred to above were motivated by a desire to explain several real world phenomena: the rapid suburbanization of population following World War II, the tendency for new residential growth to be of much lower density than the growth that preceded it, and the apparent tendency of high income households to reside at more distant suburban locations. These questions were all being widely discussed in popular publications and were hot issues of public policy debate.

Several young economists responded to these external stimuli in the second half of the decade of the '50s by attempting to develop explanations for these phenomena. William Alonso, Richard Muth, Ira S. Lowry, and Lowdon Wingo were especially prominent members of the group who began independent and simultaneous searches for answers.[6] All sought to explain the tendency for residential densities to decline with distance from the central business districts of large metropolitan areas, for higher income households to reside in suburban areas and for lower income households to reside in central areas, and for more recent growth to occur at lower densities. While the analytical tools used to explain these common historical phenomena were far from identical, all concluded from their research that the rapid suburbanization following the end of World War II and the lower density character of this growth are largely attributable to the growth in per capita income, to declines in the marginal cost of commutation, and to a postponement of the major impacts of these forces during World War II.

In contrast to these analyses by urban economists, planners and other commentators resorted to a kind of villain theory to explain the postwar changes in urban spatial structure.[7] These critics of postwar urban development alleged that rapid postwar increases in car ownership and use, extensive investments in urban highways, and a corresponding neglect of urban transit systems were responsible for the rapid changes in urban spatial structure that many planners, intellectuals, and popular writers found so distasteful.

In 1900 there were only 8,000 privately owned passenger cars in the United States. Automobile ownership grew rapidly in the decades that followed and by 1920 more than eight million privately owned passenger cars were registered in the United States. By 1972 there were nearly 100 million private cars.[8] The Depression and World War II interrupted the secular trends in transportation, just as they did the trends in urban growth. While two out of every ten Americans owned an automobile by 1930, per capita automobile ownership fluctuated around this level for the next 15 years until private car production was resumed in 1946. By 1972 there was a registered car for 6 out of every 10 Americans.[9]

Transit ridership mirrored the trends in car ownership and use after 1900 and the fluctuations caused first by the Depression and then World War II. Per capita transit ridership in the U.S. appears to have reached a peak about 1924; then it declined rapidly until 1933. From that time until World War II, when wartime controls caused transit ridership to exceed even the peak levels of the 1920s, per capita transit ridership fluctuated with per capita incomes and unemployment. When wartime controls were discontinued, transit use fell precipitously from its abnormal wartime highs, a decline that has continued at a somewhat diminished rate until the present.[10]

These trends in automobile ownership and transit ridership had important implications for the nature of the urban transportation problem following World War II and the popular perception of it. First, since the moratorium on private car production was accompanied by a freeze on highway construction during World War II, the nation's highway system was grossly inadequate for the rapid postwar growth of car ownership and use. Serious and growing congestion, and widespread public support for highway improvement programs, were the logical consequences.

To deal with the growing problems of congestion, local, state, and federal governments undertook major road improvement and construction programs, including, in particular, the federal interstate highway system. To design, locate, and build the nearly 7,000 miles of urban interstate highways included in this program was a major undertaking. When it became clear that the existing methods of traffic forecasting were inadequate to plan and design the wholly new systems of urban expressways proposed for U.S. metropolitan areas, transport engineers and planners devised and then carried out comprehensive land use transportation planning studies in all U.S. metropolitan areas during the postwar period.

The heart of the land use transport planning methodology used in these studies is the observation that the demand for urban trip-making depends on the extent, nature, and location of activity in various portions of metropolitan areas. This premise led urban transport planners to collect data on the travel habits of thousands of households in each urban area; to assemble and analyze large amounts of data on physical land use, population, and employment by location within urban areas; and to devise models to predict the physical growth and expansion in urban areas.[11] Urban economists, and notably Ira S. Lowry, had some influence on this process, but it would probably be correct to say that these studies, which were carried out primarily by transport engineers and planners, had a larger effect on urban economics than the opposite.[12]

During the 1950s there had been very little opposition to highway programs and only limited support for federal transit subsidies. But as transit use continued to decline, as the dispersal of employment and suburbanization of population continued unabated, and as highway construction began to seriously impact dense, built-up urban centers, opposition to highway and especially urban expressway programs grew. This opposition was reinforced by a widely held view that the growth of automobile ownership and the large investments in urban highways were responsible for the dispersal of employment, the suburbanization of the population, and for a host of the ills of central cities. In the hope of reversing what they regarded as undesirable trends in land use, critics of postwar urban development and transportation policy sought and obtained federal capital grants and, more recently, operating subsidies.

The principal strategy of transit planners in large metropolitan areas has been to extend existing rail rapid transit systems to suburban areas in order to compete with the private automobile for commuter trips from suburban residences to core workplaces. Major extensions to existing systems are under construction or have been completed in Boston, Chicago, New York, and

Cleveland, and plans for additional extensions are awaiting further federal subsidies. In areas that lack rail facilities, transit planners have sought funding to construct entirely new systems linking central employment centers with suburban areas. An entirely new system has been opened in the San Francisco–Oakland Bay area, a major new system is under construction in Washington, D.C., and systems have been approved or are under active consideration in Atlanta, Seattle, Denver, and several other metropolitan areas.

Both additions to existing rail rapid transit systems and new systems are extremely costly. For example, the 75 mile long BART system in San Francisco had a capital cost in excess of $2.5 billion, and few supporters claim the system has any hope of covering more than its operating costs. Worse yet, critics of this approach argue that these rail rapid transit systems will fail to provide the benefits claimed by their proponents and will serve the transit-dependent population poorly. As a result, both subsidies for the construction of rail rapid transit systems and attempts to expand urban expressway systems have been the subject of active public debate and have influenced the research agenda of urban economists.[13]

If the renaissance of urban economics during the latter half of the 1950s and the early part of the 1960s is traceable to the housing and transportation needs created by rapid increases in metropolitan income and populations and by the rapid postwar physical expansion of American cities, the boom in urban economics during the second half of the decade of the 1960s clearly resulted from the "urban crisis." Following the riots in Watts and Detroit, the federal government assigned a high priority to the problems of racial discrimination, the ghetto, and black unemployment. As bureaucrats and businessmen rushed to save the cities and students flocked to courses in urban economics, the emerging field of urban economics experienced something of an identity crisis. To many persons, urban economics was indistinguishable from an analysis of the general problems of poverty, unemployment, and discrimination that affected urban populations. Large numbers of college and university courses in urban economics gave little or no attention to the theoretical and empirical issues that previously had been the dominant concern of urban economists. As these issues have receded from the public eye, "problems" courses on poverty, discimination, and the like have become less numerous and the label "urban economics" has become a more reliable guide to courses whose central concerns are with the determinants of urban spatial structure. At the same time, the urban crisis has left its mark. Urban economists and courses in urban economics are now much less likely to overlook the effects of racial discrimination on the structure and development of urban areas.

The Vietnam War, the cooling off of the cities, policies of benign neglect, the ecology movement, and women's liberation have combined to push articles about the ghetto and racial discrimination off the front pages, and the nation's attention has turned to a consideration of other problems. The interests of economists tracked each shift in the nation's priorities, albeit with a lag. A sizeable number of urban economists turned to research on housing markets and policy, and others undertook to analyze a plethora of environmental problems.[14] The research on housing markets reflected both a wider concern about housing policies and problems, and a growing recognition among urban economists that development of an improved theory of urban housing markets was essential to the development of a useful and relevant theory of urban spatial structure.

The 17 essays included in this book, which clearly bear the mark of these historical trends and public controversies, are divided into five sections. Part I contains three chapters on the residential location choices of urban households and Part II contains two chapters on changes in the geographic distribution of employment within metropolitan areas. The chapters in Part III examine the effects of racial discrimination on the spatial structure of urban areas. The preparation of most of these essays anticipated the urban crises, but at least one is a direct response to the public debate about how to deal with the problems of racial discrimination. The final two sections present chapters on housing markets and urban transportation.

Several of the essays included have been controversial and have stimulated research designed to correct, embellish, refute, or support various propositions suggested by the analyses. A number of them are seminal works which have initiated important areas of research or have provided the first serious challenge to accepted interpretations of urban phenomena. We now briefly review the individual essays, summarizing their important conclusions and findings and indicating their relationship to the larger structure of urban economics.

ANALYSIS OF RESIDENTIAL AND COMMUTING CHOICES

Part I includes three chapters that analyze decisions by urban households on how much residential space to consume, i.e., at what residential density to reside, where to live within the metropolitan area, how far to commute, and what travel modes to use. These interrelated decisions are explained by a simple theory of the individual housing consumer, which emphasizes trade-offs by urban consumers of housing and transport costs.

The theory of the individual housing consumer, presented in Chapter One and amplified in Chapter Two, resembles in important respects theories of residential location and urban spatial structure independently developed by William Alonso, Lowdon Wingo, and Richard Muth.[15] All of these theories seek to explain the density and locational choices of urban households in terms of a utility-maximizing calculus which features the substitution of journey to work costs for savings in housing costs or location rents.

With the exception of my statement of the problem, these theories assume that all employment is located at a single workplace, or, at best, make largely inconsequential modifications of this assumption. Households can save on transportation costs by residing closer to this single workplace, and competition among households for these more accessible locations produces a decline in land values or location rents with distance from this single center.

This decline in location rents with distance from the center and the increase in commuting costs as the household lives farther from the center provide households with the opportunity to substitute commuting costs for location rents. Housing expenses or total location rents depend both on how far the household lives from the center and on the quantity of housing or residential space it consumes, while transport costs depend only on the distance the household resides from the center and are invariant with the amount of housing or residential space it consumes. As a result, households which consume more residential space obtain larger savings in location rents as they commute farther from the center than households who consume less. Therefore, households who consume more residential space or housing will, if everything else is equal, live farther from the center.

All such theories assume that residential space or housing is a superior good and that its consumption will increase with income. This tends to produce a spatial distribution of households by income similar to that observed in American cities. At the same time, all of the theories use assumptions that imply that transport costs will tend to increase with income as well. This creates something of a problem, since the location by income class becomes indeterminant. The problem is resolved in every instance by an essentially empirical argument that housing or residential space consumption increases more rapidly with income than do transport costs.

The theory of residential location developed in Chapters One and Two shares with those of Alonso and Wingo an emphasis on the consumer's preference for residential space and a neglect of the housing production function. But, like Muth's approach, it depicts consumers as choosing between only two goods, assuming that consumers allocate their budget between residential space and all other goods. Also, in contrast to Alonso, both Muth's approach and Chapters One and Two represent the disutility of travel as a cost. Muth assumes journey to work costs are a function of both distance traveled and income. Somewhat analogously, the analysis presented in Chapters One and Two assumes that location incorporates no elements of utility and that housing consumption depends on what I have subsequently termed "gross prices." The gross price of any housing unit is the sum of monthly rent and monthly journey to work costs, where journey to work costs include both money costs and the value of commuting time.

The theory of residential location presented in Chapters One and Two depicts the residential space consumption and residential location choices as a two level problem. First, the household calculates the gross price of consuming each type of housing at each location. In those cases where location rents decline regularly from the household's workplace, there will be a minimum cost location for consuming each type of housing. When residential space is the only dimension of housing services included in the analysis, there will be a minimum cost location for each quantity of residential space and the change in this minimum gross price with changes in quantity of residential space may be interpreted as the price of residential space.

The theory then assumes that the household decides how much residential space to consume by using the price of residential space, the price of all other goods, its preference for residential space, its preference for all other goods, and its income in a more or less conventional utility analysis. After the quantity of residential space consumed by the household has been determined, the household's residential location is uniquely determined; it is simply the least cost location for consuming that quantity of residential space.

The central distinguishing feature of the analysis presented in Chapters One through Three is its emphasis on the specific workplace location of individual households in explaining the housing and location choices of urban households. Alonso, Muth, and Wingo are far more interested in explaining the aggregate distributions of residential densities; the decline in land prices or location rents from the center; and the tendency for higher income groups to live further from the center. Thus, all three theories employ the convenient abstraction that all employment is located at a single center or make largely inconsequential modifications of this assumption. Muth, for example, shows the effects of secondary workplaces on the surface of location rents and includes a class of local workers in his model.[16] These local workers have no effect on the surface of location rents and densities, however, and he never considers their behavior in any serious way.

A closely related point is that theoretical analyses presented in Chapters One through Three are oriented more toward hypothesis testing and statistical estimation, a characteristic that is also strongly evident in Muth's work. Wingo provides no empirical tests and Alonso presents only an inconclusive analysis of land values in an appendix.[17] In contrast, the empirical and theoretical analyses presented in Chapters One through Three emphasize the role of multiple workplaces on the location of urban households, the length of the household's journey to work, and the residential space consumption of urban households.

Chapter One first presents the simple analytics of housing choices by urban households. As in all economic theories of urban spatial structure, households are assumed to trade off savings in location rents against higher outlays for transportation. But these trade-offs are assumed to be made with reference to a predetermined workplace that is not necessarily or even usually the central business district. The predictive power of the theory and the possibilities for empirical testing arise from the fact that workers at different workplaces face difference location rent surfaces. Or, more correctly, they view a common metropolitan surface of location rents from different vantage points.

To empirically test this theory of residential location, the analysis presented in Chapter One divides the Detroit metropolitan area into six concentric distance rings surrounding the central business district which are both workplace and resident locations. The analysis centers on the similarities and differences in the residential location decisions of workers employed in and residing in these six rings.

For purposes of the empirical analyses, it is assumed that the metropolitan surface of location rents declines monotonically with distance from the central business district until it flattens out around suburban workplaces, a shape that is consistent with the negative exponential function employed in many theories of urban spatial structure. Thus, consider two extreme cases, the CBD and the outermost workplace ring. While white CBD workers are assumed to face a rapid decline in location rents with distance from their workplace, white workers employed in the outermost workplace ring face a virtually flat surface of location rents around their workplace. These differences have two important implications: first, the price of consuming residential space is much higher for CBD workers than for suburban workers; and second, the savings from making longer journeys to work are much greater for CBD than for suburban workers. These differences in location rent surfaces analogously lead to different predictions in the commuting patterns and residential locations for workers stratified by income, sex, race, family size, and residential density—i.e., structure type. These propositions are examined empirically in the second half of Chapter One.

Chapter Two amplifies the theory of the housing consumer and presents further empirical tests using data for white workers employed in the central business districts of Detroit and Chicago. Both Detroit and Chicago CBD workers face a rapidly declining location rent schedule. But because Chicago has a much larger employment and population, the price of residential space for Chicago workers should be higher and decrease more rapidly than for workers employed in Detroit's CBD. This postulated difference in the location rent schedules of the two cities provides a series of testable propositions similar to those considered for workers employed in different portions of the Detroit metropolitan area.

Chapter Two also investigates another kind of trade-off available to urban households. Central business district commuters may choose among a fairly large number of transport modes with varying time and money costs. The time and money costs of these several transport modes in turn depend on household decisions about the consumption of residential space. Chapter Two explores these several trade-offs and presents empirical analyses of the relations between the housing and mode choices of Chicago central business district workers.

Chapter Three presents a multiequation recursive model that provides a more rigorous and systematic test of a number of the hypotheses developed in Chapters One and Two. The model attempts to explain the decisions about residential density, auto ownership, journey to work transportation mode, and the length of the journey to work of workers employed at 254 Detroit workplace locations.

The underlying consumer choice model is formulated in terms of the residential and trip-making behavior of a single white worker. The model assumes households make these interrelated decisions in a recursive manner. Specifically, it assumes that the household first chooses the residential density at which it will live on the basis of its preferences for residential space, its income, and the price of residential space. The price of residential space applicable to a particular household depends on the workplace locations of its members. A household's preference for residential space is represented in the empirical analysis by variables that measure the size and labor force participation of each family.

The household's decision on whether to own an automobile is then strongly influenced by its prior decision about residential space consumption, its level of income, and the level of transit service available at the workplace of its employed members. The decision by employed members of the household whether to drive to work or use transit is then affected both by the household's previous decisions about residential space consumption and automobile ownership and by family income, sex, and the level of transit service at their workplaces.

The model's final behavioral relation states that the mean elapsed time of the journey to work for each worker depends on the household's previous decisions, sex, family income and the price of residential space. The empirical estimates strongly confirm the importance of these several factors and particularly demonstrate the role of gross prices or the price of residential space in determining the household's consumption of residential space.

The multiequation model described in Chapter Three is estimated with data that describe the average characteristics of white workers employed at 254 work zones in Detroit or characteristics of the work zone itself. The use of work zone averages follows from the underlying consumer choice model developed in Chapters One and Two, and discussed previously, which emphasizes the role of workplace-specific gross prices as determinants of these interrelated series of choices by urban households. In the statistical model presented in Chapter Three, the gross price of residential space is represented by a crude gross price proxy, which is meant to represent the workplace-specific gross price of residential space for workers at each of the 254 workplaces.

The workplace-specific price of residential space is basic to the theoretical framework developed and empirically tested in Chapters One through Three. Yet it appears many persons still do not understand the role of gross prices in the model or why they vary by workplace location. In particular there is a tendency to confuse two concepts of price: the location rent or price of standardized housing bundles at various locations within the metropolitan area; and the function that describes how the price of residential space varies among workplaces.[18]

A number of other empirical studies of housing choices, which have followed the framework suggested in Chapters One through Three, have demonstrated the importance of gross prices as determinants of the housing and residential choices of urban households. Two of these studies, by Steven Dresch, and by H. James Brown and me are reported in *The Detroit Prototype of the NBER Urban Simulation Model.*[19] Dresch's study, like the analyses presented in Chapter Three, is based on Detroit data; but it uses 1965 data, while Chapter Three uses 1952 data. The study by H. James Brown and me uses 1965 data for the San Francisco-Oakland SMSA.[20] While both studies consider a larger number of housing attributes and employ a somewhat different and improved statistical method, their findings strongly confirm those of Chapter Three on the effects of workplace-specific gross prices on housing choices.

The central focus of urban economics is the explanation of how various economic activities, particularly employment and population, are located within urban areas, and of the patterns of land use and investment associated with these largely private location decisions. Because residential land uses comprise the preponderance of urban land uses, and because data on the spatial distribution of population are more plentiful than information on the location of employment, theories of residential location constitute the theoretical core of urban economics.

THE LOCATION OF JOBS

The principal distinguishing feature of the analyses of the residential and commuting choices of urban households presented in Chapters One through Three is unquestionably its emphasis on the importance of specific workplace location as a determinant of the housing, residential location, and commuting choices of urban households. This emphasis on the role of a specific workplace location in determining these choices was a major stimulant for the research on trends in employment location and the determinants of industry location summarized in Chapters Four and Five. An equally important factor was my collaboration with John R. Meyer on the Rand Corporation study of urban transportation.

Meyer's views on urban growth and development were strongly influenced by his previous research in transport economics. He argued persuasively for the importance of intercity transportation technologies in determining the location of employment activities within metropolitan areas, an insight that strongly complemented my thinking about the roles of commuter transportation and specific workplace location in determining household residential and housing choices. Similarly, Edgar Hoover and Raymond Vernon's rich and insightful analyses of both workplace and residence location patterns for the New York metropolitan study had a major influence and remain an important component of my views on these problems.[21]

The research on trends in industry location and on the determinants of employment location presented in Part II thus dates from the Rand study on urban transportation. Chapter Four, written during 1967–68, is something of an updating and stock-taking of analyses first completed and published in the *Urban Transportation Problem*.[22] But Chapter Four also presents new analyses of nonresidential investment and changes in the location of jobs during World War II, analyses of trends in employment location within the city of Chicago, and an evaluation of forecasts made for the Philadelphia SMSA by the Delaware Valley Planning Commission. Chapter Five, which presents a simple econometric model of industry location by John Niedercorn and me, was also completed as part of the Rand Corporation Study of urban transportation.[23]

In spite of the obvious importance of industry location in determining the spatial structure of urban areas, there have been few theoretical and empirical analyses of the problem. Indeed, with the exception of Hoover and Vernon's research and some analysis of manufacturing employment by Creamer and by Woodbury there had been almost no systematic empirical analyses at the time John Niedercorn and I began to analyze the problem.[24] Efforts to provide rigorous theoretical models are even more rare. Edwin Mills and Leon Moses are numbered among the select group of economists who have attempted to provide theoretical models of the location of employment within metropolitan areas, and these analyses are of fairly recent origin.[25]

The principal explanation is presumably the lack of suitable and convenient data on employment by geographic location in metropolitan areas. In contrast to population and housing, for which the decennial census has provided large amounts of spatially disaggregated data for many decades, there are few sources of information on the location of employment within metropolitan areas and the limited available data are difficult to analyze and interpret. Although the situation has improved somewhat recently, a lack of suitable data continues to hamper research in this area. As a result there was, and continues to be, a fundamental lack of understanding of the trends in employment location, and misconceptions continue to be widespread.

The analyses of trends in industry location and tentative projections of future urban development reported in Chapters Four and Five shocked and dismayed many persons. These analyses, which it must be admitted were based on fragmentary and highly incomplete information, suggested that rapid central city employment growth was uncommon and that in a growing number of central cities the number of jobs and the population were declining. Moreover, a survey of available data for the central business districts of large central cities indicated that the pattern of no growth or decline extended to the central business districts, although in a few metropolitan areas CBD employment levels appeared to show more resistance to decline than the remaining portions of the central city. Older areas surrounding the CBDs appeared to fare worst. The analyses, moreover, revealed that those central cities that grew during this period more closely resembled suburban areas than they resembled older central cities. They were typically the rapidly growing, newer cities of the South and West, which included large tracts of unencumbered land within their boundaries.

The descriptive analyses presented in Chapter Four assemble and evaluate much valuable data on trends in employment location within metropolitan areas. The analyses in Chapter Five are concerned with the more demanding task of formulating and estimating a behavioral model that explains changes in employment and population in large metropolitan areas. This econometric research, which centers on the explanation of central city and suburban changes in employment and population for 39 large SMSAs between 1954 and 1958, was seriously hampered by a lack of information on several variables that theory points to as important determinants of industry location. Still, the simple econometric model presented in Chapter Five provides considerable insight into the forces causing changes in the distribution of employment and population in large U.S. metropolitan areas.

The model consists of three major segments or blocks. The first segment explains aggregate changes in SMSA population and manufacturing employment for the entire metropolitan areas. The model relies on two simple theoretical concepts to explain differences among areas. First it assumes changes in SMSA employment level depend on the difference between actual manufacturing employment in the SMSA at the start of the period and the "equilibrium" or "normal" level of manufacturing employment for the SMSA. Underlying this concept is the notion that manufacturing employment is tending to become more equally distributed between U.S. metropolitan areas.

Changes in SMSA population then are assumed to depend on the growth of manufacturing employment and the age of the metropolitan area. This equation relies on the familiar export-base model in which the level of export employment determines aggregate employment and population. In this analysis, manufacturing employment is used to proxy total export employment, an assumption that is satisfactory for most metropolitan areas. The empirical findings presented in Chapter Five provide considerable support for these hypotheses.

After the growth in SMSA population and manufacturing employment has been determined, the second block of the model allocates these changes between the central city and the suburban rings. Changes in central city manufacturing employment depend on changes in SMSA manufacturing employment and the amount of vacant central city land available in the central city. Changes in central city population are then explained by changes in metropolitan area population and central city manufacturing employment. The availability of suitable industrial land within central city boundaries is the critical variable in determining the share of new manufacturing jobs that locate in the central city. The presumption is that cities with large tracts of unencumbered land within their boundaries will fare much better than land poor cities in the competition for industrial employment, a view that is strongly supported by the findings in Chapter Three. The analyses in Chapter Three also reveal that only a small fraction of SMSA population growth will occur in the central city but that this fraction is quite sensitive to changes in central city manufacturing employment.

In recent years the findings about changes in employment location presented in Chapters Five and Six have been disputed. Several recent studies of employment location, which analyze some new data sources, claim we underestimated the attractiveness of central city locations to certain kinds of employment that were not represented in the published census sources which formed the basis of much of our analysis.[26] It is difficult to determine from these critiques whether the authors' dispute our findings for the entire postwar period, or whether the trends we identified have weakened in recent years. In part, the apparent disagreements may be the result of an insufficient emphasis in our presentation on the growth in employment in new, rapidly growing metropolitan areas of the South and West. None of the critics seems to be arguing that the older central cities of the East and Midwest experienced *major* increases in employment during this period. The final section of Chapter Five evaluates these recent studies.

While theories of residential location and urban spatial structure are the theoretical core of urban economics, there is a growing consensus that changes in the location of employment within metropolitan areas has a more substantial impact on urban spatial structure than residential location. The physical form of cities and, particularly, the role of the central business district depend heavily on these poorly documented and dimly understood trends.

EFFECTS OF RACIAL DISCRIMINATION

The chapters in Part III identify racial discrimination as perhaps the major imperfection of urban housing markets and as the cause of major distortions in urban spatial structure. As a group, these essays are concerned with identifying, tracing, and quantifying the effects of racial discrimination and segregation in urban housing markets on the pattern of urban development and on black welfare. They clearly demonstrate that limitations on black residential choice resulting from housing market discrimination have much larger and more numerous effects on the welfare of black households than is generally recognized.

Chapter Six, which combines parts of two previously published papers, extends the theory of residential location developed in Part II to incorporate the effects of racial discrimination. The chapter begins with a review of the evidence on the extent of segregation in American cities which reveals that black Americans are intensely segregated and that this segregation is increasing over time. The chapter then considers three possible explanations for the intense segregation of Negro Americans: that the observed patterns of segregation are due to socioeconomic differences between black and white households, that they result from self-segregation by black households or a preference of blacks to live in segregated neighborhoods, or that they result from discriminatory actions by whites. Examination of the evidence reveals that very little of the observed pattern of housing market segregation can be explained by black-white differences in income and other characteristics and that very little support exists for a self-segregation hypothesis. Moreover, there is considerable, though unsystematic, evidence that blacks encounter substantial difficulty in attempting to buy or rent housing in all-white neighborhoods.

The second section of Chapter Six examines the implications of a segregated housing market for the economic theory of residential location developed in Chapters One and Two. This analysis, which reveals that housing market discrimination and segregation affects the metropolitan schedule of location rents in major ways, illustrates the analytical value of a model that assumes that the housing consumed by black and white households is provided in two interrelated, but quite distinct, submarkets. The analysis indicates that the price of housing services within the black submarket depends only indirectly on the accessibility consideration stressed in economic theories of residential location and urban spatial structure. Instead the price of housing in the black submarket depends on the price at which comparable units are transferred from the white submarkets. Since these transfers normally occur only when the price in the black submarket exceeds that in the white submarket by some amount, rents in the ghetto are normally higher than the price of comparable properties in the white submarket. This does not mean that the price of all types of housing in the ghetto must exceed the price outside the ghetto, however. Rapid shifts in black demand can produce an excess supply of some kinds of housing within the ghetto without causing these units to shift back to the white submarket.

Chapter Six also includes an analysis of the residential and commuting choices of black central business district workers in Chicago and Detroit similar to that presented in Chapter Two for white workers. This analysis demonstrates both the the applicability and inapplicability of the simple model of residential location and travel behavior developed in Part II.

Chapter Seven explores a number of other ways in which housing market discrimination affects the housing consumption of Negro households. The analysis reveals that while there is considerable empirical evidence of a discrimination markup for ghetto properties similar to that suggested by the theoretical analyses presented in Chapter Six, this markup may be among the least serious consequences of housing market discrimination. Thus, the analyses of the determinants of homeownership presented in Chapter Seven illustrate that the problem faced by black households may be less that they must pay more than white households for their housing, than the fact that the most desirable types of housing are unavailable to them or at best can be obtained only with great difficulty. These analyses of the effects of racial discrimination on homeownership, like several of the other essays included in this book, stimulated a number of follow-up studies along the same lines. In general, these subsequent studies have confirmed the findings reported in Chapter Eight, but in some instances they have extended or taken exception to particular findings.[27]

Chapter Seven contains two kinds of analyses of homeownership and purchase. The first, based on a large sample of St. Louis households, reveals that black households in St. Louis in 1967 were 9 percentage points less likely to be homeowners and 12 percentage points less likely to be home buyers than white households of similar characteristics. Thus, the analysis suggests that while 32 percent of black households in the sample were homeowners, an estimated 41 percent would have been homeowners if they had been white, and that while only 8 percent of Negro households who had moved in the past three years purchased homes, 20 percent would have been home buyers if they had been white.

A second analysis, which examines differences in the rates of homeownership among 18 large metropolitan areas, provides support for the hypothesis that these differences in the homeownership rates of black and white households are attributable to restrictions on the supply of housing suitable for homeownership available to black households.

The final section of Chapter Seven considers some further implications of the limitations on black homeownership. The most significant of these may be its effects on the wealth accumulation by black households. Black households at every level of income own less wealth than white households. As Terrell and others have shown, homeownership is the most important form of investment by low and middle income households and accounts for more than half of the wealth of these groups in the case of whites.[28] It follows that the lower rates of homeownership by black households over several decades, the direct result of discrimination, may be a major cause of the much smaller amounts of wealth owned by black than by white households at every income level.

The economic theory of residential location presented in Chapters One and Two assumes that the place of work of employed household members is predetermined or causally prior and that households choose where to live by trading off savings in housing costs obtained by commuting further from the fixed workplace against the increases in commuting costs thereby incurred. But because the residence choices of black households are so severely constrained, the applicability of this model to black households is more limited. Indeed, geographic limitations on the residence choices of black households are so serious that it is reasonable to ask whether these constraints may not affect the job search behavior of black households and the final geographic distribution of black employment. Black households whose residence locations are fixed by racial discrimination may trade off commuting costs against wages and working conditions and accept lower paying jobs near the ghetto in preference to better and higher paying jobs distant from the ghetto. It is, moreover, possible that some black households will choose unemployment over low paying jobs located far from the ghetto and that housing market discrimination may be responsible in part for the higher rates of unemployment of black than of white workers.

Chapter Eight examines the interrelations between housing market discrimination and Negro employment and tests empirically three hypotheses about the effect of housing market discrimination on the labor market behavior of black households. These are that racial segregation in urban housing markets (1) affects the distribution of black employment and (2) reduces black job opportunities, and (3) that the ongoing suburbanization of employment has serious aggravated the problem. These hypotheses are tested with data for Detroit and Chicago using a simple, single equation, reduced form model that assumes that the residence location of black households is limited to a few compact ghetto areas.

The findings of the empirical analyses presented in Chapter Eight can be briefly summarized as follows. First, the empirical evidence clearly indicates that housing market discrimination strongly affects the geographic location of black employment. This conclusion depends on acceptance of the evidence presented in Chapter Six that black households are severely limited in their choice of residence locations. The effect of housing market discrimination on Negro employment is less certain, but Chapter Eight presents evidence that job losses from housing market segregation could be substantial.

The final part of the analysis considers the effects of employment dispersal on black employment. For Chicago sufficient data were available to evaluate directly some of the model's predictions about the effects of postwar employment and population shifts on black employment. The Chicago SMSA had 3,000 fewer manufacturing jobs in 1960 than in 1950 and these fewer jobs were on average located farther from the ghetto. Even so, a disproportionate number of jobs remained in the central city at the end of the period and, with ghetto expansion, large numbers of white workers moved away from these centrally located jobs. These outward shifts of the white resident population would be expected to improve the labor market position of blacks relative to whites and central workplaces.

The simple statistical models presented in Chapter Eight can be used to evaluate the net impact of these offsetting trends. The estimated changes in black employment obtained by solving the simple econometric model using 1950 and 1960 data are remarkably similar to the actual changes.

A preliminary version of the empirical analyses presented in Chapter Eight was published in 1965 and an extended analysis was published four years later in the *Quarterly Journal of Economics.*[29] These papers attracted considerable scholarly and popular attention and provided an intellectual justification for several federal experiments to provide transport services from central city ghettos to suburban workplaces and for a number of manpower programs designed to help overcome the distance and information barriers that limit black employment opportunities outside the central cities.

Both the empirical results and the programs based on them proved to be quite controversial and in the ensuing years a number of analyses and critiques have been published that claim to support or refute one or more of the hypotheses outlined above. Some of the more prominent of these analyses are those by the late Joseph Mooney; Paul Offner and Daniel Saks; Roger Noll; Bennett Harrison; and Stanley Masters.[30]

Collectively, the critics present four kinds of analyses that they believe undermine the findings presented in Chapter Eight: (1) evidence on the relative tightness of central city and suburban job markets, (2) tests to determine whether relative black-white earnings or employment levels are correlated with differences among SMSAs in measures of segregation, (3) analyses that demonstrated the sensitivity of my estimates of Negro job loss to alternative model specification, and (4) statistics on the welfare of black households living in the central cities and suburbs.

Joseph D. Mooney published the first major independent test of the hypothesis that limitations on Negro residential choice reduced Negro employment in the May 1969 issue of the *Quarterly Journal of Economics.* His findings generally supported those presented in Chapter Eight, but he argued that the geographic separation of the central city Negro from suburban jobs is less important than aggregate demand conditions in determining the level of black employment.[31] Noll and others have argued that jobs are in some sense more plentiful in core areas than in suburban areas in spite of widespread employment dispersal within metropolitan areas, and at times the critics seem to argue that housing market discrimination and the resulting segregation benefits black households by forcing them to live in neighborhoods located near large numbers of available jobs. These arguments and several of the most significant extensions and critiques are examined in the final section of Chapter Eight.

The riots that broke out in Detroit, Los Angeles and other central cities in the summers of 1965, 1966 and 1967 riveted society's attention on the distressed condition of central city ghettos and their residents and spawned a plethoric array of proposals to ameliorate or eliminate entirely the ills of the ghetto. Prominent among these proposals were a number that involved economic development of the ghetto.[32] Advocates of this strategy drew a parallel between the ghetto and an underdeveloped nation and proposed policies for economic development of the ghetto in this spirit. This economic development approach included a variety of subsidies to encourage firms to locate in the ghetto, to foster black-owned business in the ghetto, to involve the nonwhite population of the ghetto in the rehabilitation and renewal of its housing stock, and to improve the physical environment of the ghetto. A moderate version of this strategy argued that regardless of the measures taken to provide housing for Negroes outside the ghetto, the ghetto will continue to grow and that, as a consequence, it is essential to renew the ghetto in order to improve conditions for the majority of Negroes. The Kerner Commission, for example, made a number of recommendations in this spirit.[33]

The findings presented in Chapter Eight on the effects of housing market discrimination and segregation on Negro employment were widely cited as justification for ghetto job creation programs and similar measures. Even so, I have long considered that this approach to improving the welfare of black Americans is misguided. In Chapter Nine Joe Persky and I enumerate the reasons. First, we assert that the continued growth of central city ghettos imposes large and growing costs on black and white Americans alike. Second, we claim that nearly all of the objectives of the proposed ghetto investment programs could be better achieved through programs that are not limited to the ghetto. And finally, we point out that the linkages between the northern ghettos and southern rural areas are so strong that efforts to increase Negro incomes and employment in northern ghettos may be dissipated by increased migration from the rural South, further exacerbating the problems associated with the rapid growth of central city ghettos.

As an alternative to these policies, Chapter Nine proposes vigorous antidiscrimination measures, manpower training, and similar programs to increase the human capital of black households; a policy of southern economic development; and, most importantly, measures to enable black households to obtain housing outside the ghetto.

ANALYSIS OF HOUSING MARKETS

The essays included in Part IV are chronologically the most recent of those included in this book. The four chapters that comprise this section of the book analyze a number of aspects of urban housing markets alluded to, but not developed, in previous chapters. For example, the analyses of residential choice presented in Chapters One through Three deal with only one dimension of bundles of residential services, the quantity of residential space or density, and concentrates on the effects of specific workplace location and residential space consumption on the residential location decisions of urban households.

This partial view, though instructive, abstracts from many important features of urban housing markets. When consumers choose a residential location they simultaneously purchase a diverse collection of housing attributes. Several of these housing attributes, in addition to lot size and arrangement, are durable and difficult to modify or require more than the action of a single housing supplier to produce. Economic theories of urban spatial structure ignore these troublesome features of urban housing markets by analyzing only long run equilibrium situations when the capital stock is assumed to adjust fully to changes in demand and by ignoring any forms of interdependence.

Chapter Ten, by Gregory K. Ingram and me, considers these issues. The first part of the chapter presents the rudiments of partial equilibrium models of individual housing consumers and individual housing suppliers and describes how these partial models are used in the NBER Urban Simulation Model.[34] The NBER model incorporates the theoretical insights obtained from traditional analytical models of residential location and urban spatial structure into a framework that employs more realistic and less restrictive assumptions.

The theory of the individual consumer presented in Chapter Ten is a generalization of the simple theory of the housing consumer developed in Chapters One and Two. It retains the emphasis of that theory on specific workplace location and gross housing prices as major determinants of the housing and residential location choices of urban households. As in the simple theory, households with varying incomes and tastes employed at different workplace locations choose the type and location of their housing on the basis of the relative gross prices of the several bundles. Gross prices are, of course, the sum of the rent or value of dwelling units and the transportation costs required to reach each residence location from a household's particular workplace.

The only difference between the theory of the individual consumer presented in Chapter Ten and in previous chapters is the definition of housing output used. The analysis presented in Chapters One and Two ignores spatial variations in all aspects of housing output other than residential space, and it deals with only the effects of variations in gross prices on the consumption of residential space and residential location. The model presented in Chapter Ten employs a much more comprehensive definition of housing services and depicts households as choosing among a finite number of distinct housing bundles, defined in terms of dwelling unit, structure, lot, and neighborhood characteristics on the basis of their preferences, incomes, and the gross prices of the various housing bundles.

The extended theory of housing and residential choice described in Chapter Ten is the theoretical basis for the demand sector of the NBER model. This demand sector consists of econometrically estimated housing bundle demand equations, which predict housing bundle choices on the basis of differences in the gross prices of specific bundles. As a result, NBER researchers have expended a great deal of effort to solve the difficult theoretical and statistical problems inherent in estimating behavioral relations of this kind and have estimated bundle or attribute demand equations for several cities.[35]

John Quigley, in an analysis of the demand for housing attributes by Pittsburgh renters, has obtained valuable evidence of the importance of gross prices in determining the choice of housing bundles. He also demonstrated the predictive power of the gross price model in explaining residential location choices.[36] The gross price model presented in Chapter Ten predicts that once a household has decided on its housing bundle on the basis of its preferences, income, and the gross prices of competing bundles, it will reside at the location where its preferred bundle is cheapest. This least cost location varies by workplace location and household characteristics. To test this proposition, Quigley computed the gross price for each household at each of 130 residence locations and sorted them in order from the households highest gross price for the bundle selected to the lowest. He found that 40 percent of renters who had moved within the last seven years were living in a residence zone that was in the lowest 5 percent of their own gross price distribution for the preferred bundle and that 68 percent were living in areas that were in the lowest 25 percent of their own gross price distribution. These results are rather remarkable when it is recognized that many of these sample households selected their residences some years earlier and that these estimates make no allowance for changes in workplace location or the spatial distribution of housing prices during the period.

The more comprehensive definition of housing output used in these econometric studies of housing bundle and housing attribute demand also has important implications for the behavior of housing suppliers. The housing services production function implicit in the analyses presented in Chapters One and Two includes only two inputs, land and nonland factors of production. In contrast, the housing production function discussed in Chapter Ten, and used in the NBER model includes specific types of durable structures, land and nonland factors of production, operating expenses, local public services, and other neighborhood attributes as inputs. Explicit recognition of the durable stocks of specific housing capital and of the role in housing production of government services and other neighborhood characteristics that are not produced and competitive firms is the most important difference between the framework outlined in Chapter Ten and long run equilibrium theories of urban spatial structure and residential location.

A major result obtained from long run equilibrium theories of urban spatial structure is a predicted decline in residential densities with distance from the center of urban areas. At the same time, the density gradients, or density functions, observed in a large number of cities have been proposed as empirical confirmations of these long run equilibrium theories.

Chapter Eleven presents an essay written with David Harrison that develops and empirically tests an alternative theoretical explanation of urban density functions. This theory assumes that the stock of residential and nonresidential capital has an infinite life and does not depreciate—precisely the opposite assumption from that used in long run equilibrium theories of urban spatial structure. The density gradients observed in cities throughout the world then are produced by a historical process of cumulative, concentric growth of urban areas.

The theory assumes that urban areas grow incrementally and that the density of urban development during each time period depends on the size of the city and on the incomes, transportation costs, and preferences that exist at the time the development takes place. Once development occurs at a particular density, that density persists. The high densities found in central areas result from the fact that they were developed during periods when average incomes, transport costs, and similar variables favored high residential densities. Analogously, the low densities found at less central locations are attributable to the fact that this development occurred when these same variables favored lower density development. Differences in density gradients among metropolitan areas are the result of differences in the timing of metropolitan development. To test this alternative theory of urban development, we first econometrically estimate incremental net density functions that explain the variation in incremental net residential density among 83 metropolitan areas over a period of 90 years. The empirical relations obtained from this analysis, and the assumption of regular, compact, peripheral growth of urban areas, are then used to calculate density gradients for U.S. metropolitan areas. The density functions derived in this way exhibit a surprising agreement with actual density gradients.

The assumption that stocks of residential capital have infinite lives is, of course, not literally correct. A more realistic theory and more accurate predictions could clearly be obtained by introducing depreciation and by allowing succession and physical transformations of the stock. Still, the simpler theory used to calculate the density function serves to emphasize the importance of the durability of existing stocks, a feature of housing markets that has received too little attention in most economic analyses of urban housing markets.

In Chapter Twelve John Quigley and I analyze the several dimensions of housing bundles and estimate implicit market prices for individual housing attributes. The estimates are based on a highly unusual sample of St. Louis dwelling units that includes both information on the characteristics of individual housing units and elaborate descriptions of adjacent units, the block face, and the surrounding neighborhood. The analysis reveals that many of those housing attributes that are not produced by individual housing suppliers are highly valued by housing consumers, a feature of urban housing markets that has very important implications. Chapter Twelve also presents an analysis of the effects of housing market discrimination on the price black households must pay for the average sample dwelling, which indicates that both rental and owner-occupied units are more expensive inside the ghetto than outside.

In Chapter Thirteen, Gregory K. Ingram and I explore the implications of this broader view of housing services for the behavior of housing suppliers. The chapter develops a simple model of housing production that emphasizes the effects of both stocks of heterogeneous and durable structures, and the nonmarket production of many housing attributes on market demand and on the production of housing services. The essential feature of our analysis is that individual housing suppliers are able to produce some, but not all, attributes of housing bundles. In particular, we distinguish between structure services, which are supplied by individual property owners using quantities of annual inputs, and capital and neighborhood services that can only be produced through the collective action of housing consumers, suppliers, or government. While neighborhood services cannot be produced by individual housing suppliers, they strongly affect the property values and the rents the landlord can obtain from supplying various types and quantities of structure services.

The model presented in Chapter Thirteen also makes a sharp distinction between the type of housing capital and its quantity. To produce a particular kind of structure services requires housing capital of a particular type. It is possible to augment the quantity of housing capital of a particular type, but structure transformations are required to produce a particular kind of housing services from the remaining types of housing capital.

The final essay in Part IV, Chapter Fourteen, considers existing government housing policy. First, it briefly reviews previous evaluations of federal housing programs and policies and discusses the failure of these evaluations to consider the effects of housing market discrimination in any serious way. The chapters' final section describes a number of policies that would be effective in combating housing market discrimination and segregation, and in reducing the welfare losses imposed on black households.

URBAN TRANSPORTATION

The three chapters on urban transportation included in Part V bear the indelible stamps of John Meyer and Martin Wohl. Indeed Chapter Fifteen, although written by me, is a summary and restatement of the findings of our joint research on the costs serving peak hour commuters by alternative technologies. Moreover, Chapter Sixteen, "How to Improve Transportation at Practically No Cost," is in many respects an extrapolation and refinement of concepts hammered out by the three of us in jointly writing *The Urban Transportation Problem.*[37] Still, while the analyses and ideas in Chapter Sixteen owe a great deal to John Meyer and Martin Wohl, I doubt if they would agree with all of its particulars and I bear sole responsibility for any errors it may contain.

Chapter Fifteen summarizes the principal findings of an analysis of the comparative costs of alternative urban passenger transportation technologies. These cost analyses, completed for the Rand Corporation study of urban transportation, were the first published attempt to develop generalized and comparable estimates of the full cost of providing peak hour commuter services by rail rapid transit, bus rapid transit, and private automobile. The cost models divide the typical journey to work into three parts: (1) line haul, (2) residential collection, and (3) downtown distribution. These different trip segments represent considerably different operating conditions and environments and frequently are performed by different technologies. A common error of all previous cost analyses and many subsequent ones was to ignore one or more segments of the typical trip in comparing the cost and effectiveness of alternative modes.

The findings summarized in Chapter Fifteen strongly contradicted the conventional wisdom about the efficiency of rail and bus transit and private automobiles. The analyses confirmed the widely held view that either bus or rail transit is considerably cheaper than the private automobile for meeting peak hour line haul transport requirements at very high corridor volumes. But at the same time they revealed that at the low corridor volumes that characterize many American cities, an automobile system, even with 1.6 passengers per car, is often cheaper than either rail or exclusive transit or bus rapid transit operating on a private right of way. The analysis further indicates that bus transit at low and medium densities is almost invariably cheaper than rail rapid transit. But the most important finding was the potential revealed by the analysis for an innovative system which we termed the freeway flier. The analysis clearly showed that express buses operating on an uncongested mixed traffic expressway and paying only their proportionate share of the facilities capital cost would be the cheapest form of high performance line haul transit, even at high population densities. The importance of this finding, given the extensive urban expressway network then under construction in U.S. cities, is obvious.

The only obstacles to the implementation of bus rapid transit systems in U.S. metropolitan areas are a policy decision to maintain congestion-free operation of urban expressways during peak hours and the development of methods to monitor expressway operations and to provide transit vehicles with priority access to urban expressways. The equipment needed for this purpose has been developed and tested and some limited experiments have been carried out. But for reasons described in Chapter Sixteen, no operational systems using these principals have been implemented.

Some of the findings of Chapter Sixteen, which examines a number of low cost improvements in urban transportation, are startling. For example, the BART system for the San Francisco–Oakland Bay area, which has 75 route miles had a capital cost of more than $2.5 billion. In contrast, cost estimates, presented in Chapter Sixteen indicate that the 314 miles of expressways existing in the bay area in 1964 could be modified to function as a joint bus rapid transit–general purpose highway system for an additional capital outlay of less than $15 million and that the needed surveillance and control system required to maintain congestion-free operation and to provide transit vehicles with priority access to these facilities could be operated for less than $8 million a year.

Chapter Seventeen, "Transportation and Poverty," written by John Meyer and me, summarizes the findings of a conference on transportation and poverty we held under the auspices of the American Academy of Arts and Sciences. The conference, sponsored by the Department of Housing and Urban Development, resulted from HUD's discovery of the probable link between housing market segregation and Negro unemployment following the Watts riots. During this period Meyer and I advised HUD on the design and implementation of a number of inside-outside transport demonstrations funded under UMTA's demonstration grant program. The conference on transportation and poverty and our paper represent something of an evaluation or stocktaking of this experience.

THE FUTURE OF URBAN ECONOMICS

This introductory essay has attempted to identify the forces influencing the formation and development of urban economics in the 30 years following the end of World War II and seeks to place the 17 essays included in this book in the context of the overall development of urban economics. In the two decades since urban economics emerged as a recognizable and finally recognized field of economics, the number of courses offered at U.S. colleges and universities, the number of practitioners, and the quantity and quality of research have grown manyfold. An indicator of the growing maturity of urban economics is the founding of the *Journal of Urban Economics* in 1974. One consequence of the rapid growth and enlargement of urban economics is that it is increasingly difficult to summarize or even identify the main currents of intellectual development in the field or to project the likely course of its development for the next few decades. Still, a number of trends in urban economics are reasonably clear and it is perhaps worthwhile to consider what they portend for the future of urban economics.

First, the basic analytical model of urban economics introduced by Alonso, Muth, Wingo, and other pioneers is rapidly being extended and deepened almost beyond recognition by a host of young economists armed with an ever growing kit of increasingly powerful analytical tools.[38] The explosive growth of what Edwin Mills has termed the new urban economics reflects a rapid expansion in the supply of mathematically gifted economists and the discovery by economic theorists that their mathematical techniques are as applicable to distance in the monocentric city as to time in neoclassical growth models. As a result, the monocentric city threatens to become the new growth theory of economics. Analyses by Mills, and more recently by Solow, appear to be the principal beacons drawing the growing numbers of young economists to this intersection between economic theory and urban economics.[39]

The second important external force impacting on urban economics and on economics generally is the growing availability of microdata sets and the rapid decline in real computational costs. Just as importantly, economists have become far more sophisticated in the analysis and the use of these microdata and have been expanding and improving the statistical methods needed for their effective analysis. Both general purpose sets of microdata, such as the one-and-one-hundred public use sample from the 1970 census, and more specialized samples, such as those collected by land use transportation studies, have enabled quantitatively trained urban economists to rapidly increase our understanding of the various aspects of behavior relevant to urban economics. Examples abound where enlarged and improved sets of microdata and increased statistical sophistication have combined to greatly increase our knowledge of aspects of behavior relevant to the urban economics. The best examples include the analyses of urban travel demand pioneered by Daniel McFadden; the analyses of urban housing markets by Mahlon Straszheim, John M. Quigley, and A. Thomas King; and the analyses of firm location decisions within metropolitan areas by Robert Leone, Raymond Struyk, Franklin James, Peter Kemper, and Roger Schmenner.[40]

A growing use of computer models is the final trend strongly evident in recent research in urban economics that is certain to have a major effect on both urban economics and the economics profession generally in the next few decades. These methods promise to allow urban economists to extend and elaborate traditional analytical models of urban economics and to digest, synthesize, and apply the rapidly growing body of behavioral research on urban behavior, particularly microanalytic, based on the ever more numerous and improved microdata sets. Urban analysts have long been attracted by the idea of using computers to handle the large amounts of data and great complexity that may be necessary to accurately depict and analyze the structure and dynamics of metropolitan areas. Indeed, computers and computer models have been used for some time in transport and land use planning.[41] Although of unquestioned value, computer models of various aspects of the urban economy have tended to lack clear theoretical foundations or at least foundations of a sort recognizable to economists.[42]

More recently, a growing number of urban economists have begun to devise, calibrate, and exercise computer simulation models rooted in economic analysis and designed to illuminate various aspects of the urban economy. The most important examples of these models clearly include the optimization models initiated by Edwin Mills and extended principally by the Hartwicks; the Urban Institute Housing model devised by Frank de Leeuw and implemented by de Leeuw, Raymond Struyk, Ann Schnare, and others at the Urban Institute; and the NBER Urban Simulation model.[43]

Computer simulation models of urban structure and development have the potential of not only enriching the theory and body of urban economics, but also of providing increasingly useful and relevant analyses of urban problems pertinent to public policy. Development of these models is still in its infancy and years of concentrated effort will be required before their full promise is attained. Still, I for one look forward to the challenge and promise before us of increasing our knowledge of urban growth and development and of making urban economics more useful to society and its decisionmakers.

Part I

Residential and Commuting Decisions

Chapter One

The Journey to Work as a Determinant of Residential Location

This chapter develops a simple theory of residential location and presents empirical evidence on the manner in which transportation costs influence the household's choice of a residential location. The central hypothesis, suggested by this and similar models, is that households substitute journey to work expenditures for site expenditures.[1] This substitution depends primarily on household preferences for low density as opposed to high density residential services.

THE MODEL

The model deals with the locational choice of a single household. It is assumed that this household's transportation costs increase monotonically with the distance it resides from its workplace. The reasonableness of this assumption may be seen if the household's monthly expenditure for transportation is broken into its component parts. These outlays may be expressed as the sum of the costs of the journey to work, of obtaining residentially oriented services within the immediate residential area, i.e., groceries, elementary school, etc., and of obtaining other services available only outside the residential area. Included are both dollar expenditures for transportation and dollar valuations of time spent in travel. Unless the distinction is explicitly made, transportation costs here will refer to these combined costs.

The household's monthly transportation costs, T, may then be expressed as the sum of its expenditures for those services obtainable within the residential area, t_r, those which vary with the residence's distance from its workplace, $t(w_1), t(w_2), t(w_3), \cdots, t(w_n)$, and those which vary with the residence's distance from other points outside the residential area, $t(o_1), t(o_2), \cdots, t(o_m)$, where n equals the number of workplace destinations for the household and m equals the number of other destinations outside the residential area. The household's total monthly transportation cost for each residential site may thus be expressed:

$$T = t_r + t(w_1) + t(w_2) + t(w_3) + \cdots + t(w_n) + t(o_1) + \cdots + t(o_m) \quad (1.1)$$

For our purposes it may be assumed that t_r is invariant with the household's choice of location. The level of t_r may vary with the kind of residential area the household chooses, i.e., low density versus high density, but there is no reason to expect a significant variation between areas of similar characteristics.

If the costs of residentially provided services—retailing, medical services, schools, etc.,—may be considered as invariant, the accuracy of our assumption depends on the relative weights placed on the trips to workplaces and on the trips made to other points outside the residential area. For the majority of urban households the sum of transportation costs to points other than work or within the immediate residential area is small, and the costs to any one other single point are almost always trivial. The journey to work costs, by way of contrast, are large and significant. Thus, if these contentions are correct, no serious violence is done in most instances by considering only journey to work costs in our residential location model.

It is not at all difficult, however, to find exceptions to these propositions. For example, there is the large and increasing number of households without a member in the labor force. For such households the worktrip term in Equation 1.1 is equal to zero and the location of other destinations may be of considerable importance. Many retired people desire to live near their children and grandchildren. Single persons and young married couples may make frequent trips to major cultural and recreational centers. The monthly travel costs of these households may vary significantly with the distance from these centers.

Despite these exceptions to the rule, the assumption used in this model is approximately correct for a very large proportion of the population, perhaps for as many as 80 or 90 percent of households having a member in the labor force.

The data in Table 1–1 illustrate the importance of the journey to work in the household's travel budget. Nearly half of all trips from home are made to work. Of the remainder, some portion of social-recreation trips and personal business trips are made to other destinations outside the residential area. The destinations of these trips may be spatially quite separated. Furthermore, many will be to points nearby the workplace, since a large proportion of cultural, recreational, personal business, and other destinations are likely to be nearby employment concentrations. Social-recreation and personal business trips made to destinations near the household's workplace may be added to the trips made to the workplace. If a small proportion of the popu-

Table 1–1.   Purpose of Trips Originating in the Dwelling Unit in 38 Cities.

Trip Purpose	Percent	Trips per 1000 Dwelling Units (Hypothetical)
Work	43.9	1010
Business	6.8	155
Social-Recreation	21.4	490
Shopping	11.9	275
School	4.8	110
All others	11.2	260
Total	100.0	2300

Source: Robert E. Schmidt and M. Earl Campbell, *Highway Traffic Estimation*, The Eno Foundation for Highway Traffic Control, 1956, Table II–4.

lation makes large numbers of these trips, the averages shown in Table 1-1 overstate their importance for the remainder of the population.

The Market for Residential Space

This analysis also assumes that the household is an atomistic competitor in the market for residential space. That is, it assumes that there is a market for residential space and that the price a single household must pay per unit for space is given. Residential space is defined as the urban land utilized by the household in its residential activities. For single family dwelling units this would be closely approximated by lot size. For multiple units it would be some proportion of the total amount of land utilized by the structure. (This glosses over a number of complex relationships among lot layout, overall neighborhood densities, and substitutability between capital and land residential space.)

This analysis further assumes that the price the household must pay per unit of residential space varies from one location to another. This price is an economic rent which landlords can obtain from households for more accessible sites. Rents on more accessible sites arise because of households' collective efforts to economize on transportation expenditures. For this model, it is assumed that these rents, which are referred to hereafter as location rents, decrease with distance from the household's workplace. Specifically, it is assumed that the unit price the household must pay per unit of residential space *of a stated quality and amenity* decreases monotonically from its workplace. Of course, the magnitude of the location rents is significant only when there is a significant concentration of employment.

It is possible, as Alonso, Wingo, and others have done, to obtain this second result using only the first assumption.[2] Since I am unable to improve on their solutions in what I consider to be the most important directions, i.e., adequate and explicit treatment of time, depreciation, obsolescence, quality, and other problems of housing market dynamics, I instead offer it as a provisional hypothesis. Common sense, the excellent theoretical works cited above, and fragmentary evidence support its acceptance; arrayed against it is the opinion of a number of knowledgeable institutional real estate economists and other urban researchers. A really adequate empirical verification or rejection of the hypothesis has yet to be accomplished.

The Household's Consumption of Residential Space

It is further assumed that residential space is not an inferior good and that the household chooses its residential location and its consumption of residential space by maximizing the utility obtainable from a given income. Thus, the quantity of residential space the household will consume depends on the household's income, the price of residential space, and its preference for residential space. These, along with the assumptions about location rents and journey to work costs, are the basic components of the model presented here. It will be seen that, if the household's workplace and transportation costs per mile are taken as given, its residential location can be expressed as a function of its space consumption. Similarly, then, the household's residential location may be expressed as a function of its income, space preference, and the price of residential space. This is the nature of the hypotheses to be tested later in this paper. First, however, it is necessary to spell out the implications of our key assumptions more completely. These key assumptions are (1) that the household's transportation cost function increases with distance from its workplace, (2) that the existence of a market for residential space in which the price per unit a household must pay for residential space of a given quality decreases with distance from its workplace, (3) that there is a fixed workplace, (4) that there is utility maximization on the part of households, and (5) that residential space is not an inferior good.

The Location Rent Function

The location rent function or schedule of location rents—i.e., the function which describes the decrease in location rents with distance from the household's workplace—describes the savings per unit of residential space the household may achieve by moving farther from its place of employment. What is of interest to the household in making a locational choice, however, is not this amount but its total savings at various distances. If rents per unit of space decrease as the household moves farther from its workplace, the absolute amount of savings possible through longer journeys to work depend on the amount of residential space consumed by the household. Since the household's space consumption has not been specified, the decline in total location rents with distance is described by a family of iso-space curves similar to the

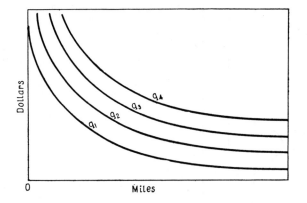

Figure 1-1. Total Iso-Location Rent Curves

economist's iso-quants. Each curve in Figure 1–1, for example, illustrates the decline in location rents with distance for a given quantity of residential space. From Figure 1–1, it can be seen that the absolute dollar savings obtainable by a longer journey to work clearly become larger as more residential space is consumed. By way of contrast, the household's transportation costs per mile, $t(d)$, are invariant with the amount of residential space consumed.

It is, however, the combined outlay for transportation costs and location rents that ought to concern the household in selecting a residential site. Since a given dollar spent for transportation or rents has the same disutility, the household's utility maximization combination of the two is included in the set which minimizes the combined outlay for rents and transportation costs for each quantity of residential space.

Marginal Savings in Location Rents and
Marginal Increases in Transportation Costs

The characteristics of the solution we seek can perhaps be more easily understood if we use functions which describe the changes in each of these substitutable costs with the household's distance from its workplace. Figure 1–2 illustrates the incremental savings in location rents obtained by commuting an additional unit of distance for each quantity of space. The area under each curve is equal to the total location rents that would have to be paid by the household if it were to reside at its workplace and if it were to consume the quantity of space specified by a given curve. Since this function describes the manner in which total location rents decrease, the area under each curve to the right of oi equals the total monthly location rents that must be paid to locate at i for each quantity of residential space. For example, the area under q_3 to the right of oi is paid for the quantity of residential space represented by the curve q_3.

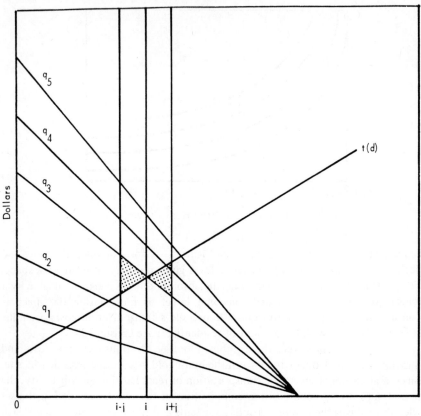

Figure 1-2.   Marginal Location Rent and Transportation Cost
Functions

Marginal Transportation Costs

The incremental increase in transportation costs can be illustrated in
the same manner. The line $t(d)$ in Figure 1–2 shows the incremental increase in
transportation costs with distance. The area under the curve $t(d)$ to the left of oi
is equal to the expenditures for the journey to work required to reside at oi.

The minimum cost location for each quantity of residential space is
given by the intersection of the marginal cost of transportation function and
each of the marginal location rent savings functions. For q_3, the minimum cost
location is at oi. For larger quantities of residential space, the minimum cost
location is farther from the household's workplace; for smaller quantities,
nearer.

This solution can be easily verified by using Figure 1–2. Locations
farther from the workplace, say $oi + j$, add the area between oi and $oi + j$ under

the $t(d)$ curve to the household's transportation costs. Its savings in location rents amount only to the area under q_3 between oi and $oi + j$. Thus, the household's total location costs for the quantity of residential space q_3 are increased by the shaded area under $t(d)$ between oi and $oi + j$.

Similarly, if the household locates closer to its workplace, say oi-j, it reduces its transportation costs by the area under the $t(d)$ curve between oi-j and oi. At the same time, it increases its rental expenditures by the quantity under the q_3 curve between oi-j and oi. Thus, a household consuming the quantity of residential space q_3 and residing at oi-j rather than oi would make uneconomic expenditures for location which equal the shaded area between oi-j and oi.

Thus, from Figure 1–2 we have obtained (1) those locations which minimize the household's locational costs for each quantity of residential space, and (2) the expenditures the household would be required to make to consume each quantity of residential space. This is all the information needed to obtain a unique locational solution for each household.

Total location costs divided by the quantity of residential space is the price the household must pay per unit for residential space. With this price information the household's locational solution is straightforward. Using conventional tools of demand analysis, and information on the price of all other goods and services—the household's preference for residential space, its preference for all other goods and services, and its income—the household's consumption of residential space may be determined. After we have determined the household's consumption of residential space, we have uniquely determined its residential location.

Empirical Testing

At the beginning of the chapter, it is emphasized that the purpose of this model is to provide some testable hypotheses. The variables employed in the model are location rents at each site and transportation costs per mile, from which we define a third variable—the price of residential space; incomes; preferences for residential space; and preferences for all other goods and services. I have already stated my willingness to specify the shape of the rent function, and money costs of transportation are fairly straightforward, although the valuation of time is complex. In the empirical tests presented in this chapter it is assumed that similar households place the same valuation on time per mile. Preferences are always difficult to quantify, but it is possible to make defensible assertions about the relative space preferences of various classes of households. For example, it is reasonable to assume that larger households, such as those with children, prefer residential space more than smaller households. Since I assume that residential space is not an inferior good, the consumption of residential space will increase with income.

Data for the empirical tests presented in this chapter were obtained from the origin and destination study conducted in 1953 by the Detroit Area

Traffic Study. The data consist of the origins and destinations of worktrips, information on the characteristics of the households to which the trip-maker belonged, and certain attributes of the trips themselves, for a stratified random sample of approximately 40,000 Detroit households.

The Location Rent Surface for Detroit

For empirical testing of the residential location model, the Detroit metropolitan area is divided into concentric distance rings, numbered from one to six from the center outward, around the central business district. It is assumed that location rents for a unit of residential space of a given quality and amenity successively decrease from ring to ring outward from the center, with rents very high near the center and very low near the outer circumference. The rate of decrease is assumed to be substantial in the inner rings and very slight in the outer. The surface in the outer rings is assumed to be quite flat, and to decrease only moderately with distance from the central business district.

These assumptions about the shape of the location rent surface are obtained from our premises about the determinants of the surface. It was stated earlier that location rents result from the competition among many workers for residential space near the same workplace or other workplaces nearby. The number of workers employed within each ring may be thought of as representing the number of demanders for residential space within the ring, and the number of acres within the ring as the supply of residential space. Ring 1 includes only .02 percent of the available space within the study area, but provides jobs for nearly 11 percent of Detroit's workers. Detroit has 60 percent of its employment located within six miles of the central business district, but only 10 percent of the land within the study area is located there. This indicates a substantial excess demand for space within the close-in rings, and a substantial lessening of demand for space in outer rings. The relatively low level of demand for urban use in the outermost ring is indicated by the large proportion of land which is not in urban use within the ring. A full 68 percent of the available land in Ring 6 is vacant; if land devoted to streets and alleys were subtracted, this figure would be even higher.

Thus it is reasonable to expect that location rents in the central business district and nearby would be very high, while in Ring 6 they would be very low. The high level of demand for residential space in inner rings is indicated by the high employment—and, for that matter, high residential densities. The low level of demand for residential space in outer levels is indicated by low employment densities, low residential densities, and the large quantities of vacant land within these rings.

EMPIRICAL ANALYSIS

If workers stratified according to income, sex, race, family size, residential density, or structure type have a common workplace, i.e., the same location rent function, the residential location model would predict different distributions of residence around this workplace for each group. At the same time, the model would predict differences in the residential distribution of the same class of workers if the workers are employed at different workplaces, i.e., have different location rent functions.

For the empirical tests presented in this section, the residential distribution of different classes of workers employed within the same ring, having by assumption the same location rent function, are compared with distributions expected a priori from the model. In addition, the residential distributions of workers belonging to the same class but employed at different workplaces, i.e., having different location rent functions, are compared for consistency with the expected relationships.

The first finding which supports the appropriateness of the residential location model is a well-known one. Journeys to work are predominately from outer residential rings to inner workplace rings. Furthermore, the proportion of a ring's workers residing within the same or adjacent rings increases with the workplace ring's distance from the central business district.

In terms of the model described above, equal transportation costs are incurred with movement in any direction. Reductions in location rents are to be found only away from the central business district. As a result, the minimization of location rents is always obtained in the direction of the periphery regardless of the household's space consumption. Secondly, as the schedule of location rents flattens out toward the periphery, the space consumption of households becomes less of a constraint and higher proportions of the workplace's employees live nearby. The model's only justification for a journey to work is to reduce the household's total expenditures for location rents. If, as hypothesized for Rings 5 and 6, total location rents do not decrease as the household makes a longer journey to work, or decrease only slightly, there is little incentive to make a journey to work, at least to economize on rents. Thus, the direction of the journey to work is from residences in outer rings where location rents are low to workplaces in inner rings; and larger proportions of worktrips are made to nearby rings as the workplace's distance from the central business district increases.

The distribution of elapsed time spent by workers employed in each ring in reaching work also exhibits the expected relationship. The fewest short trips are made by workers employed in the central business district. Few workers employed in Rings 5 and 6 make long trips. For example, 49 percent of workers employed in the central business district make trips more than one-half hour long. By way of contrast, only 17 percent of those employed in Ring 6, where the location rent surface is hypothesized as being nearly horizontal from the workplace, make trips of longer than a half-hour. The proportion is even lower for Ring 5: 14 percent. If it is assumed that the distribution of travel time valuations, money costs of transportation, incomes, space preferences, etc., are similar for each workplace ring, the model would predict longer journeys to work by workers employed in inner rings than for those employed in outer rings. The longer journeys to work made by Ring 6 workers are explained by the fact that much of Ring 6 is rural. Workers employed in isolated establishments within the ring may have to make substantial journeys to work to obtain an adequate selection of housing.

These results may seem trivial as tests of the appropriateness of the residential location model. It should be noted, therefore, that the empirical results for nonwhites, who because of housing market segregation are unable to compete freely in the market for residential space as we defined it, are exactly the opposite. The longest trips by Detroit nonwhites are made by those employed in outer rings and the shortest by those employed in inner rings. Similarly the journey to work pattern of nonwhites employed in outer rings is from residences in inner rings to workplaces in outer rings. If this economic model lacked relevance, or if residential location resulted entirely from some socioeconomic clustering as many urban sociologists and real estate market analysts have suggested, these regularities would not have to exist. Distributions similar to those observed for nonwhites might be the rule rather than the exception.

Male-Female Differences in
Work-Residence Patterns

The work-residence patterns of all workers conceal important differences among the various classes of workers. An understanding of these differences is important for a satisfactory explanation of the relationships between the journey-to-work and the selection of a residential location. Among these is a significant difference in the ring to ring movement of male and female workers. Table 1–2 compares the proportions of males and females residing in each distance ring, by ring of employment.

From Table 1–2 it is evident that the residential distribution of males around their workplaces is flatter than that of females. Higher proportions of female workers consistently reside in nearby residential rings than do the proportions of male workers. The tighter locational pattern of female workers is, in terms of the residential location model, consistent with at least three different hypotheses. The first inference that might be drawn is that the direction of causation assumed in the model is wrong for women workers. It might plausibly be argued that the residence is selected for some unspecified reason, and that the wife and mother has a greater need to find a convenient job near the home. Such an argument would correctly point out that many females, if not most, are secondary wage earners. As such, they tend to seek nearby jobs to augment their family budget, with a more casual attitude in job seeking than that of the primary wage earner. As a result, the place of employment generally has less effect on the choice of a residence. This view suggests that women's selection of a place of employment is more conditioned by the selection of residence.

Table 1–2. Proportion of Males and Females Residing in Each Distance Ring, by Ring of Employment

Employment Ring	Sex	Distance Ring						Total
		1	*2*	*3*	*4*	*5*	*6*	
One	Male	4.8	9.9	25.0	26.8	23.2	10.2	100
	Female	2.6	15.6	38.0	25.8	12.9	5.0	100
Two	Male	1.0	19.1	31.2	22.9	17.1	8.6	100
	Female	0.8	23.2	39.2	20.9	11.0	4.6	100
Three	Male	0.8	11.3	36.9	24.0	16.9	10.1	100
	Female	0.4	9.7	46.9	25.3	12.5	5.1	100
Four	Male	0.5	6.4	21.0	32.2	24.2	15.7	100
	Female	0.0	4.0	23.0	44.0	19.8	9.2	100
Five	Male	0.4	2.1	10.2	16.6	50.8	20.0	100
	Female	0.0	1.9	8.7	16.6	53.8	18.9	100
Six	Male	0.5	2.0	6.9	10.1	22.4	58.0	100
	Female	0.2	1.6	3.8	6.1	16.6	71.8	100

The second interpretation is that females make shorter journeys to work because their workplace is the same as or nearby to that of their husbands. Such households have a stronger incentive to shorten the journey to work because the combined journey to work costs are higher than for households having only a single wage earner.

Finally, it is likely that a disproportionate number of female wage earners belong to households having lower space preference, i.e., to one or two person households. For these households both the greater numbers of working wives and the lower space preferences work in favor of shorter journeys to work.

OCCUPATIONAL DIFFERENCES IN RESIDENTIAL DISTRIBUTIONS

The model would postulate that if households had the same location rent function, the same transportation cost function, the same space preference, and the same valuation of time, but different incomes, the length of the households' journey to work would increase as an increasing function of income. The Detroit origin and destination study did not obtain household income, but the occupations of wage earners can be used as a crude measure of household incomes.

Figure 1–3 shows the proportion of high, medium, and low income central business district workers residing in each residential ring. Clearly, lower income workers have the tightest residential pattern; the highest income workers, the most dispersed.

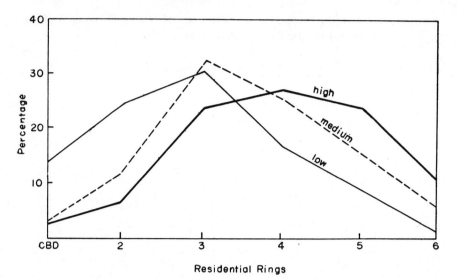

Figure 1-3. Proportion of the Central Business District's Low, Medium, and High Income Workers Residing in Each Residential Ring

Analysis of the Data for Occupations
Ranked by Median Income

Similar residential distributions were obtained for Employment Rings 1, 2, and 3, using eight occupational classifications. For workers employed in Ring 4, however, these relationships show signs of weakening. The hypothesized relationships have all but disappeared for Rings 5 and 6—an expected result. Since the location rent function is very flat from workplaces located in Rings 5 and 6, space consumption provides less of a justification for a journey to work. Additionally, the lower income workers retain their tight adhesion to the workplace observed for inner rings. Of the service workers employed in Ring 6, 77 percent reside within the same ring. The proportion is nearly as large for male service workers—75 percent.

The relationships between occupational earnings and the proportion of each occupation residing in each ring may be subjected to a more rigorous test. The proportion of workers employed in each occupation residing in each ring may be ranked by size. Table 1–3 illustrates these rankings for workers employed in Ring 2. If the hypothesis is correct, the ranks of the proportions residing in that ring should have the opposite order from those of the median earnings of each occupation. A perfect inverse ranking would show that, in all cases, as the median income increases, the proportion of the occupation residing in a residence ring would decrease. This represents the expected pattern for rings near the workplace, where rents decrease significantly with distance from the workplace. A perfect ordering in the opposite direction is expected for Rings 5 and 6. The proportions of the occupation's members residing in Ring 6 should decrease as the average income of the occupation decreases.

It can be seen in Table 1–3 that although the order generally accords with the hypothesis, it is not perfect, the imperfection being that lower percentages of sales workers and clerical workers reside in inner rings than their incomes would lead us to expect. By contrast, a higher proportion of operatives and craftsmen resides in inner rings than is consistent with their income rankings. The ordering is also very good for Residence Rings 5 and 6. If the above two pairs of occupations were exchanged, the order of occupational incomes and the ranks of the percentage residing in Ring 5 would be identical. This is a systematic discrepancy for all workplace rings. The operatives group is consistently out of order. Only operatives of the four highest income occupations reside in inner rings at higher than average proportions and outer residential rings at below average proportions. This apparent discrepancy can be largely explained in terms of differences in female participation by occupation mentioned earlier. For this reason we will present results both for all workers and for males only. For the analysis of ranked data which follows, the data for each of the six workplace rings are arranged as in Table 1–3.

The Spearman Coefficient of Rank Correlation provides a powerful and efficient tool to evaluate the degree of association among these ranked relationships. The Spearman Rank Order Correlation Technique is interpreted in a way similar to that applied to the usual correlation technique. For the relationships among these sets of ranked data to be consistent with our a priori expectations, the following relationships would have to be exhibited.

The inner employment rings best satisfy the assumptions about the schedule of location rents set forth in the model; therefore, in the innermost

Table 1–3. Ranked Residential Distributions for Occupational Groups Employed in Ring

Occupation	Median Income	Residence Ring									
		2		3		4		5		6	
		%	Rank	%	Rank	%	Rank	%	Rank	%	Rank
Managers	$4516	10.6	8	28.8	7	28.8	2	27.4	1	8.5	4
Professionals	4099	12.0	7	27.0	8	29.5	1	22.0	2	8.6	2.5
Craftsmen	3715	19.1	4	29.6	6	24.2	3	16.0	4	10.6	1
Operatives	3002	24.9	3	37.9	1	16.8	7	13.1	6	6.4	6
Salesworkers	2792	15.4	6	33.5	4	24.1	4	18.4	3	8.6	2.5
Clerical	2706	18.0	5	36.3	3	23.2	5	15.3	5	6.5	5
Laborers	2690	34.3	2	30.5	5	18.1	6	6.8	7	6.2	7
Services	2262	35.0	1	36.5	2	15.4	8	6.1	8	2.6	8

three rings, the proportion of an occupation residing in a given ring should be negatively correlated with income. For outer residential rings there should be a high positive correlation between those occupational groups ranked according to median income and ranked according to the proportion of each residing in the residential ring. As the workplace's distance from the urban center increases, the relationship should deteriorate. This would be observed empirically by a decrease in the size of the coefficient of rank correlation for both inner and outer residential rings, and perhaps a nonuniform change of sign in many cases. Where the ring of employment and ring of residence are the same, it is expected that the relationship would always be negative, because low income workers are small space consumers and thus make shorter journeys to work. Tables 1–4 and 1–5 give the coefficients of rank correlation between occupation and the

Table 1–4. Rank Order Coefficients Between Occupations Ranked by Income and Occupations Ranked by Rate of Residential Selection, for All Employment and Residence Rings: All Workers

Employment Ring	Residence Ring				
	2	*3*	*4*	*5*	*6*
CBD	−0.86*	−0.74*	0.69	0.83*	0.98*
2	(−0.81)*	−0.67	0.83*	0.89*	0.71*
3	−0.50	(−0.64)	0.76*	0.88*	0.76*
4	−0.57	−0.71	(−0.48)	0.88*	0.89*
5	−0.47	0.04	0.29	(−0.33)	0.19
6	−0.33	0.21	0.42	0.90*	(−0.61)

Note: Figures are in parenthesis where residence and employment rings are the same.
*Differs significantly from zero at the 0.05 level.

Table 1–5. Rank Order Coefficients Between Occupations Ranked by Income and Occupations Ranked by Rate of Residential Selection, for All Employment and Residence Rings: Male Workers Only

Employment Ring	Residence Ring					
	1	*2*	*3*	*4*	*5*	*6*
CBD	(−0.69)	−0.81*	−0.74	0.57	0.95*	0.95*
2		(−0.50)	−0.55	0.88*	0.88*	0.90*
3		−0.76*	(−0.95)*	0.95*	0.86*	0.83*
4		−0.88*	−0.57	(−0.17)	0.48	0.19
5		−0.43	0.29	0.29	(−0.38)	0.38
6		−0.40	0.36	0.36	0.81	(−0.40)

Note: Figures are in parenthesis where residence and employment rings are the same.
*Differs significantly from zero at the 0.05 level.

percentage of that occupation residing in the ring for all six employment rings, for all workers and for males.

The coefficients in Tables 1–4 and 1–5 are generally expected. Reading the tables from left to right, i.e., from inner residential rings to outer residential rings, the coefficients change from high negative correlations to high positive correlations. Reading from top to bottom, i.e., from inner workplace rings to outer, the relationship tends to weaken. Where the residence and workplace rings are the same, the figures are in parenthesis; these are the diagonal elements in Tables 1–4 and 1–5. The expected pattern for these rings also materializes: lower income workers reside in above average proportions in these rings, i.e., the journey to work typically becomes shorter as income falls.

The overall consistency of the pattern indicates that the locational selections of household by occupation are generally consistent with the model of residential location.

Family Size by Residence Ring

The relationships between family size and residence are neither as uniform nor as simple to interpret as those between sex and residence and occupation and residence. Family size is employed at this point as an indicator of household space preferences. Larger families undoubtedly spend a greater proportion of their time in the home, using it for a far broader range of social and recreational activities. As a result, it is expected that these households, *ceteris paribus*, would manifest a greater preference for residential space.

At the same time, residential space beyond minimum requirements is to some extent a luxury. When families reach a very large size, the greater desire to consume space is probably partially offset by a lower per capita income. The minimum levels of food, clothing and other necessities require a larger proportion of the household budget. Thus, there appears to be some tendency for the space consumption of households to fall off as family size increases beyond a certain point.

The Family Size Residence Pattern for Inner Employment Rings.

Tables 1–6 and 1–7 show the cumulative percentages of those employed in Rings 1 and 2 who reside in Rings 1 through 6. From Table 1–6 it can be seen that the proportion of one person families residing in inner rings is substantially higher than that of any other family unit size. The cumulative percentages residing in Rings 2, 3, 4, and 5 fall as family size increases, until a family size of five persons is reached. For families of six or more, the relationship reverses itself. The proportion of six person families residing in inner rings exceeds the proportions for all family groups except those having more than six persons or unrelated individuals.

The decreasing proportion of central business district workers residing in inner rings, as family size increases, is consistent with a higher space

Table 1–6. Cumulative Percentages of Ring 1 Workers Residing in Rings 1 Through 6, Family Size

Family Size (Number of Persons)	Residence Ring					
	1	*2*	*3*	*4*	*5*	*6*
1	26.1	55.6	86.0	97.8	98.5	100
2	2.5	14.8	50.3	76.2	93.4	100
3		9.7	39.8	69.3	90.5	100
4	0.4	10.2	38.8	68.8	90.8	100
5		9.8	35.7	67.3	89.5	100
6		11.2	52.0	77.0	93.4	100
More than 6		15.9	46.8	70.7	92.1	100
All	3.7	16.1	46.8	72.9	91.4	100

Table 1–7. Cumulative Percentages of Ring 2 Workers Residing in Rings 1 Through 6, Family Size

Family Size Number of Persons	Residence Ring					
	1	*2*	*3*	*4*	*5*	*6*
1	9.7	59.7	87.1	94.6	98.9	100
2	0.8	22.6	56.4	79.8	93.0	100
3		16.7	51.1	74.7	93.3	100
4	0.1	15.8	48.9	73.5	91.2	100
5	0.1	17.3	48.3	70.7	89.4	100
6		19.2	53.6	75.0	89.7	100
More than 6	1.4	21.6	58.6	79.2	90.8	100
All	1.0	21.1	54.2	76.6	92.2	100

preference on the part of these households. A higher space preference, *ceteris paribus,* leads to a greater consumption of space and a longer journey to work.

The reversal of the relationship for households having more than five members is consistent with their lower per capita incomes. Beyond a certain size, the greater space preference is offset for many very large families by an income constraint. Household demand for other needed goods and services causes them to forego higher space consumption.

Table 1–7 shows that these relationships hold for Employment Ring 2 as well, with only one unimportant difference: from Rings 3 through 6 the cumulative percentage of families having more than six persons falls below that of six person families. The percentages still exceed all but those of one and two person families, however.

Family Size by Ring of Residence—Outer Employment Rings. In the outer employment rings, we should expect either a reversal of the pattern observed in Rings 1 and 2 or no discernible relationship between family size and residential location. Table 1–8 shows that one and two person families employed in Ring 5 tend to reside in inner rings in the highest proportions of all family unit sizes. Because of the lower space requirements, living closer to the central business district is less costly for them than for those having higher space preferences. To state that the higher location rents are less of a constraint for these households fails, however, to provide any reason that smaller families should be more willing to pay higher location rents or make a longer journey to work in order to reside nearer the center. The more incomplete specification of the transportation costs of these households provides such an explanation.

It is logical to expect that many of these households make above average numbers of trips to social and recreational centers located in or near the central business district. Their locational choices, therefore, would be heavily weighted by these trips. This should be true for one person families as well. Unfortunately, one person households employed in Ring 6 exhibit the tightest locational pattern of all families but those having more than five persons. One person households employed in Ring 5 exhibit the expected behavior. From Table 1–8 it can be seen that only 33 percent of those employed in Ring 5 reside either in it or in Ring 6. By contrast, 64 percent of two person households and 73 percent of six person families reside in one of these two rings.

Also, it is likely that a large proportion of two person families have a second wage earner. If the second member of the household is employed in an inner ring, this provides an added incentive for the household to live closer to the center. It should be remembered, for all family sizes, that only small proportions of those employed in Rings 5 and 6 live in Rings 1, 2, and 3.

The final relationship exhibited by Tables 1–8 and 1–9 is an increase in the proportion of a ring's employees residing nearby the workplace as family size increases. This finding is also consistent with the lower per capita incomes of larger families. When changes in total location rents with distance are slight, minimization of transportation costs results in the minimization of total

Table 1–8. Cumulative Percentages of Ring 5 Workers Residing in Rings 1 Through 6, Family Size

Family Size Number of Persons	*Residence Ring*					
	1	*2*	*3*	*4*	*5*	*6*
1	100	89.1	78.3	52.3	32.6	10.0
2	100	99.8	96.6	83.9	63.6	20.9
3		100.0	98.3	85.6	67.8	19.7
4		100.0	98.0	89.2	72.0	23.1
5		100.0	98.8	92.5	72.5	21.2
6		100.0	99.2	88.8	73.1	27.1
More than 6		100.0	97.6	86.6	70.9	26.6
All	100	99.5	97.2	86.2	67.4	22.5

Table 1–9. Cumulative Percentages of Ring 6 Workers Residing in Rings 1 Through 6, Family Size

Family Size Number of Persons	Residence Ring					
	1	*2*	*3*	*4*	*5*	*6*
1	100	93.7	84.3	81.1	79.0	66.8
2	100	99.7	96.5	88.0	76.1	56.3
3		100.0	98.7	92.3	81.7	62.7
4		100.0	93.8	93.1	83.5	58.4
5		100.0	97.8	93.4	85.5	62.6
6		100.0	99.6	92.9	90.0	66.4
More than 6		100.0	99.4	95.1	87.3	66.7
All	100	99.6	97.6	91.4	82.2	61.0

locational costs. Households with lower per capital incomes may be more sensitive to small differences in transportation costs.

Family Size by Ring of Residence–Rings 3 and 4. Above average proportions of the very large and very small households employed in Rings 3 and 4 reside in rings near the center. Families with three to six members reside in higher proportions in Rings 5 and 6. The closeness in locational patterns of one and two person families employed in Rings 3 and 4 is even more reasonable than is that of the same size families employed in Rings 5 and 6.

Suburban living must be far less attractive to the young married or the childless couple than to those with children; their social and recreational activities are to a much greater degree directed outside the home. For the unattached person, residence in a suburban neighborhood far from the center of activity is even more unsatisfactory.

No adequate explanation in terms of the model can be offered for the locational choices of the very large families. In the case of Employment Ring 4, the divergence is great enough that a larger proportion of its workers reside in Ring 3 than in Ring 5. Even so, more workers reside in the two rings away from the central business district than reside in those nearer the central business district.

Space Consumption by Residential Rings

The model of residential location postulates that where location rents are a significant factor, households consuming larger quantities of space will, *ceteris paribus*, make longer journeys to work than those consuming lesser quantities. The distance the household resides from its workplace is expressed in the model as a function of the quantity of residential space consumed. The relationship between space consumption and length of the journey to work, like that between income and the length of the journey, should deteriorate for outer employment rings, where the schedule of rents decreases only slightly or not at all around the workplace.

In this paper, structure type is employed as a measure of space consumption. This is an admittedly inadequate index, especially for single family dwelling units, where the index fails to differentiate between very significant differences in lot size. Regardless of these deficiencies, structure type undoubtedly represents a dimension of the space consumption relationship. It is probably roughly correlated with the measure of space consumption we would wish to employ. For this reason, we will look at the relationships between residential location and occupancy of single family, two family, or multifamily dwellings.

The Residence Space Consumption Pattern for Inner Employment Rings. Table 1–10 shows the percentages of workers occupying each type of dwelling unit in each residence ring, for Employment Rings, 1, 2, and 3. As might be expected, those choosing higher density structures—two family dwelling units and multiple dwellings—reside in well-above-average proportions in the close in residential rings. For example, 30 percent of central business district workers who live in multiple dwelling units reside in the adjacent ring. In contrast, the adjacent ring is selected by only 5 percent of those choosing single family structures and 13 percent of those selecting two family structures. This

Table 1–10. Percentage of Inner Employment Ring Workers Residing in Each Ring, by Structure Type

Structure Type	Residence Ring						
	1	*2*	*3*	*4*	*5*	*6*	*Total*
Percentage of Ring 1 (CBD) Workers							
One family	–	5.4	22.1	29.8	28.9	13.8	100
Two family	–	13.1	46.7	32.8	5.8	1.5	100
Multiple	2.4	29.5	50.2	14.7	2.1	1.1	100
All	3.8	12.6	31.1	26.3	18.4	7.8	100
Percentage of Ring 2 Workers							
One family	–	8.7	25.5	28.1	25.1	12.5	100
Two family	0.2	26.2	46.8	21.4	4.0	1.4	100
Multiple	1.2	43.6	43.4	9.3	1.7	0.7	100
All	1.0	20.1	34.1	22.4	15.6	7.7	100
Percentage of Ring 3 Workers							
One family	–	5.3	27.0	29.7	24.1	13.9	100
Two family	0.1	13.8	60.0	21.4	3.7	1.0	100
Multiple	0.8	25.2	59.9	11.2	2.0	0.8	100
All	0.7	10.9	39.3	24.3	15.9	0.9	100

pattern persists through Ring 3, where 50 percent of all central business district workers who live in multiple dwelling units reside. Ring 3 also provides dwellings for 47 percent of those residing in two family units, as opposed to only 22 percent of those residing in one family units.

The proportion of those residing in multiple and two family units in Residence Rings 5 and 6, on the other hand, is very low. Less than 2 percent in each case live in Ring 6.

The Residence Space Consumption Pattern for Outer Employment Rings. The differential pattern of residence by structure type for outer workplace rings is also a basic conformity with the model. These patterns are shown in Table 1–11. A large proportion of these residents of all three structure types reside in their workplace rings or adjacent rings. Employment Ring 6 encompasses the residences of 64 percent of all single family households, 40 percent of the two family households, and 52 percent of households choosing multiple units, who work in that ring. Where the rent schedule is relatively flat, as in Ring 6, we would postulate a short journey to work regardless of space consumption. In the case of Employment Rings 4 and 5, a similar pattern exists: the residential distribution is tighter than for inner rings, but less tight than for Ring 6. In terms of the model, households employed in Ring 6 tend to live nearby, regardless of space consumption. Those employed in Ring 2, by

Table 1–11. Percentage of Outer Employment Ring Workers Residing in Each Ring, by Structure Type

Structure Type	Residence Ring						
	1	2	3	4	5	6	Total
Percentage of Ring 4 Workers							
One family	–	2.6	13.4	34.2	30.7	19.1	100
Two family	–	8.2	39.4	42.8	7.1	2.5	100
Multiple	–	21.5	43.2	25.5	5.1	4.7	100
All	0.5	6.0	21.4	34.5	23.3	14.4	100
Percentage of Ring 5 Workers							
One family	–	0.7	6.0	16.3	51.8	25.1	100
Two family	–	5.2	27.0	31.8	30.2	5.9	100
Multiple	–	12.9	34.4	24.2	17.9	10.5	100
All	0.3	2.2	10.5	18.4	46.8	21.8	100
Percentage of Ring 6 Workers							
One family	–	0.8	3.4	7.3	24.0	64.5	100
Two family	–	3.2	21.2	25.7	10.2	39.8	100
Multiple	–	9.8	18.2	10.3	9.5	52.2	100
All	0.4	2.0	6.2	9.2	21.2	61.0	100

comparison, tend to live nearby only if they consume limited quantities of residential space. They tend to make a journey to work from outer rings if they consume larger quantities of residential space. Very few of those consuming small quantities of space live in Rings 4, 5, and 6.

Somewhat larger proportions of those employed in Ring 6, and consuming small amounts of space, reside in interior rings.

Income and Substitution Effect

It was pointed out previously that in terms of the way the problem is formulated in this chapter, the price of residential space is determined by location rents and transportation costs. As a result, the households employed in inner rings, confronted by higher and steeper schedules of location rents, must pay a higher price for residential space than must be paid by those employed in outer rings. If the assumption of similar incomes, tastes, and transportation costs for those employed in each successive ring is reasonably adequate, it would be expected a priori that the relatively lower price of residential space for those in outer rings would lead to higher space consumption.

From Table 1–12 it can be seen that this pattern generally holds. A smaller proportion of central business district workers and those employed in Ring 2 reside in single family units. A larger proportion select two family and multiple units. The proportion employed in Rings 5 and 6 living in one family structures in turn exceeds those for Rings 3 and 4. Similarly, the proportion residing in multiple and two family living quarters is smaller.

DERIVED DEMAND FOR RESIDENTIAL SERVICES

There is one final question which should be considered briefly. A large number of researchers have emphasized the role of good schools and public services, and the supply of new and high quality dwelling units, in determining residential location.

It is an empirical fact that the mean quality level of the housing

Table 1–12. Percentage Residing in Each Structure Type, by Employment Ring

Structure Type	Employment Ring					
	1	*2*	*3*	*4*	*5*	*6*
One family	58.4	56.9	60.6	69.0	79.2	78.1
Two family	18.2	21.7	20.8	18.4	11.8	10.4
Multiple	17.4	17.2	15.4	10.4	6.9	7.5
Other	5.9	4.2	3.2	2.4	2.2	4.0
Total	100.0	100.0	100.0	100.0	100.0	100.0

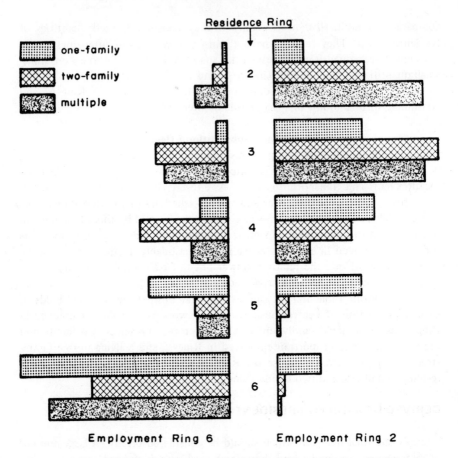

Figure 1-4. Percentage of Ring 2 and Ring 6 Workers Residing in Each Ring, by Structure Type

stock, and most likely of government services, increases with distance from the central business district. My intuition, based partially on the findings presented here and those of related research, is that an explanation of residential location in these terms is at best an oversimplification and at worst may be basically incorrect. It is my belief that housing quality is less of a determinant of residential choices than are collective residential choices a determinant of the quality of housing services and of the quality of governmental services. Among other things, the theory developed in this chapter predicts a spatial distribution of demand for residential space by different income groups. If the demand for housing quality and quality of governmental services is a derived demand, the distribution of quality predicted by my model and to some extent supported by the evidence presented in this chapter would be very similar to that observed empirically. This leads me to the tentative conclusion that observed distribution of housing quality is the result of the long run operation of an admittedly imperfect market, but one which is possibly less imperfect than often supposed.

There is one major exception to my remarks: racial discrimination represents a major market imperfection which distorts the spatial demand for residential space by both whites and nonwhites. The way in which discrimination affects the housing choice of black households and the form of urban growth and development is analyzed in Chapters Six and Seven.

CONCLUSIONS

This chapter presents a simple economic theory of residential location and evaluates this theory with data on residential distributions for Detroit whites employed in six concentric rings around Detroit's central business district. These same six distance rings are also used as the residential subareas in the analysis. The analysis assumes that workers employed in each ring face different housing costs, transport costs and trade-offs than workers employed in every other ring. These differences arise from the fact that the schedule of prices per unit of urban space in each differs with distance and direction from the workplace. As a result, differences in the length of the journey to work and in the locational choices of workers employed in each ring may be understood only when the characteristics of the metropolitan schedule of location rents is specified. For Detroit, it is reasonable to assume that the surface of location rents tends to decrease with distance from the central business district, and that the rate of decrease is greatest near the center and least near the periphery.

In addition, although housing quality was not explicitly included as a variable in the empirical work, the analysis offers some conjectures about the relationships between the distribution of housing quality and the selection of residential locations by households.

The empirical findings are generally in conformity with those expected a priori from the model of residential location. This model would predict that, where the market for residential space has the characteristics ascribed to the inner rings in Detroit, households will locate at varying distances from their workplaces according to their transportation costs, space consumption, space preferences, and incomes.

The empirical analysis revealed that the commuting pattern was largely from residences in outer rings to workplaces in inner rings, that the average length of the journeys to work decreased with the workplace's distance from the central business district, and that the proportion of a ring's workers residing in the same or nearby rings increased as the workplace ring's distance from the central business district increased.

Workers employed in higher income occupations and working in inner rings tend to make longer journeys to work and reside in outer rings. When employed in outer rings they make much shorter journeys to work and live within the same ring and adjacent rings at very high rates. Low income workers make short journeys to work and reside within the workplace ring and in nearby rings regardless of the location of workplace.

Family size as an indicator of space preference has a similar effect on residential location. The smallest and largest families make the shortest journeys to work. For the smallest families, this is attributed to low space preferences; the shorter journeys to work by the largest families are attributed to a per capita income constraint.

Structure type is used as a measure of the household's space consumption. The longest journeys to work are made by those residing in one family units and the shortest by those residing in multiple units. A marked difference between the locational choices of males and females was discovered. Female workers, regardless of workplace ring, make shorter journeys to work than male workers and reside within the workplace ring and nearby rings in much higher proportions. Finally, it was determined that the proportion of workers residing in low density structures increased as the workplace ring's distance from the central business district increased.

All the relationships summarized above are very clear cut for rings near the central business district, where the location rent function with distances from the workplace is probably very steep. For peripheral workplace rings, where the function is probably very flat, the relationships are much weaker.

In summary, the evidence in this chapter supports the simple economic model developed in this chapter. The findings are generally consistent with our a priori views on the problem as obtained both from this model and similar models by Alonso, Wingo, and others. The issues evaluated in this chapter are still far from settled; however, a number will be considered further in subsequent chapters.

Chapter Two

Commuting and Residential Decisions of Central Business District Workers

INTRODUCTION

This chapter extends and elaborates the analyses of household housing and travel behavior presented in Chapter One. Section II below presents a restatement of the simple consumer-choice model developed there and presents further empirical tests of this model using data on the housing and travel behavior of white central business district workers in Detroit and Chicago.

In contrast to the situation analyzed in Chapter 1, all of the workers included in this analysis face a rapidly declining location rent surface with distance from their workplace. Even so, because of the differences in aggregate metropolitan area employment, central business district employment, and other differences in the two metropolitan areas, the location rent surfaces are assumed to differ in predictable ways that affect the residential and travel behavior of the two groups of workers. These differences permit empirical tests similar to those presented in Chapter One for Detroit households alone. Moreover, the more varied transport alternatives available to Chicago central business district workers permit our analysis of household substitution among different travel modes and the relation of these decisions to the residential decisions of these households. These simple empirical tests illustrate more clearly the logic of the theoretical framework employed and its consistency with widely accepted empirical facts.

A MODEL OF HOUSEHOLD RESIDENTIAL AND TRAVEL BEHAVIOR

The behavioral hypotheses used here to explain the residential and travel behavior of workers employed in central locations are essentially those described in the previous chapter. Still, because of their importance to the analysis that follows, it is perhaps useful to restate them briefly. It is assumed that households try to maximize their total real income in what is undoubtely an imperfect way; that is, they try to obtain their preferred set of consumer services at lowest possible cost. It is also argued that the length of a worker's journey to work, and thus the distance he resides from his workplace, largely depends on a cost trade-off between transportation costs and housing costs.

The essence of this trade-off is that, while workers employed at central locations can lower their housing costs by living farther from their workplaces, they increase their travel costs by doing so. The second relevant aspect of this trade-off is the fact that the magnitude of such savings in housing cost increases with the amount of residential space the worker uses, greater space consumption being associated with residence in lower density structures. The utility maximizing worker lives at that distance from his workplace where the money he saves in housing costs by undertaking a longer journey to work is just offset by increased travel costs.

The assumption that the portion of housing costs variously referred to by other authors as "location," "site," or "position" rents declines with distance from major workplace agglomerations is crucial to the explanation of household travel behavior developed in this chapter.[1] These location or site rents are economic rents which landlords may obtain from households for sites more accessible to major workplace agglomerations. The rents exist because of households' collective efforts to economize on transportation expenditures. Location rent surfaces having these properties have been obtained in a number of theoretical writings.[2]

It seems probable that a surface of location or site rents would be very complex and that location rent surfaces might differ for various types of accommodations (those of varying quality, density, age, etc.). The quasi rents obtainable in one submarket defined by, say, quality differences, might differ substantially from those obtainable in another. Market disequilibrium may well be the rule rather than the exception, since there are major imperfections in the market for real property, and since housing is both durable and nonhomogeneous.

Although there is apparently no empirical information that would permit direct evaluation of the hypothesis that location rents in the various submarkets differ, there is some inferential evidence. For one thing, some kinds of residential services may be difficult or impossible to secure by renovating single units of the existing stock of housing. For example, if large lots, high levels of community services, and other than gridiron street patterns are highly preferred residential attributes, wholesale demolition and redevelopment would probably be necessary to achieve them in the older built-up portions of cities. Since large lots are rare in old residential areas near central business districts, the price of large lot residential services might vary by a greater amount with distance from the central business district and other workplace agglomerations than the price of small lot residential services would. Thus, if there are two submarkets, one characterized by modern, high quality, large lot residential structures and another by obsolete, low quality, small lot structures, the incremental savings obtainable with distance from major workplaces might well be much greater in the former than the latter. In either case, however, we would expect the price for units in either submarket to decline with distance from the central business district. Furthermore, even given the above reservation, there is no obvious reason why systematic price differentials between the various submarkets, in the absence of serious market imperfections, should persist for long periods. Housing services can be either upgraded or downgraded. Downgrading can occur through density-increasing conversions, capital consumption, and failure to maintain and renovate structures. Upgrading can occur by renovation, demolition, and reconstruction, and by other forms of private market renewal.

Since the workers dealt with in this chapter are employed in the central areas of Chicago and Detroit, where urban employment densities are highest, we would expect their housing costs per unit of residential space to decline with distance from the center. Because Chicago and Detroit differ in size and in the numbers employed in their central business districts (about two and one-half times as many in Chicago as in Detroit), it would seem reasonable to expect—assuming the above provisional hypotheses about the determinants of location rents are valid—that location or site rents would be higher in Chicago than in Detroit at each distance from the central business district. Specifically, for the purpose of the empirical testing in this study, it is postulated that the price per unit of residential space of a stated quality and amenity decreases monotonically with distance from the center, but that the price is consistenly higher for Chicago. Thus it is postulated that centrally employed workers in both cities may reduce their housing costs per density unit by commuting longer distances, but that the savings per mile will be larger for Chicago workers.

It is also crucial that, in making longer journeys to work, households incur larger costs in both time and money. Since time is a scarce commodity, workers should demand some compensation for the time they spend commuting. Both the commuting distance and the time a central business district worker will spend thus depend on his valuation of commuting time, the money cost of his commuting, and the savings in housing cost he is able to obtain from a longer journey to work. He will extend his distance only so long as his savings in location rent offset his increased expenditures of time and money.

His reductions in housing cost, however, depend not only on his commuting distance, but also upon the quantity or the amount of residential space he consumes. If he lives in very low density residential quarters, his cost savings per unit of residential space are multipled by a large number of units; if he chooses very high density quarters, his savings may be small. For many people, housing cost savings obtained from longer journeys to work may be quickly offset by increasing travel costs.

Unless the labor forces of Detroit's and Chicago's central business districts differ greatly in their socioeconomic composition, the simple economic model used in this chapter would predict that Chicago workers' trips, measured by either elapsed time or distance, should exceed those of Detroit workers. As noted previously, we would expect larger savings in housing costs to be obtainable by commuting a given distance in Chicago than in Detroit, at every level of residential space consumption. Thus, if transportation costs in Chicago and Detroit are at all comparable, Chicago workers would be expected both to commute farther and to spend more time commuting. Precisely this relationship is shown in Figure 2–1. Fifty percent of Detroit's central business district workers can get home by traveling five miles or less, and 30 minutes or less; only 32 percent of their Chicago counterparts live that nearby, and only 34 percent can get home within that length of time.

Just as certainly, the simple consumer choice model predicts that Detroit workers will consume more residential space since it costs less than in Chicago. Figure 2–2 illustrates the comparison, measuring residential space consumption according to the structure type of residence. It is assumed that the greatest amount of space is consumed by single family units, followed by two

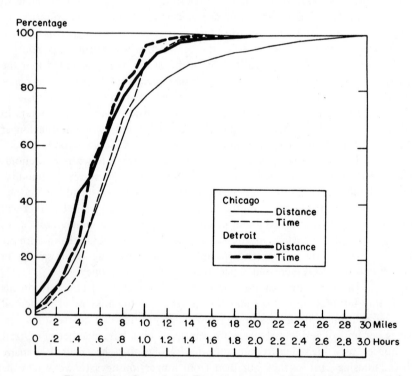

Figure 2–1. Cumulative Percentage Travel Times and Distances for Chicago and Detroit Central Business District Workers

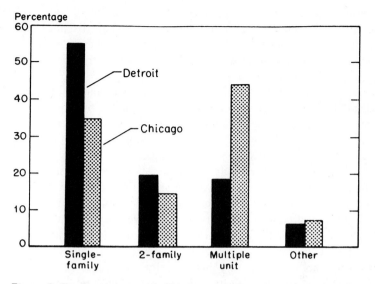

Figure 2–2. Percentage of Chicago and Detroit Central Business District Workers Residing in Each Structure Type

family units and multiple units. Both findings are well known and obvious empirical relationships. They are presented here because they are consistent with the consumer choice model previously discussed, and because they illustrate the trade-off between housing cost and travel cost.

SUBSTITUTION OF TIME AND MONEY EXPENDITURES IN COMMUTING

Trade-offs between housing and travel costs are not the only alternatives available to urban households attempting to maximize their real incomes. Journey to work travel costs have two components: dollar costs and time costs. Commuters to the central business district may choose among fairly numerous transportation means in Detroit, and even more in Chicago, with widely varying time and money costs. Differences in the relative costs of the several transport modes depend partly on distance traveled and partly on the household's choice of residential density. The choice, as discussed previously, strongly affects the amount a worker can save in housing costs by commuting longer distances. The numerous transport modes can also be used in combination to provide still more alternative time and money costs.

    If we consider only out-of-pocket costs, and if parking is free, the dollar costs of a railroad commuter and of a lone automobile commuter to the Chicago central business district are very similar; parking charges and car pooling, however, greatly affect the out-of-pocket costs of automobile commuting. These costs, for a single car commuter paying $1.00 a day for parking, exceed rail commuting costs by about $0.80 a day, assuming no collection or distribution charges for the railroad commuter. If these costs are shared by two persons, auto commuting costs 20 percent less for a trip to and from a residence area 20 miles from the Loop.

The level of transportation service, the amount of inconvenience and delay, and the portal to portal time of commuting by alternative travel means depend largely on the density of the worker's residence and workplace. Chicago's central business district has a combination of an unusually high level of transit service and high parking charges, both stemming from its very high workplace density. The result is a high rate of public transit use: 80 percent of the central business district's workers arrive there by some form of transit. The lower rate in Detroit—53 percent— is attributable to lower parking charges, lower levels of public transit services, and lower average residential density. Both high workplace and high residential densities usually mean more frequent transit service with wider coverage. Thus, there is a high probability that a worker employed at a very high density workplace, such as the CBD, and residing in a very high density residential area, will find it cheaper to use public transit than to travel by car. The probability is much lower for a worker employed at the same workplace but residing in a lower density area, and it is nearly zero for a worker having both a very low density workplace and a low density residence. Table 2–1, which lists the percentage of Detroit workers using public transit, by workplace ring and structure type of residence, illustrates just this relationship. Reading Table 2–1 from top to bottom, we find a decrease in the average workplace density and thus in the level of transit service at workplaces; and reading from left to right, we find a decrease also in the average residential density and thus the average level of transit service. The transit use figures shown in Table 2–1 are just those that would be predicted if the probability of public transit use were expressed as the joint probability of use at the workplace and at the residence, where the independent probabilities are

Table 2–1. Percentage of Detroit White Workers Using Public Transit, by Workplace Ring and Residence Type

Workplace Ring (higher to lower workplace density)	Residence Type (higher to lower residential density)		
	Multiple	*Two Family*	*One Family*
1	60.7	58.7	50.6
2	28.5	28.6	19.5
3	29.4	23.1	18.9
4	27.3	23.1	14.1
5	17.8	11.1	8.4
6	5.8	4.1	3.5

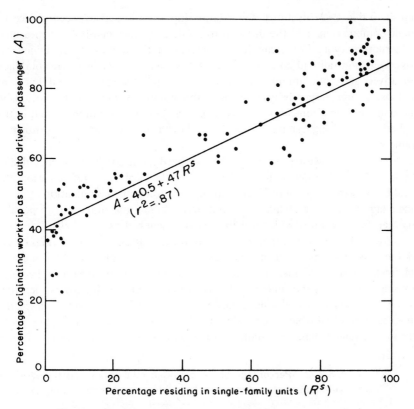

Figure 2-3. Percentage of Automobile Commuters in Each of Chicago's Residence Areas, by Percentage of Area's Single Family Dwelling Units

positively related to workplace and residence densities. The scatter diagram, Figure 2–3, illustrates the relationship between automobile use at the origin of the work trip (either by driver or rider) and the percentage of workers residing in single family dwelling units, for all white Chicago workers. From the figure, it is clear that those residence areas having fewer single family units and thus lower residential densities tend to have lower rapid transit use at the origin of worktrips.

Even among those CBD workers in Chicago who reside in low density structures, the vast majority are discouraged from commuting by automobile all the way to work, because of the high employment density and high parking charges in the CBD, and the high levels of service and abundant capacity provided by rapid transit and commuter railroads. Typically, those residing in single family units combine the use of private automobiles, either as drivers or passengers, with commuter railroad or—slightly less often—rapid transit. Table 2–2 illustrates the relationship for Chicago between choice of mode combinations and the decision to reside at various densities, as measured by structure type. For example, 85 percent of those who are combined car passengers and railroad commuters, and 82 percent of those who are combined car drivers and rail commuters reside in single family units; only 6 and 9 percent of those groups, respectively, reside in multiple units. As pointed out previously, the dollar cost and time cost properties of these combination modes result in the highest cost and highest average speed of all of the combination modes shown in Table 2–2.

The lowest money cost, lowest speed mode combination included in Table 2–2 is undoubtedly the combination of the local bus at residence and the local bus at workplace; only 17 percent of those using that combination reside in single family structures, while 51 percent reside in multiple units, and 15 percent in other dwelling units (which usually have the highest densities of all).

The interpretation offered here for the differences in the rates of use of the combinations listed in Table 2–2 is that they are the result of the cost minimization, utility maximization calculus described previously. The large housing cost savings per mile traveled for those residing at the lowest densities encourages them to travel long distances. As the distance traveled increases, the time savings obtainable from using modal combinations with higher speed encourages long distance commuters to spend more money to reduce travel time.

Table 2–2. Percentage of Chicago Central Business District Workers Residing in Various Structure Types, by Travel Mode Combinations

Travel Mode at Origin	Travel Mode at Destination	Type of Residence				
		One Family	Two Family	Multi-ple	Other	Total
Automobile						
Driver	Car driver	40.0	13.9	40.2	5.9	100.0
Driver	Railroad	81.9	8.1	8.8	1.2	100.0
Driver	Rapid transit	56.3	22.0	21.7	0.0	100.0
Driver	Bus	63.6	7.4	27.1	1.9	100.0
Passenger	Car passenger	28.3	13.4	50.9	7.4	100.0
Passenger	Railroad	85.4	6.9	5.5	2.2	100.0
Passenger	Rapid transit	60.6	13.5	25.2	0.7	100.0
Passenger	Bus	77.7	9.5	12.8	0.0	100.0
Railroad	Railroad	47.4	9.7	38.4	4.5	100.0
Railroad	Rapid transit	76.0	6.0	18.0	0.0	100.0
Railroad	Bus	57.5	1.9	29.0	11.6	100.0
Rapid transit	Rapid transit	11.4	13.3	67.6	7.7	100.0
Rapid transit	Bus	12.4	30.9	43.7	13.0	100.0
Bus	Railroad	54.7	20.5	20.2	4.6	100.0
Bus	Rapid transit	31.9	25.3	40.8	2.0	100.0
Bus	Bus	17.4	16.2	51.1	15.3	100.0
All modes		36.5	14.8	41.1	7.6	100.0

In addition, as residential density decreases, the time costs of using various travel modes from residence—railroad and rapid transit in particular and, to a lesser extent, bus—increase rapidly, usually making the private car the most economical way of originating the trip.

The situation is somewhat different for a great many people who choose to commute entirely by local bus. Their decision to reside at high density causes their potential housing cost savings by commuting longer distances to be small and to dictate minimal transportation expenditures in both time and money. Since terminal time makes up a very large proportion of total time spent on short trips by all modes, the travel time savings obtainable from the faster, more costly travel combinations are often too small to justify the larger dollar expenditures. Moreover, many small space consumers employed in the Chicago central business district can use the relatively high speed rapid transit mode for the entire trip and walk to residences and workplaces located near the rapid transit stations; of those using rapid transit for the entire trip, the percentage residing in multiple units is higher than that for any other travel modal combination—68 percent.

The relatively small percentage of whole trip automobile commuters, both drivers and riders, residing in single family units (40 and 28 percent respectively) suggests the interpretation that a majority of automobile commuters to the Chicago central business district use their cars for work-associated purposes. The finding that a disproportionate number of both car drivers and car passengers to Chicago's central business district and to the ring adjacent to the CBD, i.e. Sector O, gave "sales" as their occupation further supports this interpretation.

The importance of cars and buses in trips from residence to the higher volume grade-separated facilities is to be seen in Table 2–3, which gives the percentages of Chicago central business district workers residing within the cordon area and using each mode at their residences, and the percentages arriving in the central business district by each travel mode. (Detroit data do not permit comparable tabulations, since only the primary mode used was coded.) Table

Table 2–3. Percentage of Chicago Central Business District Workers Using Each Mode at Their Residences and Workplaces

Travel Mode	At Origin	At Destination
Car driver	19.9	12.3
Car rider	11.6	9.3
Railroad	13.1	22.1
Rapid transit	13.7	33.5
Bus	39.2	25.0
Taxi	—	0.3
Walk	1.3	1.3

2–3 shows that 20 percent of the worktrips to the Chicago central business district originate as car driver trips, 12 percent as car rider trips, and 39 percent as bus trips, while only 12.4 percent of the arrivals represent car driver trips, 4 percent car rider trips, and 25 percent bus trips. Commuter railroad, by way of contrast, accounts for 22 percent of destinations but only 13 percent of origins; and rapid transit accounts for only 14 percent of trip origins but over 33 percent of trip destinations. Table 2–4 shows that the majority of commuter railroad trips combined with another mode are serviced at the origin by auto; of the 22 percent of work trips arriving in the Loop by commuter railroad, 9 percent originate by car, about equally divided between driver and passenger trips. Car trips are only about half as important as feeders for the rapid transit lines: of the 34 percent of destinations accounted for by rapid transit, only about 4.1 percent begin by car. Buses are the important collector for the rapid transit system: almost one-half the 75,000 rapid transit trips terminating in the central business district originate by bus, while only slightly more than one-third of the 75,000 arrivals originate on the rapid transit line.

A comparison of Tables 2–3 and 2–4 illustrates the combined effect of lower parking fees and slightly poorer transit service on modes of travel used by workers employed in Chicago's Sector 0. While only about 17 percent of the central business district workers reach their workplaces by car, either as drivers or riders, more than twice that percentage (43 percent) of Sector 0's workers do so. Similarly, while 22 percent of the CBD's commuters arrive by commuter railroad, only a little more than 6 percent of Sector 0's commuters do, of whom nearly one-half start the trip as car drivers or riders; and only 8.6 percent arrive by rapid transit as opposed to nearly 34 percent of Loop employees. The bus is by far the most important transit vehicle for Sector 0 workers: 34 percent of the worktrip arrivals in Sector 0 are by bus, and 33 percent of originations; 29 percent of those workers ride the bus all the way between home and work.

The percentage distribution for the structure types given in Table 2–5 suggest how the use rate of each travel mode combination is affected by workers' choices of residential density, differences in the level of service provided by various modes, and differences in the level of parking charges

Table 2–4. Percentage of Chicago Workers Employed in Sector 0 Using Each Mode at Their Residences and Workplaces

Travel Mode	At Origin	At Destination
Car driver	36.8	34.3
Car rider	10.9	8.5
Railroad	4.2	6.4
Rapid transit	6.9	8.6
Bus	33.9	34.0
Walk	6.6	6.6
Work at home	1.0	1.0

Table 2–5. Percentage of Chicago Workers Using Each Combination of Origin and Destination Modes, by Workplace Location and Residence Type

Origin Mode	Destination Mode	One Family	Two Family	Multiple	All Residence Types
		CENTRAL BUSINESS DISTRICT			
Automobile					
Driver	Car driver	13.5	11.6	12.1	12.3
Driver	Railroad	10.5	2.5	0.9	4.4
Driver	Rapid transit	3.7	3.4	1.2	2.3
Driver	Bus	1.2	0.3	0.5	0.7
Passenger	Car passenger	3.4	3.4	5.1	4.2
Passenger	Railroad	11.6	2.2	0.6	4.6
Passenger	Rapid transit	3.2	1.7	1.0	1.8
Passenger	Bus	1.8	0.5	0.3	0.8
Railroad	Railroad	16.3	8.2	10.7	12.0
Railroad	Rapid transit	0.9	0.2	0.2	0.4
Railroad	Bus	1.2	0.1	0.5	0.7
Rapid transit	Rapid transit	4.2	12.0	20.7	13.2
Rapid transit	Bus	0.1	0.6	0.7	0.5
Bus	Railroad	1.8	1.7	0.5	1.1
Bus	Rapid transit	14.1	26.7	15.4	15.8
Bus	Bus	11.0	24.1	27.7	22.3
Other	Other	1.5	0.8	1.9	2.9
All modes		100.0	100.0	100.0	100.0
		SECTOR O			
Automobile					
Driver	Car driver	42.8	36.9	33.0	34.2
Driver	Railroad	4.4	0.6	0.2	1.4
Driver	Rapid transit	1.1	0.5	0.2	0.5
Driver	Bus	1.8	0.1	0.1	0.5
Passenger	Car passenger	7.4	9.2	3.4	8.2
Passenger	Railroad	3.9	0.6	0.2	1.2
Passenger	Rapid transit	0.8	0.2	0.2	0.4
Passenger	Bus	2.3	0.5	0.6	1.0
Railroad	Railroad	6.5	3.0	2.5	3.4
Railroad	Rapid transit	0.4	–	0.1	0.1
Railroad	Bus	1.2	0.4	0.4	0.6
Rapid transit	Rapid transit	1.8	3.6	5.1	3.9
Rapid transit	Bus	1.0	1.5	4.1	2.6
Bus	Railroad	0.9	0.2	0.2	0.0
Bus	Rapid transit	5.0	5.9	4.2	3.6
Bus	Bus	16.2	32.3	35.8	29.3
Other	Other	2.5	4.5	9.7	9.1
All modes		100.0	100.0	100.0	100.0

between CBD and Sector 0. Perhaps the features most sharply exhibited in Table 2–5 are (1) the much greater use of private automobiles by Sector 0 than by CBD workers; (2) the much greater use of commuter railroads in combination with other travel means by CBD workers residing in single family units than by any other group employed in either CBD or Sector 0; and (3) the minimal use of either rapid transit or commuter railroad by Sector 0 workers. The greater distance of a majority of the workplaces in Sector 0 from railroad and rapid transit stations than in the CBD, and the lower parking costs in Sector 0 apparently lead workers who do not live conveniently near a railroad or rapid transit station or who place a high value on their travel time to commute by car rather than by railroad or rapid transit. Nearly 43 percent of Sector 0 workers who reside in single family units drive private cars between home and work, and over 5 percent commute the entire distance as car passengers.

SUMMARY AND CONCLUSIONS

This chapter elaborates and presents further tests of the simple economic model of the residential and travel behavior of urban households developed in Chapter One. The consumer choice model used emphasizes several kinds of economic calculations assumed to be made by urban workers in deciding on the transportation mode or combination of modes used for the journey to work, the distance commuted, the time spent commuting, and the amount of residential space consumed (or the residential density at which they reside). The model presents these choices as being determined by the minimization of household's urban locational costs, which are the sum of housing costs incurred to reside near work and of work-associated travel costs. The model explicitly considers several kinds of cost trade-offs available to urban households in maximizing their real income. The first is a trade-off between higher housing costs and higher transportation costs. Workers employed at high density workplaces can save on housing costs by commuting longer distances—but thus increase transportation costs. The amount they can save on housing costs depends on both the level and rate at which housing costs per residential space unit decrease with distance from their workplaces and on the number of space units they consume.

The second important set of trade-offs embraces the substitution possibilities between travel time and money cost expenditures for the journey to work. The various modes or combinations of modes have different money cost and speed characteristics, and the differences provide another opportunity to urban households for utility maximization. Moreover, these characteristics both affect and are affected by workers' decisions about residential density.

Finally, hypotheses suggested by this model are tested empirically using data on work travel obtained from the Chicago and Detroit transportation studies. Overall, the empirical tests are consistent with the simple economic model used in the analysis.

Chapter Three

An Econometric Model of Urban Residential and Travel Behavior

This chapter presents a nine equation econometric model dealing with the decisions about residential density, auto ownership, journey to work transportation media, and length of worktrip of workers employed at 254 workplace locations.

The underlying consumer choice model is in terms of the residential and trip-making behavior of a single white worker. Because of racial discrimination, a substantially modified or at least a more elaborate model is required to explain these behavioral relationships for non-whites. These questions are considered in Chapters Six through Nine.

THE DATA

The econometric analyses of workers' choices of residential density, auto ownership, journey to work transportation media, and time spent commuting to and from work presented in this chapter are based on a 1953 survey of approximately 40,000 Detroit households by the Detroit Area Traffic Study. For the statistical analysis presented in this chapter these survey data are aggregated to workplace areas. Thus, the variables, the choices, and the attributes of the white labor force of each of 254 workplace zones are attributes of themselves. The zones vary considerably in size, being smaller geographically where employment is dense and larger where it is sparse. The relationships are estimated from cross-sectional data using least squares multiple regression techniques. The following section presents the estimating equations, designed to estimate four types of relationships: auto ownership, residential space consumption, choice of transportation mode, and length of journey to work. Each is discussed separately. Reduced form equations are obtained and presented in the paper's final section, along with the empirical findings.

THE MODEL

Equations (3.1a) through (3.4) describe the residential and trip-making model estimated in this chapter. Residential space consumption is determined by Equations (3.1a) to (3.1d), auto ownership by Equation (3.2), choice of transportation media by Equations (3.3a) to (3.3c) and elapsed travel time by Equation (3.4). The sequence or causal ordering assumed for these nine equations is critical. It is assumed that the worker first chooses the residential density at which he wishes to live on the basis of his space preference and income, and the price per unit of residential space.

His decision on whether or not to purchase an automobile is affected by his previous decision about the level of residential space consumption, and by his income, the level of transit service available at his workplace, and his preference for automobile ownership (which is strongly affected by his sex and his family's size).

The worker's decision on whether to drive to work or use public transit is affected by both of his previous decisions about auto ownership and residential space consumption. Some other factors affecting his decision about transit use are his income, sex, the level of transit service available at his workplace, and the competitive demands on the use of the family auto by other wage earners—measured by the family's labor force participation variable.

The model's final behavioral relationship states that the mean elapsed time of the journey to work by workers employed in zone j depends on their previous decisions about the consumption of residential space and journey to work transportation mode. The length of the journey to work is also influenced by the worker's sex, family income, and the price of residential space near the workplace.

The Model's Equations

$$R_j^s = a + a_1 F_j + a_2 Y_j + a_3 P_j + a_4 S_j + a_5 N_j \tag{3.1a}$$

$$R_j^2 = a' + a_1' F_j + a_2' Y_j + a_3' P_j + a_4' S_j + a_5' N_j \tag{3.1b}$$

$$R_j^m = a'' + a_1'' F_j + a_2'' Y_j + a_3'' P_j + a_4'' S_j + a_5'' N_j \tag{3.1c}$$

$$R_j^o = 1.0 - R_j^s - R_j^2 - R_j^m \tag{3.1d}$$

$$A_j = \beta + \beta_1 R_j^s + \beta_2 Y_j + \beta_3 L_j + \beta_4 S_j + \beta_5 F_j \tag{3.2}$$

$$M_j^a = \gamma + \gamma_1 A_j + \gamma_2 R_j^s + \gamma_3 L_j + \gamma_4 Y_j + \gamma_5 S_j + \gamma_6 N_j \tag{3.3a}$$

$$M_j^P = \gamma' + \gamma_1' A_j + \gamma_2' R_j^s + \gamma_3' L_j + \gamma_4' Y_j + \gamma_5' S_j + \gamma_6' N_j \tag{3.3b}$$

$$M_j^o = 1.0 - M_j^a - M_j^P \tag{3.3c}$$

$$T_j = \mu + \mu_1 R_j^s + \mu_2 S_j + \mu_3 Y_j + \mu_4 P_j + \mu_5 N_j + \mu_6 M_j^P \tag{3.4}$$

Endogenous Variables

R_j^s = the percentage of white workers employed in zone j residing in single family units;

R_j^2 = the percentage of white workers employed in zone j residing in two family units;

R_j^m = the percentage of white workers employed in zone j residing in multiple units;

R_j^o = the percentage of white workers employed in zone j residing in other types of dwelling places—rooming houses, hotels, trailers, etc.;

A_j = the mean automobile ownership of white workers employed in zone j;

M_j^a = the percentage of white workers employed in zone j who drive autos to work;

M_j^P = the percentage of white workers employed in zone j who ride public transit to work;

M_j^o = the percentage of white workers employed in zone j using other modes;

T_j = the mean elapsed time in hours and tenths spent by white workers employed in zone j in commuting to work.

Exogenous Variables

Y_j = the mean family income of white workers employed in j in hundreds of dollars;

P_j = a proxy variable for the price of residential space per unit at the jth workplace: 11.5 minus j's distance from the central business district, with a minimum value of 0.5;

S_j = the percentage of white workers employed in zone j who are male,

N_j = the labor force participation by the families of the white workers employed in zone j; i.e., the percentage of j's workers belonging to families having a single wage earner;

L_j = the level of transit service at the jth workplace; coach miles of transit service in each workplace zone in a 24 hour period in 1958, divided by the number of acres in workplace zone j; and

F_j = the family size of the white workers employed at j; the percentage of white workers employed at j belonging to families with more than 2 members.

The Residential Space Consumption Function

The preferred measure of residential space for the consumer choice model is closely approximated by lot size in the case of single family units, and by some proportion of the building site in the case of multiple units. Ideally, this would be weighted by a measure of neighborhood density and the density of the immediate community. Structure type, used here as a measure of residential density, has obvious shortcomings, the most important being its failure to account for significant differences in lot size for single family dwellings. As noted above, then, the model has three linear stochastic and one definitional equation for estimating residential space consumption.

Three of the five independent variables in Equations (3.1a) to (3.1c) might be interpreted as indicators of the relative space preferences of the workplace zones' employees; the most obvious is the family size variable—the percentage of workers belonging to families with more than two members. The male percentage of a zone's workers may also differentiate worker populations by residential space preferences. Since housekeeping burdens tend to increase with living area, many working females may actually feel that larger living areas have a negative utility. The labor force participation variable, i.e., percentage of *j*'s workers belonging to families with a single wage earner, is in some ways similar to the variable described above. A disproportionate number of multiple wage earner families are smaller families and probably spend more time outside the home than do families with a single wage earner. Consequently, these households would be expected to value residential space less.

The Detroit Traffic Study did not obtain information about family income in its home interviews. For this study, a household income variable was defined, using each worker's coded occupation. The Detroit Traffic Study coded the occupations of males and females, using the census one digit occupational codes. The family income variable used in this paper is constructed from the median income of each occupational group and sex in Detroit in 1949.[1] The family income estimate is obtained by summing these median incomes over all working family members.

The household's consumption of residential space also depends on the price it must pay to reside at lower densities. It is hypothesized that the price workers must pay for residential space varies inversely with the distance of their workplace from the central business district. A location rent proxy is defined as 11.5 minus the zone's distance in miles from the central business district, with a minimum value of 0.5.[2]

Automobile Ownership Function

Mean automobile ownership would be expected to be much lower in workplace zones well serviced by public transportation; thus there should be a negative relationship between the level of transit service in the zone and mean automobile ownership.[3] The author would also expect to find a positive correlation between mean automobile ownership and the percentage of zone *j*'s workers residing in single family dwelling units. If the worker wishes to reside at a low density site, his journey to work will probably be quickest and cheapest if he drives his own auto since, by and large, low density residential sites have poor public transportation services. Clearly, zone income should be positively related to automobile ownership, even if the effects of residential space consumption, the proportion of male and female workers, and the level of transit service are held constant. Automobiles are, of course, valued as transportation and also for their comfort, convenience, and privacy. One would also expect automobile ownership to be greater in workplace zones employing a high percentage of males. Various cultural factors make it less common for females to operate automobiles; two car families are still moderately rare, even among those households with more than a single wage earner, and workplaces with high proportions of females are represented by a disproportionate number of multiple worker families. Moreover, since women earn less than men, single women are also less likely to own automobiles. Finally, residential space consumption will usually be less in households with working wives. Presumably, automobile ownership also increases with family size. Transit travel is more bothersome, tiring, and inconvenient for adults when they have to take children along. Furthermore, the cost of automobile transportation rapidly becomes competitive with that of public transportation as more passengers use the automobile.

The Mode Choice Functions

Auto usage should be directly related, and transit usage inversely related, to the workplace zone's mean automobile ownership. Since auto usage is more common among workers who reside in single family units, the percentage of a zone's workers using transit should be inversely related to the percentage residing in single family units. Automobile use should be inversely related, and transit use directly related, to the level of transit service available at the workplace. Since higher income workers would be expected to place a higher value on their time, higher income zones should have higher proportions of auto drivers, even when automobile ownership and the level of transit service are held constant. Auto travel is nearly always faster than public transit, while the money costs per worktrip mile are frequently less by public transit. Furthermore, since females less often know how to drive, less often own automobiles, and usually have lower incomes, zones with large proportions of female workers should have lower proportions of auto drivers and higher proportions of transit riders. Finally, zones with large numbers of workers belonging to households having more than a single wage earner should have higher transit usage.

The Journey to Work Length Function

The elapsed time variable, used to measure the length of the journey to work, is a complex index measuring both the spatial separation of the household's workplace and residence, and the worker's relative valuation of time and money. Underlying it is a substitution relationship between a mode usually having higher average cost but higher speed (the automobile) and a mode having lower speed but lower cost (public transit). In addition, because of differences in the levels of transit service available from zone to zone, different sets of transportation alternatives are available to the various workers. Furthermore, for workers employed in the central parts of large urban areas, payment of location rents and transportation expenditures for the journey to work are alternative means of gaining access to the workplace. It is assumed that the worker makes marginal decisions between higher site rent expenditures and higher transportation expenditures, until his savings in location rents equal the increase in his commuting cost measured in both time and money. Given a schedule of location rents and transportation alternatives, the length of the journey to work the wage earner is willing to make depends on potential savings in location rents; these savings in turn largely depend on his consumption of residential space. Therefore, if the effects of the model's other variables are held constant, mean elapsed time spent by the zone's workers in reaching work should be positively correlated with the proportion of its workers residing in single family units.

Likewise, the time the worker spends in his journey to work should be directly related to the price of residential space. The higher the location rent function, the longer the journey to work should be at every level of residential space consumption.

Since the labor force attachment of women is generally weaker than that of men, and since they more often belong to families having low space preference and more than one wage earner, they should make shorter average journeys to work than do males; and thus the average length of the journey to work should be greater for zones with high proportions of male workers. Longer journey to work trips would be expected for zones with large proportions of workers belonging to families having a single wage earner. If the effects of residential space consumption, income, etc., are held constant, zones with high proportions of transit riders would be expected to have higher mean elapsed times than would zones with low proportions of transit usage. Similarly, zones with higher mean incomes would, *ceteris paribus,* have shorter journeys to work in terms of elapsed time.

THE STRUCTURAL EQUATIONS

The structural equations, estimated by least squares estimation techniques, consist of Equations (3.5a) through (3.8). (Sample means for the variable are shown in Table 3–1). Excepting Equation (3.5b), for the percentage residing in two family units, the proportion of total variance explained by the equations is exceptionally high for cross section and for so low a level of aggregation. Moreover, the individual regression coefficients have signs consistent with those postulated from the consumer choice model, and all but income in Equations (3.5a) to (3.5c), the percentage male in Equation (3.6), and the percentage residing in single family units in Equation (3.8) differ significantly from zero at the 1 percent level. Of these five coefficients, only the income coefficients in the three residential space consumption equations fail to satisfy a two-tailed t test at the 5 percent significance level; the regression coefficients for income in Equations (3.5a) to (3.5c) are smaller than their standard errors.

$$R_j^s = 59.40 + .254F_j + .136S_j + .023Y_j$$
$$ (.062) \quad (.050) \quad (.073)$$
$$-2.62P_j - .184N_j \qquad R^2 = 0.56 \qquad\qquad (3.5a)$$
$$(.197) \ (.043)$$

$$R_j^2 = 1.77 + .084F_j - .066S_j + .016Y_j$$
$$ (.054) \quad (.043) \quad (.063)$$
$$-1.43P_j + .141N_j \qquad R^2 = 0.23 \qquad\qquad (3.5b)$$
$$(.170) \ (.038)$$

$$R_j^m = 1.77 - .215F_j - .115S_j + .015Y_j$$
$$ (.043) \quad (.034) \quad (.050)$$
$$+ 1.235P_j + .098N_j \quad R^2 = 0.44 \qquad\qquad (3.5c)$$
$$(.135) \qquad (.029)$$

$$A_j = .466 + .004F_j + .004R_j^s - .031L_j$$
$$ (.0008) \ (.0009) \quad (.007)$$
$$+ .0007S_j + .004Y_j \qquad R^2 = 0.49 \qquad\qquad (3.6)$$
$$(.0006) \qquad (.001)$$

$$M_j^a = -18.49 + 31.56A_j + .087R_j^s - 1.788L_j$$
$$ (3.51) \qquad (.045) \qquad (.413)$$
$$+ .229S_j + .132Y_j + .337N_j \quad R^2 = 0.82 \qquad (3.7a)$$
$$(.040) \quad (.059) \quad (.029)$$

$$M_j^P = 86.06 - 22.10A_j - .088R_j^s + 3.25L_j$$
$$ (3.51) \quad (.044) \qquad (.412)$$
$$-.209S_j - .174Y_j - .358N_j \qquad R^2 = 0.83 \qquad (3.7b)$$
$$(.040) \quad (.059) \ (.029)$$

$$T_j = .302 - .0006R_j^s + .002S_j - .001Y_j$$
$$ (.0004) \quad (.0004) \ (.0005)$$
$$+ .006P_j - .0006N_j + .004M_j^P \quad R^2 = 0.65 \qquad (3.8)$$
$$(.002) \quad (.0003) \quad (.0005)$$

The generally high level of explained variance of the structural equations, and the apparent stability and significance of the net regression coefficients, lend legitimacy to the final step in our analysis, i.e., solving the structural equations in terms of the model's exogenous variables to obtain the reduced forms. Even so, great care must be used in interpreting the empirical results so obtained, especially those affected by the income variable.

THE REDUCED-FORM EQUATIONS

Equations (3.9a) through (3.12) are reduced-form equations obtained by algebraically solving Equations (3.5a) through (3.8) in terms of the model's exogenous variables. Table 3–1, obtained from Equations (3.9a) through (3.12), lists percentage changes in the endogenous variables, given a one percentage point change in each of the independent variables, with all other independent variables in the equation held constant. These percentage changes, or elasticities, are computed using the mean of both the dependent and independent variables.

The Reduced Forms

$$R_j^s = 59.40 + .254F_j + .136S_j + .023Y_j - 2.62P_j - .184N_j \tag{3.9a}$$

$$R_j^2 = 1.77 + .084F_j - .066S_j + .016Y_j + 1.43P_j + .141N_j \tag{3.9b}$$

$$R_j^m = 1.77 - .215F_j - .115S_j + .015Y_j + 1.235P_j + .098N_j \tag{3.9c}$$

$$A_j = .704 + .005F_j + .001S_j + .004Y_j - .010P_j - .007N_j - .031L_j \tag{3.10}$$

$$M_j^a = 8.896 + .180F_j + .272S_j + .260Y_j - .543P_j + .289N_j - 2.766L_j \tag{3.11a}$$

$$M_j^P = 65.27 - .133F_j - .243S_j - .264Y_j + .452P_j - .320N_j + 3.938L_j \tag{3.11b}$$

$$T_j = .599 - .0004F_j - .0011S_j - .00004Y_j + .006P_j - 0020N_j + .016L_j \tag{3.12}$$

Empirical Results for the Residential Space Equations

As noted previously, the truncated workplace distance from the central business district is interpreted as a proxy for the price households must pay for residential space. Thus, in the first equation, the proportion residing in single family units decreases 0.2 of 1 percent with a 1 percent increase in the residential space proxy. In the second Equation (3.9b), a 1 percent increase in the proxy variable results in an increase of 0.4 of 1 percent in occupancy of two-family units, and in the third (3.9c), a similar increase increases multiple unit occupancy by 0.3 of 1 percent.

It was postulated, a priori, that location rents should tend initially to decrease sharply with distance from the central business district, but then flatten out and decrease only slightly or not at all once predominantly rural areas are reached. For comparison purposes, Equations (3.1a) through (3.1c) were estimated using the location rent proxy without truncation (i.e., $P_j = 11.5 - j$'s distance in miles from the central business district). There were two important differences in Equation (3.1a), e.g., the coefficient of multiple determination was 0.56 using the truncated location rent, but only 0.47 using the proxy without truncation. The partial correlation coefficient was −0.65 in using the truncated location rent proxy and only −0.44 using the location rent proxy without truncation. Thus, this simple modification in the location rent proxy, in terms of our a priori beliefs about the determinants and the characteristics of the location rent surface, substantially increased the explanatory power of the estimating equation.

The exogenous variable in Table 3–1 having the largest elasticity at the sample means for the percentage residing in single family units, R_j^s, is the family size variable, F_j, i.e., the percentage belonging to families with more than two members. A 1 percent increase in the percentage of a workplace's employees belonging to families with more than two persons causes a 0.3 percent increase in the percentage residing in single family dwelling units, with all other exogenous variables held constant. In the equation for multiple units, a 1 percent increase in the proportion belonging to families with more than two persons leads to almost a 1.3 percent decrease in the proportion residing in multiple units.

An interesting set of interrelationships is suggested by the coefficients of the location rent proxy and family size variables in Equations (3.5a) through (3.5c). Larger families and those with children have a clear preference for single family detached units because of their privacy, greater space, attached play yards, and the like. The duplex is a logical compromise for lower income workers or for workers employed at high density locations where location rents are very high, since it has many of the attractions of a single family house but is

Table 3–1. Elasticities at the Sample Means for Equations (3.9a) through (3.12) (Percentage change in the endogenous variables resulting from a 1 percent change in an exogenous variable)

Exogenous Variables				Endogenous Variable				Mean Values
	R_j^s	R_j^2	R_j^m	A_j	M_j^a	M_j^P	T_j	
F_j	.26	.35	−1.27	.30	.20	−.53	−.07	70.2%
S_j	.14	−.28	−.69	.06	.32	−.99	−.19	71.4%
Y_j^a	.02	.05	.06	.17	.21	−.76	−.05	50.4%
P_j	−.17	.38	.46	.03	−.04	.11	.06	4.39
N_j	−.13	.40	.40	−.29	.23	−.88	−.23	48.2%
L_j				−.04	−.06	.31	.05	1.37
Mean Values	67.8%	16.8%	11.9%	1.18	61.4%	17.5%	0.42 hr.	

aIn hundreds of dollars

much more parsimonious in its use of expensive urban space. The first equation states that a large proportion of workers reside in single family units in those workplace zones where the price of residential space is low and which employ a large proportion of workers belonging to families of more than two persons. The second equation, for two family dwelling units, also states that larger proportions of two family occupancy are found in those zones having a greater proportion of workers in larger families. It differs from the first in that higher occupancy is also found in zones where the price of residential space is high. The final equation states that there is a greater tendency to choose multiple units when location rents are high and when there is a large proportion of one and two member families.

Because of the low level of statistical significance of the regression coefficients for income, little confidence is attached to the nearly zero income elasticities obtained from the residential space equations. On the basis of independent empirical evidence and on theoretical grounds, it would appear that the income elasticities for R_j^s, R_j^2, and R_j^m are understated, and that the failure to estimate a positive income-space consumption relationship is attributed primarily to inadequacies of the space consumption and income measures.

Evidence that the low significance level of the income variable is due to inadequacies of the income definition, rather than the lack of any functional relationship between the dependent and independent variables, came from stratifying the sample of workers into those belonging to one worker and two worker families, and fitting Equations (3.1a) through (3.1c) for each subgroup. This substantially improves the occupation-income transformation discussed above. The regression coefficient for income is highly significant in all six equations, being several times its standard error. It should be noted, however, that income is highly significant in Equations (3.6) through (3.8). Moreover, the choice of structure type may be relatively insensitive to variations in the income level, but there may be a significant and unmeasured relationship between lot size and income. Thus, it seems likely that there may be a significant income-structure type relationship not captured here because of shortcomings in both the independent and dependent variables.

In addition, some of the income effects may be picked up by the labor force participation and percentage male variables. Because of the manner in which the income variables are constructed, both may be expected to be positively correlated with household income. The higher occupancy of single family units in zones having a large proportion of workers belonging to families with more than a single worker supports this interpretation, as does the positive sign for "percentage male" in the first equation and the negative sign for "percentage male" in the other two equations.

Empirical Results for Automobile Ownership

As postulated above, the family size, percentage male, and income variables all have positive coefficients. The elasticity with respect to the family size variable is largest of all six exogenous variables; a 1 percent increase in the proportion having children would result in a one-third of 1 percent increase in auto ownership. A positive family-size effect on automobile ownership is exerted both directly, through a family size effect on the preference for automobile ownership, and indirectly, by means of a preference effect on the percentage of single family residency. A similar observation can be made about the percentage male variable, for which both a direct and indirect positive relationship exist.

The labor force participation variable has an elasticity with respect to auto ownership not significantly smaller than that of the family size variable. It should be emphasized that automobile ownership is measured per worker rather than per household. Mean automobile ownership per household might actually increase, even if auto ownership per worker declined. Income also has a positive effect from both sources, although the contribution of the residential space variable to the income elasticity for automobile ownership is, of course, small. If the hypothesis about the income-space consumption elasticity is correct, it is also true that income elasticity is understated for automobile ownership.

The coefficients for the remaining two exogenous variables—the residential price proxy and the transit service variable—are all negative, as postulated a priori, and their elasticities are nearly zero. One additional observation should be made about the automobile equation: the mean level of automobile ownership is very high—1.2 automobiles per worker family. At lower levels of automobile ownership, the elasticities for all six variables are much higher.

Empirical Results for the Modal Choice Relationships

Elasticities at the sample mean for the transit use equation are much higher than for the automobile driver equation; the reason should be fairly obvious. Absolute changes in modal use are very similar for auto driving or transit riding since the regression coefficients in Equations (3.11a) and (3.11b) have opposite signs, but are very similar in magnitude. The percentage changes are quite different, since the mean proportion of automobile drivers (61 percent) is more than three times the mean percentage of transit riders (18 percent). A 1 percent increase in the male percentage in a zone's labor force results in an almost equal percentage decline in transit riders. It is also significant to find a fairly high (although still less than unity) income elasticity in the transit use equation, where a 1 percent increase in income causes a 0.75 percent decline in the percentage riding transit. As in the previous equations, if the hypothesis is correct that the income-space consumption elasticity is understated, the income elasticities for M_j^a and M_j^P are also understated. Similarly, a 1 percent increase in the level of transit service would, on the average, lead to a 0.3 percent increase in the percentage using transit and a 0.06 percent decline in the proportion of automobile drivers. The remaining 0.12 of 1 percent or so would be represented by those switching from car pooling or walking to transit use.

The Elapsed Time Relationships

The signs for the coefficients of the family size, percentage male, income, and family labor force participation variables are negative in the reduced-form equation; however, the sign for the percentage male variable is positive. This difference in signs arises because the positive relationship between elapsed time and percentage male in the structural equation is more than offset in the reduced form by a negative indirect relationship. This illustrates two structural difficulties of the model, and for that matter of the problem itself: the complexity of the elapsed time variable and the two types of substitution relationships; i.e., between time and money transportation costs, and between travel and housing costs available to the worker in his efforts to maximize total real income. Both the model and other independent evidence suggest that female workers make shorter trips in miles but use slower, cheaper forms of transportation. In the elapsed time equation, the negative sign for percentage male suggests that for working females, the travel dollar cost—time cost substitution is more important than the housing cost—travel cost substitutions—a result to be expected for reasons outlined previously. The negative sign between family size and time spent in travel, with income held constant, is consistent with a positive space preference and a housing cost—travel cost trade-off. The sign of the income coefficient is negative, as postulated, but its elasticity is nearly zero. In addition to the already described weaknesses and probable understatement of income elasticity in previous equations, which also reduces its indirect effects here, the space consumption variable again has the same shortcomings as in previous applications. A better space consumption variable would improve the income elasticity estimates in Equation (3.12) in two ways: it would measure space consumption much less imperfectly, and it would not fail to net out the housing and travel cost, and money and time cost substitution effects.

CONCLUSION

The nine equation econometric model presented in this chapter provides further empirical support for the simple economic model of residential location presented in Chapters One and Two. Moreover, it extends the analysis of trade-offs among transport modes considered in Chapter Two and, in addition, considers how both of these decisions are related to household decisions about car ownership. These several decisions are shown to be highly interrelated, and to be consistent with a simple theory of consumer behavior.

Part II

The Location of Jobs

Chapter Four

The Distribution and Movement of Jobs and Industry

By any measure, metropolitan growth since World War II has been rapid but unevenly distributed. Outlying portions of metropolitan areas have been growing quickly, while the central areas have been growing very little and, in an increasing number of instances, have actually declined. During this period, what began as a relative decline became an absolute decline for a lengthening list of central cities. Losses in retail sales and property values, declining profits for central city merchants, and falling tax bases have usually followed from these employment and population declines. Moreover, depopulation was selective; the young, the employed, the well-to-do, and the white moved to suburban areas, leaving behind the aged, the unemployed, the poor, and the Negro. This selective depopulation and employment decline aggravated old problems and created new ones for central city governments.

These trends did not pass unnoticed or unchallenged. Demands that public policy do something to halt the "decay" of our central cities were and still are frequently heard and much legislation directed to this end has been enacted. Some persons even argue that this decay is in large part the result of direct subsidies, such as FHA-insured loans for low density suburban housing, indirect federal subsidies to suburban communities, and services provided to the suburbanite (especially the commuter) but paid for by the central cities. Indeed, a slavish worship of the private automobile is regarded by many as the sole, or at least primary, cause of the "undesirable" pattern of postwar metropolitan development.

Proposals to solve the "problem" are even more numerous and include central city residential and industrial renewal; increased taxation of private automobiles; a moratorium on expressway construction; the abolition of federal income tax credits for interest and real estate taxes paid by homeowners; and subsidization of public transit and construction of new high speed rail rapid transit systems.

However, among scholars who have investigated these questions, there is general agreement that central city decline is nothing new—that only perception and concern about it are new—and that there is no or little reason to expect a reversal of these trends in the foreseeable future, given current and proposed policies. And there is an equal measure of agreement about the principal causes of these declines.[1]

The relative and absolute decline of central cities, and their downtown areas in particular, is the result of several important technological and economic changes that have made decentralization a more feasible, more economic, or more desirable choice for increasing numbers of households and businesses. Developments in transportation and communication have made different parcels of land increasingly interchangeable for most manufacturing, retailing, wholesaling, residential, and other uses. Many activities once willing to pay the higher costs of central locations no longer find it to their advantage to do so. Firms previously restricted to a fairly limited number of central locations by their need to be near ports, freight and passenger terminals, rail lines, and the like now depend to an ever increasing extent on trucks. Transport costs for these firms may be lower at an outlying site near an interchange on the burgeoning metropolitan expressway system. This is particularly true of the growing fraction of wholesaling and manufacturing firms that rely mainly on truck transport. Similarly, rapid increases in automobile ownership have released many firms from their need to be located convenient to mass transit facilities in order to attract a labor force. Though experiences are somewhat mixed, firms relocating to outlying areas, with abundant free parking, often find they have an easier time attracting a labor force than they once did at their central city locations. The transportation and communications savings that caused many firms to choose central locations have become smaller or disappeared entirely.

Still other forces are affecting the location of wholesaling and manufacturing. Changes in production methods, which increasingly require spacious, single story plants, are among the most important of these. Such plants are difficult and enormously expensive to construct in built-up central city areas but easy to build on large vacant sites in outlying areas. In addition, rapid technological changes in communications and data processing appear to be reducing the need for armies of white collar workers employed in central city offices, or at least allowing them to be located in less expensive space in outlying areas. The growth in white collar employment has for the time being offset these forces in many instances, but the impact of the communications revolution is only beginning to be felt.

TRENDS PRIOR TO 1945

Interpreting these postwar changes in metropolitan structure and the spatial distribution of jobs is made difficult by the fact that they follow 15 years of "abnormal" development. Metropolitan growth and development was twice disrupted—first by the sharp reduction of employment and investment during the Great Depression, and then by the rapid expansion of employment during World War II. Wartime expansion was accompanied by government controls on materials, construction, and investment in plant and equipment. These controls affected the level and spatial distribution of economic activity both within and among metropolitan areas.

One leading interpretation of the impact of World War II on the spatial distribution of economic activity within and among metropolitan areas was advanced by Woodbury (1953) and Creamer (1963).[2] Both studies are limited to manufacturing. Their arguments about the effect of World War II on the location of manufacturing activity may be summarized as follows:

1. World War II caused a huge increase in U.S. manufacturing employment from a prewar (1939) level of approximately 9.6 million workers (nearly identical to the level in 1929) to a postwar (1947) level of 14.4 million. (By comparison, total U.S. employment in manufacturing increased by only one million more between 1947 and 1954, reaching a level of 15.4 million workers in 1954, and by 1958 had declined slightly to 15.2 million workers.)
2. Because of controls, most of this wartime increase in manufacturing employment had to be accommodated at existing manufacturing plants and was achieved principally by means of a more intensive use of facilities existing at the beginning of the war.
3. Because the big central cities were the primary recipients of this captive increase in manufacturing employment, wartime expansion reversed a long term trend toward employment dispersal within metropolitan areas.
4. Were it not for wartime controls, most of this increased manufacturing employment would have located at newer plants at less central locations and in newer metropolitan areas. The removal of controls at the end of World War II was followed by rapid dispersal.
5. Thus, much of the postwar dispersal of manufacturing (and probably by extension many other kinds of employment) was simply a delayed redistribution. It follows that employment dispersal should slow down as this backlog of relocations is worked off.

Thus, Woodbury and Creamer both conclude that the principal effect of World War II was to halt or reverse long-standing and well-documented trends toward suburbanization within, and diffusion among, metropolitan areas. They argue that prior to World War II manufacturing employment was becoming more evenly distributed among U.S. metropolitan areas with the smaller, more rapidly growing, and less industrialized metropolitan areas of the South and the West increasing their share of manufacturing employment at the expense of the older, more mature manufacturing centers of the North and Northeast.

But there is an alterative interpretation of these trends, which could lead to substantially different forecasts of metropolitan spatial structure. The key element in the Woodbury and Creamer interpretation is the assumed limitations on the construction of new plant and equipment. For example, Creamer cites data on the amount of private investment in industrial plant and equipment during and immediately following World War II: "The real net value of privately owned structures and equipment was expanded by less than 10%, from $51.5 billion in 1954 prices in 1939 to $55.7 billion in 1945 . . . By the end of 1947, the real net stock of fixed capital was about 25% larger than in 1939 and 15% above the 1945 figure."[3] However, Creamer overlooks the fact that most of the wartime investment in plant and equipment was provided by the federal government. The *Quarterly Progress Report* of the Surplus Property Administration notes: "The total government investment in war plants and equipment was more than 18 billion dollars of which 17 billion dollars was for manufacturing facilities—a staggering figure, for the entire cost of construction of all the manufacturing facilities in the United States before the war was only 40 billion dollars."[4]

Yearly data are available on the level of private and public outlays for industrial buildings and these are plotted in Figure 4–1. Government construction of industrial buildings exceeded private outlays for the same purpose by a wide margin during 1941–1944. Construction of privately owned industrial buildings had declined to $351 million by 1943, but during the same

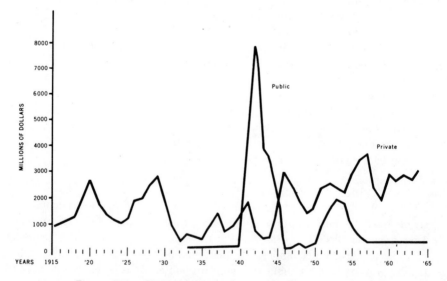

Figure 4–1.   Construction of Public and Private Industrial Buildings in the United States, 1915–1965

year $4.2 billion worth of publicly financed industrial buildings were completed. Outlays for public industrial buildings were even larger in the previous year ($8 billion), but those for privately owned industrial buildings were only about one-tenth as large ($829 million). By comparison, new construction of privately owned industrial buildings amounted to $3.1 billion in 1946, and that of publicly owned industrial buildings was only $209 million.[5]

Data presented in Table 4–1 on the mean yearly construction expenditures by use suggest a significantly different interpretation of the impact of World War II on metropolitan development. The time periods in Table 4–1 correspond to the dates of the censuses of manufacturing moved forward one year because employment at a new plant usually would lag behind its construction. The impact of both the Depression and World War II are clearly evident in the statistics in Table 4–1. Yearly outlays for the new construction of residential structures during 1938–1946 were only 35 percent of expenditures during the immediate postwar period, and the ratio for the Depression period (1929–1938) was even more unfavorable. Similarly, yearly outlays for the construction of stores and restaurants during 1938–1946 amounted to only 58 percent of those during 1946–1953. A far different situation characterized the industrial buildings category. New construction of industrial buildings during 1938–1946 was 128 percent of that for 1946–1953. Outlays for privately constructed industrial buildings were only 60 percent of 1946–1953 levels, but those for publicly financed structures were 351 percent of 1946–1953 levels.

These data indicate that whereas the construction of new residences, stores, office buildings, restaurants, and the like was severely restricted by wartime controls, a great deal of investment in industrial plant took place. Following World War II nearly all this new industrial plant was transferred to private ownership, often at nominal cost. The spatial distribution of this new

Table 4–1. Mean Yearly Value of Construction Put in Place, by Period (millions of constant 1957–1959 dollars)

Type of construction	1918–1928	1928–1938	1938–1946	1946–1953	1953–1957	1957–1962
Private residential	9,807	3,539	4,527	14,503	17,012	16,606
Public residential	14	59	736	491	371	832
Total residential	9,821	3,598	5,264	14,994	17,383	17,438
Private office buildings	914	602	220	713	1,600	2,062
Private stores, restaurants, etc.	1,569	744	625	1,069	1,847	1,936
Private industrial buildings	1,895	1,112	1,303	2,173	3,026	2,564
Public industrial buildings	–	11	2,631	875	898	409
Other public nonresidential	155	193	137	319	436	524
Total industrial buildings	1,895	1,123	3,928	3,057	3,924	2,973

Source: U.S., Department of Commerce, *Construction Statistics 1915–1964: A Supplement to Construction Review* (Washington, D.C. : G.P.O., January 1966).

investment is crucial to an analysis of metropolitan development. While there is no definitive analysis of the location of this investment, some hypotheses can be advanced.

It appears that Creamer and Woodbury were right to an important degree. A significant amount of new manufacturing employment probably did occur in the way they suggest. However, a significant portion also was accommodated by means of new plant and equipment investment. Also, much of this new investment occurred within large central cities. No data are available (or at least obtainable at reasonable cost) that describe investment in plant construction by city. However, yearly data on the value of construction and number of new structures for all nonresidential uses are available for a large number of cities. Table 4–2 lists the investment and number of new nonresidential buildings constructed in the 20 largest cities during 1939–1946. By any criterion the amount of construction during the period is very large, and in some cities phenomenal. For example, in Los Angeles alone more than half a billion dollars of new nonresidential construction and 94,346 new nonresidential structures were put in place during 1939–1946. The outlays for new construction were even larger in Chicago, even though only about a third as many new nonresidential structures were built.

In interpreting the construction data in Table 4–2 it should be recalled that central cities are large and heterogeneous. If a substantial part of the new investment took place in a different spatial pattern than existing employment, the impact on metropolitan structure might be quite large. In fact there are good a priori reasons for believing this was the case, and the data for the New York City boroughs in Table 4–2 provide some support for this view. It seems very likely that a disproportionate amount of the new industrial plant built during World War II was located at the periphery of central cities, but within their legal boundaries. At the start of World War II most central cities contained large amounts of usable vacant land. Industry by itself is a small user of urban land and the large scale housebuilding that invariably accompanied new plants in the postwar period was constrained by wartime controls on homebuilding.[6] Still more plants might have been constructed outside of their boundaries and then quickly annexed to the central city.

If this hypothesis about the wartime expansion of manufacturing employment within central cities is in part, or substantially, correct, it implies a far different interpretation of postwar metropolitan development than is usually advanced. It suggests a great deal of largely unnoticed employment dispersal (and, more important, non-population-serving employment) took place *during* World War II. If so, this wartime dispersal of jobs would provide a powerful force for postwar dispersal of housing and population-serving employment.[7] The argument is that a fundamental redistribution of employment took place during World War II within central city boundaries (or what were central city boundaries by 1947). This employment redistribution set the stage for the rapid

Table 4–2.   Value of New Nonresidential Construction and Number of New Non-residential Structures During 1939–1946: 20 Largest Cities, 1960 Population (thousands of constant 1947–1949 dollars)

City	1939–1946	
	Value	Number
New York City		
Bronx	40,382	1,414
Brooklyn	261,934	3,912
Manhattan	92,384	930
Queens	142,072	9,276
Chicago	539,134	17,364
Los Angeles	515,369	94,396
Philadelphia	305,742	3,786
Detroit	275,368	36,289
Baltimore	176,699	13,600
Houston	176,835	6,831
Cleveland	215,600	14,064
Washington, D.C.	269,715	4,518
St. Louis	165,496	10,893
Milwaukee	72,644	8,853
San Francisco	212,200	2,089
Boston	134,204	2,209
Dallas	64,278	9,219
New Orleans	129,078	1,240
Pittsburgh	56,313	2,863
San Antonio	43,336	4,436
San Diego	198,855	16,459
Seattle	150,661	9,704
Cincinnati	46,015	3,322

Source: U.S., Department of Labor, Bureau of Labor Statistics, Bulletin 693, Building Construction 1940; Bulletin 713, Building Construction 1941; Bulletin 786, Construction Industry in the United States 1942; Bulletin 918, Construction in the War Years 1942–1945; Bulletin 941, Construction and Housing 1946–1947.

dispersal of population and population-serving employment as soon as wartime controls on homebuilding and noncritical nonresidential construction were removed. Though there is a fair amount of evidence that would seem to support this hypothesis, its final acceptance or rejection must await better documentation of the changes in the geographic location of metropolitan employment during and prior to World War II.

If correct, this alternative view of the process of metropolitan dispersal could have a substantial effect on many existing forecasts of metropolitan structure and on our perception of many metropolitan problems. For example, since most projections of employment and population dispersal are based on extrapolations of historical trends, it is conceivable that we are currently overestimating the rate and extent of population and employment dispersal. Much of the rapid postwar suburbanization of population and dispersal of employment, other than manufacturing, may be due to restraints on new construction during World War II and thereby be temporary. If so, many current forecasts of land use based on this experience may be erroneous.

POSTWAR TRENDS IN THE LOCATION OF JOBS[8]

At the end of World War II, the average metropolitan area—based on the data in Table 4–3 for the 40 largest areas—had an estimated population of 1.4 million.[9] About 64 percent of these people lived within the central city and about 36 percent lived in the suburban or metropolitan ring. Manufacturing was clearly the most important of the four industry categories analyzed. The average metropolitan area had about 177,000 manufacturing workers distributed between its central city and ring in nearly the same proportions as the population. Retailing accounts for the next largest number of employees and except for manufacturing was least concentrated in the central city. Even so, at the beginning of the period an average of only 25 percent of the 81,000 employees of retailing firms worked in the ring. Wholesaling was the most centralized industry, with nearly 92 percent of its labor force employed in the central city. Selected services were nearly as concentrated as wholesaling, with 85 percent of its workers employed in the central city. The four categories of employment for which data are available account for roughly two-thirds of total employment in the average metropolitan area.

It is not surprising to find, as Table 4–4 shows, that suburban rings grew faster than central cities in the postwar period. Even so, the yearly percentage growth in ring population and all categories of employment is rather remarkable. Except for manufacturing during 1954–1958 and 1958–1963, the average yearly percentage increases in employment exceeded 10 percent for all four employment categories and three time periods. Wholesaling employment exhibits the most rapid suburban growth, amounting to 25 percent a year during the six year period immediately following the war. This rapid suburban growth of wholesaling is all the more remarkable given its extreme centralization at the beginning of the period. (Of course, this growth took place on a small base, a fact that may explain in part why its *rate* of growth declined during the postwar period.) Suburban wholesaling grew at an average yearly rate of 15 percent during 1958–1963. It should be emphasized that the employment data in Tables 4–4 and 4–6 have been "corrected" for annexations. Thus, the employment data refer to changes in employment within the boundaries of the central cities and suburban rings as defined in 1950.[10]

Manufacturing and retailing grew least rapidly in the suburban rings, a fact that may be related to their greater suburbanization at the beginning of the period. Even so, suburban retailing employment increased by 11 percent a year during its period of slowest growth (1948–1954) and averaged 13 percent a year during both 1954–1958 and 1958–1963. Suburban manufacturing employ-

TABLE 4–3.   Mean SMSA, Central City, and Ring Employment and Population in 1948 and Central City and Ring Shares: 40 Large Central Cities.

Item	Central City		Ring		SMSA	
	Number	Percent	Number	Percent	Number	Percent
Employment						
Manufacturing[a]	118,652	66.9	58,805	33.1	177,457	100
Wholesaling[b]	33,124	91.8	2,959	8.2	36,083	100
Retailing	61,048	75.3	19,992	24.7	81,040	100
Services	23,654	84.8	4,240	15.2	27,894	100
Population[c]	899,625	64.1	504,790	36.0	1,404,415	100

Source: See note 9

[a]Data pertain to 1947–1954

[b]Wholesaling data available for 39 SMSAs only

[c]Obtained by interpolation of 1940, 1950, and 1960 data

Table 4–4.   Estimated Mean Annual Percentage Changes[b] in Population and Employment for the Central Cities and Suburban Rings of 40 Large SMSAs (1950 central city boundaries)

Item	Central City			Ring		
	1948–1954	1954–1958	1958–1963	1948–1954	1954–1958	1958–1963
Employment						
Manufacturing[b]	1.9	−1.7	−0.4	13.2	6.9	6.0
Wholesaling[c]	0.8	0.2	−0.2	24.9	16.6	15.1
Retailing	−0.6	0.1	−2.0	11.3	13.5	13.4
Services	1.6	3.9	0.9	18.0	16.6	13.5
Population[d]	0.2	0.1	−0.5	8.7	6.4	5.5

Source: See note 9

[a]Simple, unweighted averages of individual city percentage changes

[b]Data pertain to 1947–1954

[c]Wholesaling data available for 39 SMSAs only

[d]Obtained by interpolation and extrapolation of 1940, 1950, 1960, and 1965 data

ment experienced the least growth in both of the two most recent periods. This lower suburban growth rate in manufacturing is consistent with the lesser restrictions on manufacturing investment during World War II and a greater wartime dispersal than other employment categories. Even so, its growth rate during the most recent, and most slowly growing, period amounted to a healthy 6.0 percent a year. Data on changes in manufacturing employment must be interpreted carefully, since they are particularly sensitive to the business cycle. Of the years studied, cyclical effects were particularly important in the recession year of 1958, although 1954 was also a year of mild recession. By comparison, manufacturing employment in 1963, buoyed by the Vietnam build-up, was unusually high. (Nationally, manufacturing employment declined by 0.2 percent a year during the four year period 1954–1958, while it increased by approximately 1.2 percent a year during the five year period 1958–1963). Yearly percentage increases in suburban population, though considerable, are only about half as large as the increases in suburban employment. This permits a guarded conclusion that these jobs, at least, were moving to the suburbs at a faster rate than people.

In contrast to the marked uniformity of suburban growth rates, changes in central city employment and population were highly irregular. Central city manufacturing employment grew at an average rate of 1.9 percent during 1947–1954. But during the next four years it declined at an average rate of 1.7 percent at year. Central cities also lost manufacturing jobs during the most recent period, but at a reduced rate, 0.4 percent a year. The previous comments about cyclical variability of manufacturing employment apply here. During slack periods, multiplant firms generally reduce production most in their older and less efficient plants. It is likely that central cities contain a disproportionate amount of this older and less efficient capacity. Thus, cyclical effects might be especially pronounced in central cities. This suggests that the very large central decline in manufacturing employment during 1954–1958 may be somewhat overstated by the recession year of 1958. By the same logic, the much smaller 1958–1963 decline may be relatively understated. Regardless of how much weight is given to the impacts of the business cycle, the nearly 2 percent decline during 1954–1958 and the 0.4 percent decline during 1958–1963 compare unfavorably with the substantial suburban growth rates during both periods.

Central city wholesaling employment exhibits only a small percentage increase in each of the first two periods. Moreover, there is a suggestive decline in the yearly rate of growth until the final period (1958–1963), when central city wholesaling employment actually decreased slightly (minus 0.2 percent per year). By contrast, ring wholesaling increased by 15.1 percent during 1958–1963. Even central city service employment shows some tendency toward decline in the later period. Central city employment in selected services increased during every time period. Its growth during 1954–1958 was especially rapid, averaging nearly 4 percent a year. However, an undetermined share of this rapid growth in central city services employment during 1954–1958 was "statistical" and resulted from the addition of establishments not previously included. During 1958–1963 the growth rate of central city employment in selected services amounted to a more modest 0.9 percent per year. Suburban growth of selected services employment exceeded 13 percent in all three periods, declining somewhat over the 15 years.

Percentage growth rates are but one way of examining changes in employment and population levels. If used alone, they give an incomplete, and perhaps even misleading, description of urban change. Where the base is very small, an employment category may have a very high mean percentage rate of growth, but a very small absolute change. Therefore, mean annual absolute changes in employment for the population for the same 40 metropolitan areas are presented in Table 4–5.

The marked importance for urban development trends of changes in the level and spatial distribution of manufacturing employment is evident from the data presented in Table 4–5. During the period 1954–1958 central cities lost an average of 2,122 manufacturing jobs each year. The yearly loss during the most recent period was even larger, averaging 3,462 jobs per year. Thus, during the nine year period 1954–1963, the central cities of these 40 large metropolitan areas lost an average of 25,798 manufacturing jobs. This loss in central city manufacturing employment was almost exactly offset by a growth of manufacturing employment in suburban areas, which averaged 25,948 jobs during the same period.

The much more unfavorable performance of central city manufacturing employment when absolute changes are used as the measure is due to the greater weight given to large cities and particularly those with disproportionate amounts of manufacturing. This is consistent with other information that suggests the most rapid declines are being experienced by the older, dense manufacturing centers of the North and East. By comparison, the newer, less dense cities of the South, West, and Southwest have suffered smaller declines and in many instances have grown.

As noted above, the location of manufacturing is, especially critical in determining metropolitan spatial structure, since the locational decisions of

Table 4–5. Estimated Mean Annual Absolute Changes in Population and Employment for Central Cities and Suburban Rings of 40 Large SMSAs (1950 central city boundaries)

Item	Central City			Ring		
	1948–1954	1954–1958	1958–1963	1948–1954	1954–1958	1958–1963
Employment						
Manufacturing[a]	218	−2,122	−3,462	2,396	1,262	4,180
Wholesaling[b]	−85	55	−198	425	767	831
Retailing	−588	188	−985	896	2,263	1,931
Services	479	1,011	294	510	874	756
Population[c]	464	25	−4,595	31,491	36,722	41,000
Population annexations	4,180	5,532	2,610	−4,180	−5,532	−2,610

Source: See note 9
[a]Data pertain to 1947–1954
[b]Wholesaling data available for 39 SMSAs only
[c]Obtained by interpolation and extrapolation of 1940, 1950, 1960, and 1965 data

most manufacturing firms are largely unaffected by the distribution of metropolitan population. Manufacturing determines the locational decisions of urban households, not vice versa.

Smaller, but persistent, declines occurred throughout the period in central city wholesaling and retailing employment as well. In both industry groups employment increased during 1954–1958 after declining during the period immediately following World War II. This improvement was short-lived, however, as larger employment declines were experienced by both industry groups during the most recent period. During 1958–1963 the average absolute decline in central city wholesaling employment increased to an average yearly loss of 198 jobs. Changes in central city retailing employment, after becoming slightly positive during 1954–1958, are heavily negative during the 1958–1963 period, when central cities lost an average of 985 jobs per year. As was true of the percentage growth rates, the absolute growth of central city services is significantly less during 1958–1963 than during 1954–1958.

Large yearly absolute increases occurred in every category of suburban ring employment during every time period. During the 1958–1963 period, suburban rings of the 40 large metropolitan areas included in Table 4–5 gained an average of 831 wholesaling, 1,931 retailing, and 756 selected services jobs each year. Suburban manufacturing employment posted especially large gains during the period with an average absolute increase of 4,180 per year, almost twice that experienced during either of the two previous postwar periods.

The pervasiveness of postwar declines in central city population and employment during the postwar period is shown even more clearly by data presented in Table 4–6, which contains a tabulation of the number of declining central cities and suburban rings in each employment and population classification during each of the three postwar periods. During the first period, retailing employment declined in 27, manufacturing employment in 15, and wholesaling employment in 16 of the central cities. During the second period, central city manufacturing employment declines were still more frequent, occurring in 30 of the 40 central cities. (The previously noted cyclical impacts should be kept in mind in evaluating these data.) Central city wholesaling employment declines were also more frequent during the second period, occurring in 18 cities. City retailing employment rebounded somewhat, with only 17 out of 40 metropolitan areas recording central city declines. However, during 1958–1963, the number of central cities experiencing a decline in employment in wholesaling, retailing, and selected services was again greater than in the earlier two periods. Central city employment declines were the rule. Wholesaling employment declined in 21 central cities, retailing in 37 central cities, and selected services, which showed considerable resistance to decline in the decade following the war, in 15 central cities. Even with the national growth in manufacturing employment during 1958–1963, manufacturing employment declined in all but 12 of the 40 central cities. These data suggest even more clearly than those presented previously an acceleration of postwar trends toward metropolitan dispersal.

Table 4–6. Estimated Number of Central City and Suburban Rings (out of 40) Having Employment and Population Declines (1950 central city boundaries)

Item	Central City			Ring		
	1948– 1954	1954– 1958	1958– 1963	1948– 1954	1954– 1958	1958– 1963
Employment						
Manufacturing[a]	15	30	28	6	9	11
Wholesaling[b]	16	18	21	4	0	1
Retailing	27	17	37	4	0	0
Services	7	4	15	2	1	0
Population[c] (legal boundaries)	17	16	18	1	2	0
Population (1950 central city boundaries)	21	22	24	1	1	0

Source: See note 9

[a]Data pertain to 1947–1954

[b]Wholesaling data available for 39 SMSAs only

[c]Obtained by interpolation and extrapolation of 1940, 1950, 1960, and 1965 data

METROPOLITAN AND CENTRAL CITY GROWTH

There is of course a great deal of variation among different metropolitan areas. The 40 metropolitan areas analyzed above range in population (1960) from a low of 514,000 (Akron, Ohio) to a high of 10,695,000 (New York). Similarly, central city populations vary from 262,000 (Dayton, Ohio) to 7,782,000 (New York). Central city and metropolitan area age and densities are also quite varied. For example, central city population densities were, in 1960, approximately 25,000 persons per square mile in New York City and more than 14,000 per square mile in Boston, Chicago, and Philadelphia, but less than 3,000 persons per square mile in San Diego, Houston, Dallas, and several other central cities. Even more important in terms of the central city and suburban employment and population growth rates presented above, the 40 areas experienced very different growth rates during the period. Between 1950 and 1960, changes in metropolitan population varied from a 6 percent decline (Jersey City) to a 100 percent increase (Phoenix).

These variations in metropolitan growth rates are of particular importance because changes in metropolitan structure are strongly affected by metropolitan growth. Since the 40 areas in Tables 4–3 to 4–6 have widely varying rates of growth, statistical averages disguise a great deal of variation in central city and ring growth. To evaluate the impact of overall metropolitan growth on central city and ring growth, these 40 areas are divided by the rate of metropolitan growth during the decade 1950–1960. Specifically, three subgroups are defined (for the 40 areas analyzed:) the 13 areas with the highest percentage rate of population growth for 1950–1960, the 13 with the second highest, and the 14 with the lowest.[11] Overall metropolitan growth strongly affects employment growth in both the central city and the suburban ring. Percentage changes in employment and population by these population growth categories are shown in Table 4–7. With a few exceptions, the areas with the highest population growth have the greatest change in employment, in both the central city and ring, and the areas with the least population growth show the least employment growth.

The absolute changes in employment and population by subgroups are ·similar to those for percentage changes, as shown in Table 4–8. Central city declines are somewhat more prevalent, suggesting that the larger central cities

Table 4–7. Estimated Mean Annual Percentage Changes in Employment and Population for the Central Cities and Suburban Rings of 40 Large SMSAs, by SMSA Growth Rate (1950 central city boundaries)

	Central City			Ring		
Item	1948–1954	1954–1958	1958–1963	1948–1954	1954–1958	1958–1963
Employment						
Manufacturing[a]						
Highest	6.0	0.3	0.2	27.5	15.7	9.0
Medium	0.1	−1.9	0.5	9.0	3.6	6.0
Lowest	−0.4	−3.5	−2.0	3.6	1.8	4.0
Wholesaling[b]						
Highest	1.2	2.0	1.1	35.4	21.8	15.1
Medium	0.5	−0.2	−0.02	33.0	16.8	16.6
Lowest	0.8	−0.2	−1.5	8.2	11.9	13.7
Retailing						
Highest	0.2	0.6	−1.3	19.2	20.2	13.6
Medium	−0.8	−0.1	−2.2	13.0	14.4	17.6
Lowest	−1.2	−0.02	−2.4	2.1	6.6	9.3
Services						
Highest	2.4	4.1	2.3	25.5	25.4	14.9
Medium	1.4	4.1	−0.1	22.2	17.3	16.6
Lowest	1.1	3.5	0.5	7.2	7.6	9.3
Population[c]						
(1950 boundaries)						
Highest	1.3	1.0	0.7	12.5	9.2	6.0
Medium	−0.2	−0.2	−0.8	9.5	6.6	6.2
Lowest	−0.5	−0.6	−1.5	4.4	3.5	4.2

Source: See note 9. The SMSAs included in each population change group are listed in note 13.

[a]Data pertain to 1947–1954

[b]Wholesaling data available for 39 SMSAs only

[c]Obtained by interpolation and extrapolation of 1940, 1950, 1960, and 1965 data

within each population growth category are the slowest growing. Services are the only central city employment or population group for which there were consistent increases for both the medium and lowest population growth categories, and even they recorded declines during 1958–1963 in the medium growth category. Between 1948 and 1963, the central cities in the 14 areas with the lowest growth rate lost on the average 117,000 people, 66,705 manufacturing jobs, 14,358 retailing jobs, and 6,493 wholesaling jobs. Offsetting these losses since the war are only 11,458 service jobs. Central cities in the 13 areas having intermediate rates of growth fared somewhat better. During the 15 years 1948–1963, they lost on the average 60,000 people (within 1950 boundaries), 17,580 manufacturing jobs, 9,043 retailing jobs, 351 wholesaling jobs, and gained 4,123 selected services jobs.

Table 4–8. Estimated Mean Annual Absolute Changes in Employment and Population for the Central Cities and Suburban Rings of 40 Large SMSAs, by the SMSA Growth Rate (1950 central city boundaries)

	Central City			Ring		
Item	*1948– 1954*	*1954– 1958*	*1958– 1963*	*1948– 1954*	*1954– 1958*	*1958– 1963*
Employment						
Manufacturing[a]						
Highest	2,332	294	−222	2,860	2,992	2,222
Medium	−549	−2,784	−630	1,945	26	2,100
Lowest	−1,035	−3,750	−9,099	2,384	806	7,929
Wholesaling[b]						
Highest	245	226	284	447	1,006	649
Medium	7	−7	−73	325	440	525
Lowest	−453	−35	−727	473	813	1,272
Retailing						
Highest	91	−312	−372	1,197	2,872	1,576
Medium	−446	−198	−1,115	898	1,628	1,657
Lowest	−1,352	227	−1,431	617	2,285	2,516
Services						
Highest	587	826	501	703	1,417	759
Medium	209	771	−43	304	513	557
Lowest	628	1,405	414	521	705	937
Population[c]						
Highest	8,000	7,000	7,000	33,000	44,000	37,000
Medium	−2,000	−2,000	−8,000	30,000	32,000	35,000
Lowest	−4,000	−4,500	−15,000	34,000	38,000	50,000

Source: See note 9. The SMSAs included in each population change group are listed in note 13.

[a]Data pertain to 1947–1954

[b]Wholesaling data available for 39 SMSAs only

[c]Obtained by interpolation and extrapolation of 1940, 1950, 1960, and 1965 data

During the same period in which the 14 central cities of the slowest growing areas lost 66,705 manufacturing jobs, their suburban rings gained 58,785 manufacturing jobs. Likewise, while these same cities lost an average of 14,359 retailing jobs, employment in their suburban rings increased by 25,422. Wholesaling employment in these central cities declined on the average by 6,493, while ring employment in wholesaling increased on the average by 12,450. On the other hand, the central city gain in services for these areas was actually greater (11,458) than in the ring (10,131).

TRENDS WITHIN CENTRAL CITIES

The gravest weakness of the employment statistics presented thus far is that they cover such large areas. Central city statistics, in particular, may hide very diverse and critical differences in employment and population growth within central city boundaries. For example, they may mask large increases in employment within central business districts (CBDs). This is especially worrisome because data presented thus far are especially deficient in the coverage of such important CBD employment activities as central office employment, banking, finance, and business services. Unfortunately, few employment data have been collected that would permit a definite answer about changes in employment levels within CBDs and other points of the central city. The fragmentary data available, however, fail to support the belief (or hope) that despite central city employment and population losses, sizable increases in CBD employment levels have occurred.[12]

For 39 of the 40 metropolitan areas discussed previously, data are available on changes in CBD retail employment levels during 1958–1963. CBD retailing employment in these areas declined by 4.2 percent a year during 1958–1963. The corresponding average absolute decline is 636 jobs per year. Thus, it appears that the losses in retailing jobs were *greatest* in the CBD.

Some data are available that provide a more complete description of changes in the spatial distribution of employment within particular central cities. In every instance there are serious problems of completeness, accuracy, and unknown bias. One such source provides statistics on workers covered by unemployment compensation by postal zones within the city of Chicago.[13] For the period 1958–1963, postal zones within the city of Chicago are aggregated into seven larger areas roughly corresponding to concentric distance rings (or parts of rings) surrounding the CBD as illustrated in Figure 4–2. During the five year period 1958–1963, the central city lost each year roughly 20,042 jobs covered by unemployment insurance, or in excess of 100,000 jobs over the entire period. In percentage terms the decline amounts to about 1.5 percent a year, a figure that is reasonably consistent with other statistics on Chicago employment.

In general the data in Table 4–9 bear out our previous speculations about the geographic distribution of employment growth and decline within

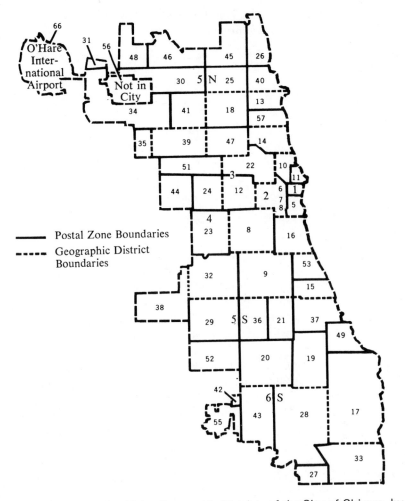

Figure 4-2. Major Geographic Districts of the City of Chicago, by Postal Zone

central city boundaries. Significantly, the most rapid growth (4.9 percent and 4,538 jobs per year) is taking place to the northwest near O'Hare International Airport (area 5N). This finding will come as no great surprise to regular air travelers, since rapid employment growth is occurring around every major airport. The far south (areas 6S) is the only other area posting a gain. Of the five remaining areas, the central business district (area 1) shows the greatest stability, with its losses being held to 1 percent and 2,120 jobs a year. The outer business ring (area 2), with a decline of 1.7 percent and 5,065 jobs a year, exhibits somewhat less resistance, and the two remaining areas (area 3 and area 5S) did

Table 4-9. Annual Absolute and Percentage Change in Employment by Subarea: Chicago 1958-1963.

Area	Number	Percent
CBD	−2,120	−1.0
2	−5,065	−1.7
3	−6,889	−3.2
4	−4,903	−1.5
5N	4,538	4.9
5S	−3,922	−3.1
6S	304	1.1
Unclassified	−1,983	−2.4
Total	−20,042	−1.5

Source: Illinois State Employment Service, *Employed Workers Covered by the Illinois Unemployment Compensation Act, 1955-1964: Chicago Standard Metropolitan Statistical Area.* (Chicago: Chicago Research and Statistics Units, ISES, 1965).

most poorly (−3.2 and −3.1 percent a year). Two facts emerge from these data. Central city declines are much greater in central (except for the CBD) than in outlying areas. Employment growth in the northern parts of the city, and especially near the airport, is much greater than in the south, especially near the Negro ghetto. Whether employers are being attracted by the airport or are fleeing the ghetto is an interesting question and an important issue for public policy.

In summary, neither the evidence presented here nor that published elsewhere suggests that the fairly general declines in central city employment levels conceal any large scale increases in employment within the most central parts of central cities. Rather, the opposite is probably the case. The evidence regarding CBD employment levels is far from clear-cut; even so, it suggests that CBD declines are somewhat smaller than in the immediately surrounding areas. This is consistent with the views of those who emphasize the importance of increased employment in central office employment. In an increasing number of central cities the most rapid declines appear to be taking place in the core areas surrounding the central business districts.

METROPOLITAN STRUCTURE AFTER
FIFTEEN YEARS

Fifteen years of rapid metropolitan growth, very unevenly distributed between the central cities and suburban rings, profoundly affected the level and spatial distribution of metropolitan employment and populations. Nearly a third of wholesaling employment in the 40 largest metropolitan areas is located in suburban rings in 1963 as compared to less than one-tenth at the beginning of the postwar period (Table 4-10). Of selected services employment, 31 percent is in the ring at the end of the period, as compared to 15 percent at the beginning.

Table 4–10. Suburban Ring Share of SMSA Employment and Population, by Selected Years (1950 central city boundaries)

Item	1948	1954	1958	1963
Employment				
Manufacturing[a]	33.1	38.6	42.0	51.8
Wholesaling[b]	8.2	14.5	20.7	28.6
Retailing	24.7	30.6	37.2	45.4
Services	15.2	21.6	26.1	31.3
Population[c]	36.0	43.5	48.2	54.3

Source: See note 9

[a]Data pertain to 1947–1954

[b]Wholesaling data available for 39 SMSAs only

[c]Obtained by interpolation and extrapolation of 1940, 1950, 1960, and 1965 data

By 1963 nearly half of metropolitan area retailing employment was located outside of central cities (as defined in 1950); in 1948 the proportion had been slightly less than one-fourth. The suburban share of manufacturing employment in 1963 exceeded 50 percent.

The proportion of metropolitan population residing in suburban areas increased during the period as well. By 1958 almost half of the population of these 40 large metropolitan areas resided outside of 1950 central city boundaries. In 1963 the percentage had reached 54 percent. Even so, the data in Table 4–10 suggest employment may be shifting toward suburban areas at a *more* rapid rate than population.

FUTURE URBAN FORM

Projecting future metropolitan employment patterns is a difficult and uncertain exercise, but such projections are needed for a wide range of urban public investment and policy decisions. The above analyses of historical trends have strong implications for forecasting. Granted the difficulties of projection, it is useful to risk some speculation about future urban form.

First, despite the many objections that might be raised about the quality and meaning of the data presented above, it is impossible not to conclude that the most central parts of metropolitan areas are losing employment to outlying areas and that this process is, if anything, accelerating. Slow growth and not infrequent decline of central areas have accumulated to the point where absolute declines in central city employment are now commonplace in other metropolitan areas.

Second, metropolitan spatial structures are undergoing rapid change. If historical trends continue, future central cities will have substantially smaller populations and employment levels. As employment is becoming more evenly dispersed over the surface of the metropolitan regions, metropolitan centers are becoming less dense. The large concentrations of employment that characterized the historic central city appear to be becoming less pronounced. Perhaps the most common visual conception of the distribution of metropolitan employment is a tent with its highest point at the center. Metropolitan growth and the agglomeration of numerous formerly independent cities into a metropolitan region meant that smaller peaks—outlying employment and commercial centers—had to be added to the traditional visualization. Figure 4–3, which shows the number of daily person-trip destinations by quarter-square-mile area in Chicago, illustrates the complex, many peaked surface of this kind. Even so, the cone or tentlike surface remains the basic spatial structure. The outlying subcenters are merely an elaboration of the historic central city model.

However, if the changes in employment distributions identified above continue, they will bring about even more changes in the shape of the metropolitan area. The extreme peaks will steadily erode away. City and suburb are already becoming similar. Over the long haul, these processes could result in a relatively "flat" distribution of employment and population that is sharply different from what we know today and even less like what we remember of the historic city.

Third, though gaps in the available data make it impossible to be certain, it appears that employment is dispersing even more rapidly than the metropolitan population. However, since the population of the rapidly growing

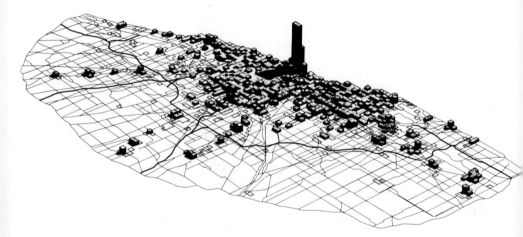

Figure 4–3. Total Person-Trip Destinations: Chicago

Source: Chicago Area Transportation Study, vol. 1, fig. 7, p. 25.

The destinations of 10,212,000 person-trips on the average weekday are distributed throughout the study area as shown in this model. The highest blocks represent 144,000 trip destinations per quarter square mile grid, the lowest blocks 5,000. The flat shaded areas represent less than 5,000 but more than 2,500.

suburban areas includes disproportionate numbers of persons who do not belong to the labor force (housewives and children), more careful analysis might disprove this hypothesis. Even so, one may conjecture that the doughnut may be the model of the future—that is, employment opportunities will be located around the periphery and workers' homes in the central city. This image of metropolitan structure is far different from that more commonly held. Obviously, such a radical redistribution of jobs would profoundly affect many urban problems, of which transportation is only the most obvious.

SOME CONTRARY EVIDENCE ON FUTURE URBAN FORM

Land use forecasts have been prepared for nearly every U.S. metropolitan area. Almost without exception these depict a much different picture of probable future developments in land use than that presented in this paper. Forecasts of employment and population for Philadelphia over a 25 year period, 1960–1985, prepared by the Delaware Valley Regional Planning Commission (the follow-up agency to the Penn-Jersey Transportation Study), are typical of these projections of urban development. For the Philadelphia Central Business District (CBD) they show "a substantial growth in office employment, modest retail growth, a stability or decline in other employment groups and little change in households."[14] Moreover, the study concludes that the city of Philadelphia will lose 3 percent of its households and 21 percent of its manufacturing jobs. However, an expected 52 percent increase in nonmanufacturing employment leads to an overall employment increase of 29 percent or 1.2 percent a year. These projections of population and employment lead the authors to conclude that: "The continued effect of these two trends—dispersed residences and relatively centralized economic activity—will be a marked spatial separation of residences from employment, which in the past led to large volumes of long, peak hour radial trips. The region's transportation need apparent in 1960 will, therefore, not only continue into the future but will increase in intensity."[15]

These conclusions are diametrically opposed to those presented in this chapter. Since both views cannot be correct, the obvious question is which one is? It is possible that this chapter's speculations about future urban form are true for some metropolitan areas but that Philadelphia is an exception. Only the future can determine which view is more accurate. Meanwhile, it is useful to examine the postwar experience of Philadelphia and the available data underlying these two very different forecasts. Table 4–11 summarizes the "historical" census data for Philadelphia and the forecasts prepared by the Delaware Valley Regional Planning Commission. These census employment data for Philadelphia differ from those for the 40 SMSAs in the earlier analyses in that active proprietors are aggregated with paid employees to obtain total employment. Projected levels of employment growth from the Delaware Valley study have been converted to simple yearly averages to simplify their comparison with the census data presented in Table 4–11 and in previous sections.

Several observations can be made about the data in Table 4–11. As noted previously, the census data categories provide incomplete employment coverage. Indeed, they account for only about 60 percent of all employment in the Philadelphia SMSA. By comparison, the Delaware Valley forecasts include all categories of employment. Thus, the census data presented in Table 4–11 and earlier sections of this paper may be providing a misleading picture of employment changes by focusing on those employment categories that are decentralizing most rapidly.[16]

As shown in Table 4–11, the largest forecast growth rates are for the "education, institutions, and communications" and "office" employment categories. Office employment is projected to have a growth of 3.1 percent per year in the central city. Central city employment in the education, institutions, and communications category has an even higher growth rate amounting to 4.4 percent per year. It could be argued on this basis that employment in central areas will increase and that increases in central office and other activities will more than offset declines in the categories for which historical data are available.[17]

It is difficult to compare the data shown in Table 4–11 since the aggregated categories used for the Delaware Valley forecasts are not precisely the same as for the census categories. Still, it is impossible to avoid the impression that the forecasts are optimistic in terms of available historical information. While the authors of the Delaware Valley forecasts project a decline of 0.3 percent and 1,357 jobs in wholesaling and manufacturing combined, they report that the declines are limited to manufacturing. This is in contrast to the postwar experience of small, but persistent, declines in central city wholesaling employment between 1948 and 1963. Similarly, the decline in central city wholesaling and manufacturing employment between 1960–1985 forecasted by the Delaware Valley report amounts to only 34,000 jobs. Yet the decline estimated from census data in these two employments groups between 1960 and 1963 amounted to over 23,000 jobs, despite a rapid expansion of economic activity on the national level. Thus, according to census data, the rate of decline of manufacturing and wholesaling employment in Philadelphia's central city appears to have accelerated in the recent 1958–1963 period, with most of the loss being offset by increases in suburban area manufacturing and wholesaling employment.

The Delaware Valley forecasts also include a retail trade and services category which, though it includes about 60,000 fewer workers, corresponds roughly to the combined census categories of selected services and retail trade. According to census data for the 1958–1963 period, the increase in selected services jobs of 245 per year fell short of offsetting a yearly decline of 3,588

Table 4–11. Yearly Percentage and Absolute Changes in Central City and Suburban Employment (paid employees plus proprietors): Philadelphia.

Type of Employment	Central City				Ring			
	1948–54	*1954–58*	*1958–63*	*1960–85*	*1948–54*	*1954–58*	*1958–63*	*1960–85*
Retailing	−3,046	−1,171	−3,588	2,440	2,398	3,815	3,261 ⎫	4,005
Selected services	529	1,843	245		534	1,978	1,660 ⎬	
Wholesaling	−284	−562	−992	−1,357	1,094	1,146	1,720 ⎬	2,012
Manufacturing	−2,648	−2,818	−6,726	5,698	4,824	285	6,505 ⎭	
Office work	—	—	—		—	—	—	
Education, institutions, and communications	—	—	—	3,689	—	—	—	2,758
Total	—	—	—	11,307	—	—	—	14,177

Percent growth per year

Type of Employment	Central City				Ring			
	1948–54	*1954–58*	*1958–63*	*1960–85*	*1948–54*	*1954–58*	*1958–63*	*1960–85*
Retailing	−1.9	−0.8	−2.6	1.8	3.1	4.1	3.0 ⎫	3.4 ⎫
Selected services	1.0	3.2	0.4		2.7	8.6	5.4 ⎬	
Wholesaling	−0.4	−0.8	−1.5	−0.3	11.9	7.3	8.5 ⎬	0.7 ⎬
Manufacturing	−0.8	−0.9	−2.2	3.1	2.4	0.1	2.7 ⎭	
Office work	—	—	—		—	—	—	2.2 ⎭
Education, institutions, and communications	—	—	—	4.4	—	—	—	5.2
Total	—	—	—	1.2	—	—	—	2.3

Source: See notes 9 and 16

retailing jobs. Yet the Delaware Valley report forecasts a yearly growth of 2,440 jobs in retailing and service trades between 1960–1985.

Clearly, discrepancies exist between the projections of future urban form presented earlier in this chapter and those developed by the Delaware Valley Planning Commission and similar groups preparing forecasts for specific metropolitan areas. The forecasts for individual metropolitan areas are almost always much more favorable than those suggested by the analyses presented here. A significant part of these optimistic projections result from reversals of the declines noted for employment groups for which census data are available. Yet neither the Delaware Valley study, nor others of its type, present these census data or identify the forces that are to "cause" these changes. This optimism may be due in part to the fact that these projections are often conditional and assume some favorable changes in government policy that will improve the prospects of central cities. However, I suspect that there is a more fundamental explanation.

The Delaware Valley Planning Commission forecasts central city declines in employment for only one category, manufacturing. Therefore, it is important that the manufacturing employment location model is the only one of those developed by the study that is based on historical data, for the period 1950–1960. The remaining models were estimated from data for a single year, 1960. It seems possible that the land use forecasting models estimated by the study from cross-sectional data fail to capture some important dynamic elements underlying employment dispersal. From this point of view, the uniform historical experience of widely different metropolitan areas presented previously may provide a sounder basis for forecasting changes in metropolitan structure, despite its partial character.

It would seem prudent to give more attention to the experience of central office employment about which so little is known and on which so many hopes for central cities and central business districts depend. In their discussion of methods used in forecasting future spatial distributions of office employment, the authors of the Delaware Valley Planning Commission report appear to be arguing that: (1) they have no information on changes in employment levels over time for office employment and a number of other categories of employment, (2) these activities are rather highly concentrated during the one year for which the data are available; and (3) it is reasonable that they will remain highly concentrated. The employment location model developed by the study from 1960 data allocates about the same proportion of employment in these categories to the central city in 1985. Since a large proportion of these activities were located in the central city in 1960 and since they are expected to grow rapidly, the model projects a large increase in central city employment. The remaining allocation models appear to have similar biases. Thus, during the entire 25 year period the projected growth of central city employment outstrips the growth of suburban employment by approximately 3,000 jobs a year. Yet all the historical evidence points to a much more rapid employment growth in suburban areas and the possibility of significant central area employment decline trends, if the postwar trends were to accelerate.

The weakness of the logic used by the Delaware Valley planners and the model based on it can be illustrated by reference to wholesaling employment for which historical data are available. In 1948 roughly 91 percent of wholesaling employment in 39 metropolitan areas was concentrated in the central city. If this fraction were used to project the central city growth of these 39 cities, wholesaling employment would increase by 1,280 jobs between 1948 and 1963. In fact, central city wholesaling employment declined by 6,003 jobs during this period.

It seems entirely possible that the Delaware Valley projections, and others obtained using similar methods, may have grossly underestimated the strength of the economic and technological forces leading to employment dispersal and as a result may have grossly overestimated future levels of employment in the central portions of U.S. metropolitan areas.[18]

Very little systematic time series information is available on employment in central city offices. One of the few sources is a "directory study" of changes in the location of a sample of the central offices of large corporations between 1950 and 1960.[19] Table 4–12 summarizes the 1950 and 1960 locations of "mover" firms located in the 40 SMSAs used in the earlier analyses. Because of the importance of New York City as a central office location, data for it are presented separately; data for Philadelphia are also listed separately.

There are a number of difficulties with the study summarized in Table 4–12 and its findings must be interpreted carefully. Nevertheless, its

Table 4–12. Central Office "Mover Firms" Locating in New Geographic Areas, 1950 and 1960

Area	1950	1960	Difference	Percentage Change
39 Large SMSAs (excluding New York)				
CBD	530	404	−126	−23.8
CC	394	392	−2	−0.5
Ring	102	235	133	130.4
New York SMSA				
CBD	314	300	−14	−4.4
CC	31	12	−19	−61.3
Ring	20	45	25	125.0
Philadelphia				
CBD	36	36	0	–
CC	44	22	−22	−50.0
Ring	4	28	24	500.0

Source: Meyer, Kain, and Wohl, *The Urban Transportation Problem,* p. 41.

results are highly pertinent to this discussion. The central business districts (CBDs) of the 39 SMSAs lost 126 mover firms over the decade, while their central cities (outside the CBD) lost two. By comparison, their suburban rings gained 133 mover firms. In New York, the CBD lost 14, and the central city 19, mover firms, while the suburban ring gained 25. Philadelphia's CBD had 36 mover firms in both 1950 and 1960, but its central city lost 22 between 1950 and 1960. By comparison, the suburban ring which had only 4 mover firms in 1950, had 28 in 1960.

Though these data are incomplete, they do raise the possibility of central office dispersal. In the past few decades, any tendency toward dispersal of central office activities has been offset by a rapid increase in employment in these activities. As a result, the growth of employment in central office and other "control" activities in CBDs has been rapid in most instances. Though these increases have offset some of the CBDs declines in wholesaling, retailing, and manufacturing employment, they have not been large enough to cause increases in the levels of CBD employment. The fragmentary evidence on CBD employment levels indicates that employment declines have been the general rule in American cities. Some observers argue that the declining employment sectors in the CBDs have run their course and that the postwar employment declines will be reversed by continued rapid growth of office employment. The location decisions of central office activities, thus, are especially critical to the future levels of employment in the CBD. It is difficult to be as optimistic about central city employment increases since the central city still contains a great deal of the kinds of employment that historically are dispersing rapidly. For example, the city of Philadelphia lost over 63,000 manufacturing jobs between 1947 and 1963, a major component of its overall employment decline. Yet in 1963 it still contained an estimated 285,000 manufacturing jobs, a number representing more than one-third of central city employment that year.

Given these observations, my prognosis remains that of a continued decline in employment within the central cities of U.S. metropolitan areas and further rapid growth in the suburban rings. However, because of the incompleteness of the data used in both this discussion and in the large number of planning studies within U.S. urban areas, I would emphasize the speculative nature of these predictions and the need for more research on the determinants of industry location within metropolitan areas.

RECENT EVIDENCE ON TRENDS IN EMPLOYMENT LOCATION

The analyses presented thus far in this chapter are reproduced largely in the form in which they were first published in *The Metropolitan Enigma.*[20] Since the employment data used in the analysis are more than a decade old, it is prudent to inquire whether more recent and more complete sources indicate a need to revise the findings and tentative projections presented previously.

The release of more recent and more complete data have prompted a fairly large number of researchers to further analyze the questions discussed in this chapter.[21] Studies by Benjamin Cohen and Roger Noll, by Alexander Ganz and Thomas O'Brien, and a critique of the Ganz and O'Brien analysis by Franklin James are representative of the recent research on employment location and illustrate the interpretative problems it poses.

Benjamin Cohen and Roger Noll, both jointly and independently, have published three papers that critically examine the findings presented in this chapter.[22] Among their most valuable contributions is an analysis of changes in the level of government employment within central cities. The analyses presented previously in this chapter do not consider government employment, which accounts for roughly one-fifth of all jobs in metropolitan areas and which has grown at twice the rate of private employment since the end of World War II. Noll and Cohen clearly demonstrate that this rapid growth in government employment has had an important effect on employment trends in central cities. For example, Noll, in a 1970 paper, reports that the growth in local government employment in the central cities of 30 large metropolitan areas between 1957 and 1962 was sufficient to offset the combined decline in manufacturing, wholesaling, retail trade, and selected services employment in the same central cities, between 1958 and 1962.[23] The former grew by 52,000 jobs while the latter declined by 33,000 jobs.

Of the 52,000 increase in local government in the central cities of the 30 large SMSAs included in Noll's analysis, 40,000 or 77 percent of the growth took place in eight large central cities. These same eight cities also benefited from a 40,000 increase in federal jobs between 1958 and 1963. The combined growth of federal and local government employment in these eight cities was large enough to offset the combined loss in manufacturing, wholesaling, retailing, and selected services, and indeed to produce a net increase in employment in these six categories of approximately 32,000 jobs. Similarly, if the 12,000 increase in local employment in the remaining 22 SMSAs is added to the 15,000 increase in employment in the four private employment sectors, a growth of 27,000 jobs is obtained for these central cities.

In evaluating Noll's and Cohen's findings, it is important to recognize two important differences between their analyses and the similar analyses of census data presented in the first part of this chapter. First, they consider only 30 large metropolitan areas, while the analyses presented in Tables 4–3 to 4–7 refer to 40 large metropolitan areas. And second, the employment change estimates shown in Tables 4–3 to 4–7 are defined in terms of 1950 boundaries, while Noll and Cohen use current boundaries—i.e., their estimates include central city employment growth due to annexations. Cohen and Noll do not correct their data for annexation both because they regard the use of legal boundaries as more appropriate for the issues they consider and because they contend the correction procedures used in this chapter tend to underestimate employment growth within central cities. It is even more evident that the failure to account for annexations overstates employment growth within constant boundaries.

As a comparison of Table 4–13 with Table 4–4 reveals, these two changes are sufficient to produce fairly large differences in annual average rates of employment growth or decline. Cohen obtains larger percentage declines in central city manufacturing and wholesaling employment between 1958 and 1963, but more favorable changes in central retailing and selected services employment than were obtained for the 40 SMSAs included in Table 4–4. For the 30 cities used by Cohen, retailing grows at an average rate of 1 percent between 1958 and 1963 within legal boundaries, as contrasted with a 2 percent decline within the 1950 boundaries of the 40 large SMSAs included in Table 4–4. Similarly, Table 4–13 indicates central city employment in selected services grew by 2.6 percent a year in the 30 SMSAs analyzed by Cohen in contrast to a growth of 0.9 percent for the 40 metropolitan areas included in Table 4–4.

In a 1971 paper, Benjamin Cohen provides data for employment changes in the same 30 cities during a more recent period.[24] These estimates, shown in the lower half of Table 4–13, reveal that the central cities of these metropolitan areas fared considerably better during 1963–67 than during

Table 4–13. Thirty Large Metropolitan Areas: Change in Employment

	Central City (1)	"Suburbs" (2)	Total Metropolitan (3)	Central City (4)	"Suburbs" (5)	Total Metropolitan (6)
	Thousands			*Annual Percentage*		
1958–63						
Manufacturing	−264	393	129	−1.3	6.0	0.3
Retail	108	546	654	1.0	7.7	3.6
Wholesale	− 48	145	97	−0.7	8.2	1.2
Selected services	173	205	378	2.6	7.9	4.1
Total above	− 31	1,289	1,258	−0.1	4.8	1.8
Local government[a]	52	n.a.	n.a.	1.6	−	−
TOTAL	21	n.a.	n.a.	0	−	−
1963–67						
Manufacturing	139	679	818	0.9	4.8	2.7
Retail	59	350	409	0.6	4.6	2.5
Wholesale	57	171	228	1.1	8.4	3.2
Selected services	141	165	306	2.4	5.9	3.5
Total above	396	1,365	1,761	1.1	5.1	2.8
Local government[b]	110	n.a.	n.a.	3.1	−	−
TOTAL	506	n.a.	n.a.	1.3	−	−

[a]1957–62

[b]1962–67

Source: Benjamin I. Cohen, "Trends in Negro Employment within Large Metropolitan Area," *Public Policy* XIX, no. 4, (Fall 1974): 614–15.

1957–62. In the latter period, central city employment in all four private sectors increased by between 0.6 percent per year for retailing employment to 2.4 percent per year for selected services, while local government employment grew by 3.1 percent per year. The combined growth rate of all five sectors was 1.3 percent per year. The gains during 1963–67 were large enough to offset the declines recorded during the previous period, and, as a result, total employment in these five sectors grew by an average of 0.6 percent per year over the entire period, 1958–67.

The growth in central city employment reported by Noll for 1963–67 took place against a background of general economic expansion and is broadly consistent with what would have been predicted from the simple econometric model presented in Chapter Five. For example, Equation 5–21 implies that the 818,000 increase in SMSA manufacturing employment that occurred during 1963–67 would cause central city manufacturing employment to increase by 139,000 if the average vacant land ratio for the 30 central cities of these 30 metropolitan areas was 0.09, an entirely plausible value.

For the same sample of 30 metropolitan areas, employment declines of 1.3 percent per year in manufacturing and of 0.7 percent per year in wholesaling during the first period, i.e., 1958–63, were transformed to annual increases of 0.9 percent (manufacturing) and 1.1 percent (wholesaling) during the second period, i.e., 1963–67 (Table 4–13). And the annual growth rate for all five categories combined, which was 1.3 percent for 1963–67, was zero during 1958–63.

This apparent improvement in the circumstances of central cities suggested by Cohen's 1971 paper should not be allowed to obscure the fact that suburban growth also accelerated during 1966–67. In the four private sectors, the percentage growth in suburban employment exceeded the percentage growth in central city employment by factors that varied between 2.5 for selected services and 7 for wholesaling. Thus, whatever the absolute growth rate of the central cities may have been during this period, suburban growth rates remained a multiple of central city growth rates.

The preceding comparisons illustrate a number of problems inherent in attempts to analyze trends in employment within metropolitan areas. First, cyclical effects make it exceedingly difficult to identify trends in employment. Central city and suburban employment levels appear to be affected differentially by fluctuations in aggregate economic activity. In particular, it has been alleged that since central cities tend to have older plants and equipment, they are more adversely affected by high rates of unemployment than suburban areas, which tend to have newer plants. In the same way, central city employment is likely to respond more strongly to economic expansion as multiplant firms press more of their marginal capacity into operation during periods of expansion. It is significant, therefore, that 1967, the terminal year used by Cohen and several other authors in their analyses of trends in central city employment levels, had a national unemployment rate of only 3.8 percent, in contrast to a 5.7 percent rate at the start of the period. Even so, this latter rate compared favorably with the 6.8 percent rate of unemployment in 1958, which was the highest annual rate of unemployment in any year since the end of World War II.

These same issues bear on the proper interpretation of recent estimates published by Alex Ganz and Thomas O'Brien, which they claim indicate a significant change in and revival of central city economies during the decade of the '60s. Ganz and O'Brien argue that "In the 1960s, the economies of our large cities rebounded from the relative stagnation of the 1950s and expanded as centers of finance and insurance, communications, business services, recreation and tourism, personal services, and government services," and that "the transformation of the economies of our large cities was accompanied by a growth in jobs and an upgrading of their quality." To support these claims Ganz and O'Brien present data which indicate that 30 large central cities gained 1.5 million jobs between 1960 and 1968. This employment growth amounted to one-fourth of the job gains in their metropolitan areas and 15 percent of the national increase in employment.[25]

To emphasize the fundamental nature of the transformation of central city economies they believe occurred recently, Ganz and O'Brien present disaggregated data for Newark and St. Louis, cities that had especially dismal records during the 1950s. These estimates indicate that while total employment in Newark grew by only 800 jobs in the 12 year period 1948–60, in the 7 year period 1960–67 it grew by 11,400 jobs. These data also illustrate the bias that may result from a partial analysis of employment statistics. If the comparisons are limited to manufacturing, wholesaling, retailing, and selected services, it would appear that the city lost nearly 4,000 jobs between 1950 and 1960 rather than gaining 800 jobs.

It would be a mistake to conclude that measurement problems are limited to the incomplete census data used for much of the analysis presented in the first part of this chapter. Ganz's estimates of employment in the omitted industry sectors are based on data on the number of workers covered by unemployment compensation programs and social security. Both have serious disadvantages as sources to use in evaluating changes in employment levels over time. Specifically, changes in program coverage frustrate efforts to interpret the data since coverage in both programs has been extended to additional industries and to smaller firms at several times during the period. Because of these changes in coverage, the 800 worker increase in covered employment between 1948 and 1960 reported by Ganz, which amounts to only 0.3 of one percent of 1948 covered employment, almost certainly corresponds to an actual decline in Newark employment. Indeed, it is even possible that the 11,400 increase in covered employment between 1960 and 1967, shown in Table 4–14, which is 4.7 percent of the 1960 covered employment, corresponds to a real decline. While the magnitude of these measurement errors is difficult to estimate, their

Table 4–14.   Employment, by Industry, in the Cities of Newark and St. Louis, and in their Metropolitan Areas (thousands of workers)

	City of Newark				Metropolitan Area	
	1948	1960	1963	1967	1948	1967
Total*	235.7	236.5	239.2	247.9	479.5	670.5
Agriculture and Mining	0.1	**	**	0.1	1.6	2.1
Construction	6.4	5.8	5.4	7.3	22.1	28.4
Manufacturing	92.3	79.8	75.5	73.9	227.8	255.7
Transportation, Communications and Public Utilities	20.7	23.2	26.2	30.9	35.2	55.1
Wholesale and Retail Trade	44.6	46.5	45.7	41.3	87.0	130.7
Finance, Insurance and Real Estate	25.1	22.1	22.6	23.4	29.6	40.0
Services	14.7	21.0	22.4	24.7	33.7	69.2
Government	31.8	38.1	41.4	46.3	42.5	89.3

	City of St. Louis				Metropolitan Area	
	1950	1962	1965	1967	1950	1967
Total*	454.5	422.5	426.5	446.1	657.6	848.5
Agriculture and Mining	1.1	0.8	0.8	0.8	3.7	3.3
Construction	16.8	12.5	17.2	17.3	24.5	42.9
Manufacturing	166.3	138.9	133.0	138.0	266.0	298.0
Transportation, Communications and Public Utilities	42.2	37.6	37.5	40.0	63.9	64.1
Whole Trade	45.3	37.4	36.1	36.2	49.0	52.2
Retail Trade	75.5	48.6	49.5	50.9	104.8	125.1
Finance, Insurance and Real Estate	24.1	26.6	26.9	27.3	28.9	45.8
Services	38.2	62.7	64.9	73.0	48.4	126.0
Government	45.0	57.4	60.6	62.6	68.4	91.1

*Excludes unpaid family workers and self-employed workers
**Less than 50

Sources: New Jersey Department of Labor and Industry, Division of Planning and Research, Trenton, Unpublished Tabulations; Missouri Division of Employment Security, Jefferson City, U.S., Bureau of the Census, County Business Patterns, New Jersey, Missouri; Wilfred Lewis, "Urban Growth and Suburbanization of Employment: Some New Data" (Brookings Institution, May 1969, manuscript), cited in Alexander Ganz and Thomas O'Brien, "The City: Sandbox, Reservation, or Dynamo?", *Public Policy* XXI (Winter 1973): 109.

direction is clear, since there appears to be no comparable bias that operates consistently in the opposite direction.

A second weakness of these data results from the fact that they are reported on a firm rather than an establishment basis. The allocation procedures used to allocate the firm's employment among branches is also a possible source of bias, although its direction is unknown. Finally, the social security or so-called *County Business Patterns* data are reported by county. In a few instances, for example St. Louis and San Francisco, the central county and central city are coincident, but the sample of city-counties is unrepresentative of large SMSAs.

The data for St. Louis, shown in the second half of Table 4–14, depict an even clearer pattern of decline, change in industry composition, and recovery. Between 1950 and 1962 total employment in St. Louis decreased by 28,000 jobs. But during the same 12 year period employment in manufacturing, wholesaling, retailing, and services declined by 44,500 while employment in the remaining sectors grew by 16,500. Then between 1962 and 1967, according to Ganz and O'Brien, total employment in the city of St. Louis grew by 23,600 or by enough to nearly reach 1950 levels. Approximately one-half of this growth occurred in the four private sectors used for the bulk of the analysis included in this chapter.

The changes in employment levels and composition in the 11 large cities analyzed by Ganz and O'Brien, which tell a similar story, enable us to evaluate the Ganz-O'Brien view that major structural transformation in central city economies that radically improved their growth prospects accelerated during the decade of the 60s. These data also permit us to evaluate possible magnitude of bias resulting from the omission of data on employment in sectors other than manufacturing, wholesaling, retailing, and selected services.

In 1950, the four employment sectors used in the analyses presented previously in this chapter accounted for approximately 70 percent of total employment in the 11 large cities shown in Table 4–15. During the 10 year period 1950–60, Ganz and O'Brien estimate employment in manufacturing, wholesaling, retailing, and services in the 11 cities declined by 52,000 jobs or by 0.1 percent a year. In contrast, jobs in the remaining five sectors—i.e., agriculture and mining, construction, transportation, communications and public utilities, and finance—grew by 94,000 or by 4.7 percent a year during the same period. If services are omitted from the first category, employment in the remaining three sectors declined by 269,000 over the decade or by 0.6 percent a year. This evidence is consistent with the view that the analyses presented in the first half of the chapter may understate central city employment growth. The Ganz-O'Brien estimates suggest employment in these 11 large central cities grew by 1.3 percent overall. This finding must be tempered, however, by the previously discussed extensions in coverage over time.

During the sixties, i.e., 1960–67, which Ganz and O'Brien depict as a kind of central city renaissance, the annual growth in covered employment in these 11 cities was actually less than during the 1950s, 0.8 percent per year as contrasted with 1.3 percent a year. In addition, the four private sectors used previously in this chapter are relatively a more important source of growth during the second period than during the first. Between 1960 and 1967, employment in manufacturing, wholesaling, retailing, and services grew by 0.2 percent per year as compared to 0.1 percent per year during the first decade. In contrast, employment growth in the remaining sectors, which averaged 4.7 percent during the first decade, declined to 1.1 percent a year during the 60s.

Table 4–15. Job Trends and Structural Change in Eleven Large Cities

	Employment by Place of Work (thousands of workers)					
	1950	1954	1958	1960	1963	1967
Total employment (11 cities)	7,812	7,831	7,826	7,900	7,910	8,340
Baltimore	384	389	374	379	374	398
Boston	498	534	525	480	467	491
Denver	143	165	203	236	248	264
Minneapolis	404	415	427	437	432	480
Newark	230	233	232	237	239	248
New Orleans	181	207	208	208	213	246
New York	3,579	3,540	3,566	3,618	3,605	3,735
Philadelphia	968	934	888	874	840	858
San Francisco	473	469	466	473	480	510
St. Louis	454	446	424	423	427	446
Washington, D.C.	498	499	513	535	585	664
Total employment	7,812	7,831	7,826	7,900	7,910	8,340
Agriculture and Mining	10	12	17	17	17	19
Construction	337	303	301	302	320	292
Manufacturing	2,163	2,095	1,952	1,953	1,827	1,804
Transportation, Communication and Public Utilities	768	763	745	721	700	740
Wholesale and Retail Trade	1,766	1,741	1,704	1,707	1,674	1,725
Finance, Insurance and Real Estate	605	646	686	713	742	780
Services	1,084	1,115	1,230	1,301	1,363	1,538
Government	1,079	1,156	1,191	1,186	1,267	1,442

Source: Alexander Ganz and Thomas O'Brien, "The City: Sandbox, Reservation, or Dynamo?", Public Policy XXI (Winter 1973): 112.

Franklin James, Jr. reached similar conclusions in a 1974 paper which critically examines Ganz's and O'Brien's interpretation of the evidence.[26] In addition, he provides data that suggest that the reversal in the fortunes of central cities documented by Ganz and O'Brien were quite transitory and primarily reflected cyclical forces. James concludes that "industrial changes is not an important factor in the substantial recent change in the growth performance of large U.S. central cities and that they simply received a portion of the enormous economic growth which occurred during the 1960s." To support his interpretation of recent events, James presents the data on covered employment in Newark, New Jersey shown in Table 4–16. James emphasizes that these data include only workers covered by New Jersey's unemployment compensation law and that significant increases in coverage were made in 1969. Even so, the recession during 1969–71 had a dramatic effect on Newark, as covered employment declined by 25,000 jobs between 1967 and 1971 and covered manufacturing employment declined by almost 25 percent.

Franklin James also presents estimates from County Business Patterns on changes in employment by industry sector between 1970 and 1971 for 8 of the 11 central cities used by Ganz and O'Brien in their analysis. As

Table 4–16.   Covered Employment in Newark, New Jersey (thousands of jobs)

Industry	1960	1963	1967	1968	1969†	1970†	1971†
Agriculture and mining	–	–	0.1	0.1	0.1	0.1	0.1
Contract construction	5.9	6.0	7.7	7.5	8.2	7.4	7.1
Manufacturing	81.8	76.2	74.4	69.9	67.1	62.7	56.6
Transportation and public utilities	23.2	27.1	30.1	28.0	30.3	27.5	26.4
Wholesale and retail trade	46.9	45.1	41.0	38.1	39.8	39.1	36.6
Finance, insurance, and real estate	22.0	22.8	23.8	24.0	24.3	24.8	24.7
Services	21.1	22.4	24.7	24.8	25.7	25.0	23.9
Total*	201.0	199.6	201.8	192.4	195.6	186.6	175.4

*Totals adjusted because of rounding

†Coverage was expanded in 1969. See text for a discussion of the coverage of the data.

Source: New Jersey Department of Labor and Industry, *Covered Employment Trends* (Trenton: Division of Planning and Research, annual), cited in Franklin J. James, Jr., "The City: Sandbox, Reservation or Dynamo? A Reply," *Public Policy,* Vol. XXII, Winter 1974, p. 43.

Table 4–17 reveals, these eight cities lost a total of 66,000 manufacturing jobs, 20,000 jobs in transportation and public utilities, 23,000 in wholesale and retail trade, and 8,000 in finance and service industries in one year. James' data strongly illustrate the cyclical sensitivity of central city employment.

These and similar results make it clear that the favorable employment experience of central cities, reported by a number of critics of my research on industry location, is primarily attributable to the rapid economic expansion during the period 1958–67. In addition, a number of the data sources used by various authors to fill the gaps in the analyses reported in the first part of this chapter are biased toward overstating central city growth or understating central city decline since the end of World War II. Even so, there is some reason to suspect that analyses limited to published statistics from the Census of Manufacturing and Trade may have exaggerated the frequency of central city declines. Still, it is difficult to find the seeds for any but very modest central city growth in the revisionist literature on employment location.

QUESTIONS OF PUBLIC POLICY

We are constantly told that public policy should do something to halt or reverse the trends described in this chapter. Several proposals directed to this end have been mentioned. Nonresidential urban renewal is the most direct attack on employment dispersal; it is a way of reducing the difficulty and cost of assembling the large tracts of unencumbered land needed for the construction of

Table 4–17. Private Employment Change in Eight Major Cities, 1970–1971 (thousands of jobs)

Industry	Employment		Change
	1970	*1971†*	
Agriculture, forestry, and fisheries	3.4	3.5	+0.1
Mining	13.5	12.6	−0.9
Contract construction	158.4	156.3	−2.1
Manufacturing	741.6	675.1	−66.5
Transportation and public utilities	325.0	304.3	−20.7
Wholesale trade	287.8	277.6	−10.2
Retail trade	508.5	495.8	−12.7
Finance, insurance, and real estate	347.9	341.4	−6.5
Services	800.8	799.2	−1.6
Unclassified	7.1	7.5	+0.4
Total*	3194.2	3074.0	−120.2

*Totals adjusted because of rounding

†1971 St. Louis employment in neither mining nor "unclassified" was disclosed separately, although both were included in the city total. These two groups employed 743 persons. As a result, employment in individual industries does not add to total in 1971, nor for change between 1970 and 1971.

Source: U.S. Bureau of the Census, *County Business Patterns,* cited in Franklin J. James, Jr., "The City: Sandbox, Reservation or Dynamo? A Reply", *Public Policy,* Vol. XXII, Winter 1974, p. 46.

modern plants and warehouses. Another proposal is to subsidize the location of plants within central city ghettos. This is justified, in the view of some, by the high unemployment rates among Negroes trapped in central city ghettos, made worse by the steady and frequently rapid movement of jobs away from these centrally located residential neighborhoods.

No detailed discussion of these two programs is attempted here, but I can offer a few general observations about their underlying rationale. First, I know of no good statement of why these trends *should* be reversed. It is not obvious that a reduction in central area employment and population densities is detrimental. The argument most frequently used against it holds that such dispersal jeopardizes the tax base of central cities; though true, there are many straightforward, and more efficient, ways of solving the admittedly difficult fiscal problems of central cities than by redirecting metropolitan growth. Attempting to reverse a massive, nationwide social and economic movement (that is, suburbanization) strikes me as the most costly method—and the one least likely to succeed—of helping pay for needed central city services.

Central city nonresidential renewal is frequently justified on the grounds that the market for urban land is imperfect and that these imperfections sharply increase the cost of acquiring and assembling the large tracts needed for modern industrial plants. Nonresidential renewal is simply a means of over-coming these imperfections and providing a locational pattern more like that which would occur in a perfect market. Far more analysis is needed, but it appears that the high costs of nonresidential renewal in central cities are due more to a need to acquire and destroy many still useful residential and nonresidential structures than to market imperfections. At a minimum it would appear that nonresidential urban renewal should be subjected to careful scrutiny to determine whether its supposed benefits are commensurate with its costs.

Ghetto job creation is a far more difficult question. Negro Americans appear severely limited in their housing choices by collusive behavior on the part of whites. If high Negro unemployment rates in central city ghettos are due in part to these housing restrictions (and perhaps, even if they are not), there would appear to be a fairly strong justification for public action.[27] But there are several serious questions that need to be raised about ghetto job creation schemes. Job creation in central city ghettos would be very expensive. The subsidy per job would almost certainly be very large. Such programs might reduce pressures for residential integration and would tend to perpetuate existing patterns of racial segregation.[28] But the most telling objection is that such policies might well fail altogether. There are strong linkages between northern ghettos and the still vast pools of rural, southern Negroes. Ghetto improvement and particularly ghetto job creation programs might well have as their principal result increased migration of southern Negroes to northern metropolitan areas. The growth rates of northern ghettos might increase severalfold, greatly aggravating the already serious problems there, while leaving the existing adverse levels of income and unemployment unchanged. Undoubtedly the well-being of many southern Negroes might be increased, but just as assuredly the distortions of metropolitan growth would be magnified, and the goal of assimilating and integrating the Negro into the urban society made far more difficult. Moreover, as with the central city public finance issue, better and more direct means exist for improving the conditions of southern Negroes. These arguments are considered more fully in Chapter 9.

Chapter Five

An Econometric Model of Metropolitan Development

with John H. Niedercorn

In this chapter we present a dynamic cross-sectional econometric model describing population and employment changes which have taken place in 39 large standard metropolitan statistical areas (SMSAs) during the 1954–1958 period.[1] The model is used first in an attempt to describe the structure of metropolitan development; later it is used to evaluate changes in the spatial structure of large urban complexes.

For years there has been a good deal of speculation about the structure of metropolitan growth. Considerable controversy has raged over the question of whether population changes lead to employment changes, whether the opposite is true, or whether the two are simultaneously determined with each exerting some influence on the other. Another frequently debated question is whether the employment and population declines taking place in some older central cities are attributable to transportation systems changes resulting from biases in public policy favoring capital expenditures for highways over those for public transit, or whether these declines are caused by shifts in employment locations attributable to changes in production techniques and household locations. The latter may result from deep-seated preferences by urban residents for low density areas, abetted by rising incomes, favorable government mortgage policies, and a lower cost and more ubiquitous form of urban transportation. Again, these changes may be taking place simultaneously and could very well be mutually reinforcing. The analysis set forth in this chapter supplies a tentative answer to the first question and offers some even more tentative conclusions about the second.

The analysis of urban structure presented in this chapter proceeds in several discrete steps. First, we determine changes in population and manufacturing employment for the entire SMSA. Manufacturing employment in most metropolitan areas is the major type of basic employment and these changes in its level have a major effect on the aggregate level of employment and population in the SMSA. Basic employment is the exogenous variable used in economic base models. It differs from nonbasic in that its output is exported and thus provides the area with income.

Several assumptions about metropolitan growth influence the model's structure. Since the SMSA is defined as a region in which significant economic interactions between its constituent parts take place, SMSA growth must be understood before very much can be said about either the central city or the metropolitan ring. The SMSA is essentially a small, mainly nonagricultural economy, which is postulated to develop like a national economy, yet differs in that it is open—i.e. trade with other countries, and the migration of labor, capital and other resources are much more important. Growth of population and manufacturing employment are the key or basic variables underlying the development process. Population is important because it largely determines the final local demand for goods and services. Manufacturing employment, as noted above, is a key variable because it usually supplies a large proportion of the region's exports, providing it with earnings to pay for its imports of raw materials and finished goods. A region's export level, together with its import level, i.e., leakage, places limits on SMSA population. Changes in the SMSA's population and manufacturing employment are assumed to depend only on predetermined variables and are assumed not to be significantly affected by population and employment distribution between the central city and metropolitan ring. Although this assumption may oversimply reality, it is not unreasonable.

Once the changes in SMSA population and manufacturing employment have been determined, they can be partitioned between the central city and the ring. This allocation is accomplished with the help of a vacant land variable—a crude measure of the land available within the central city for urban development. Changes in retailing, wholesaling, and service employment in both central city and ring can then be determined largely by population changes. Retailing and selected services employment, and to a somewhat less extent wholesaling, are considered demand, or population-oriented in this paper because they exist largely to satisfy the demands of the resident population and will tend to shift locations in response to location changes of this population.

In addition to the shifts in demand for retailing and wholesaling, the model also attempts to account for the role of certain types of technological change on the level and distribution of employment in wholesaling and retailing. Large increases in labor productivity have occurred in each area during the postwar period. Thus changes in the level of employment can occur even if the level of demand remains unchanged.

THE VARIABLES

The econometric model presented in this paper, and shown in schematic form in Figure 5–1, includes 11 stochastic equations, estimated by least squares, and 4

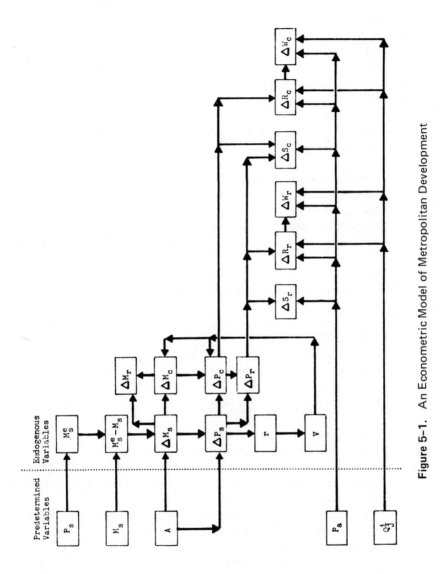

Figure 5-1. An Econometric Model of Metropolitan Development

definitional equations. As can be seen, the model's causal structure is recursive. In all, it includes 9 predetermined variables and 19 endogenous variables. We define the 28 variables below, roughly in their order of use in the model. The predetermined variables are of three kinds. The first, SMSA manufacturing employment and population, are lagged endogenous variables; for these, the model only requires the specification of initial conditions or initial values as the model itself determines their values in later periods. The second type of predetermined variable, age, varies cross-sectionally and is a prespecified characteristic of each central city. It does not vary with respect to time. On the other hand, population annexations, the four employment-sales ratios or labor productivity variables, and the time trend are exogenous variables varying over time, and their values for each metropolitan area in each time period must be specified outside the model.

Predetermined Variables

M_s = SMSA manufacturing employment.

P_s = SMSA population.

A = Number of decades elapsed since the central city reached one-half of its 1950 population. This variable is measured in deviations from its mean, which is 4.7.

P_a = Population annexed by the central city from the ring each year.

Q_c^r = The ratio of retail employment to deflated sales in central city stores in 1954.

Q_c^w = The ratio of wholesaling employment to deflated sales in central city stores in 1954.

Q_r^r = The ratio of retail employment to deflated sales in ring stores in 1954.

Q_r^w = The ratio of wholesaling employment to deflated sales in ring stores in 1954.

t = Time measured in years.

Endogenous Variables

M_s^e = Equilibrium SMSA manufacturing employment.

ΔM_s^g = Assumes only nonnegative values. Annual change in SMSA manufacturing employment in SMSAs of increasing manufacturing employment and equals zero when $\Delta M_s < 0$.

ΔM_s^d = Assumes only 0 and negative values. Annual change in SMSA manufacturing employment in SMSAs of decreasing manufacturing employment, and equals zero when $\Delta M_s > 0$.

ΔM_s = Annual change in SMSA manufacturing employment in all areas. ·

ΔP_s = Annual change in SMSA population.

V = Ratio of vacant land area to total land area in the central city.

r = Rate of vacant land absorption in the central city.

ΔM_c = Annual change in central city manufacturing employment.

ΔP_c^1 = Annual change in legal area central city population.

ΔP_c = Annual change in constant area central city population.

ΔM_r = Annual change in ring manufacturing employment.

ΔP_r^1 = Annual change in legal area ring population.

ΔP_r = Annual change in constant area ring population.

ΔR_c^1 = Annual change in legal area central city retaining employment.

ΔW_c^1 = Annual change in legal area central city wholesaling employment.

ΔS_c^1 = Annual change in legal area central city service employment.

ΔR_r^1 = Annual change in legal area ring retailing employment.

ΔW_r^1 = Annual change in legal area ring wholesaling employment.

ΔS_r^1 = Annual change in legal area ring service employment.

THE DATA

Statistical estimation of the model presented here required data from several sources, both published and unpublished. Data on the 1954 and 1958 SMSA and central city employment in manufacturing, wholesaling, retailing, and selected services were obtained from the 1954 and 1958 Censuses of Manufacturers and Business. Ring employment was obtained by subtracting central city employment from SMSA employment. (If there was more than one central city within an SMSA, as in the San Francisco–Oakland standard metropolitan statistical area, they were combined into a single central city.) The employment-sales ratios for ring and central city retailing and wholesaling were also obtained from the Census of Business. Population data were taken from the 1950 and 1960 Censuses of Population. While the raw employment data used were actual counts reported by the Censuses of Manufactures and Business, the population data were estimates made by interpolation of population counts obtained from the 1950 and 1960 Censuses of Population. Data on central city population annexations were obtained from The Municipal Year Book, 1949–59.[2] Data on the proportion of vacant land in the central cities and its rate of change were obtained by a questionnaire mailed to the city planning commissions of the 50 largest central cities, as well as various published reports. The central city vacant land data, even though far more complete than that assembled for any previous study, are still fragmentary and subject to errors.

These data have also been obtained for 1948, and relationships similar to those presented here have been estimated for the period 1948–54. We used the model's parameters for the 1954–58 period rather than for 1948–54, because our experience suggested that the earlier period contained too many disturbances and was too greatly affected by postwar adjustments to provide meaningful parameter estimates. Our belief is strengthened by the fact that the statistical results obtained for the first period, in estimating relationships similar to these, are much inferior to those obtained for the second, i.e. have fewer statistically significant regression coefficients and smaller proportions of explained variance. One disturbing characteristic of the 1954–58 period is that 1958 was a year of moderately severe recession. Thus, manufacturing employment in that year probably deviates from the secular trend. Consequently, we will feel much better about the model's coefficients once we have been able to reestimate them for the period 1954–62 using the 1962 Census of Manufactures.

THE MODEL

From Figure 5–1 it is clear that the first part of the model involves explaining changes in SMSA population and manufacturing employment. These can be described by the following three equation recursive system:

$$M_s^e = \alpha_{11} P_s, \tag{5.1}$$

$$\Delta M_s = \alpha_{21} (M_s^e - M_s) + \alpha_{22} A + \alpha_{23}, \tag{5.2}$$

$$\frac{\Delta P_s}{P_s} = \alpha_{31} \frac{\Delta M_s}{M_s} + \alpha_{32} A + \alpha_{33}. \tag{5.3}$$

The first equation states that the equilibrium or "normal" level of SMSA manufacturing employment is a linear function of SMSA population. Of course, the constant α_{11} will decrease over time because the ratio of manufacturing employment to total population in U.S. is declining. Equation (5.2) specifies that the change in SMSA manufacturing employment is a linear function of the difference between equilibrium or "normal" SMSA manufacturing employment and its existing level, the central city age variable, and a constant.

The central city age variable is defined as the number of decades elapsed since the central city reached one-half of its 1950 population and is interpreted in both equations as a lagged growth variable for the SMSA. Growth rates appear to be quite persistent; the group of most rapidly growing SMSAs has been remarkably constant in its composition for several decades. Here we have recognized that growth is a relatively continuous process and that many of the forces generating it are both pervasive and enduring. New areas, as defined by the age variable, have had more rapid growth in recent decades than older ones. We are somewhat at a loss to assign an economic meaning to the age variable. We suspect it embodies a fairly large number of exogenous forces affecting the growth rate of regions and metropolitan areas. Metropolitan growth is highly regionalized; a majority of the most rapidly growing areas are located in the Southwest and West while a majority of the stagnating ones are located on the eastern seaboard. In part, this is explainable by a change in the distribution and structure of manufacturing and other "basic" employment. The persistent growth of many areas seems to be greater than is explicable by changes in production techniques or transportation costs. A number of researchers examining this persistent growth have suggested that the better climate. better living conditions, lower levels of urban congestion, and the like in the West and Southwest are exogenous forces operating directly on the population growth rate. Having lived in Southern California and elsewhere, we feel intuitively that this view has some merit; and we suspect that the age variable may, in fact, reflect such exogenous population growth variables.

The difference between the equilibrium and existing levels of manufacturing employment is very important. This variable implies that manufacturing employment is tending to become more equally distributed between the United States' metropolitan areas, roughly in proportion to SMSA populations. In other words, as time passes, the model suggests that the variance of the manufacturing employment—population ratio for the large SMSAs will tend to decrease. This indicates that the country is moving toward a pattern of industrial location radically different from what prevailed in the past. Generally, areas that in the past had large amounts of manufacturing employment were rather highly specialized, with their unusual share of manufacturing depending on nearby raw materials and favorable location with respect to waterways or rail nets. Some areas possessed large manufacturing complexes; others had virtually none.

The reasons behind this change are many, but the most important, we feel, is the tendency for manufacturing to become less dependent on nearby sources of raw materials. This is an inevitable concomitant of the later stages of economic development because value added by labor and capital becomes a larger and larger proportion of the total value of output. Today's complex products require much more processing per unit of raw material than those of a generation ago. So, location near the source of raw materials no longer gives an area a decisive advantage in many branches of manufacturing, because raw material costs have become a smaller fraction of total costs. Of course, another reason for the diffusion of manufacturing is the increasing level of education and skills possessed by the nation's population. Industrial know how is no longer limited to the old eastern manufacturing centers. As a result of this process, manufacturing employment is increasing in newer areas of the country as markets open up, and decreasing in the older areas as they gradually lose their once gigantic skill differentials which made their products competitive throughout the country in spite of high transportation costs.

The percentage change in SMSA population depends on the percentage change in SMSA manufacturing employment, the age variable measuring the rate of past population growth, and a constant term. Thus, increases in SMSA manufacturing lead to increases in population over and above the increments caused by natural increase and the other attractions of urban life.

Obviously, changes in central city population and manufacturing employment depend in substantial part on SMSA rates of growth. In addition, they depend on the central city's amount of vacant land. Equation (5.4) defines the ratio of vacant land area to total land area in the Central City.

$$V = V_0 e^{-rt} \tag{5.4}$$

where V_0 is the ratio of total land at time $t = 0$, and

$$r = \alpha_{51} \ \Delta P_s + \alpha_{52} \tag{5.5}$$

is the rate of vacant land absorption. Therefore, the vacant land ratio declines at a rate determined by the change in SMSA populations and

$$V = e^{-(\alpha_{51} \ \Delta P s + \alpha_{52})t}. \tag{5.6}$$

Central city changes in manufacturing employment and population are then determined as follows:

$$\Delta M_c = \alpha_{71} \ V\Delta M_s^g + \alpha_{72} \ \Delta M_s^d + \alpha_{73} \ ; \tag{5.7}$$

where $V\Delta M_s^g = 0$ when $\Delta M_s < 0$ and where $\Delta M_s^d = 0$ when $\Delta M_s > 0$;

$$\Delta P = \alpha_{81} \ V\Delta P_s + \alpha_{82} \ \Delta M_c + \alpha_{83}. \tag{5.8}$$

Central city manufacturing employment changes (Equation 5.7) are assumed to depend on the change in the SMSA manufacturing employment in metropolitan areas which are losing manufacturing employment, and on the product of the change in SMSA manufacturing employment and the vacant land ratio in metropolitan areas that are gaining manufacturing employment. The division of SMSAs into growing and declining areas and the side conditions for the variables $V\Delta M_s^g$ and ΔM_s^d require elaboration. This treatment of the vacant land ratio and the change in SMSA manufacturing variables was necessitated by the asymmetry existing in the estimation procedures for the manufacturing equation and in the a priori or theoretical justifications for including the vacant land ratio in the manufacturing equation. The vacant land ratio is used here as a constraint variable. The underlying hypothesis is that if significant tracts of vacant land exist within central cities, a sizeable proportion of any new SMSA manufacturing employment will locate there. If there is little or only poorly suited vacant land within central city boundaries, increments of SMSA manufacturing employment will locate elsewhere. In the latter case, reason and some empirical evidence indicate that most new manufacturing will locate on the more proximate vacant land located in the ring.[3] As the constraint is only meaningful in those metropolitan areas having manufacturing employment increases, two changes in SMSA manufacturing employment variables are used, with the side conditions noted above, in specifying the change in central city manufacturing employment equation. This asymmetry has been introduced because vacant land is a limiting factor only when SMSA employment is increasing and there is a positive increment to be allocated between the central city and ring. When total manufacturing employment is declining, vacant land does not significantly influence the pattern of its behavior.

The change in central city population is determined by the vacant land ratio times changes in SMSA population, and the change in central city manufacturing employment. Since all except one of the SMSAs are increasing in population, the vacant land ratio constrains central city population growth in virtually all SMSAs and the problem of asymmetry noted for the manufacturing equation does not exist. Changes in central city manufacturing employment can also be expected to induce central city population changes.

So now, the changes in ring manufacturing employment and population can be determined by subtracting changes in these same variables in the central city from those in the SMSA.

$$\Delta M_r = \Delta M_s - \Delta M_c \tag{5.9}$$

$$\Delta P_r = \Delta P_s - \Delta P_c \tag{5.10}$$

Once manufacturing employment and population locational changes are determined, it is possible to specify locational changes of the three population- or demand-oriented kinds of employment for both the central city and metropolitan ring. The equations for retailing, wholesaling, and selected services are all quite similar in principle, although they differ somewhat in their detailed specification.

The change in central city retail sales should depend on the shifts in demand generated by changes in central city and ring population. If shifts in retail sales can be assumed a linear function of change in demand, and population is used as a demand proxy, then the resultant change in employment will depend largely on changes in labor productivity and changes in population in the two areas.

In this model we express the change in central retailing employment as a linear function of the product of the central city employment-sales ratio and the change in central city population, and the product of central city employment-sales ratio and the change in ring population. Symbolically the relationship appears as follows:

$$\Delta R_c^1 = \beta_{11} Q_c^r \Delta P_c + \beta_{12} Q_c^r P_a + \beta_{13} Q_c \Delta P_r^1 + \beta_{14} \ . \tag{5.11}$$

The ring equation is similar:

$$\Delta R_r^1 = \beta_{21} Q_r^r \Delta P_c^1 + \beta_{22} Q_r^r P_a + \beta_{23} Q_r^r \Delta P_r + \beta_{24} \ . \tag{5.12}$$

The annexation terms appear in Equations (5.11) and (5.12) because the employment variables are measured within legal areas, while the population variables are measured using 1954 central city boundaries. The annexation term permits estimation of changes in the dependent variable attributable to annexations alone.

The changes in wholesaling employment in both central city and ring can be explained by similar equations except that the demand proxy used is the retailing employment change instead of the population change.

$$\Delta W_c^1 = \beta_{31} \frac{Q_r^w}{Q_c^r} \Delta R_c + \beta_{32} Q_c^w P_a + \beta_{33} \frac{Q_r^w}{Q_r^r} \Delta R_r^1 + \beta_{34} , \tag{5.13}$$

$$\Delta \dot{W}_r^1 = \beta_{41} \frac{Q_r^w}{Q_c^r} \Delta R_c^1 + \beta_{42} Q_r^w P_a + \beta_{43} \frac{Q_r^w}{Q_r^r} \Delta R_r + \beta_{44} . \tag{5.14}$$

Wholesalers sell to other business establishments, in particular to retailers, rather than directly to the public; consequently, changes in the wholesaling employment distribution depend indirectly on changes in population distribution. Changes in population distribution lead to changes in the retail employment distribution which, in turn, induce changes in the wholesale employment distribution.

Changes in service employment are described by a simplified equation. Most service industries require little capital equipment, and changes in labor productivity have been minimal; thus the employment-sales ratio is not an important explanatory variable and is omitted from the services equation. The major shortcoming of the selected services category is its lack of homogeneity. The services relationships appear in Equations (5.15) and (5.16).

$$\Delta S_c^1 = \beta_{51} \Delta P_c + \beta_{52} P_a + \beta_{53} \Delta P_r^1 + \beta_{54} , \tag{5.15}$$

$$\Delta S_r^1 = \beta_{61} \Delta P_c^1 + \beta_{62} P_a + \beta_{63} \Delta P_r + \beta_{64} . \tag{5.16}$$

STATISTICAL ESTIMATION

Statistical estimation of the model is accomplished by applying least-squares regression analysis to each equation, except in the case of Equation (5.1). The parameter α_{11} used in Equation (5.1) is specified as the mean proportion of manufacturing employment to total population in the 39 SMSAs (Equation (5.17). The "normal" or equilibrium employment is then the product of this proportion and the SMSA population. Given each SMSA's "normal" or equilibrium manufacturing employment and the age variable, the equation for the change in SMSA manufacturing employment can be obtained. Using the percentage change in SMSA manufacturing employment and the age variable, the change in SMSA population can be estimated. The rate of vacant land absorption is next estimated as a function of SMSA population changes. The rate of vacant land absorption and the rates of SMSA population and manufacturing employment growth are all that are required for estimating the parameters of the change in central city population and manufacturing employment equations. The final step entails estimating the relationships for the three demand-oriented kinds of employment.

The model has not been estimated as an entire system using one of the advanced econometric techniques. Ideally, such a course would have been desirable; this was not feasible, however, because of the variation in sample sizes used. They range from 16 to 39 because the data for several variables are incomplete. A disproportionate number of the data deficiencies were for the relatively new and more rapidly growing areas. We felt that omission of these areas from the empirical estimation of the model would have significantly biased the results. The estimating equations are given below with sample size used in estimation (n), the coefficient of determination (R^2), and the standard errors of the regression coefficients. All population and employment variables are measured in thousands, with exception of the Q_j^i variables that are measured in employees per thousand dollars of deflated sales.

$$M_s^e = .115 P_s \; ; \tag{5.17}$$

$$\Delta M_s = .036 \, (M_s^e - M_s) - .642A - .645, \tag{5.18}$$
$$(.0075) (.296) \;\; (1.10)$$

where $R^2 = .58, N = 37$.

$$\frac{\Delta P_s}{P_s} = .093 \, \frac{\Delta M_s}{M_s} - .007A + .028, \tag{5.19}$$
$$\phantom{\frac{\Delta P_s}{P_s} = }(.047) \phantom{\frac{\Delta M_s}{M_s} } (.0015) \;\; (.012)$$

where $R^2 = .65$, and $N = 37$.

$$r = .0000917 \, \Delta P_s + .0104 \, , \tag{5.20}$$
$$(.0000085) (.130)$$

where $R^2 = .30$ and $N = 16$.

$$\Delta M_c = 1.970 \, V\Delta M_s^g + .722 \, \Delta M_s^d - .646. \tag{5.21}$$
$$(.854) (.084) (1.06)$$

where $R^2 = .75$ and $N = 33$; $V\Delta M_s^g = 0$ when manufacturing employment is declining and $\Delta M_s^d = 0$ when manufacturing employment is increasing.

$$\Delta P_c = .401 \ V\Delta P_s + .826 \ \Delta M_c - 2.003 , \tag{5.22}$$
$$ (.156) \qquad (.162) \qquad (1.225)$$

where $R^2 = .56$ and $N = 33$.

$$\Delta R_c^1 = 1.752 \ Q_c^r \Delta P_c + .495 Q_c^r P_a + .323 , \tag{5.23}$$
$$ (.247) \qquad (.276) \qquad (.160)$$

where $R^2 = .64$ and $N = 39$.

$$\Delta R_r^1 = 1.315 Q_r^r \Delta P_r - 1.206 Q_r^r P_a - .034 , \tag{5.24}$$
$$ (.113) \qquad (.407) \qquad (.280)$$

where $R^2 = .81$ and $N = 39$.

$$\Delta W_c^1 = 1.482 \ \frac{Q_c^w}{Q_c^r} \ \Delta R_c + .986 \ Q_a^w P_a - .030 , \tag{5.25}$$
$$ (.273) \qquad\qquad (.640) \qquad (.079)$$

where $R^2 = .59$ and $N = 39$.

$$\Delta W_r^1 = .907 \ \frac{Q_r^w}{Q_r^r} \ \Delta R_r - 1.314 Q_r^w P_a + .084 , \tag{5.26}$$
$$ (.145) \qquad\qquad (.774) \qquad (1.06)$$

where $R^2 = .59$ and $N = 33$.

$$\Delta S_c^1 = .031 \ \Delta P_c + .022 P_a + .023 \ \Delta P_r^1 + .201 , \tag{5.27}$$
$$ (.009) \qquad (.011) \qquad (.003) \qquad (.460)$$

where $R^2 = .77$ and $N = 39$.

$$\Delta S_r^1 = .027 \Delta P_r - .016 P_a - .297 , \tag{5.28}$$
$$ (.002) \qquad (.008) \qquad (.870)$$

where $R^2 = .79$ and $N = 39$.

EMPIRICAL FINDINGS

Evidently, manufacturing employment tends to close the gap between equilibrium and actual employment levels at the annual rate of approximately 3.6 percent (Equation 5.18). Furthermore, changes in population tend to widen the gap in areas of increasing manufacturing employment and narrow it in declining areas. Thus, the adjustment process is relatively slow, especially in rapidly growing areas. Age also affects the growth rate of SMSA manufacturing employment, slowing it by 642 workers for every decade in excess of the mean age of the 39 SMSAs (Equation 5.18). Finally, the negative constant seems to indicate a secular decline in manufacturing employment. This is probably spurious, however, since 1958 was a year of moderately severe recession. Analysis of aggregate manufacturing employment data for 1954, 1958, and 1962 suggests that a constant term of +0.559 might be more appropriate in the long run.[4]

SMSA population appears to grow at the annual rate of about 2.8 percent which is about 1.1 percent greater than national growth rate (Equation 5.19). The age variable and percentage change in manufacturing employment exercise a relatively moderate influence on SMSA population growth.

Central city vacant land absorption, the percentage rate of decline of vacant land, depends on the SMSA population change (Equation 5.18). This implies that rapid SMSA growth quickly absorbs any remaining central city vacant land. Since the coefficient of determination is relatively small and the vacant land variable itself is not overly reliable, this equation should be subject to some reservations.

The rate of SMSA manufacturing employment growth, although not exerting a decisive influence on SMSA population growth, has a substantial effect on the distribution of population and employment increments between the central city and metropolitan ring (Equations 5.22 and 5.23). This happens because it strongly affects changes in central city manufacturing employment, which in turn, affects changes in central city population; and the latter, in turn, affects the changes in retailing, wholesaling, and service employments.

As the vacant land ratio decreases, less and less of the SMSA increment of manufacturing employment goes into the central city (Equation 5.21). For example, if the vacant land ratio is 0.20, only about 40 percent of the increase locates in the central city. On the other hand, if this ratio is 0.10, only about 20 percent of the increase takes place in the central city. If SMSA manufacturing employment is declining, about 72 percent of the loss takes place in the central city regardless of the vacant land ratio. The negative constant in Equation (5.21) shows that manufacturing employment is, to some extent, leaving the central city. Evidently, technological change, especially the shift to one story plants, is a powerful force luring manufacturing to the suburbs.

Only a very small part of the total SMSA population increment settles in the central city. If the vacant land ratio is 0.10, only 4 percent find homes there (Equation 5.22). However, each increment or decrement of central city manufacturing employment induces a central city population change of 0.82 persons (Equation 5.22). Evidently, people move to remain near their jobs. Also, there is a strong tendency (about 2,000 people per year) to leave the central city, as indicated by the negative intercept. Many families move to the suburbs when it becomes financially possible, thus indicating a preference for low density residences. This is perhaps the strongest reason for pessimism about future central city growth.

The reason why vacant land limits the amounts of manufacturing employment and resident population that a city can absorb should be obvious. Every factory or residence constructed must occupy some space. In areas where vacant land has disappeared the only way of increasing population and employment is through the more intensive exploitation of land already in urban use. The involves demolition of old buildings and their replacement by high rise structures. Although this process has been going on for some time, there are two reasons why it has not increased urban population and manufacturing employment densities. First of all, high rise structures are not generally suitable for manufacturing. The latter usually requires a smooth flow of materials which is virtually impossible if various parts of the production process are scattered throughout a high rise building. The second reason is the desire for more open space in the cities. As old buildings are demolished some of the land reclaimed becomes playgrounds, parks and parking lots, and is thus removed from residential use. This offsets the increases in residential densities that high rise structures make possible.

The retailing, wholesaling, and services equations also provide some interesting empirical results. Retailing seems to be increasing somewhat in the central city. There is a net change of 0.088 retailing employees for every unit increase in population (Equation 5.21). In addition, there is a positive time trend. Changes in ring population do not seem to affect changes in central city retailing employment; thus, this variable is omitted from the final estimated equation (Equation 5.23). Likewise, ring retailing employment changes are not included in the central city wholesaling equation.

Retailing employment changes appear to be a good explanatory variable for wholesaling employment changes as the latter appear to follow retailing very closely. For every increase in Central City retailing employment, there is a 0.354 increase in wholesaling.

The behavior of central city employment changes in the selected service industries differs from central city wholesaling and retailing employment changes in a number of important ways. Secular increases in labor productivity have been far less important in service industries than in retailing or wholesaling; so the labor productivity variable is not included for the selected services equation. Changes in ring population that have no discernable effect on changes in central city retailing and wholesaling employment are significantly related to changes in service employment. An increase of 31 central city workers in service trades is associated with each 1,000 person increase in central city population, while an increase of 23 central city service workers is associated with each 1,000 increase in ring population. If these coefficients exhibit secular stability, this model seems to suggest that selected services is the only industry the central cities can depend on for substantial future growth. We previously indicated our reservations about this industry classification because of its lack of homogenity. Given the opportunity to construct more homogeneous classifications, we may discover some very diverse trends in the redistribution of service employment. In part, these significant central city increases are attributable to the large secular increase in service employment throughout the economy. Nevertheless, much central city service employment seems specialized enough to draw a substantial clientele from the metropolitan ring, and thus seems destined to grow rapidly as ring population increases.

The ring equations are relatively simple. In none of the three employment groups were central city changes important, so they have been omitted. Only wholesaling has a positive time trend (Equation 5.26), indicating that it is shifting to the suburbs at a rate greater than could be predicted solely by retail employment changes.

USE OF THE MODEL

Predictions made with a simpler version of the model for a representative large metropolitan area (one having average values of the variables for the sample's 39 SMSAs) indicate for the central cities moderate manufacturing employment declines, small increases in population, small increases for retailing and wholesaling, and substantial gains for services.[5] The gains in wholesaling, retailing, and service employment were more than sufficient to offset manufacturing employment declines, so there is a net gain in central city employment for the total of the four categories included here. This gain is greater than the increase in central city population and implies some increases in the demand for transportation between the ring and the central city. Although extremely suggestive of the locational trends occurring in urban areas, the employment classifications included account for only about 60 percent of total urban area employment. Construction, transportation, public utilities, finance, insurance, real estate, government, and a number of service trades are not included in the model presented here because the necessary kinds of data were unavailable. If these omitted groups have, on the average, different locational trends than do the included groups, significantly different results might be obtained.

CONCLUSIONS

Although we consider this only a first or at best a second generation model of urban development and although we admit its incompleteness, we contend that it provides a considerable amount of information, and a large number of insights useful to urban land use and transportation planning, and in the formulation of other kinds of governmental policies affecting urban development.

We have several observations to make about the first of the two questions posed in the introduction; whether population or employment is the exogenous determinant of metropolitan growth. Neither the kind of data nor the model used in this paper is the most suitable for evaluating the question. Moreover, as stated previously, this is not the central question of our inquiry. Still, we felt compelled to evaluate it and to reach tentative conclusions at least for our own satisfaction. Nor is our analysis of population and employment redistribution independent of the answer to the question; the structure of the model used in this paper rests in part on our findings and conclusions about the question. Finally, statistical estimation of the model and related empirical work have provided us with information and insights bearing on the problem.

We conclude, on the basis of our research, that the most crucial determinant of metropolitan and regional growth rates is the marked and fundamental redistribution occurring in manufacturing employment in the American economy. At the same time, we feel there is considerable merit to the suggestion by a number of researchers that there are probably exogenous forces causing higher rates of population growth in the West and Southwest than are explainable in terms of the redistribution of productive capacity.[6] Moreover, both of these exogenous manufacturing employment and population increases most certainly have multiplier effects upon one another and upon other activities within the metropolitan economy.

With regard to the more central question of our inquiry, the redistribution of employment and population within urban areas, our findings suggest that, if current trends continue, central cities will persist in having, at best, only small population and employment increases. Some will suffer declines in both categories. Moreover, the findings of this chapter illustrate that central city employment and population declines are altogether consistent with very large SMSA population and employment increases if there is little vacant land left in the central city. Only when central cities differ substantially from our conception of them, i.e. only when they contain large amounts of undeveloped land, will large increases in central city population and employment levels occur.

In the absence of radical changes in the basic underlying economic and technological trends of American society, i.e. rising family incomes, increased use of continuous processing methods of manufacturing production, lesser reliance on deep water and rail facilities for distribution, changes in the composition of output to include a smaller proportion or freight intensive output, and the like, we would expect trends of increasing suburbanization of the population, declines of population and manufacturing employment in the highest density parts of some urban areas, and substantial suburban growth of population and employment to persist. Thus, central cities will not grow at the high rates experienced in the past. We conclude from our findings thus far that any explanation which would assess the responsibility for these changes solely to the private automobile or biases in governmental transportation policy is naive and oversimplified.

Part III

Effects of Racial Discrimination

Chapter Six

Theories of Residential Location and Realities of Race

This chapter is concerned with the residential segregation of Negro Americans and the effects of this segregation on housing markets and on patterns of urban development. Existing theories of residential location ignore this serious market imperfection almost entirely. Yet it is hard to conceive of any factor that has a greater effect on either residential location decisions or the pattern of urban development. Until very recently, economists concerned with urban problems paid very little attention to race. Exceptions to this generalization were studies sponsored by the Committee on Race and Housing and research by economists at the University of Chicago, whose particular sensitivity to the problem is perhaps understandable.[1] In contrast, considerable empirical research on residential segregation and discrimination was carried out by sociologists and, to a lesser extent, by urban planners. Unfortunately this work, published in sociology and planning journals, has had little influence on urban economics.

      This chapter attempts to synthesize existing "economic" theories of location and the considerable body of empirical and descriptive research on housing market discrimination. The discussion begins with a brief survey of the empirical research on the extent and causes of residential segregation in American cities. Then a modest beginning is made at introducing racial discrimination into "economic" models of residential location. The final section uses the results of these explorations to comment on the prospects of our cities and what I regard as appropriate policy responses.

EXTENT OF RACIAL SEGREGATION

Any discussion of the contemporary role of racial discrimination in influencing the behavior of housing markets and the patterns of urban development should begin with a clear understanding of the extent and nature of residential segregation prevalent today in American cities. This proposition may seem self-evident, but previous experience with many discussions of these issues suggests the undesirability of proceeding without a clear statement of the available evidence.

An important aspect of housing market segregation is the token representation of Negroes in suburban areas. Black Americans have not participated in the rapid postwar suburbanization of the population. Unfortunately, there is more than a germ of truth to the characterization of an increasingly black central city being strangled by a noose of white suburbs. In 1960 the 216 metropolitan areas of the United States were 11 percent Negro. However, 17 percent of central city populations was black as contrasted with only 5 percent of suburban populations.[2] If southern metropolitan areas, with their suburban (agricultural) Negro population, are omitted, the underrepresentation of blacks in the suburbs is even more apparent. In 1960 Negroes were over 15 percent of the population of central cities of metropolitan areas outside the South, but less than 3 percent of their suburban populations. Much has been made recently of data from the current population surveys which suggest that suburban black populations may have grown more rapidly in the past few years. These data should be regarded with considerable caution, however, since small sample sizes do not permit any meaningful evaluation of these aggregate changes. For example, it is not possible from these statistics to determine whether the aggregate increases in black suburban populations are occurring in all SMSAs, are limited to a few SMSAs or particular sections of the country, or whether they take the form of a dispersed, integrated pattern of settlement, an acceleration in the growth of small suburban ghettos, or simply the spilling over of central city ghettos into the suburban ring. It should be clearly understood that the implications of these aggregate changes cannot be determined without more information about the nature of the changes.

Housing market segregation does not end with the exclusion of blacks from suburban areas, because Negroes also are intensely segregated within central cities. Karl and Alma Taeuber have calculated segregation indexes for central cities in 1940, in 1950, and in 1960 using census block statistics. These indexes, which assume values between zero and 100, measure the extent to which observed racial patterns of residence by block differ from a pattern of proportional representation. A value of zero indicates a completely even distribution of Negroes, that is, the proportion of Negroes on every block is the same and equal to the proportion of the entire central city. A value of 100 indicates the opposite situation of a completely segregated distribution, or, each block contains only whites or blacks, but not both. The higher the value of the index, the higher the degree of residential segregation. Values for the 156 central cities analyzed in 1960 ranged from 60 to 98 with only a few cities having values in the lower range of observations—only five cities have values below 70.[3]

DETERMINANTS OF SEGREGATION

Numerous explanations have been offered for the virtually total segregation of blacks. One of the most common is the contention that Negroes are concentrated within particular neighborhoods because they are poor, spend too little on housing, or differ systematically from the majority white population in terms of other characteristics affecting their choice of residence. This socioeconomic hypothesis is easily evaluated empirically and several studies have examined it.[4] Without exception, these studies have determined that only a fraction of the observed pattern of Negro residential segregation can be explained by low incomes or other measurable socioeconomic differences.

Although many tests of the socioeconomic hypothesis rely on elaborate statistical methods, even the most primitive analyses are sufficient to raise serious doubts. If low income explains the concentration of Negroes in central cities, it also should be true that most low income whites live in the cities. Yet, as the data presented in Table 6–1 illustrate, almost as many low income whites live in the suburban rings of the largest metropolitan areas as live in the central cities. For example, 45 percent of Detroit's poor white families live in suburbs, but only 11 percent of its poor Negro families. In fact, the proportion of low income whites living in the suburbs is not very different from the proportion of all whites.

The situation is completely different for Negroes. Relatively few high income (over $10,000 per year) Negroes live in suburbs. Indeed, the percentage of high income Negroes living in suburban areas is considerably less than that of low income whites. In Chicago 9 percent of high income Negroes live in the suburbs as compared with 55 percent of high income whites and 37 percent of low income whites. Clearly, income is not the explanation for the underrepresentation of high income Negroes in the suburbs.

Another "explanation" holds that the segregation of Negroes is the result of a desire "to live with their own kind" and that this is a "normal" and "healthy" manifestation of a pluralistic society. The immigrant colonies that are evident even today in many cities are offered as evidence of the "normality" of this behavior. It is true that a number of identifiable ethnic and nationality groups have exhibited some degree of segregation in American cities. However, the differences between their experience and that of the American Negro are so marked as to invalidate the historical analogy.[5]

The intensity of Negro residential segregation is greater than that documented for any other identifiable subgroup in American history. Moreover, segregation of these other groups has declined over time, while that of Negroes has remained at a high level, and possibly increased. Finally, metropolitan areas are very different places than they were 30 or 50 years ago. They are far less compact and employment is much more dispersed. These widely scattered

TABLE 6–1. Percent of White and Negro Families Living in the Suburban Ring of the Ten Largest Urbanized Areas* in 1960

	White			Negro		
	Family with income			Family with income		
	All Families	Under $3,000	Over $10,000	All Families	Under $3,000	Over $10,000
New York	27.8	16.3	39.2	9.4	8.2	13.9
Los Angeles– Long Beach	59.5	53.5	57.7	25.1	20.7	28.5
Chicago	47.6	37.2	54.7	7.7	5.9	9.0
Philadelphia– Camden	47.7	32.7	42.2	11.5	10.1	13.8
Detroit	58.9	44.9	63.3	12.1	11.3	12.6
San Francisco– Oakland	57.8	48.8	60.8	29.2	25.8	31.5
Boston	74.3	64.0	82.4	19.2	13.9	37.7
Washington	75.7	59.6	77.3	9.8	10.4	8.4
Pittsburgh	70.5	63.3	73.6	29.4	27.1	29.4
Cleveland	59.2	39.3	75.2	3.1	2.4	4.3

*For New York and Chicago the suburban ring is the difference between the SMSA and the urban place (central city). For all other cities it is the difference between the urbanized area and central city. San Francisco–Oakland, Los Angeles–Long Beach, and Philadelphia–Camden are counted as two central cities.

Source: U.S., Bureau of the Census, *U.S. Census of Population: 1960,* vol. I, *Characteristics of the Population.* Washington: GPO, 1961, parts 6, 10, 16, 23, 24, 32, 34, 37, and 40; chapter C; General Social and Economic Characteristics, Tables 76 and 78.

employment centers impose heavy commuting costs on many ghetto residents. No comparable disincentives existed when the ethnic colonies flourished.

To conclude that "voluntary" self-segregation is responsible for much of the current pattern of Negro residential segregation, it is necessary to assume that Negroes have much stronger ties to their community than other groups. Although there is evidence of a growing cultural pride and a sense of community among blacks in recent years as evidenced by the apparent appeal of slogans such as "Black Power" and "Black is Beautiful," it is impossible to assign much weight to this increased awareness as an explanation of these durable segregation patterns. Recognizing the difficulties of interpretation, recent surveys of Negro attitudes provide little support for the self-segregation hypothesis. In 1966, 68 percent of a random sample of U.S. Negroes interviewed by the Harris poll indicated a preference for living in integrated neighborhoods. This fraction is somewhat larger than the 64 percent expressing this opinion in 1963, in spite of the growth of Black Power rhetoric during the period. Similarly, only 20 percent of Negroes interviewed in 1963 and 17 percent in 1966 indicated a preference to live in all black neighborhoods. The fraction of northern Negroes preferring Negro neighborhoods was even smaller (8 percent in 1966); and the fraction of middle and upper income respondents in the North was still smaller (6 percent).[6]

In spite of the lack of any systematic evidence which supports the self-segregation hypothesis, it is difficult to dispose of. The problem is that it is virtually impossible to determine finally the role of self-segregation as long as strong traces of community (white) antagonism toward Negro efforts to leave the ghetto remain. The physical dangers of moving out of the ghetto probably are less today than in the past, but many subtle and indirect forms of intimidation and discouragement still exist.

Evidence of the methods used to enforce housing market segregation is more difficult to obtain today than in the past. Open occupancy laws, which forbid discrimination in the sale and rental of housing on the basis of race, and a decline in clear-cut community approval for such practices, have caused opponents of open housing to resort to more subtle and secretive methods. This is a new situation. Until very recently the most important devices used to enforce segregation could hardly be called subtle. Deed restrictions (racial convenants), the appraisal practices of the FHA and private lending institutions, the actions of local officials, and the practices of real estate agents were among the most important of these.[7] Because residential patterns have a great deal of inertia, the effect of these now discredited devices will long be felt.

Even if there were no future resistance to Negro efforts to leave the ghetto, the cumulative effects of decades of intense discrimination will have long-lasting impacts. If these inimical patterns of housing market segregation are to be destroyed, strong laws, vigorous enforcement, and powerful incentives for integration will be necessary. In determining the range of corrective action both needed and justified, it is important to recognize the extent of discriminatory actions and particularly the complicity of government and law.

ECONOMIC THEORIES OF RESIDENTIAL LOCATION

The economic theory of residential location developed and empirically tested in Part I of this book explains the locational choices of urban households by means of a trade-off between savings in location or site rents obtained by commuting further from work and the larger transportation costs thereby incurred.

For a particular household, the amount of the location rent savings obtained from commuting any particular distance increases as its consumption of residential space (the inverse of net residential density) increases. The metropolitan surface of location or site rents in these theories results from competitive bidding among households for sites that are more accessible to certain desirable locations, particularly workplaces. Most of these theories assume there is only a single centrally located workplace in order to simplify obtaining an analytical solution for the surface of location rents. However, the solution is not changed markedly by a more complex employment distribution. All that is required is that residential space be more expensive in central than in outlying areas.

In general, households choosing to live at low density will be encouraged by these larger location rent savings to travel farther from work, leaving the sites near large workplace concentrations for those consuming more modest quantities of space. The principal exception to this general rule will be those households having both an effective demand for large quantities of residential space and exceptionally large transportation costs savings.

The latter might result when an unusually high value is placed on commuting time or from a need to make unusually frequent trips to central locations. These, typically high income, households will live in central locations despite their consumption of large amounts of residential space. Still it appears that only a few households have commuting costs that are high enough to reside in central areas while consuming large quantities of residential space. Thus, "economic" theories of residential location "explain" the tendency for high income households to live in suburban areas by the fact that, on average, any upward effect of higher incomes on journey to work costs is not great enough to offset the effect of income on residential space consumption.

In the absense of serious housing market imperfections, it is possible that the simple model presented in Part I could explain household behavior adequately, especially if elaborated in terms of the heterogeneity of residential services according to attributes other than location, and in terms of the effect on travel and housing costs of other trips made by household members.

A far more serious omission in the model is its failure to consider explicitly the effects of racial discrimination on commuting and residential location. Any theory or model of the work trip and the residential location behavior of urban households, if it pretends to be realistic and reasonably complete, should explicitly consider these effects, since racial discrimination in the housing market is a potentially enormous market imperfection with great influence on the commuting and residence patterns of both whites and nonwhites.

Despite some recent improvement in the access of Negroes to previously closed portions of the housing supply, limitations on the residential choices of Negro Americans remain great enough to justify the working assumption of separate black and white submarkets. Blacks can purchase or rent property outside of neighborhoods which convention and practice have sanctioned for Negro occupancy only with great difficulty, inconvenience, and costs. These black residential areas hereafter will be referred to as the black submarket or simply the ghetto. By contrast, whites may purchase or rent dwelling units anywhere, including the ghetto, although because of prejudice or other reasons most live in predominantly white residential areas. This creates a situation whereby location rents for equally accessible sites need not be the same within the two markets.

One factor that makes the analysis of housing markets so difficult is the importance of stocks. In no area of economics is the role of stocks treated adequately. Unfortunately, this general inadequacy of economic theory is considerably more serious in the case of theories of urban location, since residential and nonresidential structures are so durable. New construction each year is but a fraction of the total housing supply. For all metropolitan areas, 29 percent of the dwelling units occupied by whites in December 1959 had been constructed during the previous decade. Stocks are an even more important portion of the housing supply in the black submarket. Only 13 percent of the units occupied by blacks in 1959 had been built during the previous ten years. These averages are strongly weighted by southern metropolitan areas, where Negro neighborhoods are more dispersed and often contain vacant land on which some new construction for blacks takes place. In the Northeast only 8 percent of the black supply was newer than ten years old and the fraction was even smaller (5 percent) in the North Central region.

Most of the increased supply needed to house the rapidly growing ghetto populations consists of units shifted from the white market, generally at the periphery of existing ghettos. For example, in the North Central region, during the decade 1950–1960, units formerly occupied by whites are nearly ten times as important as new construction in terms of additions to the black submarket (Table 6–2). The 10–1 ratio is obtained by allocating the "other" category in Table 6–2 (primarily units changed through conversions and mergers) in the same proportion as units whose previous occupant is known. Based on this assumption, more than half of North Central Negroes in 1959 lived

TABLE 6–2. Ghetto Housing Supply by Source and Region

(percent)

| | | *Previously Occupied by* | | |
Region	*New Construction*	*Whites*	*Negroes*	*Other*	*Total*
Northeast	7.5	35.3	36.6	20.6	100.0
North Central	5.3	33.2	29.2	32.3	100.0
South	19.7	14.6	44.9	20.8	100.0
West	21.8	32.1	30.4	15.7	100.0
United States	13.4	30.1	36.7	19.8	100.0
Inside central city	10.6	34.1	36.8	18.5	100.0
Outside central city	24.0	15.0	36.2	24.8	100.0

Source: U.S., Bureau of Census, U.S. *Census of Housing: 1960* vol. IV, *Components of Inventory Change,* Final Report HC (4), part 1A, no. 1 (Washington, D.C.: U.S. Government Printing Office, 1962).

in dwelling units that were occupied by whites a decade earlier. In contrast, few units shifted from black to white occupancy during the same period. For example, in the North Central region only about 7 percent as many units shifted from white to black occupancy as shifted from black to white.

Although the term location rent will be used in references to the Negro submarket, it is not a pure accessibility payment as in the white submarket. The level of location rents in ghetto areas results primarily from restrictions on Negro residential choice rather than from transport savings between a particular location and the periphery. Given the unimportance of new construction as a source of additions to the black submarket, the level of location rents in ghetto areas is determined almost entirely by the price at which units are shifted from the white market. The price of new additions to the black submarket will depend on the price level prevailing in the white market and whether black buyers are able to buy or rent units at the white submarket price, must pay a premium, or obtain them at a discount.

Whether blacks must pay a premium in order to add units to the ghetto is similar to, but not identical with, the question of whether blacks pay more than whites for housing of otherwise identical characteristics. Most researchers have concluded that blacks do pay more than whites for housing of comparable size and quality, but this view is by no means unanimous.[8] This is, of course, a factual question, and while many factual questions are easily resolved, determining the "facts" in this instance is not so simple. To determine whether there is a difference in prices paid by whites and blacks for comparable housing, it is necessary first to standardize the complex and heterogeneous bundle of residential services. Further complications are introduced by the fact that the magnitude of such discrimination would be expected to differ among metropolitan areas and over time in the same area. The size of the premium blacks must pay to shift housing from the white to the black market will depend on the extent of prejudice, the degree of organization of the market, and the instruments available to those wishing to contain the expansion of the black submarket. No one has been able to carry out the standardization in sufficient degree to demonstrate conclusively that measured price differences are not simply the result of systematic differences in the housing consumed by whites and blacks. In spite of the serious methodological and empirical problems, I conclude from my assessment of the existing evidence that a premium is required to shift units to the black submarket. This conclusion is based partially on several empirical studies, including research on rents and property values by John Quigley and me presented in Chapter 12, but it is also based on a broader range of descriptive material and a priori theorizing.

Prices at active margins of the ghetto then may be depicted as being equal to the price in the white submarket plus a premium or discrimination markup. This markup might be some constant amount, as in Equation (6.1), or be proportional to value, as in Equation (6.2).

$$p^n = p^w + \alpha \qquad\qquad (6.1)$$
$$p^n = p^w (1 + \beta) \qquad\qquad (6.2)$$

The concept of a discrimination markup bears a close resemblance to the concept of a discrimination coefficient employed by Gary Becker in his classic work, *The Economics of Discrimination.*[9] However, there is a crucial difference. Becker's discrimination coefficient is a measure of the individual seller's taste for discrimination and indicates the amount of money he would be willing to forego to avoid selling to blacks. The discrimination markup in this formulation depends only in part on an individual seller's unwillingness to sell to blacks. Becker's model depicts atomistic sellers with God-given tastes acting independently. The model presented here depicts much more collusive behavior and a relatively high level of market organization. Individual sellers may be motivated in part by individual prejudice, but real or imagined "community" pressures and the behavior of intermediaries are hypothesized to play a central role in affecting the white seller's willingness and opportunities to sell or rent to a Negro. In the not-so-distant past, these transactions were well organized and openly enforced by codes of "ethics" among market agents and even by FHA appraisers. Today the degree of organization appears to be less, or, at least less visible.

This formulation also provides a mechanism for peripheral expansion of the ghetto, something which is entirely absent from Becker's model. When excess demand within the ghetto becomes too great, that is, when the price within the ghetto exceeds the white submarket price plus the markup ($p^w + \alpha$ or $p^w [1 + \beta]$), units are shifted from white to black occupancy at the periphery of the ghetto. Sales by whites to blacks other than at the periphery of the ghetto either are not permitted at all or only at much larger discrimination markups—markups that for all blacks exceed the potential transportation cost advantages of all other locations. Markups for dwelling units far from the ghetto exceed the markups for units on the boundary of the ghetto because there is a greater consensus about keeping blacks out of these neighborhoods. When rapid growth of the black population makes it apparent that expansion must take place somewhere, it is channeled into adjacent neighborhoods. In the past, real estate agents, lenders, and local and federal officials openly enforced these rules. Although these overt enforcement activities have become less prevalent, it would be foolhardy to conclude that they have disappeared entirely.

The discrimination markup is a monetary difference in either the rent or purchase price paid by blacks in order to add a unit to the ghetto. In addition to these monetary differences there are, of course, the psychic costs of moving into a hostile environment, the transaction costs of finding a suitable dwelling and persuading the owner or landlord to make a transaction, and problems of acquiring information. These transaction and information costs also operate systematically to discourage blacks from obtaining residences outside of or far from the ghetto. If a black chooses a dwelling within the ghetto, he can expect to be courted by both white and black real estate agents and lenders. If he tries to locate outside the ghetto, the reception he receives from these agents is likely to be far less enthusiastic. There are two other explanations of ghetto expansion and price determination that are worthy of mention. The first of these, like the hypotheses outlined above, produces a positive discrimination markup. The second also provides for peripheral expansion of the ghetto but produces a negative discrimination markup.

A positive discrimination markup and peripheral expansion of the ghetto might occur if blacks prefer to live in or near the ghetto and are therefore willing to pay more for adjacent properties. In the case of blacks employed at suburban workplaces, this preference for ghetto locations must be great enough to offset the transportation cost savings available from residing in suburban areas. Under these circumstances, rents would be higher in the black submarket because blacks regard the ghetto as a more desirable location.

The other alternative hypothesis produces a negative markup. It postulates that whites residing on the periphery of the ghetto are more willing to sell to blacks than whites living farther from the ghetto because of a preference not to live near blacks, a fear of racial invasion, and a belief that property value will plummet with Negro entry. Black entry into a white neighborhood located on the periphery of the ghetto is interpreted as the first step in an inevitable process whereby the neighborhood will rapidly become all black. Since this expectation does not arise in the case of Negro entry into a white neighborhood distant from the ghetto, whites do not panic and prices remain firm. If white fears were great enough, blacks might be able to purchase or rent dwellings in these transitional neighborhoods for substantially less than in the white market. Under this circumstances, the value of the discrimination markup would be negative and the ghetto would expand as long as blacks were willing to pay a price equal to the white submarket price on the periphery of the ghetto minus the negative markup. Bargains obtainable at the periphery of the ghetto would discourage blacks from paying higher prices to reside in all white neighborhoods far from the ghetto.

CAUSES OF GHETTO EXPANSION

All three of the above hypotheses provide mechanisms for peripheral expansion of the ghetto. The first and third produce higher housing prices in the ghetto than outside, while the second produces lower prices in the ghetto. The second hypothesis seems highly implausible, given the preceding discussion of self-segregation. A choice between the first and third can be made by empirically determining whether blacks must pay a premium or obtain their units at a discount. The evidence suggests that they typically pay a premium.

The fact that the level of location rents in the Negro market depends primarily on the level in the white market and the discrimination markup does not mean that accessibility considerations may play no part in determining the surface of location rents within the ghetto. In a manner parallel to conventional models of residential location, the location rent surface within the ghetto would depend on the distribution of Negro jobs and the transport costs savings afforded by various residential locations. Given a rapid redistribution of Negro jobs, it is possible that some parts of the ghetto might become more accessible to the new employment centers and location rents would be bid up in these residential areas, causing the shape of the surface within the ghetto to deviate from that outside. However, these situations should be temporary if the previous discussion of the processes that shift housing from the white to the black submarket is valid. As long as the markup for shifting units to the black submarket is the same everywhere at the periphery, the location rent surface within the ghetto should in general resemble that in the white market plus a markup. Deviations would only occur if the markup (alpha) was larger at some boundaries than others.

There is reason to believe that differences of this kind exist. Some ethnic neighborhoods resist Negro entry more strongly than the general public. Also, suburbs with small Negro ghettos may be more successful in limiting their expansion through zoning and other political means. Forces such as these would increase the discrimination markup. Similarly, if the ghetto is bounded by groups sympathetic to the plight of the Negro, the markup might be lower.[10]

THE SEGREGATED HOUSING MARKETS
OF DETROIT AND CHICAGO

Racial discrimination may be thought of as a restraint on the housing cost–transportation cost trade-off model presented in Part I. Discrimination limits the range of choice in which nonwhites are able to exercise this market calculus. In addition the division of the market into two submarkets (a "free market" for whites, with unrestricted location choice; and a "segregated market" for nonwhites) affects the prices of housing services at various locations. Where such imperfections prevail, the schedule of location or site rents would be expected to differ from that postulated previously or obtained in the theoretical writings previously described.

Price levels in both submarkets are determined largely by supply and demand forces, but the determinants of these forces differ considerably between the two. The salient feature of both submarkets is the fact that existing housing stock makes up most of the supply. As the previous discussion shows, new construction is but a fraction of the total. A second important feature of the supply schedule is that the housing services represented by the stock are fixed by location and all but impossible to move to other locations. Urban development has usually occurred incrementally with distance from a single dominant center;

as a result, the age distribution of the housing stock varies systematically with location. An analysis of racial segregation in Detroit and Chicago and its effects on the residential and travel decisions of households in those cities provides a way to evaluate the effects of these distributions.

Chicago and Detroit contain a single dominant employment and commercial center and several much smaller subcenters around which some early peripheral growth occurred and around which, as a result, some older structures are located. Still the overwhelming majority of older structures are found in and around the primary central business districts. The segregated market in Detroit and Chicago, as in most United States metropolitan areas, is mostly located around the dominant center, frequently referred to as "the grey area." Thus, nearly all the structures in the nonwhite market are of prewar construction. Recent additions to the housing stock have been predominantly of two kinds: new lower density structures on the periphery, and high rise and other high density structures at more central locations.

A ceiling on free market rents and housing prices is established by the cost of providing new housing services, i.e., the cost of new construction. Of course, the costs of producing new housing vary considerably from one location to another. The greatest differences are due to variations in land costs, and the greatest of these are between the costs of vacant and nonvacant land. Site costs of developed sites are equal to the discounted value of the income streams of existing properties plus demolition costs. Thus it is hardly surprising that demolition is seldom carried out by the private market except to provide sites for very high density and high quality apartment developments in areas where there is substantial excess demand for them, or to provide sites for industrial or commercial use.

In any case, a price ceiling exists for any type of free market housing, dependent on the costs of providing the desired services in a new structure or location and the differential travel costs between each site and peripheral sites. The earlier discussion makes clear that price differences equal to travel cost differences may exist between two locations without providing an incentive for a household to locate in the lower cost area. The critical importance of the available stock also causes a certain asymmetry in this market; price ceilings exist for each type of housing service, but no floor, except the chain of substitutes and the ability to modify the supply characteristics of the existing stock. Conversions, renovations, redecorating, and permissive deterioration are methods used by landlords and homeowners to change the configuration of the supply of housing services to correspond to changes in the configuration of demand and to maximize their rental income.

Since nonwhites are almost entirely banned from outlying residential locations, price determination in the segregated market differs in a number of important ways from that in the free market. The price ceiling established by the cost of new fringe construction is almost entirely absent from the segregated market. The ceiling established by the cost of new construction in built-up areas still exists but, as in the free market, it is likely to be operative only at price levels considerably above those established by new construction on vacant land.

Demand for residential services in the segregated market is determined by forces similar to those in the free market. The major demand determinants for housing services in metropolitan areas during the postwar period have been increases in metropolitan populations, increases and redistribution of employment, rising incomes, and cheaper and more available housing credit. Increases in the nonwhite demand for residential services in urban areas were especially substantial during and after World War II as large numbers of rural southern Negroes and Puerto Ricans migrated to cities. Unlike whites, who can locate anywhere, nonwhites are mostly confined to areas allocated to them by convention, collusion, and the like.

While many of the same possibilities for adjusting the supply exist in the segregated as in the free market—such as the widely used device of density increasing conversions—supply determinants in the segregated market are still considerably different. Since new construction is insignificant in the segregated market, nearly all additions to its housing supply must come from spatial expansion of the segregated market. Such expansion primarily results from very substantial increases in the nonwhite demand for housing services; it usually consists of peripheral growth—almost never of the creation of "islands" in all-white areas. Thus, the prices and changes in their level in the segregated market depend almost entirely on the relative growth of the nonwhite demand within an urban area, and the rate at which the segregated market is permitted to expand.

If demand far exceeds supply in the segregated market, as it did during and immediately after World War II, rents and housing prices are sure to rise. Wartime controls on building materials and construction kept the supply of urban housing services relatively constant. At the same time, migration to cities and higher incomes caused demand to soar, especially in the segregated market, generating enormous increases in densities and sharp increases in price levels.

The postwar housebuilding boom slowly eased the supply situation, and larger peripheral expansions of the segregated market were allowed. Large price differentials between the two markets gave whites an incentive to put housing on the segregated market. They used the profits to purchase more or better housing services elsewhere. The result was a fairly rapid expansion and consolidation of the segregated market which may have erased the former price differentials. A positive differential still remains, however, and it seems likely that it will remain so long as effective segregation persists, the reason being that the nonwhite market expands only as the result of demand pressures. Unless a Negro is willing to pay somewhat more for a particular location than a white is, white owners and landlords are unlikely to sell or rent to him. Therefore, barring a sharp decrease in nonwhite demand, price levels in the segregated market will probably continue to be higher than in the free market.

This conclusion runs counter to views held and accepted by real estate brokers and white homeowners. For example, it is still commonly believed that property values plummet when Negroes move into a white neighborhood. Such beliefs are refuted by a large number of empirical investigations, but they are still held by lenders and until recently have even been approved by the Federal Housing Authority in its appraisal policies.[11] Their full acceptance—especially by mortgage lenders, whose attitudes so crucially influence the operation of the market—makes their becoming self-fulfilling prophecies an omnipresent danger.

It seems likely that discrimination raises the cost of Negro housing above that of similar free market housing, but that housing prices in the segregated market vary inversely with distance from major workplace agglomerations, just as they do in the free market. For the empirical testing that follows, it is assumed that: (1) housing costs in the segregated market are higher at every distance from the central business district than they are in the free market; (2) that Detroit housing costs in the segregated market are lower than those in Chicago at each distance; and (3) that housing costs per unit of residential space of a given quality decrease with distance from the central business district in each of the four markets.

The nearly absolute restrictions on nonwhite residential location is illustrated in Figures 6–1 and 6–2, which depict the nonwhite percentages of the total number of workers residing in residential areas of Detroit and Chicago in 1953 and 1956. Given these spatial patterns of housing segregation, the reader can easily perceive that whites and nonwhites in both cities differ significantly in the distances and elapsed times of their journey to work. The effects of these constraints on Negro residential choice are partly shown in Figure 6–3, which graphs the percentages of Chicago and Detroit whites and Negroes residing in each two mile interval from the central business district in which they work. The similarity in the patterns for the two cities is almost uncanny. The only significant difference is that the peaks of the distributions are about two miles closer to the central business district in Detroit than in Chicago. In Detroit, 36 percent of the Negro labor force in the central business district resides between two and four miles from the district; in Chicago, almost an identical percentage reside between four and six miles from the Loop. About 22 percent of Detroit's white workers reside in each of the distance intervals, four to six miles and six to eight miles; only about 1 percent less of their Chicago counterparts reside in each of the six to eight and eight to ten mile intervals. These striking similarities prevail despite the fact that the two cities differ substantially in metropolitan population, central business district employment, industrial density, and most other attributes that affect travel and residential patterns.

The discrepancy in the distances at which the profiles peak is due largely to differences in central business district employment levels and in metropolitan scale. For the same percentages of central business district workers to live within a given distance in both cities, the residential density of Chicago's

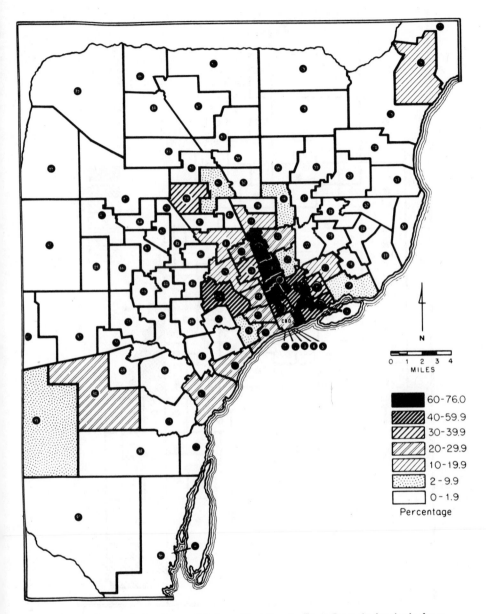

Figure 6-1. Negro Workers Residing in Each Detroit Analysis Area
as a Percentage of All Workers Residing in the Analysis Area, 1953

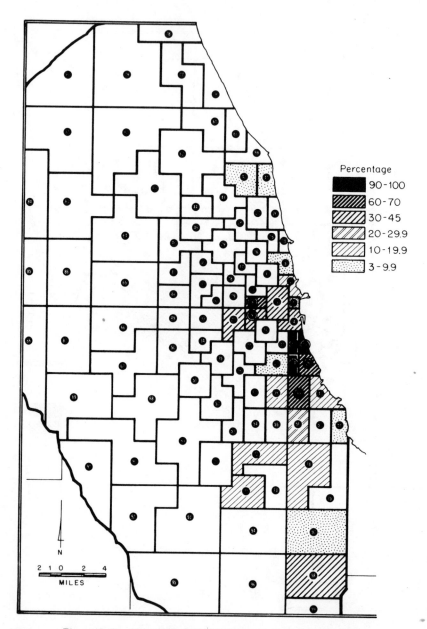

Figure 6-2. Negro Workers Residing in Each Chicago Analysis Area as a Percentage of All Workers Residing in the Analysis Area, 1956

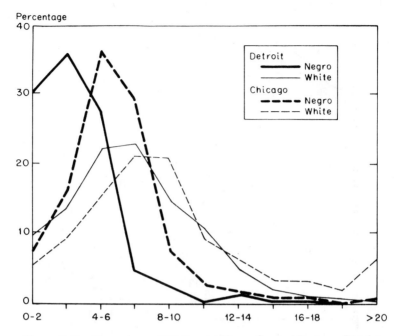

Figure 6–3. Percentage of White and Negro Central Business District Workers Residing in Each Two Mile Distance Ring from the Chicago and Detroit Centers

workers would have to be several times as great. This is accentuated by the fact that in Chicago the quantity and percentage of the total area devoted to nonresidential use near the central business district are several times as great as in Detroit.

Despite the great differences in the nonwhite and white residence profiles shown in Figure 6–3, the full effect of segregation on nonwhite commuting patterns is still greater than suggested there. From Figure 6–2 it is apparent that the few Negro residences in the outlying areas of Chicago are distributed very unequally. A large majority of Chicago Negroes live on the dismal South Side. Discrimination's full effects on the commuting of Negro central business district workers may be seen more clearly in Figures 6–4 and 6–5 which show the residential distributions of workers of both races employed in Chicago's central business district and in Sector 0 surrounding it.

Segregation also affects the residential preferences of whites, many of whom have a dual motivation: to avoid living near nonwhites, and to reside in prestige areas. In Chicago, these preferences no doubt help explain the high proportions of whites employed in the central business district and Section 0 who reside in Sections I to III (especially in Sector I, which includes Chicago's

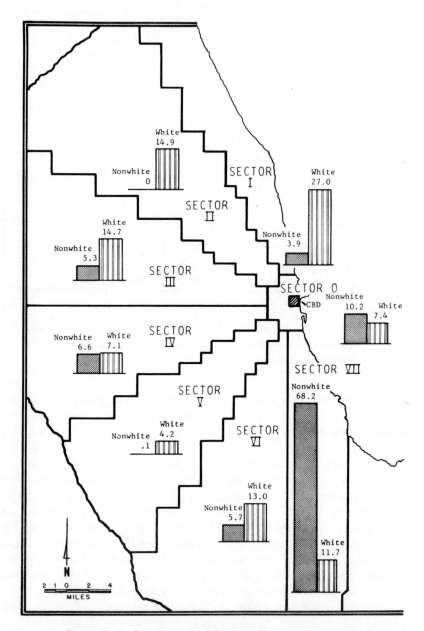

Figure 6–4. Percentages of Chicago White and Nonwhite Central Business District Workers Residing in Each Sector, 1956

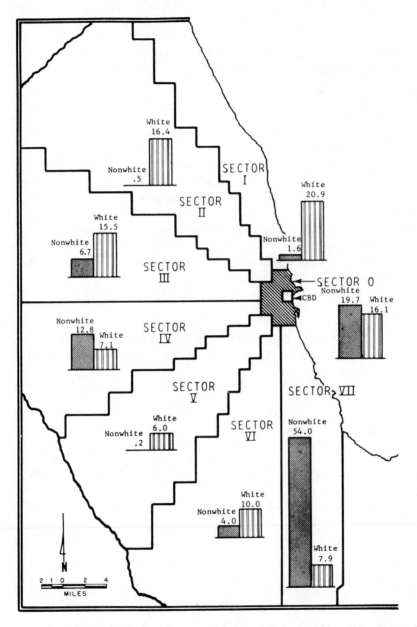

Figure 6-5.   Percentages of Chicago White and Nonwhite Sector 0
Workers Residing in Each Sector, 1956

Gold Coast, Evanston, and other high status areas), and the lower proportions residing in Sectors IV to VII (especially Sector VII, the predominantly Negro South Side).

RESIDENTIAL SPACE CONSUMPTION AND THE
LENGTH OF THE JOURNEY TO WORK

Economic theories of residential location assume that households choosing low density structures are able to obtain their largest savings in housing costs by commuting longer distances. If this proposition is correct, the journeys to work of workers residing in low density structures should be longer than those of other workers employed in the same workplaces. Similarly, since residential space is postulated to cost more for Chicago's than for Detroit's central business district workers, Chicago's workers residing in each structure type should consistently make longer work trips than those of their Detroit counterparts. Table 6–3 confirms this expectation; for both races, in fact, worktrip length increases as the density of the structure type decreases. With city and structure type held constant, whites uniformly commute longer distances and spend more time commuting farther than do nonwhites.

The simple consumer choice model underlying the analysis also

TABLE 6–3. Quartile Distance and Time of Travel for Central Business District Commuters, by Race and Residence Structure Type

Quartile and Residence Structure Type	Airline Distance (miles)				Elapsed Time (hours)			
	White		Negro		White		Negro	
	Chicago	Detroit	Chicago	Detroit	Chicago	Detroit	Chicago	Detroit
First quartile								
One family	7.7	5.0	4.0	1.8	6.4	4.5	5.1	3.3
Two family	4.3	3.1	3.3	1.2	4.8	4.0	4.2	3.0
Multiple	3.5	1.7	3.2	0.3	4.2	2.9	3.9	2.3
Second quartile								
One family	10.5	7.1	7.1	3.2	8.3	6.2	7.3	4.5
Two family	6.0	4.5	5.4	2.4	6.6	4.9	5.8	4.4
Multiple	5.7	3.1	4.5	1.6	5.5	4.4	4.8	3.8
Third quartile								
One family	15.3	9.4	9.4	4.1	9.9	7.9	8.9	6.1
Two family	7.8	6.0	7.4	3.5	8.2	7.1	7.5	5.9
Multiple	7.6	4.5	6.0	2.9	7.2	5.6	6.4	4.9

predicts—if the two cities' central business district workers do not have significantly different incomes and space preferences—that Detroit's workers will consume more than Chicago's, and whites more than nonwhites. Table 6–4 lists the relevant percentages for various structure types, revealing—among other things—that the percentage of Chicago whites residing in multiple units is more than twice that of Detroit whites. From this fact I conclude that the higher price (minimum cost combination of commuting costs and location rents) Chicago workers must pay for residential space discourages them from consuming more of it.

Part of the racial difference in residential space consumption in both Chicago and Detroit is possibly due to differences in incomes and preferences; however, much of it is due to the higher costs of residential space and restricted choices in the market for real property.

HETEROGENEITY, IMMOBILITY, AND DURABILITY

The preceding discussion of the effects of residential discrimination on metropolitan housing markets, while responding to some serious deficiencies of existing "economic" theories of residential location, fails to consider a number of factors that influence the behavior of urban housing markets and that reinforce the effects of residential segregation. Existing "economic" theories of residential location entirely ignore stocks, despite the fact that they are more important than in almost any other market. The particular importance of stocks (the durability of housing) arises from two other characteristics of the bundle of residential services—dwelling units and their associated environments are very heterogeneous and difficult to move. Were it not for this heterogeneity and immobility, the durability of housing would be much less important. For example, if dwelling units were indistinguishable, the bundle of housing services obtained by households would be the same, at all locations. Similarly, if

TABLE 6–4. Percentages of Chicago and Detroit White and Negro Central Business District Workers Residing in Various Structure Types

Structure Type	White		Negro	
	Chicago	*Detroit*	*Chicago*	*Detroit*
One family	36.5	58.4	9.2	30.2
Two family	15.0	18.2	9.5	30.0
Multiple	41.4	17.4	73.0	28.7
Other	7.1	6.0	8.3	11.1
Total	100.0	100.0	100.0	100.0

dwellings were durable, but cheaply moved (such as automobiles), neither heterogeneity nor durability would affect the location problem in any important respect, since households could locate a particular kind of dwelling unit at any location. The fact is, however, that residential structures are at once durable, heterogeneous, and difficult to transport, and these attributes complicate the residential location problem greatly.

It is also a characteristic of the bundle of residential services that external effects and collective goods are highly important. A household's preference for and valuation of a particular dwelling unit depends not only on its characteristics, but on the characteristics of surrounding structures, the attributes of the neighborhood and its residents, and the quality and quantity of services provided, for example, public and parochial schools, and police and fire protection.

Given a heterogeneous and durable housing stock, different price relationships may exist between the black and white submarkets for various kinds of housing. It is not hard to imagine circumstances where blacks have to pay a premium for adding certain types of dwelling units (of a particular size, quality, or other characteristics) to the ghetto, while other types of dwelling units may be cheaper in the ghetto. Such a result could arise if dwellings become less desirable to whites once they become part of the ghetto. It seems likely that few whites will wish to live in all black neighborhoods, and particularly deep within the ghetto. Thus, bundles of residential services located in the ghetto might be cheaper than otherwise identical ones outside the ghetto without causing large numbers of whites to buy or rent them. This difference, which might be termed the ghetto discount, could exist for some kinds of properties at the same time blacks were finding it necessary to pay a premium to add other kinds of units to the ghetto.

Assume there are only two kinds of dwelling units— high quality and low quality. The conditions outlined above could produce an excess supply (defined in terms of the white market price) of low quality dwelling units within the ghetto at the same time there existed an excess demand for high quality units. For this excess supply condition for low quality dwelling units to be consistent with the continued expansion of the ghetto and the payment of a premium for high quality units, it is only necessary that the supply price of providing high quality units by means of ghetto expansion (the price of high quality units in the white market plus the discrimination markup) be less than the cost of providing such units through the conversion of low quality units (the price of low quality units in the black submarket plus the cost of upgrading). In order for this condition to persist, it may be necessary for the depreciation rate or the filtering of high quality units to be more rapid inside the ghetto than outside.

While the growth of the ghetto has not been systematically studied in these terms, most descriptive accounts seem consistent with mechanisms of this kind. These accounts indicate that the ghetto expands into some of the best portions of the surrounding stock and that disproportionate numbers of blacks moving into previously white neighborhoods are members of higher income groups.[12] This peripheral expansion of the ghetto serves high income blacks in very much the way that the flight to the suburbs serves upper income whites. A major difference, however, is that upper income blacks are less able to protect their "ghetto suburbs" from the incursion of lower income groups. This could provide the more rapid depreciation of high quality units in the ghetto needed to produce a permanent discrepancy in relative prices between the ghetto and the white submarket.

"Ghetto suburbs" do not have the buffer of middle income housing that separates high income white suburbs from low income neighborhoods. With the continued growth of the ghetto, the neighborhoods of well-to-do blacks are continually invaded by lower income groups. This causes a decline in neighborhood quality and upper income blacks are forced to migrate to a new "ghetto suburb." Since they are unable to leap frog and establish high quality, high income residential neighborhoods far from the adverse influences of low income households in the manner of high income whites, they pass houses down to lower income groups more rapidly than do whites.

It is well to remember that the ghetto is not simply black. It is also poor. The concentration of poverty in central city ghettos produces a host of adverse environmental conditions that make the central city and its core (both ghetto and nonghetto) less attractive both to middle income whites and to middle income blacks. The only difference is that the former need not live there; they can move to independent political subdivisions a safe distance from the ghetto where they may vote service-taxation packages appropriate to their tastes and incomes. Blacks do not have this option.

In the postwar period, white central city residents, unable to obtain the desired services tax packages by political means, voted with their feet and moved out of central cities by the millions. Today, the concentrated poverty of the ghetto makes it difficult, if not impossible, for central cities to provide the quantity and quality of services demanded by middle and upper income whites and blacks.

Chicago's experience is typical of large northern metropolitan areas. During the decade 1950–1960 the central city lost 399,000 whites and gained 320,000 Negroes. The suburbs gained 1,076,000 whites but only 34,000 blacks. Similar data for other metropolitan areas are presented in Table 6–5. These trends, noticeable earlier in the century, became pronounced with the rapid migration of blacks northward beginning with World War II. Between 1940 and 1960 the white populations of the 24 metropolitan areas with populations of over a million in 1960 increased by 12 million and their Negro populations by 4.2 million. Even though these 24 areas included rapidly growing cities such as Los Angeles, San Diego, and Houston, only 0.2 percent of the white population

TABLE 6–5. Change in White and Nonwhite Central City and Suburban Ring Populations 1950–1960

(in thousands)

Rank		*Central City*		*Suburban Ring*	
		White	*Negro*	*White*	*Negro*
24	Atlanta	91	65	140	−6
12	Baltimore	−113	100	324	7
7	Boston	−130	23	278	3
15	Buffalo	− 83	34	259	4
3	Chicago	−399	320	1,076	34
21	Cincinnati	− 32	31	166	3
11	Cleveland	−142	103	367	2
20	Dallas	171	72	111	−17
5	Detroit	−363	182	904	19
16	Houston	250	90	87	7
22	Kansas City	− 9	27	204	2
2	Los Angeles–Long Beach	388	169	1,668	77
17	Milwaukee	61	41	133	−
14	Minneapolis–St. Paul	− 47	8	366	−
1	New York	−476	340	1,177	67
13	Newark	− 97	63	226	27
18	Patterson–Clifton–Passaic	3	15	286	6
4	Philadelphia	−225	153	700	38
8	Pittsburgh	− 91	18	257	7
9	St. Louis	−168	61	429	18
23	San Diego	212	20	231	3
6	San Francisco–Oakland	−148	67	554	25
19	Seattle	70	11	171	−
10	Washington, D.C.	−173	131	553	18

Source: U.S., Bureau of the Census. *U.S. Census of Population: 1960. Selected Area Reports, Standard Metropolitan Statistical Areas.* Final Report PC (3)–1D (Washington, D.C.: U.S. Government Printing Office, 1963), Table 1.

increase (net) occurred in the central cities as compared to 83 percent of the Negro increase (net). These changes became even more pronounced during the decade 1950 to 1960 when the Negro population of these 24 central cities increased by 2.1 million. Large numbers of whites were displaced by this growth of central city ghettos and these same cities lost more than 1.4 million whites during the decade. Finally, between 1960 and 1968, these same central cities lost an additional 2 million whites, while gaining an additional 1.9 million Negroes.[13] During the same eight year period the white population of the suburban rings of these metropolitan areas increased by 6.8 million while the Negro population increased by 0.6 million.

In summary, housing market segregation modifies the logic of "economic" models of residential location in several important respects. It creates a demand for certain locations (typically the inner part of large central cities) that is unrelated, or only weakly related, to their access advantages. Negro households, physically limited in their choice of residential locations, must bid sites in the segregated market away from whites who wish to be near their places of employment. The result is a radically different pattern of price (or location rent) determination than is derived in most theories of residential location. In most large U.S. metropolitan areas there exists a rapidly growing "captive" demand for residences within the ghetto. This demand is principally for low quality housing. These locations are accessible to the workplace of many Negroes, but for an increasing number of Negroes they confer no such advantages. Indeed, for those Negroes employed in peripheral areas the ghetto is perhaps the poorest location possible.

In evaluating the effect of the growing central ghetto on metropolitan development, it is crucial to keep in mind that because so many blacks have low incomes, the growth of the central ghetto also implies an increased concentration of poverty, a growing aggregation of low quality housing, and an impaired capability on the part of cities to provide urban services. These factors make the city still less attractive to higher income groups and increase the relative desirability of the suburbs.

These factors, important in a static analysis, assume even greater significance in a dynamic framework. The rapid dispersal of employment from the central parts of metropolitan areas is documented in chapters 4 and 5. The effect of employment dispersal should be to reduce the demand for centrally located residences and cause a downward shift in the location rent surface in central areas. If centrally located units become less expensive, the location rent savings from commuting to suburban locations would become much less. Under these changed circumstances, many more centrally employed middle and upper income groups would find it more advantageous to choose centrally located neighborhoods. The fact that many units would be of lower than desired quality provides no serious obstacle, providing the units can be obtained cheaply enough. The most structurally sound of these units could be renovated and modernized, while the least valuable could be demolished and be replaced by new structures. However, these possibilities have not been realized since the rapid increases in the black population for the most part have largely offset the effects of employment dispersal.

DISCRIMINATION AND LOCATION RENTS

The impact of the ghetto on the metropolitan surface of location rents is not limited to its effect within the Negro market. By reducing the white submarket supply of residential sites in particular parts of the metropolitan region, it affects the level and spatial distribution of location rents in the white market as well. The central location of the ghetto causes location rents in central areas to be higher than if this pattern of housing market discrimination did not exist. It is true that some centrally employed blacks would choose to live in these centrally located residential areas, even if there were no discrimination. However, many blacks employed at central workplaces and nearly all blacks employed in suburban areas would not bid for these central locations were it not for restrictions on their residential choices. Of course, this also means that the current demand by blacks for suburban sites is less than it would be if no housing market discrimination existed. The net effect of the present restrictions is to increase the demand for sites in central areas, where the ghetto is located, and to decrease somewhat the demand for suburban locations. The rapid growth of the Negro market represents a source of demand for central city properties that would not exist in the absence of segregation.

Were it not for Negro residential segregation, the postwar pattern of U.S. urban development would have been much different. If the suburbs had been open to low income blacks, many would have moved to suburban areas along with their jobs, much in the fashion of whites of similar socioeconomic status. This would have affected the central city housing market in two ways. First, central cities would have had a very different image. A slower rate of growth of the poverty population would have affected the prestige of central city residential areas. If more middle and high income families had remained in the central cities, the public schools and other facilities would have been maintained better and the quality of services and other aspects of the environment of their neighborhoods would have been much higher. Second, as noted previously, the prices of suburban properties would have been somewhat higher and the prices of central city properties somewhat lower if blacks had been allowed to compete for the former. The exact magnitude of these price changes are difficult to predict, but their direction is indisputable. Given these changes in relative housing prices, many more centrally employed whites would have found it to their advantage to live in the central city. Similarly, few blacks employed at suburban workplaces would commute long distances back to the central city core in order to pay more for housing. Increased Negro residence in the suburbs would also reduce the underrepresentation of blacks in suburban plants. It is hardly necessary to detail the way in which these changes in the distribution of the population by race and income would have ameliorated the problems of our cities.

So much for the counterfactual question of what might have been if there had been no housing market discrimination or if the pattern of Negro residential segregation had taken a different form. The relevant policy question is whether the situation can be retrieved by removing the barriers to Negro residential choice. Devising solutions to these problems will be difficult and will require the most vigorous efforts to undo what has been done. Turning the present situation around will be immensely more difficult than preventing it from happening in the first place would have been.

The present pattern of residence by race has created a number of adverse environmental effects that will be most difficult to correct. Because of the collective nature of many aspects of the bundle of residential services, many needed improvements cannot be made a dwelling unit at a time. Under existing political arrangements, the quality of services provided the residents of a particular neighborhood cannot be markedly better than those provided the residents of another neighborhood within the same jurisdiction. Thus, it is far more difficult to provide high quality bundles of residential services within the central city than outside, since in order to do so it is necessary to raise all city services to that level. Many recent and well-motivated actions to force school districts and local governments to provide equal services to all neighborhoods and to balance their schools racially may accelerate the departure of middle and upper income families from the central city. By comparison, the even more recent interest in decentralization, while born in the ghetto, may provide the means by which upper income neighborhoods will be able to provide higher levels of services than less fortunate neighborhoods. It seems likely that conserving or renewing central city neighborhoods requires the development of new institutions that allow the provision of higher levels of services.

While the above changes in the provision of services are essential, the first requirement is devising methods for opening suburban housing to blacks. Only when the city loses its monopoly on black poverty will it have a chance. As long as the ghetto continues its rapid growth, prices in central cities will remain at high levels and the expectation that the city will become a lower class slum will persist. If the growth of the ghetto can be arrested, positive programs aimed at making the central city attractive to middle income families, be they white or black, have a chance. Without this change in the dynamics of metropolitan development there is no way in which the trends outlined in this chapter can be reversed.

Chapter Seven

Housing Market Discrimination, Homeownership, and Savings Behavior

with John M. Quigley

The question of whether discrimination in the housing market forces Negro households to pay more than white households for identical bundles of residential services has been studied extensively. Still, it remains a controversial subject. Those who claim that discrimination markups exist in urban housing markets rely principally on a series of empirical studies similar to those presented in Chapter 12, which conclude that blacks pay more than whites for comparable housing or that housing in the ghetto is more expensive than otherwise identical housing located outside the ghetto.[1] Those who argue that price discrimination does not exist contend that studies which purport to find evidence of a discrimination markup fail to standardize completely for differences in the bundles of residential services consumed by black and white households.[2] Evaluation of the diverse empirical studies leads us to conclude that blacks may pay between 5 and 10 percent more than whites in most urban areas for comparable housing. Our own analyses of a 1967 sample of nearly 1,200 dwelling units in St. Louis, Missouri, presented in Chapter 12, suggests a discrimination markup in that city on the order of 7 percent.

Differentials of this magnitude would represent a significant loss in Negro welfare. However, we contend that researchers, in their concern about estimating the magnitude of price discrimination, have overlooked a far more serious consequence of housing market discrimination. In asking whether blacks pay more than whites for the same kind of housing, they have failed to consider adequately the way in which housing discrimination has affected the kinds of housing consumed by Negro households.

There is a great deal of qualitative evidence that nonwhites have difficulty in obtaining housing outside the ghetto.[3] Persistence, a thick skin, and a willingness to spend enormous amounts of time house-hunting are minimum requirements for nonwhites who wish to move into white neighborhoods. These psychic and transaction costs may be far more significant than out-of-pocket costs to Negroes considering a move out of the ghetto. Most blacks limit their search for housing to the ghetto; this limitation is more than geographic. There is less variety of housing services available inside the ghetto than outside; indeed, many bundles of housing services are unavailable in the ghetto at any price. This limited range of housing services within the ghetto almost certainly influences the pattern of Negro housing consumption. A full discussion and evaluation of the many ways in which discrimination may modify the housing consumption behavior of Negro households is beyond the scope of this study. However, the general principle can be illustrated by the differential propensities of Negro and white households to own and to purchase their homes.

Two statistical analyses of the probability of homeownership follow. The first is a detailed analysis of the probability of ownership and purchase for a sample of St. Louis households. It indicates there is a substantial difference in the probability of Negro and white homeownership and purchase even after accounting for most of the important differences in the socioeconomic characteristics of Negro and white households. We hypothesize that this difference results from restrictions on the location and types of housing available to Negro households. This "supply restriction" hypothesis cannot be adequately tested for a single metropolitan area. Therefore, we present a second statistical analysis of the differences in actual and expected rates of Negro homeownership among 18 large metropolitan areas. Finally, the chapter examines the implications of the apparent limitations on Negro homeownership on their housing costs and capital accumulation.

HOMEOWNERSHIP AND PURCHASE BY ST. LOUIS HOUSEHOLDS

To investigate Negro-white differences in homeownership, we developed models relating the probability of homeownership to the socioeconomic characteristics of a sample of 1,185 households in the St. Louis metropolitan area (401 black and 784 white households). Subsequently, we examined the decision to purchase or to rent for a subsample of 466 households which had changed residence in the preceding three years.

The analysis employs the regression of a binary dependent variable indicating tenure status (1=own, 0=rent) on several explanatory variables reflecting family size, family composition, employment status, household income, and race. Many previous studies have emphasized the importance of the family life cycle to household consumption patterns.[4] The life cycle hypothesis includes the combined influences of several household characteristics, which we represent by a series of family type–age interaction variables: (1) single persons (living alone or in groups) under 45 years of age; (2) singles over 45 years of age; (3) couples without children with heads under 45 years of age; (4) couples without children with heads over 45 years of age; and (5) typical families (individuals or married couples with children).

Typical families were further described in terms of age of head, family size, number of school age children, and by dummy variables for female head of less than 45 years of age, and female head of more than 45 years of age. Income, years of schooling (of head), and number of years at present job (for head) were included as explanatory variables for all households. Race was indicated by a dummy variable (1=Negro, 0=white).

The probability of ownership equation, obtained by the method of generalized least squares is summarized by Equation (7.1) (Table 7–1).[5] All the coefficients of Equation (7.1) have the anticipated signs and are reasonable in magnitude, and 12 are highly significant statistically using conventional criteria. The results indicate that old couples are more likely to be homeowners than young couples, and old singles are more likely to be homeowners than their younger counterparts. None are as likely to be homeowners as male-headed families. Female-headed families are also less likely to be homeowners than male-headed families. Income and employment are positively related to homeownership. Family size is negatively related to homeownership, but only after adjusting for the different homeowning propensities of families with school age children and with additional workers. The probability of ownership increases as the head of household gets older, and the introduction of a squared age term yields no evidence of any significant nonlinearity.

Of primary importance to this discussion is the coefficient of the race dummy variable. It indicates that, after accounting for differences in life cycle, income, education, and employment status, Negro households have a probability of ownership 0.09 less than that of whites. Thirty-two percent of Negro households in the sample owned their homes; if they were white, 41 percent would be homeowners.

There are some indications that the barriers to Negro occupancy in white neighborhoods are gradually declining. Thus, it could be argued that current ownership patterns primarily reflect historical discrimination and provide a misleading view of current conditions. To test this hypothesis, we estimated probability of purchase (1=purchase, 0=rent) equations for those sample households which changed their residence within the past three years. Equation (7.2) presents the results for the probability of purchase analysis (Table 7.1). The explanatory variables are identical to those included in Equation (7.1). The coefficients of the dummy variables representing household type and age differ in magnitude for recent movers. Aside from these contrasts, the largest differences were obtained for the income and race variables. The coefficient of the race dummy indicates that a Negro mover has a probability of purchase 0.12 lower than an otherwise identical white. Only 8 percent of Negro movers purchased homes; had they been white, 20 percent would have been home buyers. As with the ownership models, separate Negro and white equations were estimated for the probability of purchase. Except for their intercepts they were identical, and a covariance test indicated no statistically different relationship.

Previous levels of housing discrimination may affect Negro households in at least one important way that is not reflected in Equation (7.2). Because of past discrimination, Negro movers are less likely than white movers to have been homeowners in the past. This is important because when homeowners change their residence they are more likely to buy than to rent and, conversely, when renters move they are more likely to move from one rental property to another.

In large part, the association between past and present, or present and future, tenure arises because renters and owners tend to differ in terms of income, family size and composition, age, and other measured characteristics. Still,·prior tenure itself may have an independent influence on subsequent tenure decisions. Therefore, probability of purchase equations were estimated with the addition of dummy variables for prior owner, prior renter, and new households. A fourth category, "prior tenure unreported," is reflected in the intercept. Equation (7.3) in Table 7–1 illustrates these estimates.

Both the prior owner and new household variables have large and highly significant coefficients. Previous ownership raises the probability of purchase by 0.27. New households are 0.15 less likely to buy than are established households of the same age, income, and family characteristics.

Accounting for the effects of prior tenure reduces the coefficient of the race variables. Of course, the influence of housing market discrimination is reflected in prior tenure. In the sample of recent movers, only 2 percent of Negro households had previously been homeowners as compared with 17 percent of white households. Yet, even after controlling for the differences in prior tenure, Negro households are 0.09 less likely to become homeowners than white households in today's "open housing" market. A similar difference in Negro and white probabilities of home purchase was obtained by Daniel Fredland for Philadelphia.[6] Fredland's model differed in a number of respects from Equation (7.3) in Table 7–1. It included a somewhat different set of explanatory variables, was for married households only, and was estimated by ordinary least squares. Even so, he obtained a coefficient of –0.16 for a minority dummy (nonwhite or Puerto Rican) and a coefficient of 0.27 for the prior owner dummy.

Several studies of the demand for housing services have concluded that housing expenditures are more strongly related to permanent than to annual income. By extension it might be anticipated that the probabilities of homeownership and purchase would depend more on permanent than annual income. If this were true, all or part of the measured difference in the probabilities of ownership and purchase of white and nonwhite households in Equations (7.1) through (7.3) might be attributable to unmeasured white-nonwhite differences in permanent incomes.

As a test of the permanent income hypothesis, we followed the convention suggested by several authors and replaced the annual income term in

TABLE 7—1. Models of Homeownership and Purchase Equations (7.1), (7.2), and (7.3) for entire sample

	Probability of Ownership		Probability of Purchase		Probability of Purchase Given Move	
	Equation (7.1)		Equation (7.2)		Equation (7.3)	
	Coefficient	t-Ratio	Coefficient	t-Ratio	Coefficient	t-Ratio
Race (1 = black, 0 = white)	-0.088	-2.644	-0.124	-4.550	-0.091	-3.720
Income (thousands of dollars)	0.026	8.351	-0.017	3.795	0.013	3.751
Years of education (head of household)	-0.006	-1.190	0.011	2.414	0.003	0.759
Years of current job (head of household)	0.002	1.908	0.001	0.624	0.002	1.365
Retired (1 = yes, 0 = no)	0.231	4.746	-0.070	-1.493	0.065	1.530
No household member employed (1 = yes, 0 = no)	-0.011	-0.277	-0.031	-0.868	-0.014	-0.362
More than one member employed (1 = yes, 0 = no)	0.171	6.130	-0.012	-0.438	0.002	0.102
Household Types						
Single females under 45 years (1 = yes, 0 = no)	-0.403	-5.596	-0.324	-3.665	-0.191	-2.075
Single females over 45 years	-0.295	-5.278	-0.051	-0.569	-0.183	-2.033
Single males under 45 years	-0.277	-2.577	-0.283	-2.864	-0.124	-1.170
Single males over 45 years	-0.108	-1.207	-0.057	-0.539	-0.196	-1.799
Married couples under 45	-0.213	-3.407	-0.290	-3.406	-0.095	-1.106
Married couples over 45 years	-0.004	-0.070	-0.124	-1.385	-0.111	-1.159
Families						
Age of head of household	0.002	2.108	0.004	2.212	0.011	2.527
$(Age)^2$ of head of household					-0.000	-2.621
Number of persons (natural logarithm)	-0.156	-3.769	-0.138	-3.342	-0.113	-3.226
Number of school age children	-0.013	-0.986	0.032	2.626	0.018	1.518
Family headed by female under 45 years (1 = yes, 0 = no)	-0.007	-0.148	-0.145	-3.116	-0.188	-3.712
Family headed by female over 45 years (1 = yes, 0 = no)	-0.192	-2.561	-0.241	-3.663	-0.206	-3.850
Prior Tenure						
Prior owner (1 = yes, 0 = no)					0.267	4.323
Prior renter (1 = yes, 0 = no)					0.037	1.315
New household (1 = yes, 0 = no)					-0.146	-3.945
Intercept	0.409	5.747	0.126	1.354	0.122	1.212
Degrees of freedom	1166		447		443	
R^2	0.826		0.301		0.445	

Equations (7.1) through (7.3) by the mean incomes of the sample households stratified by the race and by the years of education of the head of the household.[7] Presumably, this averaging process reduces the transitory component of income and thereby provides an improved estimate of permanent income. The ordinary least squares estimates of the race coefficient for all three equations are consistently larger than those obtained for the current income models, as are the GLS estimates for the purchase model. The GLS estimate of the race coefficient in the ownership equation using the estimated permanent income is more than twice as large as the race coefficient obtained using annual income, and the GLS coefficients in the purchase models using permanent income are also larger than those obtained from the equations, including annual income (see Equation (7.4), Table 7–2).

An alternative and more dubious (both statistically and theoretically) test of the permanent income hypothesis used an estimate of housing expenditures as a surrogate for permanent income.[8] The most obvious statistical problem arises because the estimate of housing expenditures for homeowners must be imputed from housing value using a gross rent multiplier. The use of different variables (monthly rent for renters and market value for owners) transformed by a constant divisor in a regression on owner-renter may produce a spurious correlation. The coefficients of this housing expenditure variable in the ownership and purchase equations vary between 20 and 45 times their standard errors; this increases our suspicion that the relation is to a significant extent spurious and arises by construction.[9]

On theoretical grounds, moreover, there is reason to suspect that even an adequate estimate of housing expenditures would not provide permanent income measures which are neutral between Negroes and whites or

TABLE 7–2. Coefficients and *t*-ratios of Race Variable for Alternative Specifications of Income: *OLS* and *GLS*

	Probability of Ownership Equation (7.1)		*Probability of Purchase without Prior Tenure Equation (7.2)*		*with Prior Tenure Equation (7.3)*	
	OLS	*GLS*	*OLS*	*GLS*	*OLS*	*GLS*
Current annual income	−0.150	−0.088	−0.154	−0.124	−0.114	−0.091
	(5.06)	(2.64)	(3.94)	(4.55)	(2.96)	(3.72)
Permanent income	−0.163	−0.194	−0.199	−0.223	−0.138	−0.103
	(5.23)	(6.33)	(3.65)	(4.73)	(2.58)	(2.69)
Housing expenditure	−0.048	−0.035	−0.077	−0.048	−0.069	−0.029
	(1.99)	(2.33)	(2.68)	(2.76)	(2.35)	(1.63)

between homeowners and renters. If price discrimination exists in the housing market, only a demand elasticity of one for housing would prevent housing expenditures from being a biased estimate of the permanent incomes of black households. If housing demand is price elastic for blacks,[10] price discrimination would bias this measure of permanent income downward for blacks and would reduce the race coefficient when the ownership and purchase equations are estimated. This bias is accentuated if housing market discrimination reduces Negro homeownership and if homeowners spend more for housing than renters of the same incomes for any reasons. Nevertheless, the race coefficients obtained from models using this estimate of housing expenditure as an explanatory variable are summarized in Table 7–2, which presents the race coefficients for all three alternative specifications. Also included in Table 7–2 are the coefficients of the racial dummy obtained by ordinary least squares.

In addition to the equations reported in Table 7–2, estimates were obtained employing several alternative specifications of the life cycle and age variables; tests for nonlinearity in the education and income terms were also performed with negative results. For all these specifications, the magnitude and significance of the race coefficients for Equations (7.1), (7.2), and (7.3) were virtually unchanged.[11]

Taken together, the estimates summarized in Table 7–2 and the alternatives mentioned strongly indicate that Negro households are substantially less likely to be homeowners or buyers than white households of similar characteristics. It does not "prove" that this is the result of discriminatory practices in urban housing markets; and there remain several competing explanations for these results. These alternative hypotheses may be grouped into three broad categories: (1) differences in the "taste" for homeownership between whites and blacks; (2) differences in the asset and wealth positions of white and black families; and (3) racial discrimination in the housing market as the result either of simple price discrimination in the owner and renter markets or of a more pervasive restriction on the supply of owner-occupied housing available to blacks. "Supply restrictions" could be supplemented or enforced by simple capital market discrimination or by an unwillingness on the part of banks and other mortgage lenders to finance home purchases by blacks outside the ghetto.

While it is most difficult to prove that the much lower probability of homeownership of black households is not due to differences in the taste for homeownership, many of the more commonly believed determinants of the tastes of housing consumers are included as independent variables. Furthermore, stratification by race for all of the three equations discloses no statistically significant differences. We thus conclude that the "differences in tastes" hypothesis is not an important explanation for the observed differences in market behavior between races.[12]

Differences in the asset or wealth positions of Negro and white households may account for part of the differences in white and nonwhite ownership and purchase probabilities. Unfortunately, the sample used in this research shares the deficiency of most other surveys in not including information on household assets and wealth. Therefore, no direct test of the asset hypothesis is possible using these data. However, for several reasons, we doubt that much of the white-Negro differences in ownership and purchase are the result of an unmeasured difference in wealth. All three equations include income, years on the job, and life cycle variables, which may account for much of the white-black differences in assets. For most households, black and white, equity in owner-occupied housing is itself the largest component of net worth.[13] Therefore, in the probability of purchase model (Equation 7.3) prior tenure may account for much of the remaining differences in wealth. Downpayment requirements are a major reason why assets might be expected to affect the decision to purchase a home. However, FHA and VA downpayment requirements, especially for small single family homes purchased more than ten years ago, were small or nonexistent.

Housing market discrimination is the third and, to us, the most plausible hypothesis explaining the regression results in Table 7–1. The exact mechanism is hard to specify. Differential price "markups" in the owner and rental submarkets do not explain these differences in Negro and white purchase and homeownership probabilities.[14] We are forced to conclude that "supply restrictions" on Negro residential choice and on the kinds of housing available to black households may be largely responsible for the wide discrepancy between ownership rates for otherwise identical black and white households.

Further support for this position is provided by data on the average increase in the market value of Negro- and white-owned single family units in St. Louis. For this sample, the units owned by white central city residents have increased in value at a compound annual rate of 5.2 percent per year as contrasted to a 7.2 percent annual increase for the central city properties owned by Negro households. If this is interpreted as a difference in the net appreciation of ghetto and nonghetto properties, the findings of Equations (7.1) through (7.3) become even more difficult to explain. Rather than a difference in the net appreciation of black- and white-owned properties, however, this finding appears to be still another manifestation of limitations on Negro residential choice. White households wishing to improve their housing can buy newer or larger houses in better neighborhoods. Negro homeowners are much less able to improve their housing in this way; as a result we hypothesize that black homeowners spend more for renovation and repair than white households of similar characteristics. An annual increase in suburban white-owned properties of 4.1 percent provides some evidence for these inferences.

DIFFERENCES AMONG METROPOLITAN AREAS

A complete test of the supply restriction hypothesis cannot be accomplished from an analysis of a single metropolitan area. A more powerful test of the effect of supply restrictions can be obtained by analyzing differences in black homeownership among cities. Metropolitan areas and their ghettos differ in terms of the characteristics of their housing stocks, and, therefore, in the extent to which a limitation on being able to reside outside the ghetto is an effective restriction on the supply of ownership-type housing available to blacks. For example, supply restrictions should be much less important in Los Angeles, where a large portion of the ghetto housing supply consists of single family units, than in Chicago, where ghetto neighborhoods are predominantly multi-family. We analyzed the difference between "expected" and actual black ownership rates in several metropolitan areas. Expected black ownership rates were computed by multiplying a matrix of white ownership rates (stratified into income and family size groups) by the income and family size distribution of black households. Table 7–3 presents this measure in 1960 for all eighteen metropolitan areas for which the necessary census data are published.[15] The difference between the actual black ownership rate and the expected black ownership rate for each SMSA is identical in principle to the difference in the probability of ownership attributed to race in equation (7.1) for St. Louis in

TABLE 7–3. Actual and Expected Ownership Rates of Negro Households by Metropolitan Area

City	*Actual*	*Expected*
Atlanta	.31	.52
Boston	.21	.43
Chicago	.18	.47
Cleveland	.30	.58
Dallas	.39	.54
Detroit	.41	.67
Los Angeles/Long Beach	.41	.51
Newark	.24	.50
Philadelphia	.45	.66
St. Louis	.34	.55
Baltimore	.36	.61
Birmingham	.44	.56
Houston	.46	.56
Indianapolis	.45	.58
Memphis	.37	.50
New Orleans	.28	.40
Pittsburgh	.35	.59
San Francisco/Oakland	.37	.51

1967. (For St. Louis this more primitive technique yields −21.0 in 1960 as compared to an OLS estimate of −15.0 and a GLS estimate from Equation (7.1) of −8.8 in 1967.)

As a test of the supply restriction hypothesis we then regressed these estimated differences upon (1) the proportion of central city dwelling units that are single family, a proxy for the proportion of the ghetto housing stock that is single family; (2) the proportion of the SMSA black population living in the central city, a measure of the extent of suburbanization of the black population; and (3) the actual rate of white ownership in the SMSA.[16] The first two variables measure the extent of the supply restrictions among the 18 metropolitan areas, while the latter measures any differences in the level of both white and Negro homeownership that might be attributable to such factors as intermetropolitan variation in the relative cost of owner-occupied and renter-occupied housing or differences in the timing of urban development. Equation (7.4) presents the regression in difference form (expected black ownership rate minus actual black ownership rate), while Equation (7.5) presents the same equation in ratio form (expected black ownership rate−actual black ownership rate). The *t*-ratios are in parentheses under the coefficients.

$$(O_B^* - O_B) = -0.24 + 0.82 O_w -0.36 S_c + 0.12 B_c \qquad (7.4)$$
$$ (2.36) \ (4.64) \quad (6.49) \quad (2.03)$$

$$R^2 = .76$$

$$(O_B^*/O_B) = 0.89 + 1.52 O_w - 1.74 S_c + 0.90 B_c \qquad (7.5)$$
$$ (1.52) \ (1.47) \quad (5.34) \quad (2.52)$$

$$R^2 = .74$$

where,

O_B^* = expected black ownership rate in the ith SMSA

$$[\sum_k \alpha w k_i \cdot H b k_i] / \sum_k H b k_i$$

O_B = actual black ownership rate in the ith SMSA

$$[\sum_k \alpha b k_i \cdot H b k_i] / \sum_k H b k_i$$

O_w = actual white ownership rate in the ith SMSA

$$[\sum_k \alpha w k_i \cdot H w k_i] / \sum_k H w k_i$$

and

α_{wki} =proportion of whites in the kth income-family size category who are homeowners in the ith SMSA

H_{bki} =number of black households in the kth income-family size category in the ith SMSA

S_c =proportion of central city housing that is single family (number of central city dwelling units that are single family ÷ total central city dwelling units)

B_c =proportion of metropolitan Negro households residing in central city (number of Negro households in central city ÷ number of Negro households in SMSA).

The means and standard deviations of the variables used in equations (7.4) and (7.5) are shown in Table 7–4. The average expected homeownership rate for black households is 0.54 and the mean actual black ownership rate is 0.35. The actual white rate for these 18 metropolitan areas in 1960 averages is 0.65. Of the 0.30 difference between actual white and black ownership rates in these 18 metropolitan areas Negro-white differences in family size and income account for 0.11; the residual difference, 0.19, must be attributed to other factors, including the differences in supply restrictions among the areas.

Both equations strongly support the hypothesis that the differences between observed and expected black ownership rates are small (1) when the ghetto housing supply includes a larger proportion of single family units, and (2) when blacks have more access to the suburban housing market, with its preponderance of owner-occupied units. As the statistics in Table 7–3 show, the difference between the actual and expected homeownership rate of black households is relatively small for cities like Houston and Los Angeles, where the central city and its black ghetto include more single family housing, and is

TABLE 7–4. Means and Standard Deviations of Variables Used in Intercity Regression

	Mean	*SD*
$O_B^* - O_B$	0.19	0.06
O_B^* / O_B	1.61	0.36
O_w	0.65	0.07
O_B	0.35	0.08
O_B^*	0.54	0.07
S_c	0.55	0.22
B_c	0.78	0.14

relatively large for cities like Chicago, where the ghetto is predominantly multifamily and where blacks are effectively excluded from the suburbs.

The extent of black suburbanization also appears to have a significant, though small, influence on the gap between actual and expected black homeownership. In all U.S. metropolitan areas, black households are heavily concentrated in the central cities. The mean proportion of blacks residing in the central city for the sample metropolitan areas is 0.78 and the standard deviation is only 0.14. Equation (7.4) indicates that a city which is one standard deviation above the mean in terms of this characteristic (92 percent of metropolitan area blacks live in the central city) would have a gap 0.034 larger than one which is one standard deviation below the mean (64 percent of blacks live in the central city).

The findings presented in Equations (7.4) and (7.5) provide further support for the view that housing market discrimination limits Negro home-ownership.[17] Specifically, these results indicate that a limited supply of housing suitable for homeownership in the ghetto and restrictions on Negro purchase outside the ghetto strongly affect the tenure type of the housing consumed by Negro households as well as its location.

HOMEOWNERSHIP, HOUSING COSTS, AND CAPITAL ACCUMULATION

Limitations on homeownership have significant effects on Negro housing costs, income, and welfare. As is illustrated in Appendix A, an effective limitation on homeownership can increase Negro housing costs by over 30 percent, assuming no price appreciation.

Much of the savings from homeownership result from favorable treatment accorded homeowners under the federal income tax. These tax provisions favoring homeowners are widely recognized and well documented.[18] Our findings suggest that Negro households at all income levels are impeded by housing market discrimination from purchasing and owning single family homes. As a consequence, Negro households are prevented from taking full advantage of these tax benefits. Since tax savings from homeownership increase with income, this aspect of discriminatory housing markets cuts most sharply against middle and upper income black households.

Limitations on homeownership also rob Negro households of an important inflation hedge available to other low and middle income households. Calculations presented in Appendix A show that under reasonable assumptions about the appreciation of single family homes, a Negro household prevented from buying a home since 1950 would have out-of-pocket housing costs in 1970 more than twice as high as the costs which would have been incurred if the family could have purchased a home 20 years earlier.

Negro households at every income level have less wealth than white households. Current and historical limitations on homeownership may be an important reason. The importance of this method of capital accumulation among low and middle income households is apparent from a typical example. The average house purchased with an FHA 203 mortgage in 1949 had a value of $8,286 and a mortgage of $7,101.[19] Assuming that this house was purchased with a 20 year mortgage by a 30 year old household head, the owner of this unit would have saved more than $7,000 and would own his home free and clear by his fiftieth birthday. Thus, if his home neither appreciated or depreciated, at age 50 he would own assets worth at least $8,000. However, the postwar years have hardly been characterized by price neutrality. Although difficult to estimate, the average appreciation of single family houses during the past 20 years most certainly exceeded the 100 percent increase in the Boeck composite cost index for small residential structures.[20] This conservative 100 percent increase in value would mean that the typical FHA-financed homeowner by age 50 would have accumulated assets worth at least $16,000, a considerable sum that he could use to reduce his housing costs, to borrow against for the college education of his children, or simply to hold for his retirement. Perspective on this hypothetical example is obtained when it is recognized that the mean wealth accumulation of white households in 1966 was only $20,000.[21] Of course, the situation would have been different if the postwar period had been one of a general decline in the price of urban real estate. But it was not.

Homeownership is clearly the most important method of wealth accumulation used by low and middle income families in the postwar period. Equities in single family, owner-occupied structures account for nearly one-half of all the wealth of the lowest income group. As family income increases, the relative importance of home equities decreases. Still, home equities accounted for more than one-third of the wealth of all U.S. households earning between $10–$15,000 in 1962.[22]

The dominant position of home equities in the asset portfolios of low and middle income households is not difficult to understand. Other forms of investment, such as the stock market, require far more knowledge, sophistication, and discipline. In addition, low and middle income households have more leverage available in the real estate than in other investment markets.

Much of the savings imbedded in home ownership, especially among low and middle income households, is more or less involuntary or at least unconscious. Discipline is maintained by linking the investment (saving) decision to monthly payments for the provision of a necessity, with heavy penalties (foreclosure) imposed for failure to invest regularly.[23] Moreover, because of federal mortgage insurance and special advantages provided to thrift institutions, the low and middle income home buyer is able to borrow 90 percent or more of the purchase price of a new home. This may amount to $15,000 or more of capital at moderate interest rates. By comparison, in the stock market he can borrow 30 percent, a ratio which he must maintain even with price declines.

If, as our findings suggest, discrimination in urban housing markets has reduced Negro opportunities for homeownership, this limitation is an important explanation of the smaller quality of assets owned by Negro households at each income level.

Chapter Eight

Housing Market Discrimination and Negro Employment

This chapter investigates the relationship between metropolitan housing market segregation and the distribution and level of nonwhite employment.[1] The hypotheses evaluated are that racial segregation in the housing market (1) affects the distribution of Negro employment, and (2) reduces Negro job opportunities, and that (3) postwar suburbanization of employment has seriously aggravated this problem. These hypotheses are tested empirically using data on place of work and place of residence obtained from the home interview surveys of the Detroit Area Traffic Study in 1952 and the Chicago Area Traffic Study in 1956.[2]

SEGREGATION IN DETROIT AND CHICAGO

Chicago and Detroit nonwhites are highly segregated. The central city (block) segregation index for Chicago exceeds 92.0 in all three decades and the metropolitan area (tract) indexes are only marginally lower.[3] Segregation scores indicate Detroit Negroes are only slightly less segregated every year.

Negro ghettos in Detroit and Chicago, as in most other U.S. metropolitan areas, lie mostly within the central city near the central business district (CBD). Small secondary ghettos are sometimes found in the central parts of older suburbs and in previously rural areas. Both kinds of outlying Negro residential areas may importantly affect the distribution of nonwhite employment and the job loss that may result from housing segregation.

Detroit's principal ghetto, which houses approximately 93 percent of Detroit's nonwhite work force, but only about 29 percent of its whites, lies within the central city and has a slight sectoral pattern. Nearly all of the remaining 7 percent of nonwhites live in one of three small outlying nonwhite residence areas.[4]

Most Chicago Negroes live on the notorious South Side, although fingers of the ghetto extend due West and due North from the Loop. Chicago's principal ghetto houses a larger percentage of its nonwhite work force than does Detroit's: 96 percent of Chicago's nonwhite workers reside there, but only 20 percent of its white workers. The only other significant nonwhite settlement in the Chicago area straddles the suburbs of Evanston and Skokie to the North of the Loop and houses about 1,900 nonwhite workers, or just under 1 percent of the nonwhite labor force.[5]

THE DISTRIBUTION OF NEGRO EMPLOYMENT

There are several reasons why housing market segregation may affect the distribution and level of Negro employment. The most obvious are:

1. The distance to and difficulty of reaching certain jobs from Negro residence areas may impose costs on Negroes high enough to discourage them from seeking employment there.
2. Negroes may have less information about and less opportunity to learn about jobs distant from their place of residence or those of their friends.[6]
3. Employers located outside the ghetto may discriminate against Negroes out of real or imagined fears of retaliation from white customers for "bringing Negroes into all-white residential areas," or they may feel little pressure not to discriminate.
4. Similarly, employers in or near the ghetto may discriminate in favor of Negroes.

To test the hypothesis that the central location of the Chicago and Detroit ghettos and limitations on Negro residence outside these areas affect the location of Negro employment, a series of multiple regression models have been fitted for Chicago and Detroit using the Negro percentage of total employment in each of 98 workplace areas as the dependent variable and a series of proxy variables representing the factors causing Negroes to be underrepresented in distant workplaces as explanatory variables.

The Negro percentage of population residing in each of the 98 workplace zones is a proxy for the employers propensity to discriminate in favor or against nonwhite workers because of real or imagined attitudes of the resident population toward the employment of Negroes. Businesses located in the ghetto, and particularly those selling predominantly to ghetto residents, would be expected to hire disproportionate numbers of Negroes. Similarly, retailers and others located in all-white suburbs and having few or no Negro customers may feel some reluctance to employ Negroes in sales and other contact jobs. The Negro percentage of population residing in each workplace zone is unavailable. Therefore, the Negro percentage of employed residents of the workplace zone, hereafter referred to as the residence ratio, is used to measure the impact, if any, of neighborhood racial composition on the employment of Negroes in each workplace zone.

Transportation costs from the workplace area to the ghetto and the effect of distance on knowledge of job opportunities are proxied by two variables (1) the airline distance from the workplace to the nearest Negro residence area (the nearest zone having more than 2 percent Negro residents), and (2) the airline distance from the workplace to the nearest point in the major ghetto. (The residence zones used in the analysis have the same boundaries as the workplace zones.)

Distance from Negro residence areas to outlying workplaces may seriously understate transportation costs between the ghetto and many workplaces because of the indirectness or complete absence of public transit services from ghetto residential areas to outlying or suburban workplaces. Public transit systems invariably focus on the central business district and are usually badly oriented for making trips from the ghetto to outlying workplaces. Historically the principal function of these systems was to transport workers from outlying residential areas to centrally located high density workplaces, and their specialization in this regard has increased as the automobile has become increasingly competitive for off-peak and nonradial travel. As car ownership among ghetto Negroes is relatively low, the difficulty or impossibility of using public transit systems to reach outlying workplaces may severely restrict their ability to seek or accept employment there. Because of housing segregation, low-skilled Negroes are unable to move close to suburban workplaces or perhaps even to live near a direct transit line serving current or potential workplaces as do most low-skilled whites.[7]

Frequently ghetto Negroes may be forced to choose between buying a private automobile and thus spending a disproportionate share of their low incomes on transportation, making a very long and circuitous trip by public transit (if any service is available at all), or foregoing the job altogether. Where the job in question is a marginal one, their choice may frequently be the latter. More often they will not even seek out the job in the first instance because of the difficulties of reaching it from possible residence locations.

Three equations are fitted for each city. The residence ratio (R) is included in all three. In addition, the first equation for each city, (8.1) and (8.4), includes distance from the nearest ghetto, d^n; Equations (8.2) and (8.5) include distance from the major ghetto, d^m; and Equations (8.3) and (8.6) include both distance variables, d^n and d^m. Since distance from the major ghetto and distance from the nearest ghetto are highly intercorrelated, including both in the regression equation does not add much to the explained variance and greatly reduces the statistical significance of their coefficients.[8] This is especially true for the Chicago models. When only one distance proxy is used, the coefficients of all variables are highly significant.

Chicago R^2
$W = 9.18 + 0.458R - 0.521\ d^n$ 0.78   (8.1)
  (10.7) (15.6)   (4.3)   (t ratios in parentheses)

$W = 9.28 + 0.456R - 0.409\ d^m$ 0.782   (8.2)
  (10.5) (15.4)   (4.2)

$W = 9.36 + 0.455R - 0.324\ d^n - 0.176\ d^m$ 0.785   (8.3)
  (10.6) (15.4)   (1.2)   (0.8)

Detroit R^2 (8.4)
$W = 12.78 + 0.091R - 1.141\ d^n$ 0.359
          (2.9)   (4.4)

$W = 12.64 + 0.100R - 0.758\ d^m$ 0.382   (8.5)
          (2.9)   (4.7)

$W = 13.45 + 0.082R - 0.563\ d^n - 0.52\ d^m$ 0.400   (8.6)
          (2.3)   (1.7)   (2.5)

W = employment ratio, percent of zone i's workers who are Negroes =
$$\frac{\text{Negro workers employed in } i}{\text{total workers employed in } i} \times 100$$

R = residence ratio, percent of zone i's resident workers who are Negroes =
$$\frac{\text{Negro workers residing in } i}{\text{total workers residing in } i} \times 100$$

d^n = distance from the nearest ghetto, airline distance in miles to nearest boundary point of a Negro residence area

d^m = distance from the major ghetto, airline distance in miles to nearest boundary point of the major ghetto

The most obvious difference between the Detroit and Chicago models is the proportion of total variance explained. All three Chicago regressions explain more than seven-tenths of the variance in the dependent variable, while the Detroit regressions explain only about four-tenths. This difference is attributed to Chicago's greater racial segregation.[9] Detroit's major ghetto is larger and more dispersed than Chicago's, and Detroit also has more and better located outlying Negro residential areas. Thus, it is reasonable that the model explains less about the spatial distribution of nonwhite employment in Detroit, where Negro residences are not so concentrated geographically.[10] These differences are indicated by the mean distance to the ghetto in Chicago and Detroit. Mean distance from the 98 Chicago workplace areas to the major ghetto is 5.4 miles while the mean distance for Detroit is only 4.3 miles. Similar relationships hold for distance to the nearest ghetto.

The regression coefficients also differ considerably for the two cities. Coefficients of the residence ratio in the Chicago equations are much larger than those for the Detroit equations. A 1 percent increase in the number of Negro workers living in a Chicago residence area is associated with nearly a 0.5 percent increase in Negro employment. By contrast, a 1 percent increase in the residence ratio is associated with only a 0.1 percent increase in employment in Detroit. However, the distance coefficients are much larger in the Detroit models. In Detroit the percentage of Negroes employed in a workplace area declines by 0.8 percent with each one mile increase in distance from the major ghetto. The decline is only 0.4 percent in Chicago (Equations (8.2) and (8.5)). There is a similar correspondence for the distance from the nearest ghetto coefficients in Equations (8.1) and (8.4), and when both distance variables are included in Equations (8.3) and (8.6).

If the previously discussed evidence of severe restriction of Negro residential choice is accepted, these findings would seem to suggest that housing market segregation does strongly affect the location of Negro employment. However, if this evidence on housing market discrimination is not accepted, these findings could be construed as demonstrating the opposite causal hypothesis; that the location of Negro jobs strongly affects the distribution of Negro residences.[11] Some further tests of these alternative causal hypotheses are presented below.

NEGRO EMPLOYMENT BY OCCUPATION AND INDUSTRY

Since Negroes typically have less skill and less education than whites, an unequal spatial distribution of skill requirements might lead to results like those obtained for Detroit and Chicago, if the average skill level requirement of jobs increased with distance from the ghetto. Such a distribution of skill requirements could occur by chance or for historical reasons. Similarly, firms demanding many low-skilled workers might locate near the ghetto because of the plentiful supply of low-skilled workers available there. No direct evidence on the education or skill requirements of the labor force by distance from the ghetto, which would permit direct evaluation of this hypothesis, is available. However, data are available on white and Negro employment in each Chicago workplace zone by one digit occupation and industry classifications and these permit some indirect tests. Relationships, like those given in Equations (8.1) through (8.6) are estimated for each occupation and industry group for Chicago. Insofar as these industry and occupation groups have different education and skill requirements, the estimates thereby obtained will reflect differences in labor force racial composition attributable at least in part to these differences.

Equations (8.7) through (8.22) are regression equations obtained for eight one digit occupational and eight one digit industry groups. The overall consistency and goodness of fit of these 16 equations is rather remarkable given the small number of nonwhites employed in some of these occupation and industry groups and the very large sampling errors that must exist.[12] The proportion of explained variance ranges from a low of 53 percent for wholesaling to a high of 80 percent for retailing.[13]

Occupation

Professional, technical and kindred workers	$W = 0.83 + 0.392\,R$ $(1.3)\ \ (14.1)$	$R^2 = 0.68$	(8.7)
Managers, officials, and proprietors	$W = -0.04 + 0.416\,R$ $(-0.06)(16.0)$	$R^2 = 0.73$	(8.8)
Clerical and kindred workers	$W = 1.25 + 0.526\,R$ $(1.8)\ \ (17.2)$	$R^2 = 0.76$	(8.9)
Sales workers	$W = 0.48 + 0.469\,R$ $(0.65)(14.6)$	$R^2 = 0.69$	(8.10)
Craftsmen, foremen, and kindred workers	$W = 5.68 + 0.330\,R - 0.256\,d^m$ $(7.6)\ \ (13.1)\ \ \ (-3.1)$	$R^2 = 0.72$	(8.11)
Operatives and kindred workers	$W = 15.5 + 0.479\,R - 0.820\,d^m$ $(11.0)(10.1)\ \ \ (-5.3)$	$R^2 = 0.67$	(8.12)
Service workers, except in private houses	$W = 15.4 + 0.680\,R - 0.803\,d^n$ $(8.8)(11.3)\ \ \ (-3.2)$	$R^2 = 0.66$	(8.13)
Laborers and farm workers	$W = 34.9 + 0.421\,R - 1.87\,d^m$ $(16.7)\ \ (6.02)\ \ \ (-8.13)$	$R^2 = 0.62$	(8.14)

Industry

Manufacturing, durable goods	$W = 10.8 + 0.291\,R - 0.54\,d^m$ $(9.2)\ \ (7.4)\ \ \ (-4.2)$	$R^2 = 0.53$	(8.15)
Manufacturing, nondurable goods	$W = 9.7 + 0.367\,R - 0.62\,d^m$ $(8.7)\ \ (9.8)\ \ \ (-5.0)$	$R^2 = 0.64$	(8.16)
Transportation, communication, and other	$W = 5.8 + 0.317\,R - 0.36\,d^m$ $(6.3)(10.2)\ \ \ (-3.5)$	$R^2 = 0.63$	(8.17)

Retail trade

$$W = 4.07 + 0.645\,R - 0.264d^n \qquad R^2 = 0.80 \quad (8.18)$$
$$(3.8) \quad (17.8) \qquad (-1.8)$$

Finance, insurance, real estate, professional, services, etc.

$$W = 2.73 + 0.552\,R \qquad R^2 = 0.70 \quad (8.19)$$
$$(3.2) \quad (14.9)$$

Wholesale trade

$$W = 4.86 + 0.341\,R - 0.256d^m \qquad R^2 = 0.53 \quad (8.20)$$
$$(4.2) \quad (8.8) \qquad (-2.0)$$

Business, repair, personal, services, etc.

$$W = 18.2 + 0.582\,R - 0.805\,d^n \qquad R^2 = 0.55 \quad (8.21)$$
$$(9.5) \quad (8.9) \qquad (-3.0)$$

Public administration

$$W = 10.5 + 0.562\,R - 0.581d^m \qquad R^2 = 0.68 \quad (8.22)$$
$$(7.3)\,(11.6) \qquad (-3.6)$$

The regression coefficients generally have high statistical significance (as indicated by the t-ratios given in parentheses) and have the correct sign. Regression coefficients for the distance from ghetto variables, d^n or d^m, are negative and those for the residence ratios, R, are positive in all 16 equations. The problem of multicollinearity between the two distance variables remains and only the most significant relationship is presented here. Neither distance variable differs significantly from zero at the 5 percent level in Equations (8.7) through (8.10) (the first four occupational groups—professional, managerial, clerical, and sales) and both are omitted. Significantly, these four occupation groups are those for which prejudice in favor of or against employment of Negroes on the basis of the racial composition of the residential area would be expected to be greatest.

Virtually no Negroes hold jobs in these four occupational groups outside of nonwhite residence areas, and within the ghetto their representation is disproportionately large. Nonwhites were an estimated 4.6 percent of all Chicago clerical workers in 1956. Yet they were 78 percent of all clerical workers employed in ghetto workplace Zone 24 and 77 percent of these employed in Zone 13 (Table 8–1). Negroes were an estimated 98 percent of all Chicago workers residing in Zone 24 in 1956 and 96 percent of those residing in Zone 13. As the data in Table 8–1 indicate, this very large overrepresentation of nonwhite employees in ghetto workplace zones is characteristic of all occupation and industry groups. By contrast, 41 of the 98 workplace zones used in the analysis have no nonwhite clerical workers.[14] The number of zones with no reported Negro workers is even greater for the professional, technical, and kindred; the manager, official, and proprietor; and sales groups. The Negro proportion of all craftsmen in ghetto areas is generally lower than the Negro proportion in the more visible occupations, even though Negroes are a larger

TABLE 8–1.   Geographic Distribution of Nonwhite Employment by Occupation and Industry: Chicago

	Mean[a] *of 98 Work-place Zones*	*Entire*[b] *Area*	*Selected Ghetto Workplace Zones*[c]					*Number of*[d] *Areas With no Nonwhites*
			3	*4*	*12*	*13*	*24*	
Professional, technical	4.4	6.0	12.2	8.1	45.3	35.3	69.1	50
Managers, officials, and proprietors	3.7	4.2	4.6	4.6	37.0	59.9	60.1	55
Clerical	6.0	9.6	26.7	14.5	35.0	76.9	78.4	41
Sales	3.7	4.6	5.2	4.5	28.0	70.0	70.6	69
Craftsmen	7.3	9.3	10.4	15.4	28.6	45.9	54.4	20
Operatives	15.4	21.6	23.8	32.1	46.0	80.7	58.1	24
Service workers	18.3	30.2	41.2	39.4	79.1	95.8	95.5	25
Laborers	28.6	41.5	44.4	56.3	67.5	81.7	79.9	21
Durable manufacturing	10.4	12.9	16.0	23.3	32.5	42.1	49.8	24
Nondurable manufacturing	9.8	18.5	20.9	24.7	40.5	56.8	43.2	40
Transportation	6.7	11.0	13.1	19.1	26.0	38.1	41.4	45
Retailing	8.8	13.5	21.0	31.3	56.9	76.6	90.5	33
Finance, insurance, real estate	7.7	10.1	27.0	18.7	48.4	51.6	84.3	47
Wholesaling	6.5	10.1	10.0	19.7	41.1	48.4	50.0	58
Business services	20.2	26.7	23.6	30.8	71.6	94.4	92.3	23
Public administration	12.4	24.8	47.1	22.3	48.4	87.8	74.0	40
All workers	11.2	14.6	21.2	23.1	45.8	64.4	71.5	11
Employed residents	9.0	14.6	32.9	29.0	87.1	96.3	98.1	35

[a] Unweighted mean of the percent of nonwhites for the 98 Chicago analysis zones used in the analysis.
[b] Percent nonwhite for the entire area = number of Chicago nonwhites employed in industry or occupation group K divided by total Chicago employment in group K.
[c] Percent nonwhite for selected individual analysis zones.
[d] Number of the 98 analysis zones used in the analysis having no sampled nonwhite workers.

proportion of all Chicago area craftsmen. Negro craftsmen were employed in all but 20 workplace zones and Negro laborers in all but 21.

Differentiation by industry group is less great. This finding might be expected, since all industries have some jobs, such as janitors and laborers, in which Negro employment is traditionally accepted. Even so, the data in Table 8–1 indicate that nonwhites are most overrepresented in those ghetto industries having the greatest amount of customer contact—retailing, finance, insurance, and real estate; business services; and public administration. They are least overrepresented in those ghetto industries having the least customer contact—

TABLE 8–2. Coefficients of Determination and Elasticities for Distance to Major and Distance to Ghetto Centroid Models by Occupation and Industry Group

	R	d^m	R^2	R	d^e	R^2
Occupation						
Professional	0.8	0.0[a]	0.68	0.8	–0.2[a]	0.68
Managerial	1.0	0.1[a]	0.73	1.0	–0.0[a]	0.72
Clerical	0.8	0.0[a]	0.76	0.8	–0.2[a]	0.76
Sales	1.2	0.2[a]	0.69	1.1	–0.1[a]	0.69
Craftsmen	0.4	–0.2	0.72	0.4	–0.4	0.75
Operatives	0.3	– .03	0.67	0.3	–0.4	0.69
Service	0.3	–0.2	0.65	0.3	–0.4	0.70
Laborers	0.1	–0.4	0.63	0.1	0.5	0.64
Industry						
Durable manufacturing	0.2	–0.3	0.53	0.3	0.4	0.72
Nondurable manufacturing	0.3	–0.3	0.64	0.3	–0.5	0.65
Transportation	0.4	–0.3	0.63	0.4	–0.4	0.64
Retailing	0.7	–0.1	0.80	0.7	–0.2	0.80
Finance, insurance, real estate	0.6	–0.1	0.70	0.6	–0.2	0.71
Wholesaling	0.5	–0.2	0.53	0.5	–0.5	0.56
Business services	0.3	–0.1	0.52	0.3	–0.3	0.59
Public administration	0.4	–0.3	0.68	0.4	–0.4	0.70
All	0.4	–0.2	0.78	0.4	–0.4	0.82

[a]Not significantly different from zero at the 5 percent level

durable and nondurable manufacturing, wholesaling; and transportation. The converse seems to hold for Negro employment in all white areas.

Table 8–2, which gives the elasticities at the sample means for (1) d^m, distance from the major ghetto, and (2) R, the residence ratio for each industry and occupation group, provides additional information about the relative impact of the racial residential composition of a workplace area and its distance from the ghetto. Also included in Table 8–2 are elasticities calculated from regression equations in which airline distance from the ghetto centroid (d^c) is used as the distance measure. Distance from the ghetto centroid (d^c) is included because of the suspicion that the size of the workplace and residence zones used in the analysis may cause distance from the ghetto boundaries to some workplace zones to be understated. Insofar as distance proxies labor market information loss and similar concepts, these may be more closely related to the centroid of the distribution of the nonwhite population than to the ghetto's boundaries, particularly when the boundaries are as grossly measured as those used in this analysis.

Elasticities of the residence ratio variable are generally larger in those occupations and industries with frequent customer contact. Among occupations, the largest residence ratio elasticity is obtained for sales (1.2) and the smallest is obtained for laborers (0.1). Similarly, among industry groups retailing and finance, insurance, and real estate have the largest residence ratio elasticities, 0.7 and 0.6, and durable manufacturing and business services have the smallest 0.2 and 0.3.

In addition to increasing slightly the proportion of total variance explained for most occupation and industry groups, substitution of the distance from the ghetto centroid (d^c) for distance from the major ghetto (d^m) generally increases the distance elasticities and reduces slightly the residence ratio (R) elasticities. Of the nine occupation groups, the residence ratio elasticity is larger in the distance from the ghetto centroid model only for laborers, of the eight industry groups, it is larger only for durable manufacturing, although the elasticities are the same for three other industry groups. Similarly, the distance elasticities are larger using distance from the ghetto centroid for all industry and occupation groups and the differences are generally larger than for the residence ratio. The regression coefficients for distance from the ghetto centroid differ significantly from zero at the 5 percent level or better for professional, managerial, clerical, and sales occupation groups. It will be recalled that for these four residential serving occupation groups the distance coefficients did not pass the test of statistical significance using either distance from the major or nearest ghetto.

LEVEL OF NONWHITE EMPLOYMENT

This section investigates the second of the chapter's three hypotheses—that racial discrimination in housing markets reduces Negro employment opportunities. Estimates of Negro job loss caused by housing segregation are obtained by assuming the proportion of Negro workers living in every residence zone is the same. This assumption is computationally convenient and provides a smaller estimate of Negro job loss than would most other plausible assumptions. For example, it provides a lower estimate than if Negro workers were allocated to the 98 residence zones according to their income or occupational characteristics and those of the residence zones.

Solving Equations (8.1) through (8.6) (assuming the residence ratio is identical for each zone) provides three estimates each for Chicago and Detroit of what the areawide Negro percentage of employment might be, assuming that there were no racial segregation. Since all zones under these assumptions have identical racial characteristics, and distance from the major and nearest ghettos would be zero, the expected proportion of nonwhite employment is the same for every workplace zone. The expected nonwhite proportion of workplace employment is shown in Table 8–3. Once these percentages are obtained, alternative estimates of "expected" Negro employment are derived by multiplying them by the total labor force in each metrpolitan area. The loss of Negro

TABLE 8–3. Estimates of Nonwhite Job Losses for Chicago and Detroit Assuming a Uniform Residential Distribution of Nonwhites

| | *Metropolitan Area Employments* | | | | | |
| | *Actual* | | | *Estimate* | | |
Equation Variables	*Total Number*	*Number Nonwhite*	*Percent Non-white*	*Percent Non-white*[a]	*Number Nonwhite*[b]	*Non-white Job Less*[c]
Chicago						
(8.1) R, d^n	1,760,148	257,178	14.61	15.87	279,335	22,157
(8.2) R, d^m	1,760,148	257,178	14.61	15.94	280,568	23,390
(8.3) R, d^n, d^m	1,760,148	257,178	14.61	16.01	281,800	24,622
Detroit						
(8.4) R, d^n	937,555	127,395	13.59	14.01	131,351	3,956
(8.5) R, d^m	937,555	127,395	13.59	14.00	131,258	3,863
(8.6) R, d^n, d^m	937,555	127,395	13.59	14.56	136,508	9,113

[a]Obtained by solving equations (8.1) through (8.6) assuming r equals either 14.61 (Chicago) or 13.59 (Detroit) and d^m or d^n equals zero

[b]Obtained by multiplying estimated percent nonwhite times total number employed in Chicago (1,760,148) or Detroit (937,555)

[c]Obtained by subtracting estimated nonwhite employment from actual

jobs is then the difference between the actual and "expected" numbers of Negro jobs. For Chicago, the estimated losses range from 22,157 to 24,622.[15] The estimated losses in Detroit are much smaller, ranging from a low of 3,863 to a high of 9,113. Actual total employment, actual Negro employment, "expected" Negro employment, and the estimated job loss for Equations (8.1) through (8.6) are shown in Table 8–3. Part of the differences undoubtedly are due simply to the fact that Chicago's labor force is nearly twice as large as Detroit's. In addition, the much smaller estimated losses for Detroit, like the smaller explanatory power of the Detroit models, are consistent with the lesser degree of racial segregation there. Since Detroit's ghetto is larger and more extensive and there are more and better located secondary ghettos, housing constrains Negro job choices less than in Chicago. Thus, the larger estimates of nonwhite job losses obtained for Chicago are entirely reasonable.

While these estimates must be considered highly tentative, they do suggest that housing market segregation and discrimination may significantly affect the level of Negro employment in metropolitan areas. If this is true, it has grave welfare implications since the costs that housing segregation imposes on Negroes may be even larger than is generally believed. The constraint placed upon job opportunities by housing market discrimination may also partly explain the much higher unemployment rates of Negroes. Part of what is usually charged to employment discrimination may be an indirect effect of housing discrimination. This illustrates how pervasive various types of discrimination may be and how the indirect costs of discrimination may greatly exceed the direct costs.

SUBURBANIZATION AND NEGRO EMPLOYMENT

Suburbanization of employment and population has been one of the most discussed facets of postwar metropolitan development. Between 1950 and 1960 population declines occurred in over half of the central cities (based on 1950 boundaries) of the 40 largest metropolitan areas.[16] Moreover, census tract data indicate that these declines were greatest in the central parts of these central cities.

Employment dispersal is less well documented because of the unavailability of time series data on the location of employment within metropolitan areas. Even so, the fragmentary evidence strongly suggests a rapid dispersal of employment.[17] This employment dispersal is significant to this study for two reasons. Jobs traditionally held by Negroes appear to be suburbanizing at an equal, and very possibly at an above average rate, while there is only token suburbanization of Negro households.

Between 1940 and 1960 the total population of U.S. metropolitan areas increased by 40 million persons. Eighty-four percent of the Negro increase occurred in the central cities and 80 percent of the white increase in the suburbs. Suburbanization of whites accelerated between 1950 and 1960; nearly 90 percent of their metropolitan increase occurred in the suburbs. An even sharper contrast appears in the 24 metropolitan areas with populations of over one million in 1960. In the two decades between 1940 and 1960 almost 100 percent of the increase in their white populations was absorbed by the suburbs. Between 1950 and 1960 their central cities lost nearly one-and-a-half million white residents and gained more than two million Negroes.[18] Moreover, these data understate the differences in the rate of suburbanization of whites and Negroes. Negro ghettos are typically located in the most central part of central cities and expand only at their peripheries.[19]

POSTWAR DISPERSAL OF EMPLOYMENT
AND POPULATION IN CHICAGO

Postwar patterns of metropolitan development in Chicago conform closely to those described for U.S. metropolitan areas. Chicago metropolitan area population increased by 1,043,000 or by 20 percent in the 1950–60 decade; at the same time, its central city population declined by 71,000. This 71,000 decrease in central city population was the result of a 399,000 decline in the white population and a 328,000 increase in the nonwhite population. The latter is nearly ten times as large as the 34,000 increase in the nonwhite ring population. By contrast, the white population of the suburban ring increased by more than one million. As a result of these changes, nonwhites were 23 percent of Chicago's central city and only 3 percent of its ring population in 1960.[20]

Postwar suburbanization of employment in the Chicago metropolitan area mirrored these developments elsewhere. Between 1947 and 1963 manufacturing employment in the Chicago metropolitan area increased by roughly 2,000 jobs. During the same period the central city lost approximately 180,000 manufacturing jobs. Similarly, between 1948 and 1963 wholesaling employment in the metropolitan area increased by 27,000 while it declined by 17,000 in the city. Central city retail employment declined by nearly 40,000 while that for the metropolitan area remained about constant.[21]

If the equations obtained in previous sections relating the locations of nonwhite workplaces and residences are valid and hold generally over time, the implications of this dispersal for Negro employment opportunities would appear serious. Several observers have commented on the problem.[22] For example, Raymond Hilliard, Cook County (Chicago) public aid director, was quoted in a *Chicago's American* series on the Cook County public welfare as saying, "if we never have another migrant, the Negro population here will still increase 25,000 a year. And the real problem is jobs, not people . . . There are thousands of jobs now going begging in the suburbs, but the Negro can't get there."[23] James Ridgeway also referred to the problem in a recent article and noted the additional problems created by low levels of automobile ownership among nonwhites.

> In the past, the Negro ghettos provided Chicago's industries with a pool of cheap labor. The labor still is cheap—there is no minimum wage in Illinois—but there is less and less work to be had since many industries either are automating or moving to the suburbs. The rapid transit system doesn't run near the new centers of industry, and most Negroes don't have automobiles, thus they are increasingly cut off from work. Unemployment rates among men run to 40 percent in Negro districts.[24]

Sufficient data exist for Chicago to make rough quantitative estimates of the effects of postwar populations and employment shifts on nonwhite employment. Good estimates of white and nonwhite resident populations by small areas are available for census years and some data, although much less, are available on intrametropolitan employment locations. The cumulative distribution of manufacturing employment in 1950 and 1960, arrayed by distance from the ghetto centroid, is presented in Figure 8-1.[25] These 1950 and 1960 employment distributions were obtained by aggregating

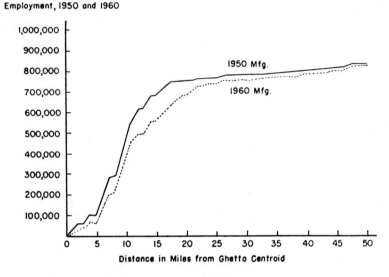

Cumulative Manufacturing
Employment, 1950 and 1960

Figure 8-1. Cumulative Manufacturing Employment by Distance
from the Ghetto Centroid, 1950 and 1960

employment data for 54 postal zones within the city of Chicago and 87 suburban communities and their surrounding unincorporated areas outside the city. While the precision of these estimates can be questioned, their general dimensions cannot. From Figure 8–1 it is apparent that Chicago Negroes were competing for an approximately constant number of jobs in 1950 and 1960, but that in 1960 the jobs were on the average located farther from the ghetto. The effect of these job shifts on Negro manufacturing employment would appear very serious at first glance. But there was an offsetting trend. Despite rapid employment dispersal in the postwar period, a disproportionate number of jobs remain located at central parts of the city. With the expansion of the ghetto between 1950 and 1960 many whites moved further away from these centrally located jobs. Thus, total population within 15 miles of the ghetto centroid remained approximately constant between 1950 and 1960, but its composition changed markedly. During the decade the Negro population within 15 miles of the ghetto centroid increased by 319,000, while the white population declined by 261,000. These outward shifts of the white resident population would be expected to improve the labor market position of Negroes relative to whites at central locations.

To provide a crude indication of how these offsetting trends net out, regression equations were obtained for total manufacturing employment and were solved using 1950 and 1960 values of the residence ratio for the 141 geographic areas (54 postal zones and 87 suburban communities). Equations (8.23) and (8.24) are the estimates for all manufacturing.

$$W = 12.3 + 0.30R - 0.29d^c \qquad\qquad R^2 = 0.65 \qquad\qquad (8.23)$$
$$(11.1)\ \ (9.3)\qquad (5.9)$$

$$W = 11.0 + 0.30R - 0.61d^m \qquad\qquad R^2 = 0.64 \qquad\qquad (8.24)$$
$$(11.3)\ \ (9.0)\qquad (5.6)$$

These estimated manufacturing employment ratios (*Ws*) were then multiplied by total manufacturing employment in each of the 141 areas to obtain two estimates of Negro manufacturing employment, one for each distance variable in each year. Both the units of aggregation and the sources of data used in estimating 1950 and 1960 Negro manufacturing employment are different from those used in estimating Equations (8.23) and (8.24), and not all of these differences can be reconciled. Still, the resulting estimates are suggestive of the impact of these population and employment shifts on Negro employment opportunities.

Estimates of Negro manufacturing employment in 1950 and 1960 obtained from Equations (8.23) and (8.24) are presented in Table 8–4. As these data indicate, total manufacturing employment declined by about 3,000 between 1950 and 1960. Negro employment declined even more: an estimated 4,000 using Equation (8.23) and an estimated 7,000 using Equation (8.24). As a result, the ratio of Negro to all manufacturing employment declined during the ten year period.

As a check, the results summarized in Table 8–4 were compared with data from the 1950 and 1960 Census of Population. Census statistics of Negro manufacturing employment are 86,000 in 1950 and 84,000 in 1960, showing a decline similar to that obtained from Equations (8.23) and (8.24). Given the differences in data used, the check is not exact. Moreover, close

TABLE 8–4. Total Actual and Estimated Negro Manufacturing Employment in the Chicago Metropolitan Area: 1950 and 1960

	Distance from the					
	Ghetto Centroid			*Major Ghetto*		
	1950	*1960*	*50–60*	*1950*	*1960*	*50–60*
Total actual (thousands)	838	835	–3	838	835	–3
Estimated Negro (thousands)	93	89	–4	86	79	–7
Percent estimated Negro	11.1	10.6	–0.5	10.3	9.5	–0.8

examination of the census statistics indicates that the similarity is not quite so great as these comparisons of Negro employment levels suggest. Census manufacturing employment statistics are for a wider geographic area, are larger in both years, and show a greater decline. Despite these difficulties, the similarity between the estimate of Negro manufacturing employment and the 1950 and 1960 census statistics of Negro manufacturing employment provides considerable support for the validity of the models presented in this paper.

The situation of Negroes is even more adverse when the relative growth of the Negro and white labor forces is taken into account. Between 1950 and 1960, the nonwhite civilian labor force in the Chicago metropolitan area grew by 31.3 percent. During the same period the white civilian labor force grew by only 3.4 percent. Thus, even if Negroes had retained the same number of manufacturing jobs their position relative to whites would have deteriorated seriously. The decline in their employment indicates a worsening situation.

THE SUBSEQUENT CONTROVERSY

The analyses included in this chapter were initiated more than a decade ago. Preliminary findings were presented at a Chicago meeting of the American Statistical Association in December 1964 and a somewhat expanded analysis of these questions was published four years later in the *Quarterly Journal of Economics*.[26]

These papers, which were the first to link discrimination in the housing market to the distribution and level of nonwhite employment in urban areas, attracted considerable scholarly and popular attention and provided the intellectual justification for several federal experiments to provide transportation services from central city ghettos to suburban workplaces and a number of manpower programs designed to limit Negro employment opportunities outside the central cities. A discussion of these policy issues is presented in Chapter Seventeen.

These papers also attracted more than the usual amount of attention from other researchers and stimulated a number of independent empirical investigations and critiques of the paper's methodology, empirical analyses, and policy implications.[27] Several of these subsequent studies have amplified, clarified, or extended by analysis in useful directions; others have added nothing but confusion and obfuscation. This section reviews and evaluates a number of both kinds of studies.

Collectively, the critics present four kinds of analyses that they believe undermine my findings: (1) evidence on the relative tightness of central city and suburban job markets; (2) tests to determine whether relative black-white earnings or employment levels are correlated with differences among SMSAs in measures of segregation; (3) analyses that demonstrated the sensitivity of my estimates of Negro job loss to alternative model specification; and (4) statistics on the welfare of black households living in the central cities and suburbs.

Noll and others have argued that jobs are in some sense more plentiful in core than in suburban areas in spite of widespread employment dispersal within metropolitan areas. "All of these findings indicate that jobs, particularly for the less skilled, are easier to find in the central city. They also suggest that suburbanization of employment may be a response to labor market conditions rather than a cause of unemployment."[28] At points these critics seem to argue that housing market discrimination and the resulting segregation benefits black households by forcing them to live in neighborhoods located near large numbers of available jobs.

It is obviously possible to devise situations where the earnings of all urban blacks or particular segments of the urban black populations will be as high or higher than otherwise similar white workers, at least for short periods of time. But these ad hoc, empirical arguments ultimately must deal with the simple, but important, observation that adding a constraint to a maximization problem of this kind must yield the result that the constrained population can do no better, and typically will do worse, than they would if their choices were not restricted.[29]

If there is a greater demand for labor and higher wages at central city and core workplaces than in the suburbs, white workers may move to convenient central city neighborhoods and accept these jobs with no transportation cost penalty. If better job opportunities are available to them in the suburbs, they can likewise move to neighborhoods convenient to these jobs. In contrast, if jobs are more plentiful and higher paying in the suburbs, black workers, in general, can hold them only by incurring large travel costs. The net hourly wage they obtain from these suburban jobs, i.e., earnings per week minus transportation costs divided by hours spent working plus hours spent commuting, typically will be substantially lower than that received by white workers who are able to obtain suburban housing near their workplace. These considerations explain the much larger amount of reverse commuting by black than by white households and the underrepresentation of black workers at suburban workplaces.[30]

Joseph D. Mooney in the May 1969 issue of The *Quarterly Journal of Economics* published the first major independent test of the hypothesis that limitations on Negro residential choice reduced Negro employment.[31] Mooney regressed the employment-population ratio of nonwhite males or females in the "poorest" census tracts of 25 SMSAs for the census week 1960 on several explanatory variables selected to measure the tightness of each metropolitan labor market, the extent of employment decentralization in each metropolitan area, and the accessibility of fringe employment areas to the central city ghetto residents. Equation (8.25) is the best of two equations he reports for nonwhite males.

$$(E/P)_M = \underset{(.052)}{.63} \quad \underset{(.56)}{-2.86U} \quad \underset{(.06)}{+.19} \quad (E_{cc}/E_{smsa}) \quad + \quad \underset{(.06)}{.24(R_M/CCM_M)} \qquad (8.25)$$

$$R^2 = .95, \quad F = 13.5, \quad n = 25$$

Dependent Variable

(E/P) = Employment-population ratio of nonwhite males or females in the "poorest" census tracts of each city for census week 1960

Independent Variables

U = SMSA total unemployment rate (census month 1960)

E_{cc}/E_{smsa} = ratio of jobs in wholesale trade, selected services, retail trade, and manufacturing in the central city to all jobs in the four sectors in each SMSA (interpolated for 1960)

R_m/CC_m = all nonwhite males over 14 years of age who work in the ring and live in the central city, divided by all nonwhite males over 14 years of age who live in the central city and work in the central city or ring (for census week 1960)

From Equation (8.25) Mooney concludes that:

> Although the geographic separation of the central city Negro from the metropolitan fringe areas reduces to some extent his employment opportunities, relative to aggregate demand conditions in a particular metropolitan area (as represented by the unemployment rates), the factor of geographic separation does not seem to be too important. [And that,] Although the model "works" in the sense that the decentralization variables ... and the proxy variables for accessibliity to the ring area from the central city have the predicted rings and are significant, the reader should not lose sight of the fact that the size of the coefficient of the unemployment rate is substantially higher than the size of the coefficients for either of the other variables.[32]

He buttresses this interpretation by appeal to the quantitative result that the beta coefficient of the SMSA unemployment rate, which has a value of 0.65 for Equation (8.25), is 50 percent larger than those obtained for the employment decentralization variable or the accessibility variable.[33]

Some reflection on Mooney's model and empirical results suggests caution in accepting his interpretation. While it is easy to agree with Mooney's reminder of the importance of full employment policies as a means of maintaining high levels of nonwhite employment, it is less obvious that his analysis demonstrates that the factor of geographic separation is unimportant.

The beta coefficients of both the employment decentralization and the accessibility variables were quite large, 0.40 and 0.35 respectively. Moreover, the relative magnitude of the beta coefficients should be evaluated in terms of the probable errors of measurement of the three explanatory variables. The aggregate SMSA unemployment rate is a rather good measure of aggregate demand conditions in a particular metropolitan area, but the measures of employment decentralization and accessibility used by Mooney are, by his own admission, unsatisfactory proxies of more subtle concepts. While bias is always difficult to evaluate, it is likely that these errors of measurement would tend to bias the coefficients of the employment decentralization and accessibility variables toward zero.

Stanley Masters, in a note published in *The Quarterly Journal of Economics,* presents analyses that are similar in spirit to Mooney's. But Masters, unlike Mooney, finds no evidence that housing market segregation limits the relative employment opportunities of nonwhites—either in total or with regard to the "better jobs".

Masters' empirical analysis involves regressions of the ratio of nonwhite to white male median incomes in 65 large SMSAs on a South dummy, the relative years of schooling of nonwhite and white males, and several segregation indexes. He finds that while the South dummy and the relative schooling variables are statistically significant in his regression equations, none of the segregation indexes are. From this result he concludes "that these results, together with those of Harrison cited earlier, suggest that housing segregation does not seriously limit the relative employment opportunities of nonwhites— either in total or with regard to 'better' jobs."[34]

But examination of the segregation measures employed by Masters, and limited reflection on the way in which housing market restraints would affect black access to jobs, indicates the inadequacy of his tests. He includes no measures of the distribution of jobs between central city and suburban workplace, of the relative degree of tightness in these submarkets, or of the juxtaposition of black residence areas and job concentrations within his sample of metropolitan areas. As a result, none of the segregation indexes he employs, either singly or in combination, begin to capture the way in which housing market discrimination and segregation affect black employment opportunities.

These failings of Master's analysis should come as no surprise. Accessibility to employment opportunities from black residence areas is difficult to describe and quantify for even a single metropolitan housing and labor market. The task becomes virtually impossible for comparisons among metropolitan areas. The very great difficulty, perhaps impossibility with available data, of devising meaningful measures of these phenomena have led me to limit my analyses to individual labor and housing markets (Detroit and Chicago). Nothing in Master's analysis or findings leads me to conclude my judgment was mistaken.

Mooney's earlier comment on my study had the same weakness, although the variables he used to represent residence-workplace separation and employment decentralization are probably somewhat more adequate than those used by Masters. In spite of the inadequacy of Mooney's measures of employment decentralization and accessibility, his analysis provided a weak confirmation of the hypothesis described in the first part of this chapter. It should come as no surprise that Masters' analysis, which failed to represent these important variables at all, found none.

The empirical findings by Bennett Harrison used by Masters and other critics to buttress their conclusions are even further from the mark. Harrison obtains frequency distributions of weekly earnings, annual employment, occupational status, marginal returns to additional years of schooling, and marginal returns to participation in five training programs for white and black males residing in central city poverty tracts, central city nonpoverty tracts, and suburban rings of 12 large SMSAs.[35] He finds that white earnings are highest in the suburbs, second highest in central city nonpoverty areas, and lowest in central city poverty areas. (He obtains similar results using the other four welfare measures.) But when Harrison examines the same frequency distributions for black male workers, he finds that the black residents of central city nonpoverty neighborhoods have higher earnings than either the black residents of central city poverty areas or suburban areas. He concludes that these findings and similar ones for the remaining welfare measures are inconsistent with the results of my analysis and cast doubt on the policy recommendation that vigorous efforts should be made to provide black households with access to suburban housing markets on terms equal to those of white households.

In fact, Harrison's findings bear almost no relation to the theoretical arguments I pose, my empirical results, or the policy prescriptions that flow from them. His finding that black and white residents of high income, central city neighborhoods have higher incomes than white and black residents of low income, central city neighborhoods, of course, follows from the definition of poverty and nonpoverty tracts. The higher income of white suburban residents in turn reflect a sorting out process where centrally employed high income whites find it to their advantage to commute to suburban neighborhoods where high quality, low density housing is cheaper than in central areas. The preponderance of white suburban workers reside in the suburbs, whatever their incomes. But the well-documented tendency of centrally employed high income white workers to reside in suburban areas at higher rates than lower income whites employed at the same workplace produces the higher mean incomes observed by Harrison for white suburban residents. This theory of residential location has been articulated and tested by a number of authors.[36]

The situation of black households is quite different. Most black suburban residents live in segregated suburban concentrations that date from the early 1900s, or in rural parts of metropolitan counties. Generally, the housing located in these outlying black residential concentrations is of relatively low quality, although in a few metropolitan areas there are pockets of relatively high quality black housing located outside of the cities. Still, the best housing available to Negro Americans is generally found in what are referred to in Chapter Seven as ghetto suburbs—i.e., relatively high quality transitional neighborhoods on the periphery of central ghetto. These are, not surprisingly, coterminous with city nonpoverty tracts. Harrison's methods of analysis, particularly the questionable pooling of the 12 SMSAs included in his analysis, eliminates any possibility of disentangling these housing quality and accessibility effects.

Harrison's use of a nonwhite, rather than a Negro, sample also tends to confuse the analysis, since the 12 SMSAs included in his analysis include at least four with large non-Negro, nonwhite populations (Houston, Los Angeles, New York, and San Francisco). While these minorities have been, and in many cases remain, intensely segregated, the geographic patterns of segregation and their implications differ in important respects from those of the Negro populations of large northern and eastern cities, with which my analysis is primarily concerned. Moreover, the large Japanese- and Chinese-American populations of Los Angeles and San Francisco are no longer disadvantaged in terms of socioeconomic status. It is of some interest in this respect that when Masters omits the 13 SMSAs where non-Negroes accounted for more than 10 percent of the nonwhite population from the analysis, the sign of the coefficient of NWT (the percentage of nonwhites living in "nonwhite" census tracts) shifts from positive to negative.[37]

No survey of the research and commentary stimulated by my papers on the effects of housing market discrimination on Negro employment would be complete without reference to the reanalysis of my Chicago data by Paul Offner and Daniel H. Saks.[38] Offner and Saks, in their valuable note, demonstrated that the equations published in my 1964 and 1968 papers and some of the findings derived from them are uncomfortably sensitive to alternative specifications. Specifically, they replaced my linear specification of the residence ratio (R) in Equation (8.1) with a quadratic form as shown by Equation (8.24), a specification they argue

$$W = 10.84 + 0.049R + 0.005R^2 - 0.67D^n \qquad R^2 = 0.82 \qquad (8.24)$$

is implied by my own hypothesis about the effect of residential segregation on the relative demand for Negro labor.

As is evident from a comparison of Equations (8.1) and (8.24) the quadratic specification employed by Offner and Saks explains a larger proportion of the variance in the employment ratio, W, (Negro workers employed in i/total workers employed in i) than the one I employed: $R^2 = 0.82$ vs. $R^2 = 0.77$. Moreover, when Offner and Saks use Equation (8.24) to estimate the loss or gain of Negro employment that would result from uniform residential integration, they find that "our estimates suggest that an end to housing segregation would have resulted in a substantial loss of employment by Negroes instead of the job gain that Kain's less satisfactory equation predicts."[39]

This neat reversal of my finding of Negro employment loss by Offner and Saks, which, to say the least, is striking, unambiguously poses the question: which result are we to believe? As I acknowledged in my rejoinder to Offner and Saks' note, their specification is obviously superior to mine if a goodness of fit criterion is employed. But neither they nor I would regard this to be the proper test. The crucial issue is not which model fits this particular sample better (particularly since both provide exceptionally good fits), but rather which model is the correct or at least the more correct representation.

The major conceptual problem centers on the interpretation of the coefficient of the neighborhood racial composition variable (R). Specifically, to what extent does it represent consumer discrimination based on the racial composition of the neighborhood, and to what extent does it act both as a measure of this effect and as a surrogate for transport cost considerations and information flows? While Saks and Offner interpret the coefficient entirely in the former terms, it is virtually certain that the coefficient combines these two effects in some unspecified way.

Offner and Saks are suitably reserved in their claims about the significance of these findings. "Our results for total employment do not prove or disprove Kain's contention that Negroes suffer a job loss as a result of residential segregation." Moreover, both they and I stressed the difficulties inherent in attempting to infer complex general equilibrium effects from a simple reduced form model such as that represented by Equations (8.1) or (8.24).

The differences between the reanalysis by Offner and Saks and my original analysis should not be allowed to obscure the numerous common elements. Both specifications suggest that Negro employment would be increased by breaking up the single, massive ghettos found in large northern metropolitan areas into a series of smaller, dispersed ghettos. If the model proposed by Offner and Saks is a better measure of the employment effects of changes in the residential locations of Negro workers, such a pattern of segregated suburbanization would have more favorable employment effects. If my specification is closer to the true relationship, the outcome would be fairly insensitive to this consideration.

Finally, Offner and Saks' reformulation of my equations produces results that are entirely consistent with the first and third conclusions of my paper: (1) that housing segregation has a substantial impact on the spatial distribution of Negro employment; and (2) that ongoing suburbanization of employment may be worsening the employment situation of urban Negroes.

Even if we accept Offner and Saks' model specification and their interpretation of it, Negroes can obtain no more employment gains from segregation since they are already segregated to the greatest extent possible. As jobs continue to move farther from the ghetto, they will suffer increasing employment losses because of growing transportation and information difficulties. Their equations, which have larger distance coefficients than my comparable ones, imply even larger employment losses from continued employment dispersal.

CONCLUSIONS

This chapter has examined the relationship between housing market segregation and the distribution and level of Negro employment. The investigation was prompted by concern that racial segregation in metropolitan housing markets may further reduce the employment opportunities of Negroes who are already handicapped by employer discrimination and low levels of education. In addition, it seems possible that the extensive growth of metropolitan areas and the rapid postwar dispersal of employment, accompanied by no reduction and perhaps even an increase in housing market segregation, may have placed the Negro job seeker in an even more precarious position.

Support for these hypotheses is provided by analyses of data for the Chicago and Detroit metropolitan areas. Housing market segregation clearly affects the distribution of Negro employment. Its effect on the level of Negro employment and unemployment is a more complex question and, consequently, the answer is less certain. While the estimates of Negro job loss due to housing market segregation presented in this chapter are highly tentative, they nonetheless suggest that housing market segregation may reduce the level of Negro employment and thereby contribute to the high unemployment rates of metropolitan Negroes.

For the Chicago area it is possible to obtain an empirical estimate of the impact of employment dispersal on Negro job opportunities during the 1950–60 decade. This is an even more complex issue than that discussed above, and the conclusions therefore must be even more guarded. Even so, the empirical findings do suggest that postwar suburbanization of metropolitan employment may be further undermining the position of the Negro, and that the continued high levels of Negro unemployment in a full employment economy may be partially attributable to the rapid and adverse (for the Negro) shifts in the location of jobs.

Chapter Nine

Alternatives to the Gilded Ghetto

with Joseph J. Persky

This chapter evaluates a series of proposals and programs for improving the ghetto through economic development, renewal, and reconstruction. The intellectual basis of many of these proposals stems from a false analogy of the ghetto to an underdeveloped country in need of economic development. This oversimplified and misleading view ignores the strong linkages that tie the ghetto to the remainder of the metropolis and to the nation. When the nature of these linkages and the complex relationship between the ghetto and metropolitan development is understood, the potential destructiveness of these proposals becomes apparent. In this article we attempt to describe these interrelationships and the ghetto's consequent culpability for an expanded list of urban problems.

THE GHETTO AND THE METROPOLIS

If we begin with the usual list of "ghetto problems"—unemployment, low income, poor schools, and poor housing—it is easy to see the appeal of proposals aimed at making the ghetto livable. Moreover, casual observation of the slow pace of school desegregation, residential integration, and fair employment practices would indicate that the promise of integration and the gains achievable from the process are to be made only at an obscure point in the future. Thus, in the short run, the argument for ghetto improvement would have us view the ghetto as something of a community into itself, a community that could substantially benefit from economic development and especially heavy investments of physical capital.

The weakness of this argument, however, is attested to by a growing body of evidence that indicates that (1) the above list of ghetto problems is much too short, because it ignores the serious implications of the growing ghetto for the metropolis as a whole, and that (2) the ghetto itself is responsible for, or seriously aggravates, many of the most visible problems of urban Negroes.

The central Negro ghetto has produced a significant distortion of metropolitan development, which has added substantially to problems in central city finance, metropolitan transportation, housing, and urban renewal. The decline of central cities has been hastened by a conviction in the white community, both individual and corporate, that the ghetto would continue its rapid expansion, carrying along its associated problems of concentrated poverty and social disorganization.

Although historically lower income groups have tended to live in central cities, this residential pattern was the result of a highly centralized employment structure. Low income households, constrained by limited housing and transportation budgets, clustered tightly around the workplaces in the densest accommodations available. High income households, by contrast, with more disposable income and preferences for less congested living conditions, found it expedient to commute to suburban areas where land costs were lower. These lower housing costs in suburban locations more than compensated them for the time, inconvenience, and out-of-pocket costs of commuting. Today, it still remains true that low income households cluster more closely around their workplaces than do high income households. However, with the accelerating pace of suburbanization of industry and jobs—itself no doubt due partly to the ghetto's expansion—these jobs are found less frequently in cities. Thus the poor are found less frequently in the central city; it is mainly the Negro poor who are found there. The inference is inescapable: central cities are poor largely because they are black, and not the converse.

This residential pattern imposed on the Negro has led to an unduly large proportion of poverty-linked services being demanded of central cities. At the same time, the expansion of the ghetto has encouraged the exodus of middle income whites. The result has been rapid increases in local government expenditures and a severe constraint on the ability of central cities to raise revenues. Hence the current crisis in city finances. Although the problem can be handled in the short run by various schemes of redistributing governmental revenues, a preferable long run solution would involve a major dispersal of the low income population, in particular the Negro. Central cities will continue to have a high proportion of the poor as long as they contain a large proportion of metropolitan jobs. However, there is no rationale for exaggerating this tendency with artificial restraints.

HOUSING, TRANSPORTATION, SCHOOLS

Housing segregation has also frustrated efforts to renew the city. At first sight the logic of renewal is strong. By offering federal subsidies to higher income whites locating within their boundaries, central cities have hoped to improve their tax base. The same logic underlies community efforts to woo industry. However, to the extent that these groups consider the city an inferior location, because of the existence of the ghetto, such subsidies will continue to fail. As long as the ghetto exists, most of white America will write off the central city. Spot renewal, even on the scale envisioned in the Model Cities program, cannot alter this basic fact.

In this context, even the small victories of central cities are often of a pyrrhic nature. So long as the central business district (CBD) manages to remain a major employment location, the city is faced with serious transportation problems, problems that would be substantially reduced if more of the centrally employed whites were willing to reside in the city. To a great extent, the CBD stakes its existence on an ability to transport people rapidly over long distances. Pressures for more expressways and high speed rail transit are understandable—and yet both encourage the migration to the suburbs. The city must lose either way, so long as the ghetto is a growing mass that dominates the environment of its core and the development of its metropolitan area.

From the above argument, it is clear that the impact of the ghetto on the processes of metropolitan development has created or aggravated many of our most critical urban problems. These costs are borne by Negroes and whites alike. However, the same interaction between the ghetto and metropolis has produced other important distortions whose costs fall almost exclusively on the Negro community. The ghetto has isolated the Negro economically as well as socially. In the first place, the Negro has inadequate access to the job market. For him, informal methods of job search, common to low skilled employment, are largely limited to the ghetto. Jobs may be plentiful outside of the ghetto, yet he will know little or nothing of these opportunties. Moreover, the time and cost necessary to reach many suburban jobs, frequently compounded by the radial character of public transit services, often will discourage Negroes from taking or even seeking such jobs. Granted that the ghetto generates a limited number of service jobs, this effect is more than offset by the discriminatory practices of nonghetto employers. Research on the distribution of Negro employment in northern metropolitan areas indicates the importance of these factors, by demonstrating that the proportion of Negroes in an area's work force is dependent on that area's distance from the ghetto and the racial composition of the surrounding residential neighborhoods. These distributional characteristics also affect the level of Negro employment. Estimates indicate that as many as 24,000 jobs in Chicago and 9,000 in Detroit may be lost to the Negro community because of housing segregation.[1] These figures are based on 1956 and 1952 data and may well underestimate the current situation. The continuing trend of job decentralization also may have aggravated the situation.

De facto school segregation is another widely recognized limitation of Negro opportunities resulting from housing market segregation. A large body of evidence indicates that students in ghetto schools receive an education much inferior to that offered elsewhere. Low levels of student achievement are the result of a complex of factors including poorly trained, overworked, and undermotivated teachers; low levels of per student expenditures, inadequate capital plants; and the generally low level of students' motivation and aspiration. This last factor is, of course, related to the ghetto's poverty and social disorganization.

The continued rapid growth of central city ghettos has seriously expanded the realm of de facto segregation and limited the range of possible corrective actions. For example, in 1952, 57 percent of Cleveland's Negro students went to schools with more than 90 percent Negro enrollment, in 1962, 82 percent went to such schools. By 1965, Chicago, Detroit, and Philadelphia all had more than 70 percent of their Negro students in these completely segregated schools.[2]

In addition to sharply curtailing Negro economic and educational opportunity, the ghetto is an important disorganizing force. It represents the power of the outside community and the frustration of the Negro. The sources of nourishment for many of the psychological and sociological problems too common to Negro Americans can be found here. Drug addiction, violent crime, and family disorganization all gain a high degree of acceptance, creating a set of norms that often bring the individual into conflict with the larger society. Kenneth Clark puts the case well: "The dark ghetto is institutionalized pathology; it is chronic, self-perpetuating pathology. . ."Although this pathology is difficult to quantify, it may well be the ghetto's most serious consequence.

In reviewing our expanded list of problems, it may seem that we have made the ghetto too much the villain. Physical segregation may have only been the not-so-subtle way to avoid discriminatory practices that might otherwise be rampant. Many ghetto problems might still exist in some other guise. Nevertheless, the problems as structured *now* must continue as long as the metropolis harbors this "peculiar institution."

Nothing less than a complete change in the structure of the metropolis will solve the problem of the ghetto. It is therefore ironic that current programs which ostensibly are concerned with the welfare of urban Negroes are willing to accept, and are even based on, the permanence of central ghettos. Thus, under every heading of social welfare legislation—education, income transfer, employment, and housing—we find programs that can only serve to strengthen the ghetto and the serious problems that it generates. In particular, these programs concentrate on beautifying the fundamentally ugly structure of the current metropolis and not on providing individuals with the tools necessary to break out of that structure. The shame of the situation is that viable alternatives do exist.

Thus, in approaching the problems of Negro employment, first steps could be an improved information system at the disposal of Negro job seekers, strong training programs linked to job placement in industry, and improved transit access between central ghettos and outlying employment areas. Besides the direct effects of such programs on unemployment and incomes, they have the added advantage of encouraging the dispersion of the ghetto and not its further concentration. For example, Negroes employed in suburban areas distant from the ghetto have strong incentives to reduce the time and cost of commuting by seeking out residences near their workplaces. Frequent, informal contact with white coworkers will both increase their information about housing in predominantly white residential areas and help to break down the mutual distrust that is usually associated with the process of integration.

Prospects of housing desegregation would be much enhanced by major changes in urban renewal and housing programs. Current schemes accept and reinforce some of the worst aspects of the housing market. Thus, even the best urban renewal projects involve the government in drastically reducing the supply (and thereby increasing the cost) of low income housing—all this at great expense to the taxpayer. At best there is an implicit acceptance of the alleged desire of the poor to remain in central city slums. At worst, current programs could be viewed as a concerted effort to maintain the ghetto. The same observation can be made about public housing programs.[3] The Commission on Civil Rights in its report on school segregation concluded that government policies for low cost housing were "further reinforcing the trend toward racial and economic separation in metropolitan areas."

An alternative approach would aim at drastically expanding the supply of low income housing outside the ghetto. Given the high costs of reclaiming land in central areas, subsidies equivalent to existing urban renewal expenditures for use anywhere in the metropolitan area would lead to the construction of many more units. The new mix by type and location would be likely to favor small, single family homes and garden apartments on the urban periphery. Some over-building would be desirable, the object being the creation of a glut in the low income suburban housing market. It is hard to imagine a situation that would make developers and renters less sensitive to skin color.

These measures would be greatly reinforced by programs that increase the effective demand of Negroes for housing. Rent subsidies to individuals are highly desirable, because they represent the transfer of purchasing power that can be used anywhere in the metropolitan area. Other income transfer programs not specifically tied to housing would have similar advantages in improving the prospects of ghetto dispersal. Vigorous enforcement of open housing statutes would aid the performance of the "impersonal" market, perhaps most importantly by providing developers, lenders, and realtors with an excuse to act in their own self interest.

SUBURBANIZATION OF THE NEGRO

Even in the face of continuing practices of residential segregation, the suburbanization of the Negro can still continue apace. It is important to realize that the presence of Negroes in the suburbs does not necessarily imply Negro integration into white residential neighborhoods. Suburbanization of the Negro and housing integration are not synonymous. Many of the disadvantages of massive, central ghettos would be overcome if they were replaced or even augmented by smaller, dispersed Negro *communities.* Such a pattern would remove the limitations on Negro employment opportunities attributable to the geography of the ghetto. Similarly, the reduced pressure on central city housing markets would improve the prospects for the renewal of middle income neighborhoods through the operations of the private market. Once the peripheral growth of central city ghettos is checked, the demands for costly investment in specialized, long distance transport facilities serving central employment areas would be reduced. In addition programs designed to reduce de facto school segregation by means of redistributing bussing, and similar measures would be much more feasible.

Although such a segregated pattern does not represent the authors' idea of a more open society, it could still prove a valuable first step toward that goal. Most groups attempting to integrate suburban neighborhoods have placed great stress on achieving and maintaining some preconceived interracial balance. Because integration is the goal, they feel the need to proceed slowly and make elaborate precautions to avoid "tipping" the neighborhood. The result has been a small black trickle into all-white suburbs. But if the immediate goal is seen as destroying the ghetto, different strategies should be employed. "Tipping," rather than something to be carefully avoided, might be viewed as a tactic for opening large amounts of suburban housing. If enough suburban neighborhoods are "tipped," the danger of any one of them becoming a massive ghetto would be small.

Education is still another tool that can be used to weaken the ties of the ghetto. Formal schooling plays a particularly important role in preparing individuals to participate in the complex urban society of today. It greatly enhances their ability to compete in the job market with the promise of higher incomes. As a result, large scale programs of compensatory education can make important contributions to a strategy of weakening and eventually abolishing the Negro ghetto. Nevertheless, the important gains of such compensatory programs must be continually weighed against the more general advantages of school desegregation. Where real alternatives exist in the short run, programs consistent with this latter objective should always be chosen. It is important to note that truly effective programs of compensatory education are likely to be extremely expensive and that strategies involving significant amounts of desegregation may achieve the same educational objectives at much lower costs.

Bussing of Negro students may be such a program. Like better access to suburban employment for ghetto job seekers, bussing would weaken the geographic dominance of the ghetto. Just as the informal experience of integration on the job is an important element in changing racial attitudes, integration in the classroom is a powerful learning experience. Insofar as the resistance of suburban communities to accepting low income residents and students is the result of a narrow cost-minimization calculus that attempts to avoid providing public services and in particular education, substantial state and federal subsidies for the education of low income students can prove an effective carrot. Title I programs of the Elementary and Secondary Education Act of 1965 and grants to areas containing large federal installations are precedents. Subsidies should be large enough to cover more than the marginal cost of educating students from low income families, and should make it profitable for communities and school districts to accept such students. The experience of the METCO program in Boston strongly suggests that suburban communities can be induced to accept ghetto school children if external sources of financing are available.

Because the above proposals would still leave unanswered some immediate needs of ghetto residents, a strong argument can be made for direct income transfers. Although certain constraints on the use of funds, for example rent supplements, might be maintained, the emphasis should be on providing resources to individuals and not on freezing them into geographic areas. The extent to which welfare schemes are currently tied to particular neighborhoods or communities should be determined, and these programs should be altered so as to remove such limitations on mobility. Keeping in mind the crucial links between the ghetto and the rural South, it is essential that the southern Negro share in these income transfers.

THE GHETTO AND THE NATION

Although there are major benefits to be gained by both the Negro community and the metropolis at large through a dispersal of the central ghetto, these benefits cannot be realized and are likely to be hindered by programs aimed at making the ghetto a more livable place. In addition to the important objections discussed so far, there is the very real possibility that such programs will run afoul of major migration links with the Negro population of the South. A striking example of this problem can be seen in the issue of ghetto job creation, one of the most popular proposals to improve the ghetto.

Although ghetto job creation, like other "gilding" programs, might initially reduce Negro unemployment, it must eventually affect the system that binds the northern ghetto to the rural and urban areas of the South. This system will react to any sudden changes in employment and income opportunities in northern ghettos. If there are no offsetting improvements in the South, the result will be increased rates of migration into still restricted ghetto areas. While we need to know much more than we now do about the elasticity of migration to various economic improvements, the direction of the effect is clear. Indeed it is possible that more than one migrant would appear in the ghetto for every job created.[4] Even at lower levels of sensitivity, a strong wave of in-migration could prove extremely harmful to many other programs. The South in 1960 still accounted for about 60 percent of the country's Negro population, more than half of which lived in nonmetropolitan areas. In particular, the number of potential migrants from the rural South has not declined greatly in recent years. The effect of guaranteed incomes or jobs available in the metropolitan ghetto can be inferred from an analysis of the patterns of migration from the South.

Historically, the underdeveloped nature of the southern region has proven a spur to the migration of both whites and Negroes. What recent progress has been achieved is overwhelmingly "whites only." The 1950s were the first decade in this century in which there was net white in-migration to the southern region as a whole. This change is very likely the result of the expansion of industrial activity throughout the South and particularly its border areas. White male agricultural employment losses of about 1 million were more than offset by strong gains in manufacturing, wholesale and retail trade, and professional and related services. By way of contrast, Negroes concentrated in the slowest growing and most discriminatory states of the Deep South showed no major gains to offset the almost 400 thousand jobs lost in agriculture. Thus, despite rapid contraction of the agricultural sector, 1960 still found 21 percent of all southern Negro males employed in agriculture as compared to 11 percent of southern whites. It is not surprising, in terms of this background, that nearly 1.5 million Negroes (net) left the South in the 1950s.

The major result of the massive migrations of the 1940s and 1950s was to make the metropolitan areas of the North and West great centers of Negro population. In 1940 these areas accounted for only 20 percent of all Negroes in the country, whereas in 1960, 37 percent of all Negroes lived in these same areas. Moreover, statistics on the migration of Negroes born in southern states indicate a definite preference for the largest metropolitan areas of the country over smaller cities.

DEVELOPING THE SOUTH

Some appreciation for migration's contribution to the growth of northern ghettos is provided by a comparison of the components of Negro population increase. Fifty-four percent of the 2.7 million increase in northern Negro populations from 1950 to 1960 was accounted for by net in-migration of Southern Negroes. Although the data on more recent population changes are scanty, the best estimates suggest that Negro net migration from the South has been averaging about 100,000 per year for the period 1960 to 1966. It therefore appears that the contribution of southern migration to the growth of northern ghettos, even though it may now be on the decline, remains substantial.

The pattern of Negro migration is in sharp contrast with the pattern of white out-migration from the same areas of the South. Thus, there are about

2.5 million southern-born whites and 2.5 million southern-born Negroes in nonsouthern metropolitan areas greater than a million, but 1.42 million whites and 4.2 million Negroes in nonsouthern cities of 250,000 to a million. Cities greater than 250,000 account for 89 percent of Negroes who have left the South, but only 60 percent of whites. The framework of opportunities presented to the individual Negro migrant is such as to increase the desirability of a move out of the South and to stress the comparative desirability of large cities as against rural areas and medium sized cities.

Although the differential in white and Negro migration is clearly related to differential economic opportunity, the overall level of southern out-migration must be ascribed to the underdeveloped nature of the region. A more rapid pace of southern economic development could change these historic patterns of Negro migration. Tentative research findings indicate that both manufacturing growth and urbanization in the South reduce Negro out-migration. Although the holding effect of these changes is not so strong for Negroes as for whites, the difference between the two responses can be substantially narrowed. If development took place at a higher rate, the job market would tighten and thus encourage Negroes to stay. Moreover, the quid pro quo for large scale subsidies for southern development might be strong commitments to hire Negro applicants. A serious program of southern development is worthwhile in its own right as a cure for a century of imbalance in the distribution of economic activity in the nation. From the narrow viewpoint of the North, however, the economic development of the South can play a crucial role in providing leverage in the handling of metropolitan problems.

Belated recognition of the problems created for northern metropolitan areas by these large scale streams of rural migration have led in recent months to a large number of proposals to encourage development in rural areas. Not surprisingly the Department of Agriculture has been quick to seize the opportunities provided. A "rural renaissance" has been its response. Full page advertisements headed, "To save our cities, We must have rural-urban balance," have appeared in a large number of magazines under the aegis of the National Rural Electric Cooperative Association. These proposals invariably fail to recognize that Negro migration from the rural South differs in important respects from the rural-urban migration and has different consequences. Failing as they do to distinguish between beneficial and potentially disruptive migration, these proposals for large scale programs to keep people on the farms, everywhere, are likely to lead to great waste and inefficiency, while failing to come to grips with the problem that motivated the original concern.

IMPROVING SKILLS

A second important approach to easing the pressure on the ghetto is to improve the educational and skill level of incoming migrants. An investment in the underutilized human resource represented by the southern white and Negro will pay off in either an expanded southern economy or a northern metropolitan job market. Indeed, it is just this flexibility that makes programs oriented to individuals so attractive in comparison to programs oriented to geography. To the extent that a potential migrant can gain skills in demand, his integration into the metropolis, North or South, is that much eased. In light of these benefits, progress in southern schools has been pitifully slow. Southern Negro achievement levels are the lowest for any group in the country. Southern states with small tax bases and high fertility rates have found it expedient in the past to spend as little as possible on Negro education. Much of the rationalization for this policy is based on the fact that a large proportion of southern Negroes will migrate and thus deprive the area of whatever educational investment is made in them. This fact undoubtedly has led to some underinvestment in the education of southern whites as well, but the brunt has been borne by the Negro community.

Clearly it is to the advantage of those areas that are likely to receive these migrants to guarantee their ability to cope with an urban environment. This would be in sharp contrast to migrants who move to the ghetto dependent on the social services of the community and unable to venture into the larger world of the metropolis. Nor are the impacts of inadequate southern education limited to the first generation of Negro migrants. Parents ill-equipped to adjust to complex urban patterns are unlikely to provide the support necessary for preparing children to cope with a hostile environment. The pattern can be clearly seen in the second generation's reaction to life in the ghetto. It is the children of migrants and not the migrants themselves who seem most prone to riot in the city.

Thus, education of potential migrants is of great important to both the North and South. The value of the investment is compounded by the extent to which the overall level of Negro opportunity is expanded. In the North, this is dependent on a weakening of the constricting ties of the ghetto. In the South it depends on economic development per se.

CONCLUDING THOUGHTS

This article has considered alternative strategies for the urban ghetto in light of the strong economic and social link of that community to the metropolis in which it is imbedded and to the nation as a whole. In particular the analysis has centered on the likely repercussions of "gilding programs."

Included prominently among these programs are a variety of proposals designed to attract industry to metropolitan ghettos. There have also been numerous proposals for massive expenditures on compensatory education, housing, welfare, and the like. Model Cities programs must be included under this rubric. All such proposals aim at raising the employment, incomes, and well-being of ghetto residents, *within* the existing framework of racial discrimination.

Much of the political appeal of these programs lies in their ability to attract support from a wide spectrum, ranging from white separatists, to liberals, to advocates of black power. However, there is an overriding objection to this approach. "Gilding" programs must accept as given a continued growth of Negro ghettos, ghettos which are directly or indirectly responsible for the failure of urban renewal, the crisis in central city finance, urban transportation problems, Negro unemployment, and the inadequacy of metropolitan school systems. Ghetto gilding programs, apart from being objectionable on moral grounds, accept a very large cost in terms of economic inefficiency, while making the solution of many social problems inordinately difficult.

A final objection is that such programs may not work at all, if pursued in isolation. The ultimate result of efforts to increase Negro incomes or reduce Negro unemployment in central city ghettos may be simply to induce a much higher rate of migration of Negroes from southern rural areas. This will accelerate the already rapid growth of black ghettos, complicating the already impressive list of urban problems.

Recognition of the migration link between northern ghettos and southern rural areas has led in recent months to proposals to subsidize economic development, educational opportunities, and living standards in rural areas. It is important to clarify the valuable, but limited, contributions well-designed programs of this kind can make to the problems of the metropolitan ghetto. Antimigration and migrant improvement programs cannot in themselves improve conditions in northern ghettos. They cannot overcome the prejudice, discrimination, low incomes, and lack of education that are the underlying "causes" of ghetto unrest. At best they are complementary to programs intended to deal directly with ghetto problems. Their greatest value would be in permitting an aggressive assault on the problems of the ghetto—their role is that of a counterweight which permits meaningful and large scale programs within metropolitan areas.

What form should this larger effort take? It would seem that ghetto dispersal is the only strategy that promises a long run solution. In support of this contention we have identified three important arguments:

1. None of the other programs will reduce the distortions of metropolitan growth and loss of efficiency that result from the continued rapid expansion of "massive" Negro ghettos in metropolitan areas.
2. Ghetto dispersal programs would generally lower the costs of achieving many objectives that are posited by ghetto improvement or gilding schemes.
3. As between ghetto gilding and ghetto dispersal strategies, only the latter is consistent with stated goals of American society.

The conclusion is straightforward. What alternatives exist, and it has been a major effort of this article to show that they do exist, considerable weight must be placed on their differential impact on the ghetto. Programs that tend to strengthen this segregated pattern should generally be rejected in favor of programs that achieve the same objectives while weakening the ghetto. Such a strategy is not only consistent with the nation's long run goals, but will often be substantially cheaper in the short run.

Part IV

Analysis of Urban Housing Markets

Chapter Ten

The NBER Urban Simulation Model as a Theory of Urban Spatial Structure

with Gregory K. Ingram

Two major approaches to representing patterns of urban spatial development and residential location have emerged in the past two decades. First, a number of concise analytical models of urban residential location and urban spatial structure have been developed and explored in the literature.[1] These models, which we refer to in this chapter as traditional theories of residential location and urban spatial structure, are formulated in the calculus, treat a highly idealized urban area, and have strong basis in the utility maximizing postulates of economic theory. Second, numerous simulation models of residential location or land use have been developed. Typically these models are formulated as computer logarithms, represent a particular city, and have little or no theoretical content or structure.[2]

Both the analytical and the simulation models have serious deficiencies when they are appraised as tools for analyzing urban development patterns, for investigating the behavior of urban housing markets, or for evaluating urban programs and policy. The analytical models are relatively straightforward and easy to manipulate and understand, but their clarity is paid for in terms of unrealistic and often misleading restrictive assumptions. For example, traditional theories of urban spatial structure usually assume that all production and employment occurs in a single center in an urban area, that the standing stock of physical capital is perfectly malleable and does not influence the long run equilibrium solutions obtained, and that interdependencies among decision-makers are minimal or nonexistent. Since such assumptions are strongly at variance with conditions found in urban areas throughout the world, traditional models are of limited value either as explanations of urban phenomena or as guides to public policy. (We recognize that the authors of these traditional theories would be the first to counsel caution in drawing policy conclusions from their analyses. Yet we are equally persuaded that these models are widely used in this way, often unconsciously.)

213

The simulation models usually relax one or more of the restrictive assumptions used in the analytical models, but they also typically abandon the theoretical structure and behavioral relations that distinguish the analytical models. The form of many simulation models, instead, reflects relations that are consistent with the data used in calibrating the model. At best, some of these models can be viewed as reduced form estimates of behavioral structures that are not specified; at worst, they are collections of spurious, accidental, or temporary relations between variables. In the latter case, the models have no content at all; in the former, they are useful only as long as the underlying behavioral structure is unaltered. Since their structure is poorly specified, their value even as forecasting tools is questionable.

For the past three years, the National Bureau of Economic Research has been sponsoring studies that focus on the determinants of urban spatial structure. A major goal of the NBER studies is the development of an urban model that can be used for policy analysis.[3]

The urban simulation model that has been developed at the NBER incorporates the theoretical approach of traditional analytic models of residential location and urban spatial structure into a framework with more realistic and less restrictive assumptions.[4] First, the NBER model relaxes the monocentric assumption of the analytic models and explicitly incorporates multiple workplaces. The assumption that urban areas have a single center is analytically convenient but inconsistent with the growth pattern of many cities in this century. Second, it abandons the long run equilibrium framework used in the analytic models. By treating only long run equilibrium, analytic models can ignore the standing stock of physical capital and the processes of adjustment of the supply side. Since buildings are heterogeneous, durable, and expensive to alter, ignoring their effect on development patterns considerably reduces the credibility of the analytic models. To overcome this weakness, the NBER model represents the standing stock of physical capital in the metropolitan area and incorporates the supply side of the housing market in detail. Finally, some preliminary steps have been taken to represent the interactions among decisionmakers in the housing market. Neighborhood quality has been introduced as a dimension of the housing bundle, and racial discrimination will soon be incorporated in the model.

Relaxing the assumptions of the analytic models has definite costs in terms of clarity and ease of manipulation. Several attempts have been made to develop more complex models using the calculus, but such models often cannot be solved analytically, and numerical solution techniques are employed to obtain results. Of course, simulation models are also solved by numerical manipulation, so they have no inherent advantage over other techniques in obtaining solutions. The NBER model has been developed using computer simulation techniques because we believe that simulation is more flexible and easier to use for constructing complex models than other possible methods of analysis.

A BRIEF MODEL OUTLINE

The NBER urban simulation model is primarily a model of urban housing markets. It represents other urban phenomena, such as industry location and changes in the demographic structure of the population, but the behavior of housing consumers, suppliers, and the "market" are its central concerns. For this reason, it is convenient to describe the model in terms of a demand sector, a supply sector, and a market clearing sector.

The demand sector of the NBER model represents changes in the level and mix of employment at each of several workplaces, the decisions of households to move, and the choice of housing bundles by households. The supply sector of the model represents changes in the quality of the standing stock of units; alterations of the standing stock through additions, subdivision, or combination; and the construction of new units on vacant land. The market clearing sector then matches households that have chosen each type of housing bundle with the available supply of each type of bundle and alters the expected prices of each housing bundle in each residence zone in a manner that reflects both demand and supply conditions. The activities in each of the three sectors are carried out in one or more of the seven submodels that make up the overall model. A brief description of the seven submodels is shown in Figure 10–1, and the relation of the submodels to the demand, supply, and market clearing sectors is shown in Figure 10–2.

The NBER urban simulation model has a number of distinctive characteristics. First, existing distributions of activities in the metropolitan area influence the pattern of metropolitan development because only a portion of households relocate and only a portion of the existing stock of dwelling units and vacant land is available for alteration or new construction during each time period. Adjustments in employment and residential locations, alterations to the housing stock, and changes in the distribution of worktrips are produced in an incremental fashion. This approach can be contrasted with that of other simulation models and with all analytical models, which locate the entire population at once to produce target year solutions. Second, although the model incorporates a market clearing sector, the demand for each type of housing is not made exactly equal to the supply of each type during each time period. Individual housing submarkets can have either an excess supply of units (high frictional vacancies) or an excess demand. Disequilibria in individual submarkets influence expected prices, which in turn produce countervailing supply responses in subsequent periods. Finally, the model produces expected prices for each type of housing in each residence zone during each period. These prices influence the behavior of households in the demand sector of the model and of firms in the supply sector.

Most of the variables within the model are represented by discrete categories rather than continuous distributions. For example, within the model

---

EMPLOYMENT LOCATION SUBMODEL

Revise level and composition of employment at each workplace and by each of nine industry types. Translate employment changes by industry to changes in employee characteristics.

MOVERS SUBMODEL

Generate households vacating housing units, and modify them to produce households seeking housing this period.

VACANCY SUBMODEL

Generate vacancies in housing stock created in intermetropolitan moves, outmigration, and household dissolution by residence zone and house type.

DEMAND ALLOCATION SUBMODEL

Combine transportation costs from work zones to residence zones with expected housing prices to form gross housing prices. Form expected gross housing prices by workplace for each housing type. Allocate households to housing types with demand equations and expected gross prices.

FILTERING SUBMODEL

Change quality classification of available housing stock according to quality premiums derived from expected prices and exogenous maintenance costs.

SUPPLY SUBMODEL

Calculate profitability of construction and transformation activities from expected prices and exogenous building costs. Perform stock transformation according to profit levels and several constraints.

MARKET CLEARING SUBMODEL

Match moving households to available units of the type chosen by households in the Demand Allocation Submodel. Each house type or submarket is solved separately. Shadow prices are used to generate prices for the next time period. Worktrip patterns are updated.

Figure 10-1. Block Diagram of Submodels as Encountered in NBER Model

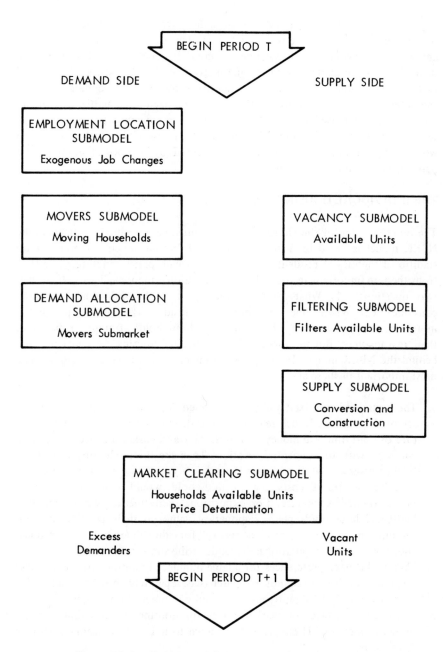

Figure 10-2. Relation of Submodels to Demand, Supply, and Market Clearing Sectors

space is represented by a system of zones. One set of zones represents workplaces and another the residential areas. The zonal systems are congruent, and workplace zones consist of one or more residence zones. Transportation detail is then summarized in interzonal matrices of travel costs, worktrips, and travel times. Housing bundles are identified by type, depending on their characteristics, and the housing stock is summarized in a matrix defined by housing type and residential location. Households are similarly categorized by several attributes and are summarized in a matrix defined by household class and workplace location. Finally, time is represented by a series of discrete time periods, each assumed to be one year in length.

THE INDIVIDUAL HOUSING CONSUMER

The representation of the choices made by individual housing consumers in the NBER model is based on a theory of demand that has much in common with traditional theories of residential location and urban spatial structure, yet differs from them in important respects. Like the traditional theories, it seeks to answer two questions: (1) What kind of housing does the individual household consume? (2) Where does the household reside? The theory postulates, moreover, that in answering these questions households attempt to maximize their real incomes. But the theory of the individual housing consumer that lies behind the NBER model also employs a number of additional assumptions. The most important of these are:

1. The household has fixed and predetermined demands for travel to a known set of destinations. Since reaching these destinations requires the expenditure of both time and money on travel, the travel costs for a given household will vary with its residential location. To make the model operational, we further assume that the journey to work accounts for most of the spatial variation in travel costs that a household would make to reach its predetermined workplace. For expositional convenience, we assume that individual households place a monetary value on their travel time. This assumption is not strictly necessary for the theory, but it reduces enormously the computational demands of the simulation model.
2. Households have preferences for a large number of housing attributes. These attributes ordinarily cannot be purchased separately, but are available in combinations that are represented as a finite number of housing bundles.
3. There exist surfaces of market prices for housing bundles that vary by residence location. These prices are known to individual consumers who are pricetakers.

The first of the specific assumptions, which is analogous to, but less restrictive than, the monocentric assumption (the convention followed in traditional theories of assuming that all employment is located at a single center), allows an important and powerful simplication. Since we assume that the household makes a fixed set of trips to predetermined locations, and that households impute a monetary value to their travel time, housing prices and travel costs are merely alternative kinds of expenditures that a household may make to acquire particular housing bundles. For each housing bundle, and for each household, a surface of gross prices can then be defined as

$$GP_{h,i,j,k,m} = P_{k,i} + V_h \times (H_{i,j,m}) + C_m \times (M_{i,j,m}) \tag{10.1}$$

where

GP = monthly gross prices
P = monthly bundle prices
V = values of travel time per hour
H = hours of travel per month
C = out-of-pocket costs per mile
M = the miles of travel per month
h = households
i = residential locations
j = travel destinations (workplaces)
m = travel modes
k = housing bundles

The definition of gross prices enables us to formulate the question of "Where does the household locate?" into a cost-minimization problem. Since all the housing attributes of interest to the consumer are included in the definition of the housing bundle, k, the optimal location of a given type of housing bundle for the household is that location where the gross price of the bundle is a minimum.

Furthermore, these minimum gross prices are the appropriate housing prices for use in answering the question: What kind of housing does the housing consumer choose? The answer to this problem can be derived by the use of more or less traditional demand analysis. The household's choice of a housing bundle is a function of its income, tastes, and the minimum gross prices of each of the housing bundles. The analysis of the demand for housing bundles differs from more traditional analysis only in terms of the side condition (an expectation rather than a requirement) that each household choose only a single bundle.

Although we do not consider the issue at any length in this chapter, it should be noted that the theory of the individual housing consumer outlined above also provides a basis for analyzing the household's choice of journey to work travel modes. Equation (10.1) incorporates the travel time and costs of each travel mode. For any housing bundle and residence location there exists a least cost method of commuting to and from work that may differ by both workplace and the household's value of time. This statement of the problem makes it apparent that the choices of travel mode, housing bundle, and residence location are highly interdependent and that all three choices depend heavily on the household's workplace.

SOME SIMPLE ANALYTICS

The use of gross prices makes it relatively easy to examine the effect that alternative workplace locations and variations in travel costs have upon the types of housing consumed and the selection of residential locations by urban households. Some geometric examples are useful in illustrating the power of this simple theory of individual housing consumers.[5]

Assume that there exists a hypothetical urban region comprised of many workplaces with gradients of bundle prices such as those shown in Figure 10–3. The origin of Figure 10–3 refers to an employment centroid at which, by coincidence, the prices of all bundles are highest. The housing bundle price gradients shown in Figure 10–3 resemble the location rent gradients obtained or used in traditional theories in that they decline with distance from the employment centroid (in more traditional theories this corresponds to the single employment location). Not too much should be made of these simplifying assumptions, however. They are not required by the theory and are employed merely to simplify the diagrams. The framework itself can accommodate metropolitan surfaces of bundle prices of any shape or complexity. Indeed, one

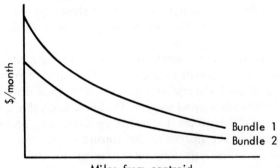

Figure 10-3. House Prices

important use of the NBER model is as a tool to examine the implications of complex surfaces of bundle prices for consumer behavior.

The prices shown in Figure 10–3 are what might be termed net housing prices. To obtain gross prices it is necessary to add the household's monthly travel costs to the bundle prices. Figure 10–4 graphs monthly travel costs of two households employed at the employment centroid, drawn on the assumption that journey to work costs are the only elements of monthly travel costs that vary with residence location, and that Household A has a higher travel cost per mile (hour) than Household B. For example, Household A might have two members employed at the centroid and Household B only one.

In Figure 10–5, we add the bundle prices and transport costs to obtain gross price surfaces for Households A and B. From Figure 10–5 it is apparent (1) that there is a minimum cost location for each household type and

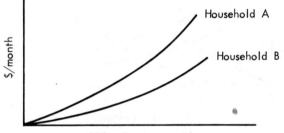

Figure 10-4. Travel Costs

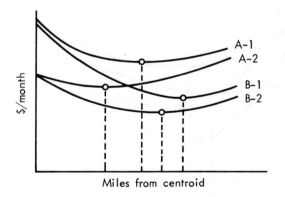

Figure 10-5. Gross Prices

each bundle, and (2) that the household with higher monthly travel costs will face higher gross prices and live closer to work within each bundle type. This does not mean, however, that Household B will in fact live farther from work than A. As is evident from Figure 10–5, this conclusion will hold only if Households A and B choose the same housing bundle.

In Figures 10–6 and 10–7 we illustrate the gross price computations for Household A and a third household, C, which has the same travel costs per

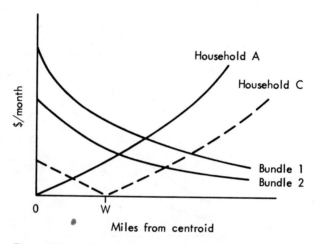

Figure 10-6.   House Prices and Travel Costs for Two Workplaces

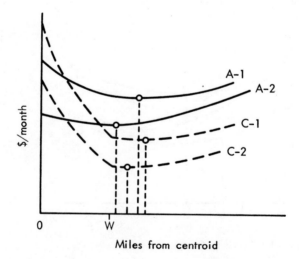

Figure 10-7.   Gross Prices for Two Workplaces

mile as Household A but is employed at an outlying workplace, W, rather than the employment centroid. The curves shown in Figure 10–6 and 10–7 illustrate several important propositions: (1) the gross prices of each bundle type will differ for otherwise identical households employed at a central and an outlying workplace; (2) Households A and C, if they consume the same housing bundle (which is unlikely), will live at different residence locations and travel different distances to and from work; (3) relative gross prices will differ for the Households A and C; indeed the gross prices do not even have the same ordinal rankings.

The above analysis, simple though it may be, illustrates that a number of important and quite specific conclusions and predictions can be obtained from our model if a few parameters can be specified in even general terms. These parameters are (1) preferences or demands of households with different sociodemographic characteristics for different bundles; (2) the general shapes of bundle price surfaces within urban regions; and (3) the variation in monthly travel costs by households with differing socioeconomic-demographic characteristics. If even crude answers can be obtained for these questions (and we believe reasonable answers can be provided), the theory of the individual housing consumer can provide useful, quite specific, and testable hypotheses about the behavior of housing consumers.

DETERMINATION OF HOUSING PRICES AND QUANTITIES

Traditional theories of residential location and urban spatial structure are not concerned solely with the behavior of individual consumers. Indeed, for most of these theories the behavior of individual households is clearly of secondary interest, and a few of them do not consider the location decisions of individual households at all. The central focus of most traditional theories of urban spatial structure is on providing explanations of observed spatial variations in land values or location rents and patterns of population density within urban regions.

In our formulation of the problem, the parallel aggregate questions are: (1) How are the bundle prices, which the individual consumer takes as given, determined in the market? (2) What are the adjustment mechanisms that provide for changes in the bundle prices and for changes in the number and location of various types of housing bundles?

In seeking to answer these questions, the NBER model and its theoretical underpinnings abandon the long run equilibrium framework employed in all traditional theories of residential location and urban spatial structure. Traditional models assume that a full adjustment of the capital stock occurs in response to changes in incomes, tastes, and technology. Although we recognize the usefulness of simplifying assumptions in theory building, we fear the resort to long run equilibrium may miss the essence of urban phenomena. Metropolitan areas are composed of capital stocks that are extremely durable and expensive to modify. In addition, the moving costs of both households and firms are often large. Finally, the long run equilibrium of an area changes over time as incomes rise, tastes change, the transport system is altered, and new technologies are introduced. A more appropriate characterization of urban areas would be that they are in disequilibrium and that their path of adjustment is dependent on the particular configuration of their existing capital stocks as well as on many other factors. Moreover, once the interdependence in the location decisions of households, firms, and other decision units is acknowledged, there is a substantial possibility that a stable long run equilibrium might not exist.[6]

For these reasons, and for others explained subsequently, we explicitly reject the concept of long run equilibrium as it applies to urban housing markets. Therefore, the NBER model includes stocks of durable capital and a market mechanism that allows transformations in these stocks to occur over time. Hence, the NBER model is capable of providing some description of the stock adjustment processes, although it would be incorrect to claim that the NBER model is fully dynamic.

Although the characterization of supply adjustments in the NBER model differs in important respects from those employed in traditional theories of residential location and urban spatial structure, there are also important common elements. For example, both the NBER model and the traditional theories assume that housing production is responsive to market demands and prices, and that individual housing suppliers are pricetakers in both factor and output markets. Moreover, both theories assume that housing is produced by profit-maximizing firms.

As was true of the theory of the individual consumer, however, the NBER urban simulation model employs some specific assumptions that differentiate it in important respects from traditional theories. The most important of these are:

1. Housing outputs are heterogenous and produced using combinations of existing durable structures, current inputs, and neighborhood attributes.
2. Most of the supply in each market period is produced from used structures. Only a small fraction of each period's supply involves new construction and the production of customized bundles.
3. Many important housing attributes are not produced by competitive firms. Some of these attributes are produced by the actions of local governments; some by the interaction of local government services with neighborhood residents; some by the aggregate location and investment decisions of individual households and firms; and some may be inherent characteristics of particular locations. This aspect of housing bundles places important

constraints on the production possibilities available to individual housing suppliers.

To examine the implications of these specific assumptions, it is useful to classify the attributes of housing bundles into two general categories: (1) attributes of the dwelling unit or structure, and (2) attributes of the neighborhood, including the socioeconomic and demographic structure of the neighborhood; the density and other physical aspects of the neighborhood as a whole; and the types and quality of local public services provided to dwelling units in the neighborhood. Traditional theories of demand ignore neighborhood attributes entirely, although a few efforts have been made to examine the impact of variations in government services and tax rates on patterns of housing demand.[7]

A number of the most important differences between the NBER model and traditional theories of urban spatial structure arise from their respective definitions of housing output and the nature of housing production relationships implied by these different definitions. The best way to illustrate the differences in production relationships used in traditional theories and in the NBER model is to describe the production functions employed in each. Traditional models employ a housing production function, such as that illustrated by Equation (10.2):

$$H_i = f(L_i, N) \tag{10.2}$$

where

H = housing outputs
L = quantities of land
N = nonland factors of production
i = specific locations.

The production function employed in the NBER urban simulation model is depicted by Equation (10.3):

$$B_i = f(S_i, L_i, N, O, G_i, A_i, P_i) \tag{10.3}$$

where

B = particular bundles
S = durable structures of well-defined characteristics
L = vacant land
N = nonland factors of production

O = current outlays (operating costs)
G = local public services
A = physical attributes of the neighborhood
P = the sociodemographic characteristics of the neighborhood population
i = specific locations.

Individual housing suppliers can do little, if anything, about the production of the last three attributes within built-up areas, and there are limits on their ability to produce them even when they develop vacant tracts. Therefore, our discussion of the behavior of housing suppliers will be limited to the first four input variables.

If we abstract, for the moment, from the problem of neighborhood attributes, the housing-production function implied by Equation (10.3) can be represented by an input-output format, such as the one shown in Table 10–1. The statistics in Table 10–1 give the incremental cost of producing a particular output bundle using a particular input bundle. These costs summarize the least cost method of achieving each particular transformation by the most efficient technology and, of course, assume a particular set of factor prices. A change in factor prices could alter both the incremental cost and the technology used.

The cost of input bundles accounts for a significant part of the cost of producing a particular output bundle. The NBER model calculates market prices by bundle type and location, and these prices are used in the model along with transformation costs to compute a supply price for each type of bundle in each residence area. As inspection of Table 10–1 makes clear, there are potentially n different supply prices for each output bundle in each area corresponding to the n input bundles. Moreover, in those areas where vacant land is available, each output bundle can be produced on vacant land. Its supply prices would be equal to the cost of new construction for that bundle type, shown in Table 10–1, plus the price of the vacant building lot.

TABLE 10–1. Transportation Cost Array (1968 dollars)

Dwelling Unit Input	Dwelling Unit Output						
	1	*2*	*3*	. . .	. . .	*19*	*20*
1	0	7460	17470	. . .	. . .	68300	500600
2	1580	0	10010	. . .	. . .	68700	501000
3	2090	1680	0	. . .	. . .	. . .	501400
. . .	. . .	. . .	. . .	. . .	. . .	. . .	. . .
. . .	. . .	. . .	. . .	. . .	. . .	. . .	. . .
18	5470	5530	. . .	. . .	. . .	18800	504200
19	20520	26740	35080	. . .	. . .	0	0
20	66400	72660	81000	. . .	. . .	123600	0
Land	10440	16660	25000	. . .	. . .	67680	500000

The transformation costs and the prices of land and bundles by location guide the actions of housing suppliers. Since the NBER model assumes a competitive housing industry, changes in the quantities of various bundles at various locations result from the efforts of competitive firms to maximize profits. Housing suppliers make their investment and production decisions on the basis of expected revenues and transformation costs. Their revenue calculations are based, in turn, on the market prices for existing bundles and vacant land.

This formulation of the problem makes it clear that housing production requires both durable structures and current outlays. Specific types of durable structure can be transformed into other types of durable structures by transformations that are represented as specific input-output activities. We are unable to fully explore the implications of this feature of housing production functions at this time, but it is clear that the explicit recognition of the role of spatially distributed stocks of durable, heterogeneous housing capital in these housing production relationships has profound effects on the composition of housing output and even greater effects on its location.

As mentioned above, there are many housing attributes that competitive firms cannot produce. The definitions of housing bundles used in the NBER model include neighborhood attributes and they are fully represented in the theory of demand. On the supply side, however, the treatment of neighborhood attributes is incomplete. In current versions of the NBER model, the locations of neighborhood attributes must be specified exogenously, although the number of units having particular neighborhood attributes does change in response to changes in demand and expected prices. As discussed in the final section of this chapter, we are now attempting to modify the design of the NBER model to make the location of several neighborhood attributes endogenous.

MARKET CLEARING AND
PRICE DETERMINATION

The theories of the individual housing consumers and housing producers that lie behind the demand and supply sectors of the NBER urban simulation model are firmly rooted in neoclassical comparative static theories of house-hold demand and of the firm. Although these constructs are enormously valuable, they take us only part of the way to our objective of producing a dynamic theory of the urban housing markets. To achieve this objective, these micro theories of household and firm behavior must be imbedded in a framework capable of providing a way (1) to match the demand for and supply of housing bundles during each market period and (2) to modify the market prices that guide the future consumption and production decisions of house-holds and firms.

The heart of the market clearing and price determination sector of the NBER model is a rather novel application of linear programming that simultaneously matches demands and supplies in each housing submarket and provides information that can be used to alter the market prices of housing bundles in each residence zone. The approach used in the NBER model follows closely the theory of the individual housing consumer presented previously; in particular it exploits the important distinction that theory makes between the household's choices of housing bundle and its choice of residence location.

The household's selection of a housing bundle is represented in the NBER model by econometrically estimated demand functions for housing bundles. These equations express the probability that a particular household will consume a particular type of housing as a function of the household's socioeconomic-demographic characteristics (tastes and income) and the minimum gross price of each bundle for that household. Solution of these housing bundle demand functions gives the number of persons employed at each workplace who will demand each type of housing bundle.

The demands for each housing bundle by workplace are summed to produce an aggregate regionwide demand for each type of housing bundle during each time period. The building industry attempts to produce enough bundles of each type to satisfy these target demands. Decisions about which kinds of bundles to produce and where to produce them depend on the criterion of profit maximation. The efforts of firms to satisfy the excess demands for each housing bundle in the most profitable manner produces a supply of bundles by type and location.

At this point in the model, the number of housing bundles of each type available in each residence location is fixed, and the use of the comparative static theory of the individual consumer to match demands and supplies begins to break down. Once a household has selected the housing bundle it wishes to consume, the theory states that the household will locate in that zone where the gross price of its chosen type of bundle is a minimum. But since the supplies of each type of bundle in each zone are fixed, the demand of households for particular locations may exceed the supply of bundles of the requisite type that are available there. Therefore, the notion of households competing for these desirable locations must be introduced into the model.

Spatial competition among households competing in the same housing submarket for bundles located in residence zones accessible to their workplaces is represented in the NBER model by a linear programming algorithm. The objective function of this programming problem, which is specified as one of the Hitchcock type, is the minimization of aggregate travel expenditures of all households competing in the same housing submarket. Since travel to and from work is the only component of a household's travel costs included in the model, within each housing submarket the programming problem obtains the least cost matching of the demands of households with known workplaces to the supplies of housing bundles available at each residence location. (Although the objective function in the current model minimizes travel costs, it may be more correct to minimize gross prices within each housing submarket. Altering the objective function would not dramatically transform the structure of the NBER model. Needless to say, such a change might be quite important in terms of the theoretical integrity of the model.)

Because each submarket or housing bundle type is solved separately, the linear programming problems produce shadow prices for each bundle type in each residence zone. These shadow prices are translated into location rents that in turn are used to alter the expected market prices of each housing bundle in each residence location.

CURRENT STATUS OF THE NBER MODEL
AND PLANNED EXTENSIONS

While we have made significant progress in developing a computer analog of our theoretical view of urban housing markets, in many respects the existing versions of the NBER model are still incomplete representations of the theory. We are attempting to improve and extend the model in a number of ways. Some of the improvements have long been on our model-building agenda; others reflect presumed increases in our theoretical understanding of urban housing markets and of the problems of developing a satisfactory analytical representation of these markets and related urban phenomena.

Our first attempt to calibrate the NBER urban simulation model used data from Detroit and San Francisco,[8] but we encountered serious problems. Although the crude calibration achieved for the Detroit prototype allowed us to test some aspects of design model, it would not support further model development. Therefore, when more suitable data became available for Pittsburgh, we shifted development of the NBER model to this Pittsburgh data base. Ingram made significant progress in calibrating a second version of the model to Pittsburgh data, but satisfactory estimates of the crucial submarket demand equations (bundle demand equations) remained as much a goal as an accomplishment.[9] We are now engaged simultaneously in major efforts to solve these estimation problems and to extend and elaborate the model's structure. These improvements in parameter estimation and model design will form the basis for the third version of the NBER model, Pittsburgh II.

It is impossible at this time to fully describe Pittsburgh II, since its final structure will depend both on econometric studies that are currently underway and on further experimentation with Pittsburgh I. We are certain, however, that Pittsburgh II will hew closely to the theoretical constructs discussed in this chapter. Our experience with the Detroit prototype and Pittsburgh I and the findings of our econometric research on urban housing markets have made us more confident of the theory underlying the NBER

Model. Moreover, we are reasonably certain of a number of lines of model development. For example, we are convinced that neighborhood characteristics should be included as part of the definitions of housing submarkets. Pittsburgh I contains the modifications in model design and programming needed to accommodate this change, and Pittsburgh II will incorporate a far larger number of neighborhood types than Pittsburgh I.

The variables most likely to be used to describe neighborhoods in Pittsburgh II are (1) the average quality or value of dwelling units in the neighborhood, (2) the average socioeconomic status of the residents of the neighborhood, and (3) some measure of neighborhood density, such as net residential density or the percentage of units that are single family. It should be possible to make a neighborhood classification scheme based on these three characteristics endogenous to the model. A classification of neighborhoods by density or dwelling unit quality could be modified over time within the model in response to new construction, transformations, and demolitions in each zone. Similarly, indices of socioeconomic status could be altered by neighborhood in response to the moving and relocation decisions of households.

The use of more types of neighborhoods is appealing on several grounds. For a given number of residential zones, the use of a larger number of neighborhood types reduces the maximum size of the linear programming problems that must be solved by the market clearing submodel. Since 80 percent or more of the running time of the Detroit prototype and Pittsburgh I is accounted for by these linear programming problems, and since the largest problems account for nearly all the program solution running time, the gains from using more neighborhood categories may be quite large.

Even more significant is the promise that housing types defined by more extensive neighborhood characteristics may allow us to increase substantially the number of residential zones. Use of a larger number of residential zones would allow us to define more homogeneous neighborhoods and provide a much more precise description of the bundle price surfaces. The advantages of greater zonal detail and more homogeneous neighborhoods for most planning and policy applications of the model are obvious.

The computational efficiency of this approach will be even greater if the use of a larger number of neighborhood types permits us to use a smaller number of house types within each neighborhood type. This trade-off is evident already from a comparison of the Detroit prototype and Pittsburgh I. In the former, each zone potentially contains 27 structure types; in the latter, no zone may contain more than 20 structure types. Although these lines of development must still be regarded as somewhat tentative, they appear to have considerable promise.

Definition and use of additional neighborhood types is also a promising method of incorporating housing market discrimination and variations in the level and quality of local public services in the model, since both may be thought of as characterizing neighborhoods in particular ways. That the racial composition of particular neighborhoods strongly influences the location choices by both black and white households can hardly be doubted.[10]

Racial discrimination could be represented in the NBER model in several ways. The approach we now favor would apply price markups and discounts to the bundle prices paid by white and nonwhite households in particular residence areas. These premiums and discounts would modify the minimum gross prices of various bundles for both white and nonwhite households and thereby affect their choice among housing bundles. In the assignment model, moreover, travel to certain zones would become more costly for white or black households.

A more elaborate neighborhood classification scheme may also be the most promising method of representing variations in local public services, such as schools, in the NBER model. The major obstacle to the introduction of local public services into the model is not computer or programming limitations. Instead, the chief obstacle is the lack of any good empirical evidence on the independent effect of public schools or other public services on the housing choices of urban households. This question has been a major issue in NBER econometric studies of the housing market. The findings, however, are quite inconclusive, and more research is required to isolate the determinants of neighborhood quality and their effects on the housing choices of various classes of households. Preliminary investigations in this area suggest that neighborhood attributes are highly correlated. Residential zones with high income levels typically also have good schools, few dilapidated structures, and a low proportion of rental units. Existing data have not permitted us to isolate the effects of public services from other aspects of neighborhood quality.

In addition to probable changes in the definition of housing types and the use of a larger number of residence zones, Pittsburgh II will also incorporate a number of less substantial modifications. First, Pittsburgh II will treat population-serving employment endogenously. The most likely formulation would make the level of population-serving employment depend on the levels of population and basic employment in each zone. At the same time, workers employed in the outlying, predominantly residential zones will be included in the model. Such workers are excluded from both the Detroit prototype and Pittsburgh I. These workers probably will be allocated to available units in nearby zones before the linear programming model is used to allocate workers employed in major workplaces to the remaining supply of available units.

A more detailed representation of the land market is still another high priority extension of the model. Pittsburgh II will include a primitive representation of the nonresidential land market. In both the Detroit prototype and Pittsburgh I, all land used for nonresidential purposes must be specified exogenously in each period. For example, the demolition of residential structures required by nonresidential expansion must be specified exogenously.

Pittsburgh II will include a simple nonresidential expansion function that will remove residential structures in zones where there is a substantial expansion of nonresidential land uses and limited amounts of vacant land available.

CONCLUSION

In this chapter we have attempted to provide a brief description of the NBER urban simulation model and to sketch the outlines of the theory of urban spatial structure that underlies the model. Because this theory relaxes many of the restrictive assumptions embodied in traditional theories, we believe that it offers a more promising approach to many challenging problems in urban economics than the more traditional analytic theories. This does not mean that there is no place for analytical methods in urban economics. The NBER model and its theoretical structure is substantially indebted to these methods and the models that employ them. Indeed, in many ways the NBER model can be viewed as a generalization of the theory used in traditional analytic models of residential location and urban spatial structure. Still, we are strongly persuaded that an excessive reliance on traditional analytical models has limited urban economics and has channeled it along some misleading and unproductive paths.

Computer simulation models are not a panacea, but they do offer the potential for removing many of the barriers to the development of a more pertinent urban economic theory. Of course, many questions about the calibration and validation of computer simulation models must be resolved. These questions are not very different from those that should be asked of any theory. However, because computer simulation models tend to be more complex and make greater efforts to achieve "realism" than simple analytic models, these questions are more often asked of computer simulation models.

We believe current versions of the NBER model should be viewed as a preliminary effort to write down a relatively complex theory of urban spatial structure. It is not a realistic depiction of any city, nor has its overall structure been validated. Indeed, as we make clear in this discussion, the NBER model is even an incomplete representation of the theory it seeks to represent. Our experience in developing the model has persuaded us that urban economics will make more rapid progress when more economists begin to exploit computer simulation techniques to extend and enrich urban economic theory.

Chapter Eleven

Cumulative Urban Growth and Urban Density Functions

with David Harrison, Jr.

INTRODUCTION

Economists have long been interested in explaining urban spatial structure, i.e., the location and density of residential and nonresidential activity in urban areas and their spatial linkages. Because of the widespread availability of information on the level of population by geographic subareas for large numbers of cities at different points in time, much of their attention has focused on population density gradients, that is, the functional relationship between population density and distance from the center of the city. Colin Clark provided the first systematic empirical analysis of these density gradients and suggested the use of the negative exponential function to describe the decline in population densities with distance from the urban center.[1] Numerous authors have attempted to provide theoretical explanations of these empirical regularities, and Edwin Mills and Richard Muth have both made some effort to use density functions to test their models of urban spatial structure.[2]

All of these economic models of urban spatial structure explain observed differences in the intensity of land use by distance from the center by using a framework which explains the gradients as resulting from equilibrium adjustments to changes in the level of employment in the urban core, commuting costs, and family incomes. We propose an alternative model which emphasizes the durability of residential and nonresidential capital and the "disequilibrium" nature of urban growth.[3] This alternative model depicts urban growth as a layering process and urban spatial structure at any point of time as the result of a cumulative process spanning decades. Current levels of population, commuting costs, transport costs, and other factor prices determine the density of development during this period, but the density of past and future development depends on the level of these variables during those time periods. In this chapter we also demonstrate how this model of cumulative growth can be

233

used to generate plausible density functions for U.S. metropolitan areas. We thereby illustrate that an alternative model, markedly different in its assumptions and implications, provides at least as good an explanation of these widely studied phenomena as traditional theories of urban spatial structure.

THE DENSITY OF RESIDENTIAL DEVELOPMENT

Our model of urban spatial structure represents urban densities at any point in time as resulting from cumulative urban development spanning decades. The density of a particular urban area at a point in time, as Equation (11.1) illustrates, is then the sum of the density of development in each time period.

$$D_t = \frac{d_0 u_0 + d_1 u_1 + \cdots + d_t u_t}{u_0 + u_1 + \cdots + u_t} = \sum_{i=0}^{t} d_i u_i \bigg/ \sum_{i=0}^{t} u_i , \qquad (11.1)$$

where

D_t = average net residential density of the metropolitan area at time period t
d_i = net residential density of the dwelling units added to the area in time period i (number of dwelling units added minus demolitions and conversions ÷ change in land devoted to residential uses)
u_i = number of dwelling units added to the area in time period i.

Equation (11.1) shifts the emphasis from total residential density at one point in time to the density of each of the various increments to the housing stock added in successive time periods. The major difference between our model and the dominant equilibrium models consists of our hypothesis that current spatial structure can be explained more adequately as the aggregation of historical patterns of development rather than as an equilibrium adjustment to current conditions.[4] To explain current differences in residential density among major urban areas, we need to consider the forces which have affected the density of residential development over time.

Many factors influence the density of residential development in each time period: the price of residential land, the price of nonland factors, the preferences of consumers for relatively more land (i.e., lower residential density), the per family incomes of likely purchasers, and the transportation costs incurred in locating at various positions within the metropolitan area are among the most important. The theoretical influences of these factors on urban densities are discussed in the major equilibrium models. Equation (11.2) depicts a model to explain incremental net residential density.

$$d_t = F(x_t^i, x_t^2, \cdots, x_t^n), \tag{11.2}$$

where d_t is the net residential density of the increment of the housing stock added to the metropolitan area in time period t, and the x_t^i's are the value of the above-mentioned forces in time period t. The combined effect of these forces on the decisions of those who produce and consume dwelling units determines the density of residential development in that time period.

The values of these explanatory variables will change over time, and, with them, the residential density of successive increments to the housing stock. Total residential density will change gradually in response to these changes in the determinants of net residential density. The reason for the gradual nature of changes in urban form is apparent from the definition of net residential density at the time t as depicted by Equation (11.1). Urban form changes primarily as a result of changes in the density of incremental development; and changes in the X_ts only affect incremental density. Since incremental development is only a fraction of existing development, the impact of changes in the X_ts on urban structure from one time period to the next is relatively small.

This does not mean that there is no scope for changing the density of existing development. Urban densities can be modified by the conversion, merger, or demolition of existing units. However, changes of this kind historically have had only a limited impact on urban form.[5] It appears that the stocks of residential and nonresidential structures are so durable that it is usually too costly to alter them in this way. As a result, urban densities have been modified principally through new construction.

The preceding discussion suggests the principal differences in urban form among U.S. urban areas are due to differences in the timing of their development. Boston and Los Angeles are good illustrations of this principle. Critics adversely compare postwar development in Los Angeles and Phoenix with that in Boston and other northeastern cities. Yet recent growth in Boston has been more scattered and of lower density than that in Los Angeles. What gives the contrary impression is the fact that recent low density development is quantitatively so much more important in Los Angeles than in Boston. In the rapidly growing Los Angeles metropolitan area (SMSA), dwelling units constructed between 1950 and 1960 accounted for almost 40 percent of the total number of dwelling units existing in 1960. (See Figure 11–1) In the Boston metropolitan area, buildings erected between 1950 and 1960 accounted for only 16 percent of the total dwelling units in the Boston SMSA in 1960. Not all of the differences in Los Angeles's and Boston's spatial structure can be explained by their different time profiles, but much can.

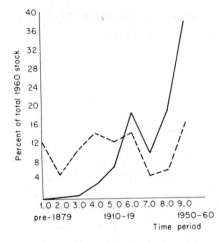

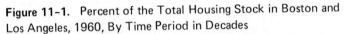

Figure 11-1. Percent of the Total Housing Stock in Boston and Los Angeles, 1960, By Time Period in Decades

EMPIRICAL TESTS

To test our model of cumulative urban growth, we estimated a series of econometric models designed to explain incremental residential density in 83 metropolitan areas over a 90 year period. These analyses require a consistent measure of the density of urban development for a large number of urban areas and over a long period of time. Net residential density (dwelling units or population per residential area) is probably the best single measure of urban form, but the required estimates of net residential density do not exist for the large numbers of cities and long time periods required by the analysis. Therefore, we used the percentage of dwelling units built in each time period made up of single family detached units (subsequently referred to as S^*) as a proxy for this more desirable measure of incremental density.[6]

For most of the 90 year period included in the analysis S^* is a reasonably adequate surrogate for net residential density. Until World War II most of the variation in net residential density among areas and over time is due to differences in the fraction of units that are single family. In the decades since World War II, when S^* approaches 100 percent in many areas, differences in average lot size become more important as a determinant of net residential density. In spite of its shortcomings, S^* is used as a measure of net residential density because Bureau of the Census data are available which permit us to estimate this proxy measure for 83 metropolitan areas and as far back as 1879.

Data problems are not limited to the dependent variable; data on transport costs, per capita incomes, and other explanatory variables were even less available. Because of these data constraints, we estimated several statistical models for different subsamples and years. The simplest of these, hereafter referred to as the basic model, contains only two variables: a time trend, used to represent secular changes in transportation costs, incomes, tastes, and the like; and metropolitan size at the beginning of the period (the total number of dwelling units) used to represent the differences in land costs among metropolitan areas. All the factors represented by the time trend are assumed to have a uniform effect on incremental net residential densities in all metropolitan areas.[7] Since most of these secular changes—i.e., higher incomes and improvements in transportation—have fostered a lower density of urban development, the value of S^* should increase over time to the present and the coefficient of the time trend should therefore be positive. All economic models of urban spatial structure indicate that land rents will be higher in larger cities.[8] Since higher land rents encourage higher density development, the coefficient of city size should be negative.

Estimates of incremental net residential density, S^*, and city size, H, were obtained from the 1940, 1950, and 1960 census of housing for 83 metropolitan areas and 13 time periods from pre–1879 to 1955–1960. The time trend variable, T, was constructed by arbitrarily assigning the pre–1879 decade a value of 1.0, the 1880–1889 decade a value of 2.0, the first half of the decade of the '50s (1950–1954) a value of 8.5, and the second half of the decade (1955–1960) a value of 9.0.

1.0	pre-1879	6.0	1925-29
2.0	1880-89	6.5	1930-34
3.0	1890-99	7.0	1935-39
4.0	1900-09	7.5	1940-44
5.0	1910-19	8.0	1945-49
5.5	1920-24	8.5	1950-54
		9.0	1955-60

All of the values of S^* and H for periods prior to 1940 are based on a cross tabulation of structure type by year built from the 1940 census of housing.

Two functional forms of this simple model were tested: the first, using the total number of dwelling units at the beginning of the period, H_{ij}, is portrayed by Equation (11.3); the second, using the logarithm of H_{ij}, is summarized by Equation (11.4). The t-test statistics are given in parentheses.

$$S_{ij}^* = 17.06 + 8.34T_i - 0.015H_{ij} \qquad R^2 = 0.678 \qquad (11.3)$$
$$\phantom{S_{ij}^* =} (16.3) \quad (47.4) \quad (-12.1)$$

$$S_{ij}^* = 25.66 + 10.58T_i - 5.99 \text{ Log } H_{ij} \qquad R^2 = 0.714 \qquad (11.4)$$
$$\phantom{S_{ij}^* =} (23.8) \quad (46.4) \quad (-17.3)$$

where

$$S_{ij}* = \frac{\text{number of single family detached units added}}{\text{total dwelling units built}} \text{ X } 100$$

T_i = time period

H_{ij} = total dwelling units (in 1000s) at the beginning of the period

Log H = log total dwelling units (in 1000s) at the beginning of the period

i = time period

j = urban area

     The linear estimates, Equation (11.3), indicate that the percentage of single family units ($S*$) added to urban areas has increased by over 8 percent each decade, when the size of the area is held constant. With time period held constant, the percentage is decreased on the average by 1.5 percent for each increase of 100,000 dwelling units. The equation using the log of city size suggests an even more pronounced secular trend toward lower residential densities. The explained variance is 68 percent in the linear formulation and 71 percent in the logarithmic formulation. Despite their simplicity, Equation (11.3) and (11.4) are powerful predictors of the incremental density of metropolitan development during each time period. The hypothesis that these equations were designed to test—namely, that differences in net residential density are due largely to the interaction of the timing of development and size of the metropolitan area—is strongly supported by these results.

ALTERNATIVE FORMULATIONS

While the basic model appears to be useful for predicting the density of residential development, the functional forms used are quite restrictive. They require both that those forces influencing urban form over time affect $S*$ equally in each decade and that the effect of city size on $S*$ be the same in every time period. In our earlier study other formulations of the model were estimated in which both these restrictions were relaxed: a brief discussion of these results is given below.[9] While these alternative formulations are conceptually preferable to the basic model, both the spirit of the analysis and the empirical results are not markedly different.

    The technological and socioeconomic forces represented by a time trend in the basic model have undoubtedly varied in a more complex manner than can be captured by a simple linear relationship. The trend toward lower density has probably been more rapid during some time periods than others. An estimate of the combined effects of those forces in each time period can be obtained by using time period dummies. The form of the model is identical to that used in Equations (11.3) and (11.4) except that the linear trend variable is replaced by 12 separate dummy variables representing each time period.

This formulation also permits us to test some a priori expectations as to the relative importance of various time periods in forming the long term secular trend toward lower density. An obvious example is concerned with the effect of the automobile on urban spatial structure. The invention and widespread adoption of the automobile is perhaps the most significant, and certainly the most frequently discussed, change in intraurban transportation that has occurred during the past century. Although mechanically powered vehicles appeared in the United States in the early 1880s, the automobile did not become an important means of transportation until the second decade of the twentieth century. There were less than half a million cars registered in 1910; by 1919 the figure had jumped to nearly seven million—almost a fifteenfold increase in ten years. Unless there were countervailing forces, this rapid change should be evident as a noticeable increase in the slope of the nonlinear time trend.

Measurement error in the dependent variable is the second major factor which we anticipated might influence the estimated time trend. As noted previously, the percent of all dwellings added during a period that are single family is not a completely satisfactory measure of incremental net residential density. In particular it does not allow for differences in lot size over time and among areas. Yet several published studies and our own research indicate average lot size does differ among metropolitan areas and over time.[10] In earlier periods, changes in residential density resulted primarily from a shift from multifamily to single family structures. However, as the percentage of single family dwelling units approaches 100 it becomes less sensitive as a measure of change in net residential density. While the trend toward lower density residential development may still be strong, our model will show a leveling off in S^* in the later time periods.

Thus, because of the presumed influence of the introduction of the automobile and the measurement errors in S^* for recent periods, we anticipated that the use of dummy variables would reveal a nonlinear low density time trend having at least two major inflection points. The slope should increase in the 1910–1919 period and should later show a tapering off, probably by the post–World War II period.

Equations (11.5) and (11.6) illustrate the results for linear and semilogarithmic specifications using time dummies.

$$S_{ij}^* = 41.8 - 6.0 \log H_{ij\pi} + 2.6d_2 + 10.2d_3 + 20.9d_4 + 34.0d_5 + 46.3d_{5.5}$$
$$+ 51.2d_{6.0} + 59.2d_{6.5} + 65.1d_{7.0\pi} + 56.4d_{7.5} + 68.8d_8 + 73.8d_{8.5}$$
$$+ 75.4d_{9.0} \qquad\qquad R^2 = 0.755 \qquad\qquad (11.5)$$

(t ratios of all coefficients but $d_2 > 5.0$; for d_2, $t = 1.4$)

$$S_{ij}^* = 34.8 - 0.016 H_{ij\pi} - 2.0d_2 + 1.1d_3 + 8.0d_4 + 18.7d_5 + 29.9d_{5.5}$$
$$+ 34.1d_{6.0} + 41.9d_{6.5} + 47.5d_{7.0} + 38.4d_{7.5} + 50.3d_8 + 54.8d_{8.5}$$
$$+ 56.1d_{9.0} \qquad\qquad R^2 = 0.726 \qquad\qquad (11.6)$$

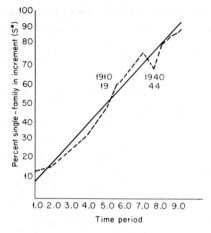

Figure 11-2. Time Trends for Areas of 100,000 Dwelling Units: Comparison of the Two Formulations

(t ratios of all coefficients exceed 4.0 except for those for d_2 and d_3; for d_2 and d_3, $t < 1.5$)

The two inflection points in the 1910–1920 period and after 1945 are evident in Figure 11–2, which compares the linear trend from Equation (11.4) with the nonlinear trend obtained from Equation (11.5). Both graphs are drawn for areas of 100,000 dwelling units.[11] While these inflection points are not necessarily due to the introduction of the automobile and the growing inadequacy of the dependent variable, the graphical results of the dummy variable formulation are very suggestive.[12]

While the dummy variable specification permits the effect of time-related forces to vary, it still requires that the effect of city size on S^* be the same in every time period. The logical next step in the analysis is to relax this assumption and allow city size ($H_{ij\pi}$) to affect S^* differently from one time period to another. This is done by estimating cross-section regressions. The form of these regressions is given by Equations (11.7) and (11.8); the empirical results for each time period are summarized in Table 11–1.

$$S_j^* = A + A^1 H_j \text{ for each time period} \tag{11.7}$$

$$S_j^* = B + B^1 \log H_j \text{ for each time period.} \tag{11.8}$$

The intercept values of both equations clearly show the strong secular trend toward lower densities. The only departures are 1940–1944 in both models and 1950–1954 in the log H model. In the log model, the values of the coefficients of log H appear to fall into three time period groups. In the

TABLE 11-1.   Cross-Section Models of Net Residential Density

Time Period	Constant	Log H	R^2	Constant	H	R^2
Pre–1879	39.2	–3.84	0.24	37.1	–0.22	0.15
1880–89	40.7	–4.15	0.21	35.1	–0.13	0.17
1890–99	49.0	–4.92	0.21	38.0	–0.070	0.17
1900–09	66.4	–7.08	0.27	44.8	–0.045	0.17
1910–19	84.6	–8.21	0.24	55.3	–0.034	0.16
1920–24	98.9	–8.58	0.28	66.2	–0.027	0.18
1925–29	110.3	–9.95	0.35	70.3	–0.024	0.24
1930–34	109.5	–7.90	0.35	77.4	–0.020	0.28
1935–39	105.5	–5.72	0.22	82.0	–0.014	0.20
1940–44	97.8	–5.93	0.12	72.9	–0.014	0.11
1945–49	114.3	–6.78	0.27	84.8	–0.014	0.27
1950–54	111.8	–5.26	0.32	88.0	–0.0096	0.31
1955–60	115.4	–5.66	0.40	89.2	–0.010	0.46
Overall R^2	.		0.74			0.76
Explained by Stratification			0.68			0.68

three periods before 1900, the coefficient of log *H* varied between 4 and 5; in the period 1900–1935 the values ranged between 7 and 10, and in the most recent period 1935–1960 they again fell into the narrow range of 6 to 7.

The much lower R^2s obtained for the individual cross-section regressions shown in Table 11–1 indicate that most of the explanatory power of the pooled regression is provided by the trend variables. Equations (11.7) and (11.8) are not, however, poorer representations of the determinants of net residential density. The appropriate comparison with the pooled regressions is not the R^2s for the individual equations, but the R^2s of all the equations considered together, including the variance explained by stratifications. The overall explained variance of Equation (11.7) is 74 percent, and for Equation (11.8) it is 76 percent. Of this total explained variance, 68 percent in both equations is accounted for by the time period stratification. Again, this illustrates that the time series variance of S^* is much larger than the cross-section variance.

INCREMENTAL DENSITY AND URBAN DENSITY FUNCTIONS

The incremental density equations provide good explanations of the average density of urban development in United States metropolitan areas. If it is assumed that urban areas grow at their periphery, these equations can be used to obtain urban density gradients.[13] A theoretical rationale for peripheral growth is provided by the importance of the central business district as the major employment center, the desire by workers to minimize commuting costs, and the external economies of urban agglomeration for most firms.

Real world exceptions to the assumption of uniform peripheral growth are commonplace, particularly in recent decades when the boundaries of many metropolitan regions have expanded to encompass previously independent cities. In addition, growth may be greater in some directions than in others because of the presence of large secondary employment centers, topographical and water barriers, and the like. Still, a simple model of urban growth and development that assumes regular peripheral growth is of considerable theoretical and empirical interest.

To estimate a gross density gradient from our incremental density model, we need only (1) to determine the size of each metropolitan area during each time period; (2) to estimate incremental density, S^*, during each time period using one of the incremental density equations—i.e., Equations (11.3) through (11.8); (3) to convert the estimated percent single family, S^*, to an estimate of gross population density, GD, the measure used in most previous analyses; (4) to estimate the number of square miles of new development in each area during each time period; and (5) to specify the number of degrees—i.e., radians—around the urban center that are available for development in each urban area. These data allow us to estimate the average gross density of development for each period and the width of the band of development during each period.

The figures shown in Table 11–2 illustrate these computations for Chicago. The values of S^* in Table 11–2 are obtained by substituting the time period and total dwelling units in Equation (11.5) (the dummy variable version).

TABLE 11–2. Illustrative Computations of Density Gradients: Chicago

Period	Total DUs	S^*	Incremental Gross Density (GD)	Area of Development (M)	Distance midpoint (r)
Pre–1879	31,002	21.2	15,505	6.8	1.0
1880–89	108,968	16.2	16,494	16.1	2.9
1890–99	284,434	18.1	16,123	37.0	4.9
1900–09	507,712	25.3	14,676	51.7	7.1
1910–19	760,001	36.0	12,514	68.5	9.3
1920–24	923,026	47.1	10,281	53.9	11.2
1925–29	1,177,005	50.5	9,584	90.1	12.9
1930–34	1,208,880	58.4	7,996	13.6	14.1
1935–39	1,239,479	64.1	6,850	15.2	14.4
1940–44	1,302,386	55.2	8,653	24.7	14.8
1945–49	1,404,885	67.0	6,260	55.7	15.6
1950–54	1,597,998	71.3	5,403	121.5	17.2
1955–60	1,846,028	72.0	5,252	160.6	19.5

To estimate incremental gross population density, *GD*, from *S**, we had to develop a conversion formula. This formula, Equation (11.9), was obtained by regressing gross population density on the percent of dwelling units that were single family detached for 40 large cities in 1960. Estimates obtained from 1950 data yielded virtually identical results.

$$GD = 19,740 - 201 \; SF \qquad\qquad R^2 = 0.59 \qquad\qquad\qquad (11.9)$$
$$(12.1) \qquad (7.4)$$

where

GD = gross density (person/square mile)
SF = percentage single family detached

Square miles of new development in each time period (M_i) is equal to population growth during the period, (P_i), divided by the estimate of incremental gross density.

$$M_i = P_i/GD_i. \qquad\qquad\qquad (11.10)$$

Incremental population growth is obtained by multiplying the increase in total dwelling units during the period by 3.4, an estimate of the average population per dwelling unit.

Estimates of the distance midpoint, the last column in Table 11–2, are derived from Equations (11.11) through (11.13). The total area of development at time period *t* is, of course, the sum of the square miles of new development from period 1 to period *t*–i.e., Equation (11.11).

$$A_t = \sum_{i=1}^{t} M_i . \qquad\qquad\qquad (11.11)$$

The radius of development up to time period *t*, b_t Equation (11.12), may be computed from the formula for the area of a circle and the estimated number of degrees available for development, θ.

$$b_t = (A_t 360/\pi\theta)^{1/2} \qquad\qquad\qquad (11.12)$$

Estimates of θ were made by inspection of maps of each urban area. For Chicago, θ equals 190°. The midpoint radius of development (r_t) is then easily calculated from the boundaries of development in time periods *t* and *t* – 1.

$$r_t = b_{t-1} + (b_t - b_{t-1})/2 \qquad\qquad\qquad (11.3)$$

Gross population density functions for 1960 then are obtained by regressing the estimated incremental gross density on the estimated midpoint distance for all thirteen time periods. A scatter diagram of these for Chicago is shown in Figure 11–3. In contrast to the theoretical models developed by Muth and Mills, our formulation implies no particular functional form for the relationship between distance and gross density. But to make our estimated density functions comparable to those reported by earlier authors, we use the negative exponential form of the density function shown by Equation (11.14).

$$GD(d) = D_0 e^{-D_1 d},$$ (11.14)

where $GD(d)$ equals gross population density at distance d, and D_0 and D_1 are the function parameters which are to be estimated.[14] For Chicago, these parameters computed from the data shown in Figure 11–3 and Table 11–2, are 20.9 and 0.070.

The procedures described above were used to estimate density gradients for all 47 urban areas included in the analysis. Values of D_0 and D_1 in 1960 for several of these urban areas are shown in Table 11–3. Estimates for all 47 cities are shown in Appendix B, Table B–1. Tables 11–3 and B–2 include four density functions for each metropolitan area in 1960; functions based on estimates of S^* obtained from the dummy variable model [Equation (11.5)],

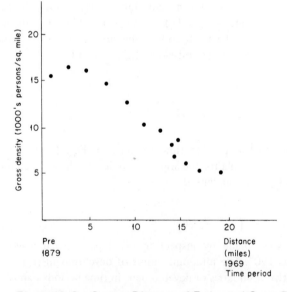

Figure 11–3. Scatter Diagram of Estimated Gross Density by Distance and Time Period: Chicago, pre-1879–1960

TABLE 11-3. Estimated Density Functions for Selected Urban Areas, 1960[a]

$$GD = D_0 e^{-D_1 r}$$

City	Dummy Variables D_0	D_1	Basic Model D_0	D_1	Cross Section D_0	D_1	Actual S^* D_0	D_1
Albany	25	.47	30	.51	27	.47	31	.53
Birmingham	11	.17	13	.22	12	.18	11	.15
Cleveland	20	.15	20	.16	20	.15	22	.18
Dallas	11	.17	11	.18	11	.18	14	.22
Denver	14	.25	15	.27	15	.26	13	.23
Hartford	21	.42	22	.45	18	.42	27	.52
Los Angeles	14	.06	14	.06	13	.06	11	.05
Milwaukee	19	.19	20	.20	20	.19	18	.16
Seattle	12	.14	13	.14	13	.14	12	.14
Utica	27	.79	30	.85	26	.78	26	.72
Wichita	10	.27	12	.41	11	.37	12	.38

[a]Estimated by log $GD = \text{Log } D_0 - D_1 r + e$.

the basic model [Equation (11.4)], the cross section model (Table 11–1), and actual values of S^*.

The parameters of the density functions for a particular urban area are not very sensitive to which equation specification is used to predict residential density, but large differences in the estimates of D_0 and D_1 are obtained among urban areas. Intercept estimates based on values of S_t^* and r_t obtained from the dummy variable data range from a low of 10,000 persons per square mile in Wichita, to a high of 27,400 persons per square mile in Albany. The slope coefficients range from a low of 0.06 in Los Angeles to a high of 0.79 in Utica. If these density functions are interpreted as measures of urban form, our model clearly predicts very different urban structures among urban areas in 1960 and differences, moreover, that seem to conform rather closely to generally perceived differences among areas.

COMPARISONS WITH OTHER ESTIMATES

Muth has published estimates of density functions for 46 United States cities in 1950, computed from samples of 25 census tracts in each city. Some of Muth's estimates have been updated to 1960 by James Barr. Mills has published estimates for 18 United States cities for a number of postwar years, computed using an ingenious, if somewhat heroic estimating technique. In Table 11–4, we compare our estimates of density functions (calculated from the dummy variable model) with those obtained by Muth and Mills for 11 urban areas that appear in all three studies. The estimates obtained by Barr for six of these urban areas are also reported.[15]

From Table 11–4 it is evident that our estimates of the parameters of the density functions for these 11 cities are of the same order of magnitude as those obtained by Muth, Mills, and Barr. Indeed, the similarities for a number of cities are striking. At the same time, there are noticeable differences in the mean values. Our mean estimates of the intercept for common samples of cities are considerably smaller than those obtained by Mills, Muth, or Barr. Our estimates of the gradient parameter are also generally smaller than those obtained by Muth and Mills, although the mean value of our estimates is identical to Barr's for the sample of 22 common cities. But not too much should be made of these aggregate sample comparisons. Differences in mean values may mask significant relationships between our estimates and those of Mills, Muth, and Barr.

In Equations (11.15a) through (11.17b) we perform a more direct comparison of our estimates of the intercepts and gradients of the density functions for these 11 cities with those obtained by Mills, Muth, and Barr. In Equation (11.15a) we regress our estimate of D_0 on Mills' estimate of D_0 and in Equation (11.15b) we regress our estimate of D_1 on Mills' estimate of D_1. Similarly, Equations (11.16a) and (11.16b), and (11.17a) and (11.17b) present regressions of our estimates of D_0 and D_1 on those obtained by Muth and Barr. The t ratios for the individual regression coefficients are shown in parentheses.

Harrison-Kain on Mills (11 cities)

$$D_0{}^{\text{Mills}} = 5.5 + 1.16 D_0{}^{H\text{-}K} \qquad\qquad R^2 = 0.43 \qquad\qquad (11.15a)$$
$$\phantom{D_0{}^{\text{Mills}} =\ } (0.7)\ \ (2.6)$$

$$D_1{}^{\text{Mills}} = 0.093 + 1.23 D_1{}^{H\text{-}K} \qquad\qquad R^2 = 0.65 \qquad\qquad (11.15b)$$
$$\phantom{D_1{}^{\text{Mills}} =\ } (1.1)\ \ \ \ \ (4.1)$$

Harrison-Kain on Muth (11 cities)

$$D_0{}^{\text{Muth}} = -8.1 + 2.09 D_0{}^{H\text{-}K} \qquad\qquad R^2 = 0.27 \qquad\qquad (11.16a)$$
$$\phantom{D_0{}^{\text{Muth}} =\ } (0.4)\ \ (1.8)$$

$$D_1{}^{\text{Muth}} = 0.292 + 0.263 D_1{}^{H\text{-}K} \qquad\qquad R^2 = 0.03 \qquad\qquad (11.16b)$$
$$\phantom{D_1{}^{\text{Muth}} =\ } (2.0)\ \ \ \ \ (0.5)$$

Harrison-Kain on Barr (6 cities)

$$D_0{}^{\text{Barr}} = -20.0 + 2.39 D_0{}^{H\text{-}K} \qquad\qquad R^2 = 0.31 \qquad\qquad (11.17a)$$
$$\phantom{D_0{}^{\text{Barr}} =\ } (0.6)\ \ (1.3)$$

$$D_1{}^{\text{Barr}} = 0.281 - 0.059 D_1{}^{H\text{-}K} \qquad\qquad R^2 = 0.02 \qquad\qquad (11.17b)$$
$$\phantom{D_1{}^{\text{Barr}} =\ } (1.7)\ \ \ \ \ (0.2)$$

Muth on Mills (11 cities)

$$D_0^{\text{Mills}} = 18.2 + 0.242 D_0^{\text{Muth}} \qquad\qquad R^2 = 0.30 \qquad\qquad (11.18a)$$
$$\phantom{D_0^{\text{Mills}} = }(4.4)\ \ (2.0)$$

$$D_1^{\text{Mills}} = 0.386 + 0.083 D_1^{\text{Muth}} \qquad\qquad R^2 = 0.01 \qquad\qquad (11.18b)$$
$$\phantom{D_1^{\text{Mills}} = }(3.0)\quad\ \ (0.3)$$

TABLE 11–4. Comparison of Muth, Barr, Mills, and Harrison-Kain Estimated Density Functions

City	D_0				D_1			
	Muth (1950)	*Barr* (1960)	*Mills* (1958)	*H-K* (1960)	*Muth* (1950)	*Barr* (1960)	*Mills* (1958)	*H-K* (1960)
Baltimore	69	46	37	23	0.52	0.39	0.36	0.22
Columbus	10	7	35	16	0.19	0.11	0.58	0.34
Denver	17		20	14	0.33		0.38	0.25
Houston	14		12	11	0.28		0.24	0.14
Milwaukee	61	48	38	19	0.44	0.38	0.32	0.19
Pittsburgh	17		22	23	0.09		0.24	0.18
Rochester	43	31	24	23	0.64	0.41	0.47	0.45
Sacramento	15		17	11	0.36		0.48	0.29
San Diego	18	11	13	11	0.39	0.15	0.21	0.14
Toledo	6	4	32	20	0.20	0.14	0.67	0.43
Wichita	19		20	10	0.53		0.63	0.27
Mean	26	24	24	17	0.36	0.26	0.42	0.26
S.D.	20	18	9	5	0.16	0.13	0.14	0.11

	Muth (32 cities) H-K				Mills (12 cities) H-K			
	D_0	D_1	D_0	D_1	D_0	D_1	D_0	D_1
Mean	25	0.39	16	0.28	22	0.37	16	0.26
S.D.	17	0.27	5	0.16	7	0.13	5	0.10

	Barr (22 cities) H-K			
	D_0	D_1	D_0	D_1
Mean	20	-0.29	17	-0.29
S.D.	15	0.25	5	0.18

These results indicate that, for these 11 cities at least, our density function parameters are quite closely related to those obtained by Mills, but much less closely related to those obtained by Muth and Barr. Indeed, our density gradient estimates are essentially uncorrelated with those reported by Muth and Barr for these cities. It should be added, however, that the density gradients obtained by Mills for these same 11 cities are even less closely related to Muth's estimates, as revealed by Equation (11.18b).

If we limit the analysis to two way comparisons, larger numbers of observations are available for a comparison between our estimates and those obtained by Muth for 1950 and by Barr for 1960. Because only 12 cities are included in both our sample and that used by Mills, a two way comparison of these cities adds little. Equations (11.19a) and (11.19b) present simple regressions of our intercept and slope coefficients on Muth's estimates for a sample of 32 urban areas. Similar results are reported for the 22 cities common to ours and Barr's sample in Equations (11.20a) and (11.20b). In Equations (11.21a) and (11.21b) we report regressions of our intercept and slope estimates on Muth's 1950 estimates for this 22 cities sample.

Harrison-Kain on Muth (32 cities)

$$D_0{}^{Muth} = 14.4 + 0.677 D_0{}^{H\text{-}K} \qquad R^2 = 0.04 \qquad (11.19a)$$
$$(1.3) \quad (1.0)$$

$$D_1{}^{Muth} = 0.033 + 1.26 D_1{}^{H\text{-}K} \qquad R^2 = 0.53 \qquad (11.19b)$$
$$(0.5) \quad (5.8)$$

Harrison-Kain on Barr (22 cities)

$$D_0{}^{Barr} = -13.6 + 1.98 D_0{}^{H\text{-}K} \qquad R^2 = 0.41 \qquad (11.20a)$$
$$(1.5) \quad (3.8)$$

$$D_1{}^{Barr} = 0.018 + 1.26 D_1{}^{H\text{-}K} \qquad R^2 = 0.60 \qquad (11.20b)$$
$$(0.3) \quad (5.4)$$

Harrison-Kain on Muth (22 cities)

$$D_0{}^{Muth} = -15.8 + 2.68 D_0{}^{H\text{-}K} \qquad R^2 = 0.47 \qquad (11.21a)$$
$$(1.4) \quad (4.2)$$

$$D_1{}^{Muth} = -0.050 + 1.32 D_1{}^{H\text{-}K} \qquad R^2 = 0.63 \qquad (11.21b)$$
$$(0.6) \quad (5.8)$$

Use of the larger sample yields much more favorable results, particularly for the 22 cities in the Barr sample. Our estimates of both the intercept and the gradient are very highly correlated with those obtained by Barr in 1960 and Muth in 1950 for these 22 cities. Our gradient estimates are also highly correlated with those estimated by Muth for the 32 city sample, although the intercepts are not closely related.

The analyses summarized by Equations (11.16a) through (11.21b) reveal a strong relationship between our estimates and those reported by Mills,

Muth, and Barr. While substantial differences exist between our estimates and theirs for individual cities, much of the difference appears to be systematic. These differences may reflect differences in method, definitions, or data sources. For example, our estimates of gross population density in each ring of new development are partially based upon estimates of gross population density for the entire city [see Equation (11.9)]. These estimates include both residential and nonresidential land. Muth and Barr, by contrast, use only predominately residential tracts to calculate their density function estimates. This difference in method presumably would cause our estimates of D_0 and D_1 to be systematically lower than those obtained by the Muth procedure. It is possible that the lower means of D_0 and D_1 we obtain as compared to Mills, Muth, and Barr are attributable to systematic measurement differences of this kind. When regression equation results are used to adjust our density function for these systematic differences, our estimates are quite similar to those reported by Mills, Muth, and Barr.

CHANGE IN DENSITY FUNCTIONS OVER TIME

Muth's long run comparative static approach to urban spatial structure does not lend itself to considering changes in urban spatial structure over time in a very realistic way. His formulation implicitly assumes that urban spatial structure will adjust instantaneously to changes in the values of the forces he identifies as the principal determinants of residential density gradients. Mill's stock adjustment model also makes the gross density function depend on current conditions in each urban area, but it adds the caveat that the adjustments "required" by changes in the underlying forces only occur after a time lag.

To estimate the parameters of his stock adjustment model, Mills computes estimates of population density functions in 18 U.S. metropolitan areas for four post–World War II years and for six urban areas as far back as 1910. Our model can also be used to compute density functions at different points in time. Comparisons of the density functions obtained by our model with the density functions estimated by Mills are shown in Table 11–5 for five of the six urban areas for which Mills' estimates go back to 1910. The two sets of estimates are quite similar for the later periods, but quite different for the early periods. Our estimates and those computed by Mills imply quite different spatial structures for these five urban areas in early time periods.

The differences in urban spatial structure predicted by Mills and by us for early periods can be illustrated by Denver. Figure 11–4 presents a graphical representation of the density function obtained from our model for Denver in 1910. The parameters of this density function are $D_0 = 14,500$ and $D_1 = -0.103$.[16] Our model suggests that Denver's early growth was low to moderate density and that the boundary of major development in 1910 extended to slightly more than two miles from the city center. Some

TABLE 11–5. Historical Changes in Density Functions, Mills and Harrison-Kain Models: 1910, 1920, 1930, 1950, 1960

		1910		1920		1930		1950		1960	
		D_0	D_1	D_0	D_1	D_0	D_1	D_0	D_1	D_0	D_1
Baltimore											
	Mills	111	0.97	80	0.75	68	0.64	51	0.48	37	0.36
	H-K	18	0.08	20	0.14	23	0.21	25	0.25	23	0.22
Denver											
	Mills	28	0.87	35	0.87	36	0.83	28	0.59	20	0.38
	H-K	13	0.01	14	0.11	15	0.24	17	0.32	14	0.25
Milwaukee											
	Mills	109	0.88	114	0.81	74	0.56	58	0.47	39	0.32
	H-K	15	0.04	16	0.08	17	0.14	19	0.17	19	0.19
Rochester											
	Mills	82	1.44	96	1.37	58	0.96	40	0.73	24	0.47
	H-K	16	0.12	17	0.21	19	0.32	23	0.45	23	0.45
Toledo											
	Mills	41	1.13	86	1.43	56	1.01	41	0.83	32	0.67
	H-K	14	0.08	15	0.17	17	0.30	19	0.41	20	0.43

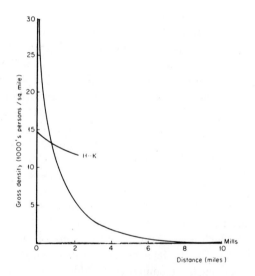

Figure 11–4. Estimated Density Functions for Denver in 1910

development no doubt existed beyond the two mile boundary in 1910, either in scattered suburban units or in small mining or agricultural communities largely independent of, or even in competition with, Denver; but our model implies that this fringe development was quantitatively very unimportant.

Mills' estimated density function for 1910 is also graphed on Figure 11–4. Mills' estimates are obtained using information on the distance of the

Denver city boundary from the center of the city, the population of Denver central city, and the population of the total Denver urbanized area. These data for each decade from 1910 to 1960 are shown in Table 11–6.[17] The parameter estimates are derived by substituting the city and area population estimates into formulas obtained by integrating a negative exponential function to k, the city boundary, and infinity, the boundary of the urban area.

The density function Mills computes for Denver in 1910 is very different from the one we obtain using our model of cumulative urban growth. Our model suggests the density function in 1910 is discontinuous, consisting of two segments. One segment describes a relatively homogeneous, low to moderate density developed area extending about two miles from the center of the city. Beyond this developed area the model suggests a very low density fringe, which we portray as having zero density in Figure 11–4. Since the city boundary of Denver in 1910 is about four miles from the center, our predictions imply a great deal of vacant land within the city limits. Mills, in contrast, describes Denver's development in 1910 in terms of a continuous density function which has a much higher value at the center and which declines regularly to a zero value at infinity. As shown in Figure 11–4, Mills predicts an extremely dramatic decline in density with distance for Denver in 1910.

Both of these characterizations of Denver's spatial structure in 1910 cannot be correct. Unfortunately no solid evidence is available to determine which view is more accurate. Data were not reported for small geographic areas, such as census tracts, in 1910, so a procedure such as that used by Muth for 1950 cannot be used to derive an independent estimate. Some rather

TABLE 11–6. Denver Development 1910–1960 Mills Estimates[a]

Year	CC boundary (mi)	CC population (1000)	Metropolitan population (1000)	Suburban population (1000)	Percent Suburban	Density function Estimates	
						D_0	D_1
1910	4.29	213	239	36	15	28.9	−0.87
1920	4.29	255	287	32	11	34.9	−0.87
1930	4.29	287	330	43	13	36.3	−0.83
1940	4.29	454	541	87	16	35.3	−0.76
1950	4.61	416	564	158	28	29.2	−0.57
1960	4.61	456	929	473	51	19.2	−0.36

[a]Some of the population figures used by Mills appear to be inaccurate. The largest discrepancy is the Denver city population for 1940, which is reported as 322,000 in the 1940 census. The other major discrepancy is for 1960, where the 1960 census reports a Denver city population of 494,000. The other city figures correspond closely to the census figures. Since the metropolitan area boundary is not clearly defined, it is hard to determine the accuracy of the metropolitan population estimates. The 1940 figure appears suspect however. Whether these uncertainties in the basic data significantly affect Mills' density function estimates is difficult to determine. In our discussion of Mills' results we refer to the data used by Mills rather than the corrected figures.

impressionistic early information is available for Denver, however, which seems to support our characterization of Denver in 1910. For example, a map prepared by Clason Map Company in 1912 shows the boundary of developed area well within the Denver city limits.[18] Moreover, photographs of Denver around 1910 depict the residential areas surrounding the city center as relatively homogeneous low to moderate density areas.[19]

While the density functions we obtain from our model differ markedly from those computed by Mills in early periods, the estimates of Denver's urban spatial structure become quite similar in recent decades. Our estimates of the nature of Denver's development in the 13 time periods from pre–1880 to 1960 as well as our estimates of the cumulative population and boundary of development at the end of each period are shown in Table 11–7. The growing similarity over time of the two estimates is consistent with our characterization of the growth process, although the trend certainly does not constitute proof of the accuracy of our early estimates. As Denver urban development expanded in the decades after 1910, the discrepancy diminishes between our discontinuous density function estimates and Mill's continuous estimate.

In the later time periods, when our model projects Denver's new development as low density development extending well beyond the city limits, the difference between our discontinuous estimate and Mills' continuous estimate virtually disappears. The 1960 density function estimate obtained from our model of cumulative urban growth and the estimate obtained by Mills are graphed in Figure 11–5. While Mills' estimated gradient for 1910 was almost

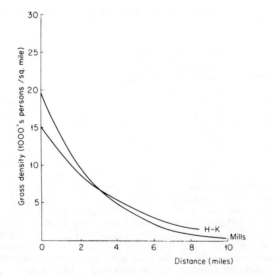

Figure 11–5. Estimated Density Functions for Denver in 1960

TABLE 11–7. Denver Development Pre–1879–1960, Harrison-Kain Estimates

Time period	Actual S* (percent)	Estimate S* (percent)	Estimate GD (1000)	Boundary of development (mile)	Total population (1000)	Suburban population (1000)	Percent Suburban	Density function Estimates	
								D_0	D_1
pre–1879	35	39	11.9	0.4	5	0	0		
1880–89	32	32	13.4	0.8	29	0	0		
1890–99	38	33	13.2	1.4	83	0	0		
1900–09	46	39	11.9	2.1	174	0	0	14.5	-0.10
1910–19	61	50	9.6	2.5	233	0	0	14.6	-0.11
1920–24	74	62	7.3	2.8	276	0	0		
1925–29	72	66	6.5	3.2	324	0	0	15.1	-0.24
1930–34	68	73	5.0	3.4	345	0	0		
1935–39	74	79	3.9	3.8	375	0	0		
1940–44	71	69	5.8	4.1	418	0	0		
1945–49	77	80	3.6	5.0	517	50	10	17.2	-0.32
1950–54	84	84	2.9	6.8	708	240	34		
1955–60	81	84	2.9	8.4	925	457	49	14.3	-0.25

nine times ours, the Mills estimate for 1960 is only 50 percent larger. Muth's estimates for 1950 are midway between our two estimates for 1960.[20]

In addition to the similarity of the estimated density functions in later time periods, our model and Mills' estimates suggest very similar patterns of post war suburban growth. Included in Table 11–7 are estimates of the percent suburban population in the Denver SMSA as estimated by our model for each year.[21] According to our model, suburban growth in Denver was truly a postwar phenomenon. Since our model does not project the boundary of development beyond the Denver city limits until the 1945–1949 period, we predict no suburban population prior to that time. But by 1960 we predict a suburban population that is as large as the total population of the city of Denver. It should be emphasized, however, that the low density development in Denver began long before the postwar period. The postwar period in Denver was different primarily because the added development took place in the areas beyond the largely arbitrary city boundaries.

The data used by Mills to estimate his density functions also include information on the percent of the population living outside the city of Denver in each time period. The pattern of suburbanization revealed by his data is strikingly similar to our predictions. In the four prewar decades, Mills estimates that between 11 and 16 percent of the Denver urban population lived outside the city limits. While it is difficult to determine whether these persons were legitimate suburbanites, tied to the city economy, or residents of outlying areas, largely independent of the city of Denver, the decline in their numbers between 1910 and 1920 suggests that many of them may have been employed in mining or agricultural pursuits. In any event, the population located outside the city of Denver was a small fraction of the areas population until 1950, when the suburban percentage almost doubled. By 1960, the suburban percentage reported by Mills was almost identical to the percentage estimated by our model for 1960.

ELABORATIONS OF THE MODEL

While it is difficult to assess the accuracy of our estimated density gradients, it is clear that the use of additional data would enable us to improve our estimates. Within the framework of our model, additional data on two important relationships would be especially valuable. First, it would be desirable to obtain a more accurate specification of the relationship between S^* and the gross and net residential densities of new development in each period; and second, it would be useful to be able to account for changes in population density in built-up areas. Determination of these relationships requires more historical information on the nature of urban growth in each time period. While these data are not available for all urban areas, we have collected sufficient information for

Chicago to illustrate how more detailed information on these relationships could be used to improve our density function estimates.

Regressions of S^* on gross population density in 40 large central cities in 1950 and 1960 indicated that the relationship between the percent single family detached and gross population density was quite stable for the decade. Over the eight decades considered in our analysis, however, significant changes could have occurred in this relationship. At least four major influences could have caused a shift in the relationship between GD and the incremental percentage of single family units, S^*. These are (1) changes in average lot size for various structure types; (2) changes in the mix of multiunit structures; (3) changes in the proportion of residential to nonresidential land; and (4) changes in population per dwelling unit.

Equation (11.22) indicates how these various influences affect gross population density.

$$GD = \frac{27{,}878{,}400 \quad (\beta) \quad (\gamma)}{\alpha^1 H^1 + \alpha^2 H^2 + \cdots + \alpha^n H^n} \tag{11.22}$$

where

GD = gross population density (persons/square mile)

H^i = dwelling units of the ith structure type added/total dwelling units added.

α^1 = residential land per dwelling unit for the ith structure type (square feet)

27,878,400 = square feet/square mile

β = family size (population/dwelling unit)

γ = acres of residential land added/total land added

The information required to estimate gross population density from Equation (11.22) is unavailable for most urban areas. But for Chicago, sufficient information can be pieced together to support some useful analysis. For early time periods the analysis must draw on largely nonquantitative studies, but they support crude estimates of changes in the structural parameters.[22] Since considerable uncertainty remains about the true value of the parameters of Equation (11.22), we compute several estimates of incremental gross density for each period based upon different assumptions about trends in these parameters. Estimates of Chicago's density function in 1920, 1930, 1945, 1950, and 1960, based on a variety of assumptions about the true values of these parameters, are shown in Table 11–8.

The first set of density functions in Table 11–8 assumes constant values of the αs, the Hs, β and γ, and are comparable to those estimated for all

TABLE 11–8. Historical Changes in Chicago Density Function, for Model Elaborations, 1920, 1930, 1945, 1950, and 1960

	Intercept (D$_0$)				
	1920	*1930*	*1945*	*1950*	*1960*
Dummy variable model	17	19	20	20	21
Lot sizes vary	28	28	36	39	38
Land use proportions and lot sizes vary	28	28	36	40	40
Family size and lot sizes vary	28	28	36	32	28
All above vary	28	28	36	34	29

	Slope (D$_1$)				
	1920	*1930*	*1945*	*1950*	*1960*
Dummy variable model	.03	.05	.06	.06	0.07
Lot sizes vary	.05	.05	.11	.13	0.12
Land use proportions and lot sizes vary	.05	.05	.11	.13	0.13
Family size and lot sizes vary	.05	.05	.11	.11	0.10
All above vary	.05	.05	.11	.12	0.11

urban areas in 1960. The second set of density functions allow the mix of multi-family units (the Hs) and average lot sizes (the αs) to change over time.[23] Persons per dwelling unit, β, and net residential land/gross urban land, γ, were set at 3.3 and 0.33 respectively for these calculations. These numbers are rough estimates based on various censuses and land use surveys.

The third set of density gradients in Table 11–6 assumes γ is equal to 0.33 for periods up to 1944, but declines to 0.25 for periods after 1945. This shift in γ is consistent with a more scattered pattern of urban development in the postwar period. The postwar value of γ was selected rather arbitrarily to illustrate the sensitivity of the density gradients to changes in this parameter. In fact, although there is a widespread criticism about the scattered and "wasteful" character of recent development, there is little evidence that development following World War II is markedly less compact than development in earlier periods.[24]

Changes over time in average family size (population per dwelling unit) also affect gross density. Although no data are available on the average size of households occupying new units in each period, the relative constancy of family size for the urban area as a whole over the 80 year period considered in the study suggests that the size of families occupying new units has not varied a great deal over time. But even if size of families occupying new units has remained relatively consistent over time, the size of families living in the oldest structures may have changed considerably. Quantification of these changes would enable us to account for changes in population densities within built-up areas and would provide a second major means of improving our estimated density gradients.

To analyze these changes in gross population density, it is useful to distinguish between structure density (dwelling units per square mile) and population density (persons per square mile). Spatial patterns of population density are determined largely, but not entirely, by structure density. Thus far, our models of cumulative urban development assume that neither the dwelling unit nor the population densities of built-up areas change as new areas are developed. Because residential structures are so durable, the assumption of unchanging dwelling unit density is quite plausible. Of course, conversions and mergers of existing dwelling units occur as conditions change, and some older structures are demolished and replaced by new residential or nonresidential structures, and these processes alter the density of older areas somewhat. But most changes in the gross population density of built-up areas over time result from changes in the size of families who occupy old units. While old, centrally located units often housed "typical families" (i.e., 3.3 persons per dwelling unit) when they were built, they have come increasingly to house young married couples, retired or childless couples, and single people. Racial discrimination insures that many old, centrally located units house relatively large, poor black families; but overall family size in built-up areas has decreased.

Unfortunately the census does not provide cross-classifications of family size by the year dwelling units were built. But since the age of the housing stock of most census tracts is quite uniform, changes in census tract population provide an indication of changes in family size for existing units. Because we are concerned primarily with population declines in centrally located, built-up areas, our empirical analysis is limited to the 935 census tracts in the city of Chicago. From the 1940, 1950, and 1960 censuses, we obtained census tract statistics on total population, total dwelling units, occupied dwelling units by year built, and median persons per dwelling unit.[25] The distance from the Loop was measured to the nearest tenth of a mile. The census tract information on structures by year built allows us to consider two other important issues: (1) how valid is the assumption of regular peripheral growth used to obtain density functions from our model of incremental density; and (2) how much change in structure densities occurs within built-up areas?

The data on the number of dwelling units built during each time period by distance from the Loop, displayed in Table 11–9, indicate that the assumption of regular peripheral growth corresponds reasonably well to the process of urban growth in Chicago. Since only city census tracts were used in the analysis, recent suburban growth is not represented. Most of the close-in residential development in Chicago during the decade 1950–1960 is probably

TABLE 11—9. Percentage of Housing Units Added in Each Time Period by Distance from the Loop, Chicago[a]

Distance (miles)	Total Units in 1960 (1000s)	Pre-1920	1920-30	Year Built (percentage) 1930-40	1940-50	1950-60	All Years
0-1	41	68	15	2	1	14	100
1-2	156	83	8	2	1	6	100
2-3	253	78	16	2	1	3	100
3-4	264	65	28	2	1	4	100
4-5	231	36	42	6	4	12	100
5-6	138	16	37	6	12	29	100
6-7	49	25	21	7	22	25	100
7-8	41	36	17	5	20	22	100
City Total	1,173	56	26	4	4	10	100
Suburban Total	920	20	16	6	14	44	100

[a]U.S., Bureau of the Census, *Census of Population: 1950* vol. III. *Census Tract Statistics* (Chicago, Ill.: U.S. Government Printing Office, 1952); and U.S., Bureau of the Census, *Census of Population and Housing: 1960 Census Tracts, Final Report PHC (1)—26*, Chicago, Ill.: U.S. Bureau of the Census, *Census of Housing: 1950* vol. I, *General Characteristics,* part 3: "Idaho—Massachusetts," (Washington, D.C.: U.S. Government Printing Office, 1953); Table 13—20; U.S., Bureau of the Census, *Census of Housing, 1960* vol. 1, *States and Small Areas,* part 3: "Delaware—Indiana (Washington, D.C.: U.S. Government Printing Office, 1963), Table 15—14.

accounted for by urban renewal and public housing programs. Edward Hearle and John Niedercorn have shown that the urban renewal process usually produces lower densities.[26]

The analysis of changes in numbers of dwelling units was much less conclusive. We planned to use the distributions of dwelling units by year built to estimate the net changes in the housing stock by age for each census tract. These net changes would reflect the combined effect of mergers, demolitions, and other transformations of the housing stock. Unfortunately, the results obtained were generally quite implausible. They indicated an increase over time in the number of dwellings at most distances (see Appendix B, Table B—5). The estimated increases between 1950 to 1960 were especially large, a result that is inconsistent with other information. It is probable that a change in the census reporting unit from a "dwelling unit" to a "housing unit" is responsible for these unanticipated results. The later definition includes single rooms without kitchen facilities while the former does not. In spite of these definitional problems, the analysis supports the general impression that transformation of the stock had only a modest effect on dwelling unit density over the period studied.

The analysis of census tract data was carried out primarily to determine whether the size of families occupying existing units changed in a systematic way. In particular, we suspected that central area population and, thereby, gross population densities declined in the postwar period because of a decline in the average size of families in areas of older housing. This pattern is evident from Table 11–10, which gives average population per dwelling unit by distance from the Loop in 1940, 1950, and 1960. The final density functions in Table 11–8 incorporate these changes in family size.

CONCLUSION

Regular declines in gross population density with distance from the center of urban areas have been observed and analyzed for many years. But rigorous theoretical explanations of these phenomena have been provided only recently. In general, these theoretical explanations have been obtained from long run equilibrium models which derive the form of these density functions from equilibrium values of employment locations, commuting costs, and family incomes. In this chapter, we present an alternative theoretical explanation of these empirical regularities which emphasizes the disequilibrium nature of urban growth and the durability of residential and nonresidential capital.

Our model views urban growth as a cumulative process and explains current residential densities as a weighted average of the density of new development over several time periods. In this framework, current levels of explanatory variables, such as commuting costs and family incomes, determine the density of development during this period, but the character of past and future development depends on the levels of these variables during those time

TABLE 11–10. Average Population Per Dwelling Unit by Distance from the Loop, Chicago, 1940, 1950, and 1960[a]

| | *Year* | | |
Distance	1940	1950	1960
0–1	2.41	2.45	2.05
1–2	3.07	2.93	2.70
2–3	3.20	2.93	2.81
3–4	3.22	2.89	2.60
4–5	3.13	2.89	2.80
5–6	3.35	3.28	3.02
6–7	3.17	3.32	3.15
7–8	3.64	3.38	3.15
City of Chicago	3.6	2.9	2.6
Suburban Chicago	3.9	3.4	3.3

[a]Same as Table 11–9 plus, U.S. Bureau of the Census, *Census of Housing: 1940,* vol. II, *General Characteristics Reports by States,* part 2, "Illinois"; U.S., Bureau of the Census, *Census of Housing: 1950* vol. II, part 2. *Nonfarm Housing Characteristics.* (Washington, D.C.: U.S. Government Printing Office, 1953).

periods. Analyses of data for 82 urban areas indicate that a simple econometric model provides good predictions of the density of residential development in each urban area for discrete time periods between 1880 and 1960 and of variations in current residential densities among these areas.

If it is assumed that urban growth occurs in a regular way at the periphery of built up areas, this simple model can be used to compute density functions for sample cities. For the analyses presented in this paper we estimated density functions for 47 of the 82 urban areas used in our analysis of intermetropolitan variations in residential density. Estimates of both the intercepts and gradients of the density functions varied considerably among the 47 cities included in the analysis, and the differences corresponded to generally perceived differences among cities. Edwin Mills, Richard Muth, and James Barr have computed density functions using different estimation techniques. Comparison of our estimates with comparable ones obtained by Mills for 11 urban areas, by Muth for 32 urban areas, and by Barr for 22 urban areas indicates a fairly strong degree of correspondence between our estimates and theirs. These results provide additional evidence of the usefulness of our approach.

The methods used to compute density functions in our analysis involve a number of unrealistic assumptions. The actual historical process of development in each urban area is certainly far more complex than this simple model implies. There are no theoretical impediments to incorporating more realistic assumptions; the constraint is empirical. No consistent data exist on changes in lot size, rates of demolitions, urban redevelopment, and population shifts for our sample metropolitan areas.

To evaluate how these omitted variables may affect our results, we collected additional historical data for Chicago and used these data to evaluate changes in Chicago's density functions under a variety of assumptions. While these more complex analyses changed the estimated intercepts and gradients for Chicago, the changes were not dramatic. More detailed historical information on development would certainly be revealing, but we doubt if these data would change our findings in any fundamental way.

Chapter Twelve

Measuring the Value of Housing Quality

with John M. Quigley

INTRODUCTION

In buying housing, families jointly purchase a wide variety of services at a particular location. These include a certain number of square feet of living space, different kinds of rooms, a particular structure type, an address, accessibility to employment, a neighborhood environment, a set of neighbors, and a diverse collection of public and quasipublic services including schools, garbage collection, and police protection.

Several published studies have tried to obtain statistical estimates of the individual contribution of these specific attributes to the total payments (rent or purchase price) for residential services. For example, Ridker and Henning used census tract data to estimate the effect of variables such as air pollution, accessibility to downtown, school quality, and substandardness on the average value of single family homes.[1] Similar analyses have been published by Muth, Oates, Pendelton, and others.[2]

All these attempts to estimate the market value of specific attributes of the bundle of residential services are deficient because they fail to represent adequately the complexity of residential service bundles, because they lack adequate measures of residential quality or rely exclusively on aggregate (published census tract) data. This article seeks to correct these deficiencies by using information for individual dwelling units, by more completely describing the bundles of residential services, and, in particular, by seriously trying to measure their physical and environmental quality.

Quantitative value estimates of individual attributes of the bundle of residential services are obtained by regressing market price (value for owner-occupied dwellings and monthly rent for renter-occupied dwellings) on the individual quality and quantity measures. The coefficients for individual variables then measure the market value of varying amounts of each attribute. If

261

the housing market could be assumed to be in long run equilibrium, this would be a fairly unambiguous measure, since it would also be equal to the supply price of adding an increment of that attribute to the bundles. However, given the importance of stocks in the housing market, substantial departures from long run equilibrium may be expected. Even so, knowledge of the market value of specific attributes of the bundles of residential services is of considerable theoretical interest and is valuable for many kinds of public and private decisions. For example, market value estimates of residential quality, obtained from earlier regressions, were used to obtain lower bound estimates of the benefits of urban renewal programs.[3] Similarly, models of this kind would be of enormous value to appraisers in estimating the market value of real estate for tax and other purposes.

The coefficients may also be considered as weights in a hedonic price index.[4] In the September 1969 *Journal of the American Statistical Association,* John C. Musgrave describes census bureau research to develop such an index for new single family homes.[5] If the various measures of quality used here could be reproduced over time, it should be possible to develop similar indexes for the housing stock. This article provides a partial test of the importance and feasibility of such an effort.

MEASUREMENT OF RESIDENTIAL QUALITY

Difficulty in measuring the physical and environmental quality of the dwelling unit and surrounding residential environment is perhaps the most vexing problem encountered in evaluating the several attributes of bundles of residential services. These problems are so serious that the Bureau of the Census omitted all measures of dwelling unit quality from the 1970 housing census.

Evaluations of the quality of sample dwelling units, structures, and blocks used in this study were obtained from three separate surveys of approximately 1,500 households and dwelling units in the city of St. Louis completed in the summer of 1967.[6] In the first survey, interviewers were instructed to rate the quality of particular aspects of each dwelling unit, e.g., the walls, on a scale ranging between one ("excellent condition") and five ("requires replacement"). A second survey, conducted by city building inspectors, provided quality ratings for specific aspects of the exterior of each sample structure and parcel, and of those on either side of the sample dwelling. Building inspectors also rated aspects of the quality of the block face (both sides of the street) on which the sample dwelling units were located; recorded the presence of specific adverse environmental influences, such as noise, smoke, heavy traffic, and noxious odors; and estimated the extent of nonresidential activity on the sample blocks.

These surveys provided 39 variables indicating the physical or visual quality of the bundle of residential services, including seven measures of the quality of dwelling units (e.g., condition of floors, windows, walls, levels of housekeeping, etc.), seven measures of the quality of the structure and parcel (e.g., condition of drives and walks, landscaping, structure exterior, etc.), eight measures of the quality of adjacent properties (e.g., condition of structures, parcels, etc.), and 17 variables pertaining to the residential quality of specific aspects of the block face (e.g., condition of street, percent of nonresidential use, etc.).

Detailed quality judgments about many components of the bundle of residential services were obtained on the premise that individual interviewers and building inspectors would provide more consistent and precise evaluations of narrowly defined individual components than they could about broader aggregates. A second premise was that subsequent statistical aggregation of many separate judgments would provide more consistent and meaningful quality measures than the subjective aggregation implicit in obtaining overall quality judgments from individual evaluators.[7]

Although this procedure reduced the danger of interviewers' inconsistent and arbitrary aggregation, it created the corollary problem of how to reduce the 39 separate quality measures to a more manageable number. It would have been possible to include all 39 variables in the regressions with the remaining attributes of the residential services bundles. But, besides the statistical problems, such as multicollinearity and the loss of degress of freedom, which would arise from doing so, there is reason to believe that both the market and individual households evaluate residential quality in terms of fewer broader aggregates.

Two different methods of aggregation were used in constructing these composite quality variables, with generally consistent results. The first set of composite quality indexes were simple, unweighted means of the individual quality measurements for the dwelling unit, the structure, the adjacent structures, and the block face. The second set, used in the regressions reported here, were derived from the original 39 variables by factor analysis. Since there is no way of unambiguously determining the appropriate number of factors, four, five, and six factor representations of the 39 quality variables were computed and evaluated.

The five factor solution, summarized in Table 12–1, accounts for 60 percent of the variance among the 39 original variables and seems to provide the most meaningful description of the quality dimensions of the bundles of residential services. Each of the five factors appears to represent a separable and intuitively meaningful quality dimension of the bundles.

The first factor accounts for 38.8 percent of the total variance of the original correlation matrix and loads heavily on 17 variables describing the overall condition of the structure and parcel; amount and quality of landscaping; cleanliness of the parcel and block face; and condition of the streets, walks and driveways (Table 12–1). In other words, the index appears to measure the

Table 12–1. Factor Loadings on Individual Quality Variables

Variable	Factor 1	2	3	4	5
Dwelling unit					
1 Overall structural condition	–	0.93	–	–	–
2 General housekeeping	–	0.66	–	–	–
3 Condition of ceilings	–	0.88	–	–	–
4 Condition of walls	–	0.88	–	–	–
5 Condition of floors	–	0.88	–	–	–
6 Condition of lighting	–	0.82	–	–	–
7 Condition of windows	–	0.83	–	–	–
Structure and parcel					
8 Condition of structure exterior	0.74	–	–	–	–
9 Overall parcel condition	0.72	–	–	–	–
10 Quality of exterior	0.52	–	0.62	–	–
11 Parcel landscaping	0.56	–	–	–	–
12 Trash on parcel	0.65	–	–	–	–
13 Nuisances affecting parcel	–	–	–	–	–
14 Condition of drives and walks	0.57	–	–	–	–
Adjacent structures and parcels					
15 Condition of structures	–	–	0.91	–	–
16 Condition of parcels	0.86	–	–	–	–
17 Structural quality of poorer	0.71	–	–	–	–
18 Structural quality of better	0.70	–	–	–	–
19 Parcel quality of poorer	0.81	–	–	–	–
20 Parcel quality of better	0.81	–	–	–	–
21 Nuisances affecting adjacent properties	–	–	–	–	–
22 Sample relative to adjacent properties	–	–	-0.78	–	–
Block face					
23 Neighborhood problems	–	–	–	–	–
24 Percent residential	–	–	–	0.77	–
25 Percent commercial and residential	–	–	–	-0.81	–
26 Percent vacant	-0.55	–	–	–	–
27 Percent in poor condition	-0.77	–	–	–	–
28 Percent in fair condition	–	–	–	–	-0.89
29 Percent in good condition	0.65	–	–	–	0.56
30 Block landscaping	0.58	–	–	–	–
31 Trash on block	0.70	–	–	–	–
32 Condition of sidewalk	0.50	–	–	–	–
33 Condition of street	–	–	–	–	–
34 Condition of curbs	–	–	–	–	–
35 Amount of commercial traffic	–	–	0.62	–	–
36 Nuisances affecting block	–	–	–	–	–
37 Condition of alleyways	–	–	-0.61	–	–
38 Cleanliness of alleyways	0.61	–	–	–	–
39 Overall block condition	0.77	–	–	–	–

Note: – indicates standardized factor loading less than 0.5.

overall quality of the exterior physical environment. For this reason, it is termed basic residential quality (BRQ).

The second factor, dwelling unit quality (DUQ), representing both the structural condition and housekeeping inside the sample dwelling unit, accounts for an additional 8.2 percent of the variance in the original correlation matrix. All seven variables with factor loadings of more than 0.5 for DUQ refer to the interior of the dwelling unit and were obtained by the interviewers as part of the home interview survey. This raises the possibility that the differences in the indexes may be the result of different evaluators rather than independent quality dimensions. However, the relatively large number of home interviewers reduces this danger.

The third factor, quality of proximate properties (QPP), which explains an additional 6.0 percent of the total variance, amplifies the BRQ index by specifically accounting for the cleanliness, landscaping, and condition of nearby properties.

The fourth factor, nonresidential use (NU), measures the presence and effect of commercial and industrial land uses in the immediate vicinity and accounts for another 4.2 percent of the total variance. It undoubtedly represents the effect of nonphysical characteristics such as noise, smoke, and traffic as well as the proportion of property on the block devoted to nonresidential use. The variables with factor loadings of more than 0.5 are microneighborhood or block face variables.

The fifth factor, average structure quality (ASQ), adds another 3.2 percent to the explained variance and loads heavily on only two variables, measures of the average quality of structures on the block face as a whole.

Besides the measures of residential quality, home interviewers obtained much information about characteristics of the occupants, objective characteristics of the dwelling units (e.g., number of rooms and bathrooms in a unit and whether it had hot water and central heating), and rent or value of the unit. Data on other aspects of the bundle of residential services, such as quality of neighborhood schools, incidence of crime, age of the structure, and various measures of accessibility were obtained from public records. These extensive data permitted us to estimate the market value of both quantitative and qualitative attributes of the bundle of residential services.

Because of the lack of comparability between price data for rental and owner-occupied units, separate models were estimated for rental and owner submarkets. Also, because the small suburban subsample is incomplete in some important aspects, separate models were estimated for the city and for the entire sample.

THE CITY EQUATIONS

Though the owner and renter equations are generally comparable, there are some differences. The renter equation is considerably more complicated and includes 25 explanatory variables compared with 15 for the owner model. Both the owner and renter equations include five quality indexes, number of rooms, number of bathrooms, age of structure, parcel area (parcel area per dwelling in the case of multifamily units), distance to central business district, median schooling of adults in the census tract, estimated percentage white of the census tract population in 1967, mean achievement levels of the neighborhood public school, and an index of the level of criminal activity in the neighborhood.[8]

Besides these common variables, the renter equation contains six dummy variables for structure type, four dummy variables describing the rental terms (whether the rent includes payment for heat, water, furniture, and major appliances), two dummy variables indicating whether the dwelling unit has central heating and hot water, a variable indicating the duration of tenant occupancy, and a dummy variable indicating whether the owner lives in the same building.

The only variable included in the owner-occupied model not in the renter model is first floor area, a surrogate for total floor area. It would have been desirable to include total floor area in the renter model as well, but it was unavailable; and first floor area, used in the owner model, is not meaningful for multifamily structures.

The owner equations are limited to single family units because there is no adequate way of imputing an appropriate share of the value of owner-occupied, multifamily dwelling units to each dwelling unit. The four contract rent corrections and the owner in building and years rented variables are not applicable to owner-occupied structures. The dummy variables representing both hot water and central heat are omitted from the owner sample because almost no single family, owner-occupied structures included in the sample lack hot water and central heat.

Although more complex specifications involving quality-quantity interactions were investigated, most of the estimation relied on linear or semilogarithmic models. (In one instance an independent variable was transformed to logarithms as well.) For the renter models, the linear specification fit the data better; for the owner models, the semilog form provided better results. Table 12–2 shows the estimated coefficients for the 579 rental units and the 275 owner-occupied, single family homes in the city.

The results obtained for the five quality indexes are particularly interesting. In the renter model, the basic residential quantity, dwelling unit quality, and average structure quality variables are statistically significant. The coefficient for basic residential quality is almost six times its standard error; more importantly, the magnitude of the coefficients indicates that the rental market values these dimensions of residential quality very highly. Basic residential quality has an estimated value of $7.22 per unit. Dwelling unit quality is valued at $4.02 per unit and average structure quality at $2.80 per unit. If they are added together, the five quality coefficients total $18.43. The mean value of contract rent for the sample is $63.19 with a standard deviation of $27.71. Thus, these aspects of residential quality account for a significant portion of monthly rent.

The table also indicates that households purchasing single family units place a high value on some of these quality dimensions. The coefficients

Table 12–2. Regression Equations for City Renter and Owner Markets

Variable	Renter Coefficient	Owner Coefficient
Basic residential quality	7.22[b]	0.104[b]
Dwelling unit quality	4.02[b]	0.059[b]
Quality of proximate properties	2.95	0.035
Nonresidential usage	1.44[a]	0.062[b]
Average structure quality	2.80[b]	−0.016
Proportion white in census tract	−4.20[a]	−0.050
Median schooling of adults in census tract	2.55[b]	0.075[b]
Public school achievement	2.62[a]	0.037
Number of major crimes	−0.00	−0.001
Age of structure	−0.28[b]	−0.007[b]
Number of rooms (natural logarithm)	23.23[b]	0.220[b]
Number of bathrooms	8.89[b]	0.036
Parcel area (hundreds of square feet)	0.06	0.005[b]
First floor area (hundreds of square feet)	−	0.370[b]
Single detached	8.18[b]	−
Duplex	11.46[b]	−
Row	4.35	−
Apartment	4.21	−
Rooming house	4.45	−
Flat	5.16[a]	−
No heat included in rent	−9.13[a]	−
No water included in rent	−2.63[a]	−
No major appliances included in rent	−11.17[b]	−
No furniture included in rent	−6.97[b]	−
Hot water	4.89[a]	−
Central heat	4.59[b]	−
Duration of occupancy (years)	−0.27[b]	−
Owner in building	−4.31[b]	−
Constant	13.57	7.93[b]
R^2	0.72	0.73
Observations	579	275

[a]Significant at 0.05 level
[b]Significant at 0.01 level
NOTE: With the exception of the dummy variables for structure type, the relevant tests are one-tailed

indicate that property owners will pay over $1,400 more for an otherwise comparable property that is one standard deviation better than average in terms of basic residential quality, and they will pay over $750 more for a structure one standard deviation unit better in terms of dwelling unit quality. Neither the quality of proximate properties nor average structure quality has a coefficient that is statistically different from zero. The final index of quality (nonresidential use), evaluated at the sample mean, suggests that a buyer of a single family house would pay $850 more for a house one unit better than average.

Sixteen other coefficients are significant at the 5 percent level in the renter equation; an additional five variables are significant in the owner equation. Also highly significant is the number of rooms in the renter equation: the difference between a two and three room unit is $10.17; the difference between a four and a five room unit is $5.87. Dwellings with hot water rent for $4.89 more per month than cold water flats, and central heating increases rent by $4.59 per month (the effect of dwelling unit size and quality being held constant). For owners, the coefficient for the number of rooms indicates that a six room house costs $550 more than a five room house with the same floor area, and a nine room house costs $400 more than an otherwise identical eight room house.

Age of structure is also strongly related to monthly rent and housing value. The results suggest that a new structure will sell for $3,150 more than an otherwise identical one that is 25 years old. Monthly rent decreases by about $2.82 per month for each increase of ten years in age of structure. Since the average rental structure is nearly 60 years old, age has a considerable effect on monthly rent. It is worth emphasizing that this difference remains after the effects of the five indexes of quality and the presence or absence of central heating and hot water have been accounted for. This strong age effect is probably attributable to further differences in quality or style not accounted for by other variables.

The surrogate for neighborhood prestige (median schooling of residents of the census tract) is statistically significant in both models. The coefficients indicate that an otherwise identical bundle located in a census tract in which the median adult has only completed the eighth grade will rent for $5.24 less per month than one located in a census tract where the median adult has completed the tenth grade; if owner-occupied, it will have a market value of $1,900 less.

For owners, the lot size and floor area variables are statistically significant. The coefficients suggest that a 600 square foot house can be purchased for $2,900 less than an otherwise identical 1200 square foot house; a house on a 10,000 square foot lot would cost $4,300 more than an identical unit located on a 5000 square foot lot.

Of those variables specific to the renter model, three of the dummy variables representing structure type are significant, as well as three of the contract rent corrections. For renters, duration of occupancy and whether or not the owner lives in the building are also highly significant. Although the regression coefficient for the duration of occupancy variable is small—only 27 cents per year of occupancy—it is highly significant. It is likely that this small difference measures a lagged adjustment of monthly rent. Landlords are less likely to raise rents when their properties are occupied by stable tenants than when the properties change occupancy.

A different landlord-tenant interaction may be responsible for the larger and highly significant coefficient of the owner in building variable. The lower rents for units with resident landlords may result either from less sophistication and professionalism on the part of these smaller operators, or they may be due to different policies for selecting tenants. When the owner lives on the property, he may select tenants more carefully to achieve lower vacancy rates and lower maintenance and repair costs. The critical impact of these factors on the profitability of rental properties has been emphasized in other studies.[9]

The findings also suggest that standardized dwelling units located inside the ghetto may be somewhat more expensive than those outside, a finding consistent with Ridker and Henning's study of St. Louis and with other investigations of housing market discrimination. The coefficient for racial composition is statistically significant at the 5 percent level in the rental equation and is approximately equal to its standard error in the owner equation. Taken at face value the coefficient in the renter (owner) model indicates that a comparable unit in an all-white area would cost 8 percent (5 percent) less than one located in an all-black area.

Although the ghetto markups indicated by estimates in Table 12–2 are consistent with most studies of housing market discrimination, serious questions may be raised about the specifications used for both the owner and renter models.[10] If housing market discrimination exists, it is doubtful that its effects can be represented merely by an intercept shift. The phenomenon may be far more complex—with discrimination more or less strongly evident in various submarkets defined by quality and structure type.[11] To test one such hypothesis, separate equations were estimated for rental units located inside and outside the ghetto.

When the coefficients of these stratified models were applied to the mean values of the explanatory variables for units in the two submarkets, the results indicated that the average ghetto unit would rent for about 2 percent less in all-white city neighborhoods, but the average nonghetto unit would rent for 10 percent more in the ghetto. Moreover, as we have shown in Chapter 7 of this book, price discrimination may be only one of the adverse consequences of housing market discrimination.[12] The virtual unavailability of certain kinds of housing inside the ghetto, and the difficulties Negroes experience in obtaining housing outside the ghetto at any price, may be more important.

In evaluating these results, it should also be remembered that the equations in Table 12–1 are estimated for city dwelling units only. Yet it is clear that for most households, particularly whites, the relevant housing market is the entire metropolitan area.

The accessibility measure, miles from the CBD, is insignificant for both tenure types.[13] This result is at variance with most economic theories of residential location, which would predict the price of a standardized bundle of residential services to decline with distance from the city center.[14] The fault could be inadequate standardization, improprer specification of the equations, the measure of accessibility used, or existing theories that fail to consider effects of such important factors as stocks or housing market discrimination.

The results obtained for the school quality and crime variables are somewhat disappointing, but hardly surprising. Stronger school and crime effects might have been anticipated given the frequent references to school quality and crime in discussions of how households make residential choices and how the urban housing market operates.[15]

For several reasons, part of the influence of better schools on value may be represented by the residential quality variables. Mean school achievement is highly correlated with the indexes of residential quality. There is reason to believe that school quality is measured with considerable error. If so, the residential variables may be proxying the effects of school quality.[16] Moreover, if better schools attract higher income households who spend more on housing maintenance, part of these measured effects of residential quality are logically the result of school quality.

Further evidence of the effect of school quality on monthly rents was obtained by estimating separate regressions for properties located inside and outside the ghetto. Ghetto schools are uniformly bad. The standard deviation of school quality is only half as large for rental properties in the ghetto as for those located outside the ghetto. It is not surprising, therefore, that an insignificant school quality coefficient was obtained in a separate ghetto regression, while the coefficient in the nonghetto stratification was larger ($5.05 versus $2.63 per month) than that obtained for the entire renter sample.

Measurement problems are even more acute in obtaining an adequate measure of neighborhood public safety. Including a neighborhood crime index in the model is more a statement of good intentions than any serious effort to come to grips with the conceptual and measurement problems of defining a neighborhood's perceived safety. The index of neighborhood crime used in the analysis is also highly correlated with the indexes of residential quality.

A final reason for anticipating weak school and crime effects is that the sample was restricted to the city of St. Louis. The largest variation in school quality and level of criminal activity is found not within the city but rather between the city of St. Louis and its suburbs.

EXPANDING THE SAMPLE

Although the data and the empirical results represent a significant improvement over previous studies, the analysis is deficient in several important respects. Perhaps its most serious shortcoming is the lack of information on suburban alternatives. For most households, the relevant housing market is the entire region, and much of the variation in the bundles of residential services is in the suburban part of the market. Legal and budget limitations on the data collection program precluded a large scale sample of suburban households; however, nearly comparable data were obtained for 26 suburban rental units and 136 suburban owner-occupied, single family units. These observations differ from those used in estimating the city equations in only two respects; no information was available on school quality or neighborhood crime. These omissions are particularly unfortunate since, as noted previously, variation in these services between the central city and the suburbs is probably far greater than variation within the city. Even so, the small increment to the sample appears to add appreciably to the sample information.

Table 12–3 shows the renter model for the entire sample of central city and suburban units. The variables for school achievement and neighborhood criminal activity are deleted, and the variable distance from CBD had been

Table 12–3. Regression Equations for Renter Model With Suburban Observations, School, and Crime Variables Deleted

Variable	Including St. Louis County	City Only
Basic residential quality	8.48[b]	7.61[b]
Dwelling unit quality	5.14[b]	4.18[b]
Quality of proximate properties	5.22[b]	2.95
Nonresidential usage	1.87[b]	1.48[a]
Average structure quality	3.49[b]	2.97[b]
Proportion white in census tract	−2.62[a]	−1.94
Median schooling of adults in census tract	1.57[a]	2.29[b]
Age of structure	−0.30[b]	−0.29[b]
Number of rooms (natural logarithm)	25.00[b]	23.33[b]
Number of bathrooms	9.01	8.71[b]
Parcel area (hundreds of square feet)	0.08	0.07
Single detached	8.93[b]	8.26[b]
Duplex	11.81[b]	10.98[b]
Row	4.32	4.52
Apartment	5.22[a]	3.93
Rooming house	5.06	4.27
Flat	5.67[a]	5.42[a]
No heat included in rent	−8.73[b]	−9.00[b]
No water included in rent	−3.10[a]	−2.61[a]
No major appliances included in rent	−11.14[b]	−10.98[b]
No furniture included in rent	−7.76[b]	−7.40[b]
Hot water	4.28[a]	4.67[a]
Central heat	4.46[b]	4.74[b]
Duration of occupancy (years)	−0.27[b]	−0.27[b]
Owner in building	−4.73[b]	−4.38[b]
Miles from CBD	−	−0.05
County dummy	8.66	−
Constant	40.55[b]	34.71[b]
R^2	0.75	0.72
Observations	605	579

[a]Significant at 0.05 level

[b]Significant at 0.01 level

NOTE: With the exception of the dummy variables for structure type, the relevant tests are one-tailed.

replaced by a dummy variable with a value of one for the county observations.[17] For comparison, the table also shows the coefficients for the city renter model when the school and crime variables are deleted.

The most striking difference when the model is re-estimated for the entire metropolitan area is the increase in the significance of the coefficients. Of the 25 variables common to both specifications of the renter model, 21 have larger t–values. Moreover, both the magnitude and the significance of the quality variables' coefficients are greater for the more representative sample. When the crime and school variables are deleted from the city model, the magnitude and significance of the quality variables similarly increase. This indicates that there is some interrelationship between the five indexes of residential quality and the level of these public services within the city.[18]

Aside from the differences in the coefficients of the quality variables, the largest changes in regression coefficients are observed for the racial composition variable. These changes in the magnitudes of the regression coefficients indicate that dwelling units in the ghetto are somewhat more expensive than other units when differences in public services are accounted for. However, this measured price difference between ghetto and nonghetto units disappears when the differences in the quality of schools and other services are not accounted for.

When the owner models are re-estimated incorporating the 136 county observations, similar results are obtained. Estimates of the semilog value model for the city and for the larger sample are presented in Table 12–4. In both the linear and semilogarithmic forms, the t–values and the magnitude of the quality variables increase when the county observations are added. The significance of all seven remaining variables common to both equations also increases.

QUANTITY-QUALITY RELATIONSHIPS

One important difference between the renter and owner models described previously is the way in which residential quality and dwelling unit size are interrelated. In the renter models, total monthly rent is computed by simply adding premiums for higher residential quality to payments for the dwelling units' objective characteristics. This specification assumes that the premium for residential quality is the same regardless of dwelling unit size.

The semilog specification used for owner models is only slightly more flexible. It requires that the premium for higher quality be proportional to the payment for size (number of rooms). The market values of owner-occupied units of various sizes at different quality levels are illustrated in Figure 12–1. With the remaining variables evaluated at their sample means, a four room unit one standard deviation better than average in terms of basic residential and dwelling unit quality (i.e., index values of 1.0 versus index values of zero) costs

Table 12–4.   Regression Equations for Owner Model With Suburban Observations, School, and Crime Variables Deleted

Variable	Including St. Louis County	City Only
Basic residential quality	0.117[b]	0.114[b]
Dwelling unit quality	0.083[b]	0.064[b]
Quality of proximate properties	0.005	0.049
Nonresidential usage	0.071[b]	0.068[b]
Average structure quality	−0.012	−0.015
Proportion white in census tract	−0.004	−0.014
Median schooling of adults in census tract	0.039[b]	0.078[b]
Age of structure	−0.006[b]	−0.007[b]
Number of rooms (natural logarithm)	0.271[b]	0.224[b]
Number of bathrooms	0.039[a]	0.031
Parcel area (hundreds of square feet)	0.005[b]	0.005[b]
First floor area (hundreds of square feet)	0.039[b]	0.036[b]
Miles from central business district	—	0.005
County dummy	−0.235[b]	—
Constant	8.290[b]	8.170[b]
R^2	0.77	0.73
Observations	411	275

[a]Significant at 0.05 level
[b]Significant at 0.01 level
NOTE: All relevant tests are one-tailed

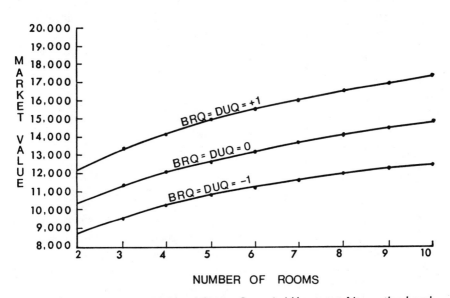

Figure 12–1. Value of Owner-Occupied Homes at Alternative Levels of Quality and Size

$2,100 more than one of average quality. For a nine room unit, the extra quality costs about $2,500 more. This incremental payment for higher quality is the same proportion, approximately 22 percent, of the payment for dwelling unit size.

These features of both the renter and owner models are disquieting. Although it seems plausible that the premium for higher quality should increase as dwelling unit size increases, there is no persuasive reason why it should be a constant fraction of payments for dwelling unit size. The constant payment for quality regardless of size is even less satisfactory.

To test other hypotheses about the interrelation between payments for quantity and for quality, several alternative specifications were estimated in which additional terms were included to represent the joint effect of quality and quantity on monthly rent or market value. In general, the resulting estimates were almost indistinguishable from the simple linear and semilogarithmic models. The coefficients of the remaining variables were virtually the same for all of these alternative specifications.

To illustrate these alternative specifications, the renter model for the entire sample (Table 12–3), summarized in Equation (12.1), was re-estimated to include variables representing the joint effects of the quality variables and the size (number of rooms) of the units. The alternative estimate, summarized in Equation (12.2), includes two interaction terms: the product of the logarithm of the number of rooms (log R) with the basic residential quality index (BRQ) and with the dwelling unit quality (DUQ) index. Because the quality indexes have mean values of zero and admit negative values, a constant was added to the index scores.

$$V = \$32.93 + \$8.48 \; BRQ + \$5.14 \; DUQ + \$25.00 \log R \qquad (12.1)$$
$$R^2 = 0.7503$$

$$V = \$28.77 - \$0.51 \; BRQ - \$1.49 \; DUQ - \$6.03 \log R$$
$$+ \$6.91 \; [(BRQ + 3.00) \cdot \log R] + \$4.78 \qquad (12.2)$$
$$[(DUQ + 3.00) \cdot \log R]$$
$$R^2 = 0.7606$$

The regression coefficients of all other variables, represented by the constant terms, are within 10 percent of those shown in Table 12–3, and R^2 is about 1 percent larger. The t–values for the coefficients of the interaction variables are 4.04 and 2.86, respectively; the t–values of the other three coefficients in Equation (12.2) are considerably smaller than 1.0.

Thus, the more elaborate specification fits the data only marginally better than the simple additive one. Nevertheless, it represents a substantially different relationship between quantity and quality. The premium for higher quality units increases with the size of the dwelling unit; it is not proportional to the payment for dwelling unit size. For example, according to Equation (12.2), the difference between the cost of a three room unit with basic residential and dwelling unit quality one standard deviation better than average (i.e., index values of 1.00) and the cost of an average quality unit (index values of 0.00) of the same size is $10.85. For a five room unit, the difference in monthly rent at comparable quality levels is $16.89. The simple additive specification indicates that the same quality premium is $13.62 regardless of dwelling unit size. Figure 12–2 illustrates monthly rent of dwelling units of various sizes at different levels

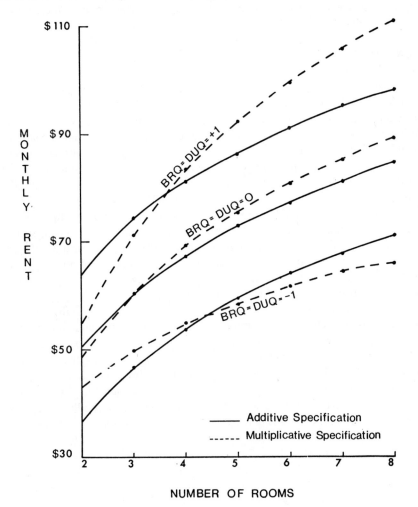

Figure 12–2. Monthly Rent at Alternative Levels of Quality and Size

of quality for both formulations of the model (assuming average values for the remaining explanatory variables).

Within the range of data used in this analysis, there is little basis for choosing among these alternative specifications empirically. A priori, it might be argued that the second specification is more reasonable, but even within the limits of the fairly substantial data base used here, the simple additive specification performs about as well. Understanding the nature of the urban housing market requires a better grasp of these kinds of interrelationships. The difficulty of establishing which model is more "correct" merely illustrates the urgent need for performing similar analyses for larger and more representative samples of data.

CONCLUSION

The analyses presented in this chapter clearly illustrate the complexity of the bundle of residential services consumed by households and, by implication, the inadequacy of so much previous empirical and theoretical work on urban housing markets. Moreover, it clearly indicates the value of more complete bodies of survey data in developing a better understanding of housing markets.

The research findings emphasize the complexity of the bundle of residential services and the importance of residential quality. The quality of a bundle of residential services has at least as much effect on its price as such quantitative aspects as number of rooms, number of bathrooms, and lot size. For example, the monthly rent of a dwelling unit one standard deviation larger than average as measured by number of rooms, number of bathrooms, and lot size is about $16 more than that of an average unit. On the other hand, the additional rent for a unit one standard deviation better than average in basic residential quality and dwelling unit quality is more than $13.

The chapter also provides some weak confirmation on the influence of neighborhood schools on the value of residential properties and indicates that rental properties in the ghetto may be more expensive than those in all-white areas. In these and other respects, the research is hampered by the inadequate sample of suburban properties. Thus, though this analysis represents a substantial improvement over previous studies, the development of truly useful models will require collecting still larger and more extensive bodies of data. In particular, examination of the entire metropolitan housing market is crucial.

Chapter Thirteen

A Simple Model of
Housing Production

with Gregory K. Ingram

INTRODUCTION

This chapter presents a partial equilibrium model of the behavior of individual suppliers of rental housing. This simple model of housing production emphasizes the effects of both existing stocks and heterogeneous and durable structures, and the nonmarket production of many important housing attributes on market demand and the production of housing services.

Most previous systematic analyses of the housing market have treated housing as a single homogeneous good that is fully described by monthly rent or market value.[1] Our analyses have led us to conclude that viewing housing outputs as quantities of a homogeneous good is analytically insufficient, failing as it does to acknowledge important aspects of housing heterogeneity and a number of crucial interdependencies that have important effects on both supply and demand.

It is clear that households demand specific housing attributes or bundles of attributes. Econometric studies have shown that the determinants of demand for individual housing attributes differ in important respects and that at least four separable dimensions of housing output exist: (1) dwelling quality, (2) interior space, (3) interior quality, and (4) neighborhood quality.[2] Moreover, these studies have demonstrated that the metropolitan surfaces of attribute prices differ and that specific attribute prices, particularly gross prices, influence household consumption of particular housing attributes. Gross prices include both monthly rent or monthly housing expense and anticipated monthly travel costs. The latter depend principally on workplace location.

Heterogeneity is important on the supply side, because the costs and profitability of producing each type of housing in each neighborhood depend on the physical characteristics and spatial distribution of the existing stock of housing capital.[3] Interior space and dwelling unit quality can usually be provided by individual housing suppliers, although the cost of producing them will vary markedly from one type of structure to another. For existing structures the amount and arrangement of exterior space can be modified only with great difficulty by individual housing suppliers. The cost of making these changes are so great that they are seldom made.

The problem is further complicated by the fact that not all housing attributes are produced by competitive firms. Individual housing suppliers can do almost nothing to affect several dimensions of neighborhood quality. These invariably depend on the aggregate decisions of large numbers of individual housing suppliers, the location decisions of large numbers of housing consumers, and the collective decisions of units of local government.

SOME ANALYTICS OF HOUSING PRODUCTION

The model presented here assumes that landlords produce distinct bundles of housing comprised of dwelling unit, structure, parcel, and neighborhood attributes. In the simple examples developed in this paper, these housing bundles are represented by discrete levels of structural services, Q_i, that are combined with discrete levels of neighborhood quality, N_j, to produce bundles of housing, B_k. Landlords can alter the level of structural services, Q_i, that they provide, but they cannot individually alter the level of neighborhood quality, N_j, that is available where their structures are located. Of course, a landlord might form expectations about future levels of neighborhood quality, and these expectations might influence his behavior. For the time being, however, we will assume that the level of neighborhood quality is fixed at some level known to the landlord.

The prices that consumers are willing to pay for housing vary by bundle type and location.[4] Since the structure operated by a landlord has both a fixed location and a fixed neighborhood quality, the prices or rents that a landlord can obtain for his units vary only with the level of structural services that he provides. The landlord knows the rents, R_i, corresponding to each Q_i that holds in his zone, and he attempts to provide that level of structural services that maximizes his profits. In Figure 13–1, we illustrate how the rents of housing bundles in these neighborhoods vary with the quantity of structural services produced. From Figure 13–1, it is apparent that the returns from producing larger quantities of structure services can differ greatly by neighborhood.

On the supply side, various levels of structural services are produced by means of a production function defined as

$$Q_i = f(A, H, S_m) \tag{13.1}$$

where

$A =$ annual inputs required to operate and maintain the structure;

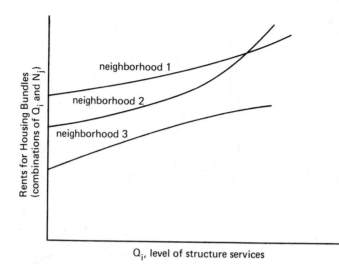

Figure 13-1. Rents, Structure Services, and Neighborhood Quality

H = annual inputs of physical capital from the structure that are not replaced
    (real depreciation);

S_m = various structure types or configurations of specific physical capital.

Since structure service levels, Q_i, and structure types, S_m, are discrete, there is a different production function for each structure type and level of structural services. Figure 13–2 illustrates four production functions that would correspond to two structural service levels (Q_1 and Q_2) and two structure types (S_1 and S_2) where Q_2 represents a higher level of structural services than Q_1.[5]

The production functions in Figure 13–2 illustrate the combinations of quantities of annual operating and maintenance inputs (A) and specific structure capital inputs (H) that can be used to produce each quantity of structure services. The quantities of each input used to produce each kind of structure services depend, of course, on the prices of A and H. The manner in which the isoquants are drawn indicates that more depreciation and fewer operating and maintenance inputs will be used as physical capital becomes less expensive relative to annual inputs. The production functions in Figure 13–2 also indicate that the extent of this substitution is limited, however, and that some minimum operating inputs must always be supplied. Furthermore, as physical capital becomes more expensive, physical capital inputs will eventually fall to zero as they are offset by operating and maintenance expenditures.

Given production functions such as those summarized in Equation (13.1) and illustrated in Figure 13–2; the level of rents in his neighborhood, R_i;

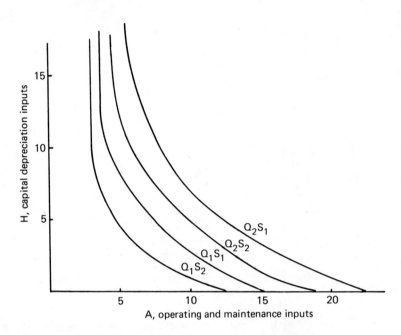

Figure 13-2. Production Functions for Two Output Levels and Two Structure Types

and the price of annual inputs, P_A; the landlord produces that level of structure services that maximizes the present value of his future stream of net revenues

$$V_{i,m} = \sum_{t=1,L} \frac{(R_i - P_A A_{i,m})}{(1+r)^t} \tag{13.2}$$

where r is the landlord's discount rate and L is the life of the structure. The structure's life is a function of the production technique used and is defined as

$$L = \frac{K}{H} \tag{13.3}$$

where H is the net amount of capital depreciation each time period, and K is the amount of physical capital embodied in the landlord's existing structure.

By solving Equation (13.2), the landlord calculates the present value of his revenue stream, which is the value of his structure or physical capital.[6] In order to solve Equation (13.2), however, the landlord must know what production technique to use, which is defined by the ratio of the price of annual inputs to the price of physical capital. Since the price of physical capital is defined as

$$P_H = \frac{V}{K} \tag{13.4}$$

Equation (13.2) must be solved using the production function as a constraint. The solution will be illustrated for the two structure types, two service level cases shown in Figure 13–2.

Because the useful life of a structure varies with the production technique used, each point on the four production functions implies a life for an existing structure. Figure 13–3 shows the relation between structure life and annual inputs that is implied by the production functions in Figure 13–2, assuming that structure types S_1 and S_2 both have 100 units of physical capital. Figure 13–3 makes the trade off between annual inputs and physical depreciation (capital mining) quite apparent. Once the structure lives are known, it is possible to calculate the present value of annual inputs used in each of the four production activities. Figure 13–4 illustrates the relations between structure life and the present value of annual inputs. These relations have simply been derived from Figure 13–3, assuming that the price of annual inputs (P_A) is equal to one and the interest rate is 5 percent.

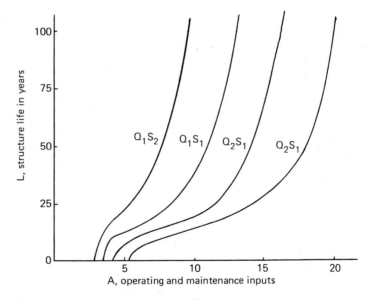

Figure 13-3. Structure Life as a Function of Operating and Maintenance Inputs

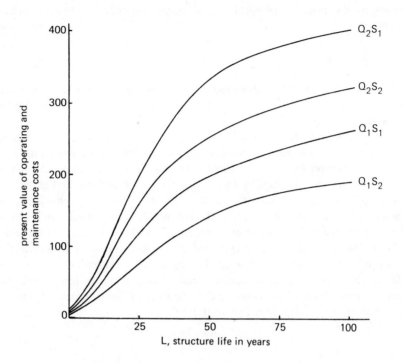

Figure 13-4. Present Value of Operating and Maintenance Costs

When the landlord knows the rent levels for Q_1 and Q_2, he can calculate the present value of future rents for each possible structure life and choose the structure life and level of annual inputs that maximize the difference between the present value of rents and annual input costs. Figure 13–5 shows how the present value of rents varies by structure life for the case where R_2 equals 18 and R_1 equals 10. By calculating the maximum difference in present values between annual costs and rental income for each possible rent level, curves relating rent levels to the present values of the structures can be constructed. Figure 13–6 shows the relations between rental levels and the maximum present values for the cases considered here. From Figure 13–6 it is apparent that the prevailing rental levels for the two levels of structure services will jointly determine the service level produced by each structure type as well as the value of the physical capital embodied in each structure type. For example, if $R_1 = 10$ and $R_2 = 15$, then structures of type 1 will be used to produce structure services of level 2 and structures of type 2 will be used to produce structure services of level 1. If R_2 falls to 13 while R_1 remains at 10, then structures of type 1 will also be used to produce structure services of level 1.

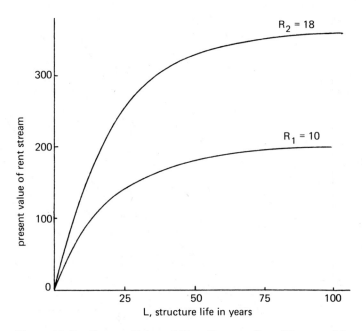

Figure 13–5. Present Value of Rent Streams Over Structure Lives

THE SIMPLE ANALYTICS AND
ABANDONMENT

The simple model of the behavior of housing producers suggests that structures will be withdrawn from production when their value becomes zero. This can happen, first, when the amount of physical capital embodied in the structure goes to zero, or second, when the structure still embodies physical capital but the value of that capital is zero. We will term the former situation "scrapping," and the latter situation "abandonment." A structure is scrapped when it is worn out or in a condition that no longer allows habitation, i.e., its physical capital has been completely depleted. An abandoned structure is not removed from production solely because of its physical condition, however. For example, structures that are abandoned in one part of the city may be in much better condition, i.e., embody more physical capital of the same kind, than structures of the same specific type that are still being using to provide housing in other parts of the city. Indeed, it is precisely this phenomenon that has precipitated widespread concern about abandonment and led observers to conclude that abandonment must signify some malfunctioning of the housing market. The distinction between scrapping and abandonment is drawn here, because scrapping would presumably cause less concern than abandonment.

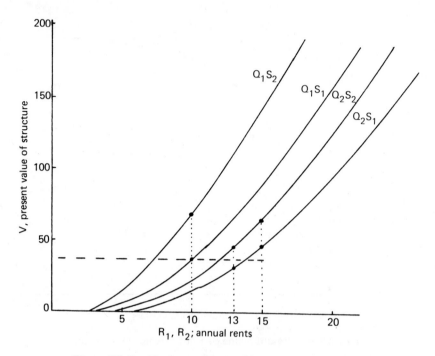

Figure 13-6. Maximum Present Value Obtainable by Activity and Rent Level

Factors that lead to abandonment or scrapping of structures will be differentiated according to their effect on the curves shown in Figure 13–6. Changes in housing market parameters that tend to rotate the curves in Figure 13–6 clockwise about their x–axis intercepts will encourage housing producers to adopt production techniques that reduce structure lives and encourage scrapping. Changes that shift the curves to the right away from the origin will raise the minimum rental required to keep a structure in production, and therefore will encourage abandonment.

Parameter changes that reduce structure lives and promote scrapping include increases in r (the discount rate used by landlords in their present value calculation), and decreases in K (the amount of physical capital embodied in a structure). Parameter changes that promote abandonment include shifts in the production function that require larger amounts of annual inputs for any level of physical capital consumed, and increases in P_A, the price of annual inputs. Finally, reductions in R_i (the market prices of various levels of structure services) will reduce structure lives and promote scrapping if the prices remain above the withdrawal level. As soon as prices fall below the withdrawal level, however, structures will be removed from production regardless of the amount of physical capital they may embody. Shifts in the production function and changes in P_A correspond to supply side explanations of abandonment, while substantial reductions in price correspond to demand side explanations.

To see the implications of the model more clearly, we consider a simple case where the two structure service levels and two structure types shown in Figures 13–2 through 13–6 are located in two different neighborhoods, A and B. In period t_0 these neighborhoods have identical stocks of the two structure types, as well as identical neighborhood quality levels, rent levels, and production functions. The equality of these parameters insures that the structure service output levels in each neighborhood will be the same.

If there is an exogenous shift in demand or change in neighborhood quality in neighborhood A that reduces the level of rents in period t_1, the value of the structures in neighborhood A will decline, and the landlords will alter their production techniques to use more capital depreciation and fewer annual inputs to produce structural services. The new production techniques will tend to shorten the lives of the structures in neighborhood A, and they will be scrapped sooner than those in neighborhood B. In addition, Figure 13–6 suggests that rent decreases in neighborhood A might lead landlords to alter the level of structural services that are produced with the structures in that neighborhood. The particular outcome of this process will depend on the specific rent levels and production functions that exist in the neighborhood.

INTERDEPENDENCE

Thus far, we have implicitly assumed that the level of neighborhood quality in a neighborhood is independent of the actions of individual housing suppliers or the level of structure services provided. Empirical studies of neighborhood quality indicates that neighborhood characteristics are highly correlated. Neighborhoods with large, expensive, high quality dwelling units typically have good schools, high quality local public services, and resident populations with high incomes. As a result, it is difficult to determine empirically the contribution of individual neighborhood attributes to a neighborhood's overall quality level. It is likely, however, that neighborhood quality is determined in part by the mix of structural service levels that are provided in the neighborhood. Thus, neighborhood quality might be given by the expression:

$$N_j = f(Q_1, Q_2, ...Q_n, O) \tag{13.5}$$

where N_j is the neighborhood quality level; Q is the numbers of units provided at each structure service level; and O is a vector of other characteristics that influence neighborhood quality.

Equation (13.5) suggests that the production decisions of individual landlords can aggregate in ways that influence neighborhood quality. Nonetheless, the effect on neighborhood quality of an individual landlord's actions will typically be so small that it will be ignored by a landlord when he decides what level of structure services to produce. However, the interdependence between the production decisions of individual housing suppliers, neighborhood quality, and bundle rents can produce circumstances where relatively small changes in projected rent levels lead to aggregate supply responses that significantly alter the mix of structure services, the level of neighborhood quality, and the schedule of rents in a neighborhood. This possibility can be illustrated with the aid of some additional diagrams.

Figure 13–7 shows how the production of the two structure service levels, Q_1 and Q_2, will vary for the two structure types, S_1 and S_2, as rents vary. For combinations of equilibrium rents that are northwest of the lines labeled S_1 and S_2, service levels of Q_2 will be produced; while for rent combinations southwest of these lines, service levels of Q_1 will be produced. For example, when R_1 is eight and R_2 is twelve, structures of type S_1 will produce level Q_1, and structures of type S_2 will produce quality level Q_2. Rent combinations

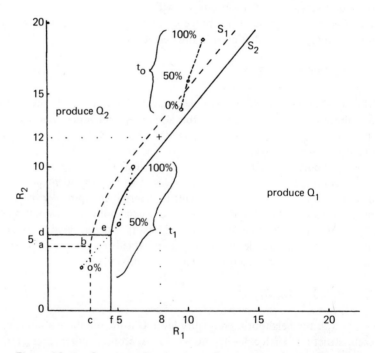

Figure 13–7. Structure Service Level Produced by Structure Types S_1 and S_2 As Rents Vary

within the rectangles *odef* and *oabc* will cause abandonment of structures of type S_1 and S_2 respectively.

Suppose that the number of S_1 structures equals the number of S_2 structures in neighborhoods A and B. The equilibrium proportion of units that have structure service levels of Q_2 can then be either 0, 50, or 100 percent, depending on whether the rents fall below line S_1, between S_1 and S_2, or above S_2 on Figure 13–7. Let us further assume that neighborhood quality is affected by the proportion of units at structure service level Q_2 and that the equilibrium relation between rents and the proportion of units of the type Q_2 changes between period t_0 and t_1 as shown in Figure 13–8. The rents labeled t_0 and t_1 in Figure 13–8 have been plotted onto Figure 13–7.

Partial equilibrium analysis suggests that at time t_0 the equilibrium rent levels are consistent with the decisions of housing suppliers. For example, if neighborhood A originally produced only structure service levels of Q_1 (zero percent Q_2), the equilibrium rents at time t_0 would encourage owners of structures of type S_1 to alter their output from level Q_1 to level Q_2. This would change the mix of structure level outputs from 0 to 50 percent Q_2 and raise the

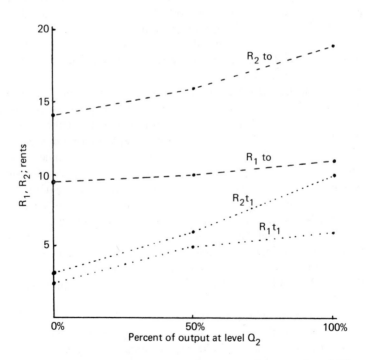

Figure 13-8.   Relation Between Rents and Structure Level Mix Produced at Times t_0 and t_1

rental level in neighborhood A enough to encourage owners of structure type S_2 to begin producing structure services of level Q_2. When all structure services were produced at level Q_2, the supply and demand side of the market would be in stable equilibrium.

When rents fell to their new equilibrium levels in period t_1, owners of structure type S_2 would find it profitable to produce structure services at level Q_1 rather than level Q_2. Their switching would lower rents further, however, and cause owners of type S_1 structures also to produce services at level Q_1. This decision would lower rents still further and lead to abandonment of structures of types S_1 and S_2. By incorporating interdependencies between the production decisions of landlords and the determination of neighborhood quality levels, we have shown that it is possible to generate production responses that lead to abandonment.[7] However, it is clear from Figures 13–7 and 13–8 that this will happen only where particular relations hold between the demand and supply sides of the housing market.

EXPECTATIONS

Thus far the housing production decisions of landlords have been treated within a simple partial equilibrium framework that assumes that landlords use a naive forecasting rule for predicting rents over time. This assumption permits us to treat the landlords' multiperiod decision problem within a one period equilibrium framework. The preceding analysis suggests that abandonment can occur when costs rise or rents fall unexpectedly.

An interesting question is whether abandonment could occur in a multiperiod setting where landlords had perfect foresight or if only scrapping would be observed. In terms of the definitions used in the model and with perfect foresight, could the value of a structure, V, ever become zero before the physical capital embodied in the structure, K, was completely consumed? Abandonment *could* still occur in situations with perfect foresight if the maximum possible capital depreciation rate was insufficient to consume the physical capital in the structure before V became zero. The production functions in Figure 13-2 are drawn in a way that suggests that there is a maximum rate at which physical capital can be consumed. If standards for construction require that structures be built with large amounts of physical capital, then even with perfect foresight a landlord might construct a building, operate it for several periods, and abandon it before its stock of physical capital was completely depleted.

The existence of building codes that are enforced would also promote abandonment rather than scrapping in a situation with perfect foresight. Building codes could be implemented in two general ways. First, they might alter the production function of the landlord by forcing him to make minimum annual expenditures on maintenance and repair. Then, instead of the production functions shown in Figure 13–2, a landlord would face production functions such as those shown in Figure 13–9. The maximum rate at which the capital in the structure could be depleted would be reduced, and structures would be more likely to be abandoned than would be the case if building codes did not exist.

A second and more likely form of building codes would specify a minimum amount of physical capital required of a structure for it to be occupied. A landlord would have to operate his structure subject to the constraint.

$$K \geq K_{code} \tag{13.6}$$

where K is the amount of physical capital in the structure, and Kcode is the minimum amount of physical capital required by the building code. In this situation, scrapping would never occur and buildings would be abandoned when their value was zero, even though they still contained physical capital. Of course, this would occur even if landlords had perfect foresight.

Perfect foresight, therefore, does not imply that abandonment would never occur. It could still be observed in situations where there were limits on the rate at which physical capital consumption could be substituted for

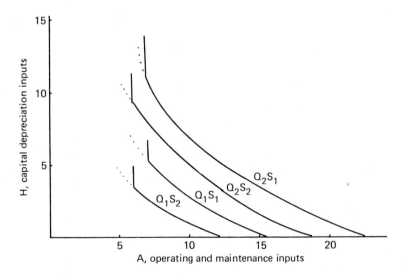

Figure 13-9. Production Functions Subject to Building Code Restrictions

annual expenditures, or where minimum amounts of physical capital were required for production. Errors in forecasting future rents or costs (overestimation of future rent levels or underestimation of future costs) would tend to promote abandonment, however.

Although the representation of abandonment sketched in the simple model presented here can be extended in several directions,[8] it is essentially a partial equilibrium model whose major inputs are the level of rents for various levels of structure services in a particular neighborhood. The model assumes that landlords are pricetakers and that they adapt their production of structure services given these rents and their production functions. In order to use the model effectively to investigate abandonment, it is necessary to determine the level of rents and predict how they will change over time. Determining rents in a given neighborhood is a general equilibrium problem, so the partial equilibrium analyses sketched thus far must be incorporated into a broader framework that determines prices.

Chapter Fourteen

What Should America's Housing Policy Be?

INTRODUCTION

In March 1973 President Nixon suspended all federal low income housing programs and instructed the Department of Housing and Urban Development to undertake a comprehensive review of government housing programs and policies. The report of the National Housing Policy Review, completed in October 1973, drew heavily on earlier economic analyses. Both the national housing review and earlier studies are quite critical of existing housing programs.

These studies contain a serious flaw; they give insufficient attention to the nature and extent of racial discrimination in urban housing markets and, thus, they fail to consider how these effects should influence housing policy. All of the studies contain the usual obligatory references to racial segregation and comment unfavorably on the high proportion of black households living in substandard housing. None documents the extent and nature of black welfare losses attributable to racial discrimination; none points the serious distortions of the processes of urban growth and development caused by this most serious of market imperfections; and none gives serious consideration to remedies. The principal goal of this paper is to correct this oversight. In order to sharpen these distinctions, however, I first summarize the conventional economic analyses of housing markets and of existing policy, which underlie these studies.

CONVENTIONAL ECONOMIC ANALYSES

Both the National Housing Policy Review and the economic analyses that preceded it agree that existing housing programs should receive low marks in terms of both equity and efficiency. Economists emphasize that the bulk of housing subsidies accrue to middle and high income homeowners in the form of favorable tax treatment under the internal revenue code. Roughly two-thirds of federal housing subsidies are indirect and accrue disproportionately to high income households.[1]

These subsidies to middle and high income households, find almost no support among economists. They are most often justified by the argument that the total supply of housing will be increased and that lower income households will obtain improved housing as units previously occupied by higher income groups "filter down." For a filtering strategy to benefit low income households, however, subsidies for the production of expensive units must cause a decline in the price of housing services consumed by low income households.

If the housing market operated in this way, filtering might be an attractive method of solving the low income housing problem. However, neither my review of recent economic analyses of urban housing markets nor my own research provides any support for this view of filtering. Subsidies to high quality units primarily reduce the price of these units. The price of close substitutes may also decline somewhat, but the effect on the price of low quality units appears to be small or nonexistent.

In addition to the estimated $9 to 10 billion in indirect subsidies to housing consumption which largely benefit high income households, the federal government in 1972 provided approximately $2.5 billion in direct subsidies targeted primarily at low income households. With a single exception these programs link the provision of subsidies to new construction. Economists point out that subsidies to specific factor inputs are almost always inefficient, and there is ample evidence that this general dictum applies to housing programs.

The federal government has not funded existing low income subsidy programs at levels that would make subsidized units available to all low income households. As a result, a few lucky families receive very large benefits while most receive none. The combination of very large subsidies for a few poor households and zero subsidies for the many has led economists to recommend instead some form of direct cash assistance to all low income households, either an unrestricted income transfer or a housing allowance. With a given budget, recipient households would receive much smaller subsidies, but all households would be treated equally. Moreover, since existing production-oriented programs are inefficient—i.e., provide a low ratio of benefits to subsidy—total benefits would be increased as well.

When asked to choose between an unfettered cash allowance and a housing allowance on strict efficiency or welfare grounds, few economists will choose a housing allowance. But economists who favor greater redistribution will often support housing allowances on the grounds that Congress can be persuaded to vote larger quantities of tied transfers than untied transfers.

The most frequent objection to housing allowances is based on the belief that such subsidies would simply increase housing prices. I can find very little support for this view among economists. They argue that income transfer or housing allowance programs would affect metropolitan housing markets in approximately the same way as increases in aggregate metropolitan area incomes. They find no evidence that these "natural" increases in income have caused large increases in housing prices and point out that the magnitudes proposed under housing allowance programs are considerably smaller.

In addition, economists question whether construction programs that do not increase effective demand will lead to permanent increases in the housing supply. Their predominant opinion is that federal subsidies may cause a temporary increase in residential construction or influence the kind and location of units built, but that production subsidies will generally produce a smaller permanent increase in the housing supply than unrestricted subsidies. If production subsidies expand the stock more quickly than effective demand, the rate of housing depreciation merely increases. The coincidence of a rapid growth of federal subsidized production programs and abandonment provides some support for this pessimistic view.

The high cost of providing subsidized housing through new construction and the apparent unwillingness of Congress to budget sums large enough to house all households eligible for these programs have produced another undesirable feature of low income subsidy programs. In an effort to hide or at least disguise the budgetary cost of these housing subsidies, proponents of low income housing subsidies have turned to back door financing. Their intent is to minimize the apparent budgetary impacts of housing subsidies by relying on accelerated depreciation, abatement of local property taxes, tax exempt local bonds, and advantageous, federally insured or subsidized financing terms. Since these measures invariably have resource costs and costs to the treasury that far exceed the amounts that appear in the expenditure budget, they are universally disliked by economists.

In summary, the large number of economic analyses of housing problems in recent years have produced remarkably similar diagnoses and prescriptions. They conclude that housing is primarily a private good, that substandard housing conditions are largely the result of poverty, and that existing housing policies are inefficient and inequitable. Specifically, they find these programs are characterized by a low ratio of benefits to real resource costs, and that they are designed so that a small percentage of poor households obtain large subsidies while the overwhelming majority receives none whatsoever.

It is generally agreed that most of the deficiencies of current programs result from a mistaken emphasis on new construction and that standard housing for low income households could be more efficiently provided through programs that employ existing housing stocks. Moreover, programs that exploit existing housing stocks would provide low income households with a wider selection of housing at much lower subsidy cost per unit. These common findings have led virtually every economist who has studied housing to recommend the replacement of existing housing assistance programs with a general income transfer or a housing allowance. Although the report of the

National Housing Policy Review does not present any recommendations, it is clear that its authors would agree.[2]

RACE AND HOUSING POLICY

If economists paid more attention to the heavy costs imposed by housing market discrimination on black Americans and to the distortions to metropolitan growth produced by existing patterns of racial segregation, they might still recommend that existing housing programs be discontinued. But they would be much slower to embrace a pure market solution.

When the full range and magnitude of these costs are recognized, it is difficult to escape the conclusion that federal housing policy should be reoriented to provide equal opportunity in housing and to redirect historical patterns of ghetto expansion. Moreover, when these are accepted as primary goals for federal housing policy, even the clear-cut case in favor of housing allowances becomes cloudy. Indeed, a strong "theoretical" justification for production subsidies emerges. First, however, we must examine the range and magnitude of welfare losses resulting from housing market discrimination.

COSTS OF HOUSING MARKET DISCRIMINATION

Any discussion of the welfare losses caused by racial discrimination in urban housing markets should distinguish between three kinds of welfare losses: those borne by blacks, those borne by the white majority, and general efficiency losses. In the case of blacks it is useful to distinguish further between those costs associated with housing consumption and losses resulting from limitations on residential location.

Insofar as economists have considered housing market discrimination at all, they have generally asked only whether housing market discrimination causes black households to pay more than white households for identical bundles of housing services. A definitive answer even to this apparently simple question has proved elusive because of the inherent methodological questions it involves. There is now general agreement, however, that blacks typically pay more than whites for the same housing bundles.[3] These discrimination markups appear to be higher in areas with larger and more rapidly growing black populations and in areas where black populations are restricted to the central city. There is some indication, however, that these differentials may have declined in recent years.[4]

Although discrimination markups of this magnitude represent serious welfare losses for black Americans, they are only the tip of the iceberg. Nearly all available estimates of discrimination markups implicitly assume that housing is a homogeneous good and that housing in the ghetto is the same as housing outside the ghetto, except for price. In fact, housing is a bundle of heterogeneous attributes, the characteristics of housing bundles available in the ghetto differ from those available in the rest of the metropolitan housing market, and the discrimination markups of these numerous housing bundles or attributes are not uniform.[5]

Using the methodology employed in earlier studies, Chapter Twelve presents estimates of discrimination markups of 5 percent for owner-occupied units and 9 percent for rental units in St. Louis, Missouri, in 1967.[6] But, when the heterogeneity of housing markets is taken into account, the estimated welfare loss is much larger. More extensive analyses by John Quigley and me published in *Housing Markets and Racial Discrimination,* reveal that the typical ghetto rental unit could be obtained for 13 percent less in all-white areas, while the typical nonghetto rental and owner-occupied units would cost 14 percent and 15 percent more respectively in the ghetto than in the nonghetto housing market.[7]

Worse yet, many desirable housing bundles are either very scarce or completely unavailable in the ghetto. To consume these desirable kinds of housing, Negro households have to seek housing in neighborhoods not sanctioned for Negro occupancy. There, without guarantee of success, they must devote inordinate amounts of time and money to househunting, and subject themselves and their families to humiliation and harassment. As a result, most blacks limit their search for housing to the ghetto. Housing market discrimination thus operates to restrict black access to the newest, highest quality housing in the best neighborhoods. It is hardly surprising, as a result, that black households consume less of both neighborhood and dwelling unit quality and exterior space and spend less on housing than would be predicted from a knowledge of their incomes and other characteristics.[8]

As the analysis presented in Chapter Seven reveals these same supply restrictions insure that blacks are much less likely to be homeowners than white households of similar income and family structure. For example while only 18 percent of black households in Chicago were homeowners, 47 percent would have been homeowners in the absence of housing market discrimination.[9] Similar differences were obtained for 17 other large metropolitan areas; the differences between actual and "expected" black ownership rates among these 18 areas appear to be related systematically to the extent to which the central city ghetto contained units suitable for owner occupancy and the extent of black access to suburban housing.

Restrictions on Negro homeownership opportunities have far greater ramifications than may be evident at first glance. As Chapter Seven also illustrates, an effective limitation on homeownership can increase Negro housing costs by over 30 percent, assuming no price appreciation. Moreover, given reasonable assumptions about increases in housing prices, a Negro household prevented from buying a home in 1950 would have out-of-pocket housing costs in 1970 more than twice as high as the costs would have been if the family had purchased a home 20 years earlier. These increases in housing costs are in addition to any discrimination price markups.

Of course, much of the savings from homeownership results from the favorable treatment accorded homeowners under the federal income tax. Since Negro households at all income levels are impeded by housing market discrimination from purchasing and owning single family homes, they are prevented from taking full advantage of these tax benefits. The loss of tax benefits is greatest for middle and upper income black households, since tax savings from homeownership increase with income.

INDIRECT EFFECTS ON BLACK HOUSEHOLDS

The restrictions on black access to homeownership documented in Chapter Seven may explain why Negro households at every income level have less wealth than white households. Moreover, the full effects of housing market discrimination extend far beyond housing and include additional, more subtle, costs and welfare losses for the black population. Segregated housing patterns create unequal educational opportunities, increase insurance and other living costs, and contribute to employment discrimination for blacks.

De facto segregation, rooted in racial discrimination in urban housing markets, has displaced *de jure* segregation as the principal cause of segregated education and the inferior quality it typically signifies.[10] Again, it is middle class and upwardly mobile blacks, who wish their children to have the best education possible, who suffer most from existing patterns of segregated education. Blacks who buy homes in the ghetto either are forced to pay more for theft and fire insurance than would be the cost in suburban communities or are unable to obtain coverage at all.[11] Mortgage financing will be more difficult to obtain and often will be obtained only on less favorable terms than in the suburbs. These premiums will be in addition to the discrimination markups and homeownership considerations discussed previously. Ghetto residents, moreover, will usually pay more for auto insurance than suburban whites.

As the analysis in Chapter Eight shows, housing segregation and discrimination reinforce more direct forms of employment discrimination. Geographic limitations on the residential choice of nonwhites insure that blacks can reach many jobs only by making timeconsuming and expensive commutes. If blacks seek, obtain, and accept these distant jobs, their real wages (money wages minus the money and time outlays for commuting) will be less than those of comparable white workers. Often they will not even learn of available jobs far from the ghetto or will not bother to apply because of the cost and difficulty of reaching them. Faced with these difficulties, they may accept low paying jobs near the ghetto or no job at all, choosing leisure and welfare as rational alternatives to low pay and poor working conditions.

As the discussions in Chapters Six and Nine point out, racial discrimination imposes heavy costs on the majority white population as well as on minorities. Commuting costs of centrally employed whites are appreciably higher than they would be if housing market discrimination and segregation did not exist. The steady growth of central city ghettos has forced centrally employed high and middle income whites to move farther and farther from their places of employment, increasing commuting time and costs. The intense pressures for expensive high speed highway and transit links to declining central employment areas is one of the consequences.

Moreover, racial discrimination and the steady growth of central city ghettos have seriously distorted the patterns of urban growth and development in recent decades. If racial discrimination had not existed in urban housing markets, private location decisions would have produced a far different geographic distribution of the low income, black population. If the suburbs had been open to middle and low income blacks, many would have moved to suburban areas along with their jobs, much in the fashion of whites of similar socioeconomic status. But discriminatory practices have effectively restricted black households to central city neighborhoods and the poverty of entrapped minority and other disadvantaged populations insured that central city housing would deteriorate. The result has been a steady expansion of slum housing, deterioration of urban services, and an expectation that the process would continue until the entire central city became a black slum. This pattern of urban development presents us with the current policy dilemma: can these historical trends be reversed or is the economic, physical, and social decline of our great cities inevitable?

IMPLICATIONS FOR GOVERNMENT HOUSING POLICY

Conventional economic analyses of government housing programs implicitly recognize as legitimate only a single goal for America's housing policy—to improve the housing condition of the poor. Because economists generally consider the housing market as the epitome of the competitive market, it is hardly surprising that they are unable to justify housing programs per se, as contrasted to income redistribution programs. They conclude that existing housing programs should be phased out as quickly as possible and should be replaced by either an unrestricted income allowance or a housing allowance.

Recognition of the large welfare losses borne by black Americans and of the large distortions in metropolitan growth and development resulting from a continuation of existing patterns of racial segregation greatly complicates the analysis. Three goals must be considered seriously: (1) to provide black households with a full range of housing alternatives at prices and on terms comparable to the majority; (2) to eliminate existing geographic or spatial barriers on the residential location of black households; and (3) to correct the distortions of metropolitan growth and development caused by the growth of large concentrations of poor black households. When these three goals are added to the goal of redistribution, the case for a federal housing and urban development policy is greatly strengthened.

Federal housing programs and policies should be designed to encourage individual minority households to consider housing outside of established minority neighborhoods and to facilitate minority groups in locating and securing housing throughout the entire metropolitan housing market. In particular, if the numerous interest and construction subsidies to builders and developers are continued, even greater efforts should be made to insure that these agents pursue active open occupancy and equal opportunity programs as a condition for continued federal subsidy.

The need for effective policies to combat racial discrimination and segregated living patterns is the strongest rationale for a major federal role in housing. There is considerable evidence that federal officials, who are insulated from local pressures, are able to take a longer view of urban development trends than local officials and are better able to reduce discriminatory practices. If current federal responsibilities for housing and urban development are transferred to state agencies, adequate safeguards must be developed to insure that active open occupancy policies are instituted and enforced.

There is a need, however, to evaluate the indirect effects of all federal programs to insure that they do not operate to maintain and to support existing patterns of racial segregation. This objective could be accomplished by requiring all federal programs to file racial segregation impact statements, similar to the environmental impact statements. Although there is always the danger that such provisions would become pro forma, they would tend to make policymakers consider explicitly the indirect effects of their programs and policies on the patterns of racial segregation in American cities.

If the paramount importance of changing existing patterns of residence by race is recognized, a credible argument for the much criticized production subsidies can be made. In theory, production subsidies could be a powerful instrument to entice builders and state and local governments to provide housing for minority households outside of established areas of racial concentration. Unfortunately, these programs have tended to operate in precisely the opposite way in the past, and the politics of housing location probably will not change in the near future. Most subsidized projects will continue to be built in high cost central locations with unfavorable neighborhood environments, where high land costs will insure that the required subsidy per assisted unit will be quite large. Moreover, these heavily subsidized units, in general, will not be the kinds of housing in strong demand by black households and in short supply in the ghetto.

The preceding discussion makes it clear that efficient operation of any housing program depends critically on modifying existing patterns of residence by race. To accomplish this objective, a number of economists have proposed the use of payments to encourage whites to move into predominantly black neighborhoods and to encourage blacks to move into all or predominantly white neighborhoods. The size of these payments would be scaled to the degree of integration existing in the neighborhood. No payments would be provided to blacks who wish to live in all-black neighborhoods or to whites choosing all-white neighborhoods. Although simple incentives of this kind are hard to fault on grounds of narrow economic efficiency, they have little chance of gaining public acceptance. Still, a number of more modest schemes in the spirit of this proposal might be accepted by the public, particularly if they were aware of the full cost of existing patterns of racial discrimination.

In principle, a housing allowance program could be a nearly ideal instrument to achieve an orderly reduction in the geographic isolation of black Americans. The allowances could be structured to encourage greater racial and economic integration and, more importantly, to discourage the intense concentration of black and poverty populations that produce unfavorable neighborhood effects in urban housing markets. Specifically, allowances either could be scaled to the social and economic concentration of particular neighborhoods or quotas could be employed. In the first instance, housing allowance recipients would be given larger allowances for housing in neighborhoods where few allowance recipients currently resided. A quota system might operate with a uniform allowance, but refuse to approve units in neighborhoods once the number of recipients reaches a certain prescribed level. Quotas and sliding subsidy scales might be justified as a way to spread the burden, to insure that no community or neighborhood is forced to accept a disproportionate number of disadvantaged households, and to minimize the likelihood of adverse neighborhood effects. HUD is currently engaged in a large scale program of housing allowance experiments. Although HUD officials obviously hope the program will reduce racial concentration somewhat, they, to my knowledge, have given no consideration to using the program in the manner described. In addition, they are fearful that fears of too rapid a dispersal of the black population might provoke opposition to the proposal.

A housing allowance program also could provide attractive opportunities to aid minority households in locating housing outside the ghetto and to monitor the activities of lenders, builders, and housing suppliers. The success of such measures, of course, depends on adequate and sympathetic staffing and on high level support for the aims of the program. Extreme care would have to be taken to insure that these information and counseling programs did not operate in precisely the opposite way, i.e., to discourage black households from searching for housing outside the ghetto and to channel them into the ghetto housing supply.

Recognition of the full range of effects of housing market discrimination on black housing consumption at once undermines the case of housing allowances and strengthens the case for an unrestricted income transfer. As long as minority households do not have access to the entire metropolitan housing supply, measures to increase the amounts available for them to spend on housing will be far less effective in reducing the housing deficiency of minority households than similar measures would be for the majority. If these minority households are given the freedom to spend the increased purchasing power in the manner they deem best, they will spend less on housing than white households of similar incomes and circumstances. If they are forced to spend all of the increased resources on housing, they will obtain less housing than similar white households.

Of course, if a housing allowance program was designed to assist black households in locating and acquiring housing outside the ghetto or, better yet, if the subsidy formula reflected the racial composition of the neighborhood where the housing is acquired, these criticisms would have less force. Moreover, even if there is no reduction in housing market discrimination, increases in black expenditures for housing would undoubtedly induce some additional housing investment and improve housing conditions somewhat within the ghetto. But the improvement obtained in this way would generally be much smaller than that which would be achieved if blacks had free access to the entire metropolitan housing market, where the possible supply responses are more varied.

The overwhelming evidence that discrimination reduces the opportunity of black households to be homeowners provides a powerful rationale for a special minority mortgage loan program. At minimum, the large impact of this impairment on Negro housing costs and on the ability of black households to save and to accumulate wealth justifies a special effort to insure that the mortgage applications of black households receive sympathetic review under existing programs, regardless of the location of the properties concerned. Moreover it is crucial that these programs give full credit to the earnings of black females in the assessment of the financial strength of potential black borrowers. Female earnings are, of course, far more important for black households than for white households.

Blacks wishing to buy properties outside of established minority concentrations should be assured that these mortgage applications receive rapid and sympathetic review under existing programs. In addition, it would be desirable to develop legislation that would enable FHA to give more favorable terms (lower interest rates, smaller down payments, and longer terms) to minority households purchasing properties in areas distant from the ghetto.[12] Unfortunately, the effectiveness of both existing programs and any special minority mortgage loan program would be appreciably diminished by the limited supply of suitable housing in existing black neighborhoods.

Negro households are a large potential market for homeownership. As Negro incomes continue to increase, this potential demand will grow. It is well to emphasize, however, that these higher levels of homeownership will not be realized unless Negro households gain access to a supply of suitable housing. A combination of favorable terms, good service, and aggressive marketing by FHA would be a powerful force to loosen the barriers to Negro entry into middle and high income neighborhoods. Such policies would enable black households to obtain the higher quality housing which existing patterns of discrimination and segregation now appear to prevent them from consuming. A minority mortgage loan program would help redress the effects of earlier FHA policies that had made it difficult or impossible for minorities to acquire housing in white residential areas, policies that were among the most effective instruments for maintaining segregated living patterns.

In the aftermath of the Detroit and Watts riots a number of banks and insurance companies instituted minority mortgage loan programs. Valuable lessons in how not to design a minority mortgage loan program can be gleaned from this experience. The BBURG (Boston Banks Urban Renewal Group) program was typical. It provided mortgages on more favorable terms to minority households. Unfortunately, eligibility for BBURG loans was limited to a few neighborhoods adjacent to Boston's ghetto. The consequences were completely predictable. Black demand for homeownership was channeled into these few neighborhoods, accelerating the process of racial transition and consolidating Boston's black ghetto. Racial antagonism in the neighborhood was heightened, and many white occupants who might have remained in an integrated neigborhood were forced out. A minority mortgage problem should be designed to reduce the pressure on transitional neighborhoods in the path of ghetto expansion rather than to exacerbate it. At minimum, it should be neutral in terms of residential location. Preferably, it should encourage minority households to seek out housing in predominantly white middle and upper income neighborhoods distant from existing minority concentrations.

Government price guarantees for properties located in the path of ghetto expansion should also be considered. It is widely believed that racial integration causes property values to decline. Although this belief would appear to be inconsistent with the evidence that housing prices and rents are higher in the ghetto than outside, a number of studies of the trends in housing prices in transitional neighborhoods have identified a pattern of short run price movements that may explain this apparent contradiction.[13]

White demand for properties in threatened neighborhoods may suddenly fall off in anticipation of their transition to Negro occupancy. Although prices are eventually re-established at an even higher level, they may reach quite low levels during the hiatus between white flight and large scale black entry. Owners who panic and sell their properties during this period may suffer large capital losses. Even a few experiences of this kind, no matter how atypical, may be sufficient to perpetuate white fears about the effect of integration on the value of their properties.

If a program could be designed to support prices during critical periods in transitional neighborhoods, it would remove a source of racial hostility, inhibit panic selling, and perhaps help stabilize neighborhoods in the path of ghetto expansion. It would be difficult to design a program of this kind because of the complexity of urban housing markets and the difficulty of disentangling the short run dynamics accompanying racial integration from longer run influences in housing markets. Even so, the feasibility of such a program should be investigated. Extreme care should be taken, however, to insure that the program does not encourage more rapid transition.

The evidence that housing market discrimination significantly reduces Negro homeownership supports the case for revision of the current treatment of homeownership expenses under the federal income tax. These provisions, which encourage high income households to increase their housing consumption and which provide far fewer benefits and inducements to low income households, cannot be justified either in terms of equity or of efficiency. They are even more difficult to justify when the differential access of black households to homeownership is recognized. If there is a strong policy preference to encourage homeownership, a simple tax credit would be far more effective.

SOME CONCLUDING OBSERVATIONS

Rapid expansion of the Negro ghetto into good quality neigborhoods adjacent to it is the most likely way in which black housing conditions would be improved under current market circumstances. In some metropolitan areas, a large increase in Negro purchasing power would cause relatively large amounts of good housing to be added to the ghetto fairly quickly. In other metropolitan areas, where the supply of appropriate housing on the boundaries of the ghetto is less plentiful, rapid peripheral growth would do little to improve Negro housing conditions. But if the social costs of continued peripheral expansion of massive central city ghettos are as high as I believe, these desirable short term improvements in black housing conditions may exact a very high long run price in adverse impacts on metropolitan growth and development.

A major goal of federal housing and urban development programs has been to arrest the physical and economic decline of central cities. These programs have been unequal to powerful market and nonmarket forces that operate in the opposite direction and thus have not been particularly successful. Discriminatory practices in urban housing markets and the resulting rapid growth of central city ghettos are the most important of these countervailing forces.

As long as the ghetto continues its rapid growth, land and housing prices in central cities will remain at high levels, the expectation that the city will become a lower class slum will persist, and government programs aimed at reversing these trends will fail. If the growth of the ghetto could be arrested, positive programs to make the central city attractive to middle income families, either white or black, would have a chance. Without this change in the dynamics of metropolitan development, the development trends outlined in this paper cannot be reversed. The first objective of federal housing policy, therefore, should be to open suburban housing to minority households.

Although black Americans remain intensely segregated, there are some indications that increasing numbers of black households are moving to the suburbs. A full evaluation of these changes and their implications must await more detailed analyses, but the limited evidence available suggests that the forces of housing discrimination in a number of metropolitan areas are waning. At the same time, other metropolitan areas, particularly those in the South, may be becoming more segregated. Historically, southern metropolitan areas, particularly older ones, did not exhibit the massive concentration of black households which characterized northern ones. Unfortunately, they appear to be developing patterns of racial segregation similar to those found in large northern metropolitan areas.

Qualitative changes in recent decades in the nature of the forces that maintain housing market segregation provide even more basis for optimism. A few years ago, government actively supported and maintained segregated living patterns. The most effective weapons to maintain segregation, for example racial covenants and FHA mortgage loan policies, are no longer available. Racial discrimination in urban housing markets is now unlawful, and the federal government and numerous state and local governments have promulgated a number of important regulations that would limit the ability of lenders, brokers, sellers, property owners, and developers to discriminate against minorities.

These changes in law and in government policy and practice reflect long term trends in the attitudes of the American population toward racial discrimination.[14] Whereas a short time ago an individual who would openly discriminate in housing could expect strong vocal approval from his friends and neighbors, today he often will feel obliged to hide his actions and motives. Brokers, who once openly refused to serve blacks, must now disguise their discriminatory actions. Because of changes in law and community attitudes, brokers are increasingly willing to show property in white neighborhoods to black households.

Because racial prejudice persists and because discriminatory acts in urban housing markets are so difficult to detect and prove, policies that insure that minority households have access to the entire metropolitan housing market on an equal basis with the white majority will be very difficult to formulate. It would be irresponsible to design and implement housing programs and policies that depended on minority access to the entire housing market without a sober evaluation of the likelihood of breaching the barriers which currently limit the housing choices of these households. The task is clearly a difficult and demanding one. But changes in the extent and nature of discriminatory practices suggest such policies could succeed, and the benefits to the entire population of the successful eradication or even significant amelioration of existing discriminatory are inestimable.

Part V

Urban Transportation

Chapter Fifteen

Comparative Costs of Alternative Urban Transport Technologies

This chapter summarizes the principal findings of an analysis of the comparative costs of alternative urban passenger transportation technologies. The central (but not the exclusive) focus of the cost analyses was the provision of services to commuters traveling between home and downtown workplaces during rush hours. The systems analyzed thus incorporate high performance, high volume capabilities seldom encountered or needed for other than urban radial, CBD-oriented transportation facilities. For analytical purposes the total CBD commuter trip pattern was separated into three functional parts for analysis: (1) residential collection and distribution; (2) line haul service; and (3) downtown distribution. These different trip segments represent considerably different operating conditions and environments and frequently are carried out by different technologies. Thus, it is analytically convenient (in fact, nearly essential) to develop cost models for each trip component separately and then to combine them into different total systems.

SYSTEM SPECIFICATION

The cost analyses emphasized evaluation of different technological systems for carrying specific passenger volumes under approximately the same conditions of service.[1] Costs may be considered precise only for the assumed conditions of service, volume, and design. The following are examples of major input variables considered to be relevant: (1) transport type; (2) hourly volume level (and its origin and destination pattern and distribution); (3) route length; (4) station (or ramp) spacing; (5) overall trip speed or travel time; (6) schedule frequency; and (7) seating space (or comfort level).

Analyses of transport technologies were restricted to those in current use: (1) automobile, (2) bus, and (3) rail transit. In each case, attention was concentrated on that representative of each type which seemed best suited for the peak hour commuter function. (That is, we suboptimized for vehicle type—where this was ambiguous each was costed explicitly.)

Choice of specific volume levels, while arbitrary, was directly related to available peak hour, cordon count data for most urban downtown or core areas throughout the nation. The corridor volume levels used in the cost analyses—5,000–50,000 per peak hour—cover most American cities plus a generous allowance for peaking and growth. (For example, the Boston Highland branch has fewer than 5,000 peak hour passengers, the Cleveland Westside line approximately 5,000, the much-heralded Chicago Congress Street Expressway—Douglas Park line approximately 10,000, and the Toronto Young Street line 20,000.)

In costing these systems, they were assumed to be special purpose, journey to work facilities, and all system costs were charged to peak hour users (e.g., it was assumed the systems operated only four hours per day, five days per week). From the demand analysis it is clear that this costing assumption favors those systems with private line haul facilities most, and those using shared highway facilities least.

LINE HAUL SYSTEMS

Line haul cost analyses were carried out for: (1) three modes—private auto, bus transit (operating both on private and shared right of ways), and rail transit; (2) three route lengths—six, ten, and fifteen miles; (3) passenger volumes varying between 5,000 and 50,000 per hour; and (4) systems constructed in high density and medium density metropolitan areas, since facility construction and right of way costs depend crucially on the intensity of urban development.[2]

Specific service, volume, and operating characteristics hypothesized for the line haul cost analyses are as follows:

1. Passenger volumes are distributed uniformly along the route length. This greatly simplifies the costing and does little harm to the generality of the findings and analytical techniques employed.

2. Cost comparisons are made both with and without along the line and reverse direction or minor direction service incorporated into the systems. This permits evaluation of the costs of providing such services and indicates how their provision modifies the quality of services as measured in other directions—for example, provisions of along the line service almost invariably reduces the quality of service rendered to "through" travelers moving from along the line stations directly to the CBD.

3. At all line haul stations, at least one bus or train must run every two mintues. This assumed two minute schedule frequency restriction does not materially affect rail transit operations and costs, but it strongly affects bus operations and costs at low volume levels. Thus, alternative operating schemes for buses are considered in which transfers and multiple stops are permitted.

4. The line haul bus systems evaluated are operated over grade-separated highways reserved exclusively for buses, or over mixed-traffic expressways with input control devices to prevent congestions, so that maximum speeds and efficiency can be attained.

5. Total travel time per vehicular trip must be either less than ten minutes or at an average speed for the entire trip of not less than 35 miles per hour, whichever is greater. The ten minutes constraint is generally binding on route lengths of two miles or less and the 35 mile constraint on all others.

6. Equal seating space standards are used for rail and bus—the same number of square feet per passenger are allowed for seating. An automobile is always assumed to have a capacity of 1.6 persons.

7. Line haul stations or ramps are located at one mile intervals, with the first station one mile from the downtown stub terminal.

8. Underground stub terminals are included for all transit systems, and parking charges are included in the automobile system.

9. Fares are collected (whenever it is more economical) in the terminal mezzanine, much as they are now on rail transit systems. A third door is added to each bus, and double side loading and unloading is permitted. These changes greatly reduce loading and unloading time, reduce the terminal area lengths required, increase utilization rates for bus equipment and labor, and thereby reduce both capital and labor costs. These changes amount to adapting some principles of rail transit and high capacity toll facility operations to buses. When coupled with the improvements permitted by operation over grade-separated and exclusive-use highways, they allow high speed and high quality bus transit services vastly superior to today's usual poor, local street bus service.

10. No real innovations are assumed for the automobile system analyzed, but the car occupancy and parking requirements assumed are powerful determinants of final system costs. The occupancy rate is particularly important since nearly proportional reductions in automobile travel costs may be achieved by increasing the occupancy rate. Parking charges or costs are the single most important cost item entering the automobile cost estimates; they can account for as much as 40 percent of total passenger car system costs.[3]

SOME COST COMPARISONS FOR
LINE HAUL SYSTEMS

Figure 15–1 summarizes several of the more important findings of the line haul cost analyses. Shown in Figure 15–2 is a comparison of the cost per trip incurred by the different transit modes for a complete inbound and outbound service for medium and high population density, a ten mile route length and volumes ranging from 5,000 to 50,000 passengers per peak hour. Also shown are private automobile costs, assuming an average passenger occupancy of 1.6 persons.

The cost comparisons reveal that either bus or rail transit is

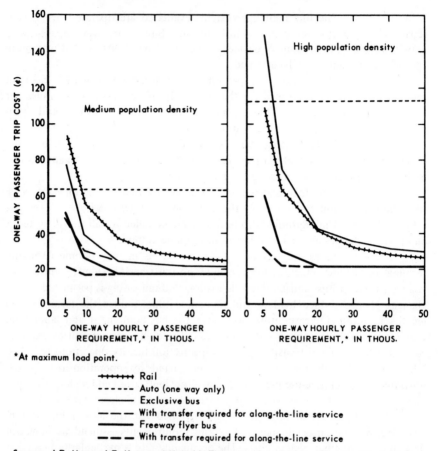

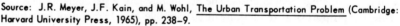

*At maximum load point.

┼┼┼┼┼┼ Rail
‑ ‑ ‑ ‑ ‑ Auto (one way only)
——————— Exclusive bus
— — — With transfer required for along-the-line service
━━━━━ Freeway flyer bus
▬ ▬ ▬ With transfer required for along-the-line service

Source: J.R. Meyer, J.F. Kain, and M. Wohl, The Urban Transportation Problem (Cambridge: Harvard University Press, 1965), pp. 238‑9.

Figure 15‑1. Line Haul Systems: Ten Mile Route Length With Complete Two Way Service

considerably cheaper than the automobile for meeting peak hour line haul transportation requirements at very high corridor volumes. (Although not shown in Figure 15‑1, the advantage of transit over private automobile tends to be inversely related to route length.) However, at low corridor volumes, an automobile system, even with only 1.6 passengers in each car, is often cheaper than either rail or exclusive bus transit, if transfers are not permitted in the bus systems. This is particularly true under medium to low population density assumptions. Automobile system costs can be reduced further simply by increasing the number of passengers per vehicle, which results in an almost proportional reduction in costs. With five passengers per vehicle, automobile

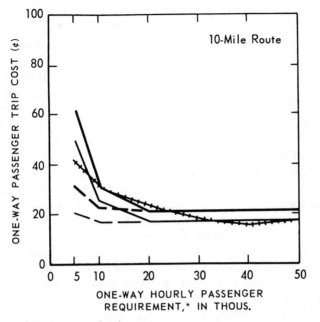

*At maximum load point.

++++++ Rail (operating and equipment costs only)
———— Freeway flyer bus: high population density
— — — With transfer required for along-the-line service
━━━━━ Freeway flyer bus: low population density
▬ ▬ ▬ With transfer required for along-the-line service

Source: J.R. Meyer, J.F. Kain, and M. Wohl, <u>The Urban
Transportation Problem</u> (Cambridge: Harvard University
Press, 1965), p. 240.

Figure 15–2. Low Cost Line Haul Systems: Complete Two Way
Service, Ten Mile Route Length

costs per trip drop close to and sometimes below those for public transit, even at
the highest volumes. Of course, such a reduction must be "paid for" in reduced
quality of service, and the low automobile occupancy rates observed in U.S.
cities suggest that many commuters regard the drawbacks of car pooling as not
worth these cost savings.

A somewhat surprising result of the cost comparisons is that bus
transit at low and medium densities is almost invariably cheaper than rail.
Indeed, a freeway flier system (an express bus system operating on a
mixed-traffic expressway and paying only its proportionate share of the
facilities' capital costs), if afforded congestion-free travel, is always the cheapest

form of high performance line haul transit, even at high population densities. Low costs of the freeway flier are attributable, of course, to line haul facilities that can be employed for other purposes, namely, the movement of private passenger vehicles and trucks.

A bus system operating on its own reserved or exclusive right of way (express bus on exclusive right-of-way) yields cost characteristics very much like those of freeway fliers, except that the absolute cost level is usually 15 to 20 percent higher. These additional costs are enough so that at high population densities exclusive bus systems generally have higher average costs per trip than rail systems. Even at medium densities, bus systems do not have a pronounced cost advantage over rail at the higher volume levels.

Rail systems are clearly at their best when population densities are high, runs are short, and trip volumes are high. Such findings are hardly unexpected. They mainly reflect the well-known facts that rail systems require less right of way than do highway systems for handling high volume or high density work loads, and that rail has a very heavy fixed cost burden.

Rail costs compare somewhat more favorably when the very heavy costs of rail structural investments are ignored. Ignoring such costs may be appropriate when structures already exist and there is no plan or necessity for replacing them in the future. Figure 15-2 presents comparisons between the two lowest cost forms of line haul transport—an existing or "sunk cost" rail system, and freeway flier buses operating without congestion hindrances. These comparisons exclude the very heavy costs of rail structural investments, but include investment costs associated with equipment that needs or shortly will need replacement. Also, the rail operations hypothesized are probably somewhat more efficiently tailored to specific levels than could be expected in existing systems, especially when demand levels have undergone change.

With structural investments eliminated from the rail cost calculations, a freeway flier system is still somewhat cheaper in most cases at low and medium population densities, but not by a large margin. On the other hand, an existing rail system often would be as attractive an alternative when population and trip densities are high. The fact that an existing rail system is already in operation and devoid of "starting up" costs could increase its attractiveness. However, these findings hardly constitute a carte blanche endorsement of efforts to maintain existing rail systems at any or all costs, particularly when hourly trip volumes have declined or were never high. In such cases, it might be better to pave the roadbed and run buses.

As might be expected, the automobile is clearly the fastest line haul mode. In general, an automobile system—through its operation, occupancy, and parking characteristics—offers flexibility and other advantages unmatched by virtually any other type of urban transport. Above all else, private automobile travel lends itself to being "tailored" to meet the specific needs of users. If a traveler wants the maximum in comfort and convenience, he may drive alone, he has unexcelled schedule frequency, and he can park close to his workplace. Automobile travelers can also pool five or six persons to a car, drive cheap used cars, park at cheaper, less centrally located parking lots, and reduce trip costs to as low as 10 or 15 cents per passenger.

Somewhat less expected, however, is the finding that bus systems' line haul travel times are generally on a par with those of rail systems. This is because buses make fewer stops under the service and operating conditions hypothesized. An express bus operation on a congestion-free right of way should be an inherently faster form of travel than rail transit, because the bus is a smaller unit of operation and therefore requires fewer stops to acquire a full load.

ROADWAY AND RIGHT OF WAY COSTS

From Figure 15–1 it is obvious that these cost findings depend importantly on assumptions about the relationship of costs to the intensity of urban development. Right of way and roadway construction costs are the most important of the cost differences attributable to variations in the intensity of urban development. Because of their importance in determining the relative line haul systems costs, the methods of estimating right of way and roadway construction costs are discussed somewhat more fully here.

Estimation of roadway and right of way costs is a most uncertain exercise. These costs to a great extent depend on traits peculiar to each urban area—on topography, for example, and, more importantly, on the kind and intensity of urban development. Despite the importance and variability of these capital costs there has been little systematic analysis of their characteristics. For urban rail systems there is even less systematic cost analysis, and, even worse, virtually no actual cost experience has been obtained in recent years on which to base cost estimates.

HIGHWAY CONSTRUCTION COSTS

Highway construction costs appear to be a nonlinear function of the number of lanes constructed, with the costs increasing less than proportionally with the addition of lanes. These costs normally have an important relationship to the intensity of urban development, rising as intensity increases because of demands for more frequent and more elaborate bridges, underpasses, overpasses, utility relocations, and the like.

Estimates of highway construction costs are based primarily on a predictive formulation obtained for the Chicago area by Hyman Joseph.[4] Joseph fitted least squares regressions to data on construction costs of the Congress Street, Edens, and Calumet Kingery Expressways as a function of net residential density. Net residential density is generally considered a good proxy for the overall intensity of urban development. Joseph obtained the following regression:

$$Y = \$999,000 + \$70,800X, \tag{15.1}$$

where Y is the construction cost per mile for a standardized eight land facility in dollars, and X is the net residential density (NRD).

It would be preferable to have an estimating function based on a wider range of experience and encompassing a larger number of urban situations. More particularly, it would be desirable to have a function that better accounted for the independent effects of the intensity of urban development, the ramp and interchange spacing, block length, and the number of lanes. The Joseph function tends to intermix all these effects.

Certain construction costs would be expected to be invariant to width changes, some variable with width, and some directly variable with the number of lanes.

In particular, the width of both the depressed rail and the highway facilities is clearly not proportional to the number of lanes or tracks. A somewhat similar relationship would prevail between the facility width and number of lanes for other kinds of structures.

Construction costs for facilities with various numbers of lanes are estimated by assuming that all but base and paving costs are proportional to width, and that base and paving costs are proportional to the number of lanes.[5] A construction cost model for expressways with varying numbers of lanes was derived from Equation (15.1) by subtracting the costs of providing base and paving for eight lanes and making these costs dependent on the number of lanes, and by making the remaining cost dependent on facility width.

Highway cost allocation studies provide a basis for estimating the costs of constructing facilities for various weight classes of traffic. These studies suggest that construction costs related to number of lanes, or base and pavement costs, for a six lane or eight lane, all—passenger car highway would be only about 61.5 percent of those for a mixed-traffic highway. The equivalent figure for an all-bus highway is about 97.8 percent. The remaining costs (for grading and structure), assumed to be related to width, are approximately 80.9 percent of the mixed-traffic highway and grading and structure costs for automobile, and 92.6 percent for bus.[6]

RAIL TRANSIT CONSTRUCTION COSTS

Obtaining satisfactory construction cost models for rail rapid transit is even more difficult because of the limited postwar rail transit construction. In addition to roadbed construction and structure costs similar to those for highways, rail transit systems require capital expenditures for electrification, amounting to $250,000 to $250,000 per single track-mile, and for signals and train control facilities, ranging from as low as $50,000 per single track-mile for conventional signals to $175,000 or more for automatic train operation. In addition, per-mile trackage costs must be taken into account. One approach to obtaining comparative costs would be to use the highway construction-cost model with a narrower right of way, with an incremental cost for electrification and train control, and with roadbed trackage costs replacing roadway pavement costs. Instead, estimates of average rail construction costs for open-cut (or fill), elevated, or subway construction, obtained from several postwar engineering studies were used. It was assumed that elevated construction would be necessary at net residential densities above 40,000 persons per square mile, and that open-cut or fill construction would be suitable at lower densities.

With a 6 percent interest rate and a 50-year life (rather than the 35-year life used for highway construction), a yearly capital cost for construction of $251,000 per mile is obtained for the two-track systems at densities of over 40,000 per square mile and $209,000 at lower densities. The annual capital costs for three-track systems were assumed to be 50 percent more plus an allowance for extra switches, crossovers, and signaling.

RIGHT OF WAY COSTS

It is even more hazardous to generalize about right of way costs than about construction costs. Right of way costs are entirely specific to a given locale, while fairly large segments of construction costs vary with the kind of construction and to a much lesser extent with locale. Also, analysis of data on actual right of way costs is considerably more treacherous than the analysis of construction-cost data because construction often uses varying proportions of existing right of way or of land previously owned by government bodies. Still, analysis of right of way costs from data obtained from the Bureau of Public Roads and information from other sources provide strong evidence that right of way costs as a percentage of construction costs increase with net residential density from 5 percent or less at very low density to 50 percent or more at high densities. Equation (15.2) gives yearly right of way costs

$$S_{row} = W_{row} \; (\$299.70X_i + \$21.27X^2_i), \tag{15.2}$$

where S_{row} is the yearly right of way cost for the ith mile of rail or bus facility using an infinite life and a 6 percent interest rate, X_i is the corresponding net residential density (NRD), and W_{row} is the average right of way width required by the various highway and rail systems as a ratio of the right of way requirements for an eight lane highway.[7]

Because of indexing, overestimates or underestimates of right of way costs impose about equal disadvantages on all systems, but the more right of way a system uses, the greater the underestimate (overestimate) resulting from an underestimate (overestimate) of right of way costs.

COSTS OF RESIDENTIAL
COLLECTION AND DISTRIBUTION

Residential collection and distribution costs account for postwar declines in transit use probably more than any other aspect of system costs. Yet most urban transportation analyses have either ignored or dealt casually with these costs. The practice has been to pass over any transit or nontransit costs and time that travelers incur, and to neglect accurate costing of additional parking or feeder bus operations created to feed passengers to or away from the line haul facility. This neglect is indefensible. It hardly can be stressed enough that it is the cost and service characteristics of the entire trip between home and work that determine the modal choice of urban commuters. Thus, the emphasis of most postwar transit plans on increasing line haul travel speeds by means of fewer and less frequent stations is questionable. A relationship clearly exists involving station spacing, time and cost of reaching line haul stations, and speed on the line haul (largely dependent on station spacing) that should be subject to a careful suboptimization. Postwar transit plans have emphasized increasing line haul travel speeds and have virtually ignored the implications of these decisions for the cost and time of residential collection and distribution.

Cost analyses were carried out for five residential collection and distribution modes: (1) kiss-and-ride (the commuter's wife or other family member drives him to and from the station and returns the automobile to the residence); (2) park-and-ride (the communter drives his automobile to the station and parks it there); (3) separate feeder bus (a separate bus is used to reach the line haul rail or bus transit station); (4) integrated feeder bus (passengers remain on the same bus for both residential collection and for the line haul segments of the trip); and (5) incremental automobile (automobile is used for both residential collection and line haul segments of the trip).[8]

The residential collection cost models assume the entire residential collection and distribution for a given line haul station is accomplished by each mode individually. Obviously this is not an accurate description of reality. For any line haul system, a mix of residential collection modes would exist simultaneously and some proportion of commuters would use each mode. However, the objective of this analysis was not to estimate residential collection costs for any existing or proposed system but rather to determine how the costs of alternative residential collection technologies are affected by differences in trip generation or residential density. (Data obtained from the Chicago Transportation Study indicate peak hour trips made to the CBD vary from as many as 75 to less than one per block.) Once the maximum walking distance has been specified, the number of stops required for each bus and thus the time needed for and the cost of residential collection becomes a function of the number of peak hour passenger trips per block destined for the line haul station. This latter quantity depends heavily, though not entirely, on residential density, being the product of the number of employed persons per block and a trip generation rate, e.g., the proportion using the line haul travel mode per peak hour. Distance to the line haul station from the residential collection area is the remaining variable importantly affecting cost. If trip originations per block are held constant, the geographic size of the residential collection area, or "commuter shed," increases as the peak hour volume per line haul station increases. Thus for any given number of trip originations per block per hour, residential collection costs increase as the line haul volumes increase and as line haul costs decline. With these assumptions, residential collection costs are identical for each line haul station, given the number of peak hour trip originations per block, peak hour volumes per station, and the residential collection mode. Thus the cost analyses are carried out for one line haul station only, and for peak hour volumes per line haul station of 333; 1,000; 3,000; and 5,000 corresponding to 3,333; 10,000; 30,000; and 50,000 peak hour passengers, in the case of the ten mile route length. Figure 15–3 illustrates the results of these calculations for the five residential collection modes.

The residential collection cost models indicate that most residential collection technologies have roughly comparable cost characteristics. Park-and-ride, often several orders of magnitude more costly than the other modes, is the only major deviation. This finding is of considerable significance, given the emphasis put on park-and-ride by most current rapid transit proposals. The costliness of park-and-ride results primarily from the parking, insurance, and ownership charges it must absorb, costs which are invariably ignored in transit plans. The principal cost saving for park-and-ride is the difference in the cost of parking at outlying and central locations. Against this must be set the increase or decrease in line haul operation costs. (Whether this is positive or negative will depend on line haul volumes and mode.)

For all modes, including park-and-ride, costs diminish as trip originations per block increase, and these costs tend to approach an asymptote quickly, usually at or near a density of ten trip originations per block per hour. Furthermore, the estimated differences in costs for modes other than park-and-ride become small in absolute terms as density increases, suggesting that at higher trip origination rates residential service choices are not too critical. Of course, these higher trip origination rates are becoming less common as residential densities decline and jobs disperse.

Both automobile modes that do not incur parking charges—kiss-and-ride and incremental automobile—are extremely cheap methods of residential collection. The low costs obtained for the kiss-and-ride are possibly misleading, however, since they do not allow for the driver's inconvenience and time.

The cheapest residential feeder mode is clearly the extension of an

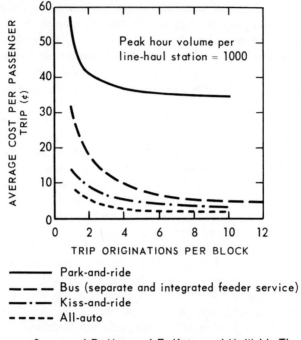

Source: J.R. Meyer, J.F. Kain, and M. Wohl, The
Urban Transportation Problem (Cambridge:
Harvard University Press, 1965), p. 265.

Figure 15–3. Residential Cost Relationships Under Different Trip
Origination Densities and Volumes Per Block

automobile trip, wherever the automobile performs the basic line haul system,
even aside from the service advantages it provides. This finding helps explain the
popularity of the automobile where corridor volumes are low, and its almost
complete dominance for peripheral trips. The service advantages of the
automobile modes (time, principally) are very large, and increase rapidly as trip
originations per block decline. Assuming an hourly station volume of 1,000 and
one trip origination per block, estimated average passenger travel time from
home to the line haul station would be approximately 17.4 minutes by separate
feeder bus, 15.6 minutes by integrated feeder express bus, 6.4 minutes by
park-and-ride automobile, 5.3 minutes by kiss-and-ride automobile, and 7.3
minutes by integrated automobile. (The high average travel time by integrated
automobile results from a three-minute allowance for car pooling.) At ten trip
originations per block the travel times are: 7.8 minutes by separate feeder bus,
6.0 minutes by integrated feeder bus, 3.5 minutes by park-and-ride automobile,
2.5 minutes by kiss-and-ride automobile, and 4.1 minutes by integrated
automobile.

An important conclusion that emerges strongly from the costs and service comparisons is that integrated systems, either bus or automobile, have certain inherent advantages as residential collectors. They not only have better performance times and lower costs than "separated" versions of the same technologies, but they also tend to eliminate transfers and other disagreeable service aspects.

From the viewpoint of both residential area cost and service, it would appear that the bus modes lose attractiveness at lower volume levels and as trip originations drop below five per block per hour, particularly relative to incremental automobile and kiss-and-ride. The automobile's strength in residential collection and distribution at low densities and volume levels undoubtedly helps explain the attractiveness of automobile commutation in many cities, and this attractiveness will grow if residences and workplaces continue to disperse.

SOME FINDINGS ON THE COSTS
OF DOWNTOWN DISTRIBUTION

The cost, service, and operational characteristics of downtown distribution are an especially important part of high performance, CBD-oriented transportation systems. Downtown distribution costs were analyzed on an incremental basis, that is, as the additional costs that would be incurred for the local distribution of travelers within downtown areas while assuming the existence of line haul facilities.

Five different types of downtown distribution services were costed: (1) integrated rail transit subway (pairs of line haul transit routes are extended in subways through the downtown area and connected); (2) integrated bus transit subway (pairs of line haul bus highways are extended in subways through the downtown area and connected); (3) integrated bus transit on downtown streets (pairs of line haul bus highways are interconnected by operating line haul buses over downtown surface streets); (4) separate feeder bus transit on downtown streets (local downtown buses shuttle or "loop" back and forth between the stub terminals or fringe parking places of each pair of line haul routes); and (5) integrated automobile on surface streets (automobile travelers continue to downtown destinations—or leave origins—on surface streets directly from—or onto—the line haul facilities).[9]

Each of these five alternative downtown distribution modes was costed at the same six volume levels used for the line haul. Costs were computed for four different downtown or CBD sizes: 144 block (1 square mile); 270 blocks (1.88 square miles); 378 blocks (2.63 square miles); and 648 blocks (4.51 square miles) to be served by four, six, and eight entering line haul corridor facilities, respectively.

All analyses are based on an arbitrary walking distance of three blocks, which, along with the assumptions about CBD size and the number of entering line haul routes, determines the number of passenger stops or stations

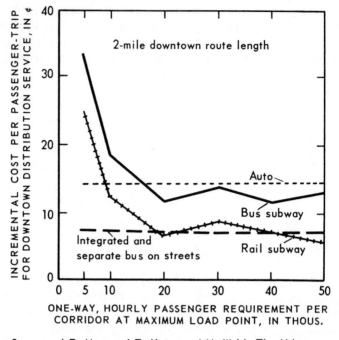

Source: J.R. Meyer, J.F. Kain, and M. Wohl, The Urban
Transportation Problem (Cambridge: Harvard University
Press, 1965), p. 287.

Figure 15–4. Comparative Costs of Downtown Distribution Modes

required on each route.[10] Figure 15–4 presents results obtained in costing each
of the five types of downtown distribution modes for a 2 mile downtown route
length. (Also costed were 1.5 mile, 3 mile and 4 mile route lengths.) The three
surface systems—integrated bus, separate feeder bus, and integrated automobile—
exhibit near-perfect divisibility for all downtown route lengths, and the two
types of surface bus (integrated bus and separate feeder bus) have practically
identical unit costs. By contrast, the rail and bus subway modes are both highly
indivisible, thus producing high unit costs as volumes approach a one way hourly
maximum load point volume of 20,000. (The subway cost undulations above
20,000 passengers can be ignored for most comparisons.)

CONCLUSIONS

The findings about residential collection and distribution costs help explain the
postwar decline in transit use and rise in automobile commutation and at the
same time raise serious questions about most existing rapid transit plans.

Highway vehicles are particularly well suited for residential collection and distribution. In recognition of this fact, all pending rail transit proposals incorporate a heavy reliance on feeder buses and private automobiles to bring passengers to suburban rail stations, and contain plans for large numbers of parking spaces at outlying points along the rail facility. Unfortunately, these residential collection costs are almost never included in system costs. If they were, these plans would appear even less promising than they do under existing cost analyses.

Somewhat surprisingly, rail rapid transit systems seldom have the lowest costs (even when the costs of residential collection are ignored). The line haul segment is usually the most costly (and longest) part of trips made to and from the CBD, though its relative importance diminishes as workplaces and residences disperse. A striking finding of the line haul cost comparisons is that a highway-oriented system is almost always as cheap or cheaper than rail transit. Rail transit remains economically attractive for the line haul only where population densities are extremely high, facilities are to be constructed underground, or rail roadbed structures are already on hand and can be regarded as sunk costs. Most American cities with enough population density to support rail transit, or even with prospects of having enough, possess it already.

An even more surprising finding of the line haul cost analysis is the extent to which a private automobile system remains competitive with transit up to quite high volume levels. A private automobile system, even with a car occupancy of only 1.6 persons, will usually be cheaper than either bus or rail transit when specific channel or corridor demands fall much below 10,000 persons per hour—a level exceeding the maximum found in a significant proportion of metropolitan areas.

The optimum overall transportation system for a city will depend on a large number of factors: the age of the city; the existing supply of arterial streets and rail transit rights of way, the density and spatial distribution of its workplaces and residences; the income level and tastes of its population; and its future prospects and patterns of population and employment growth. At present, only a handful of U.S. metropolitan areas seem to have enough rush hour CBD cordon crossings or sufficiently optimistic prospects for the future to justify even serious consideration of elaborate grade-separated transit system investments, whether bus or rail. For American cities of moderate size, efficient urban transportation seems most readily obtainable by using private automobiles, complemented by various amounts and types of bus transit using common rights of way.

The most important finding is that the means exist for an order of magnitude improvement in the quantity and quality of passenger transportation services available in large metropolitan areas. Moreover, these improvements would generally require only modest capital investment, would lend themselves to considerable experimentation, and would have great flexibility, in terms of both their operation and implementation. These large improvements in the quality and quantity of urban transportation services depend only on the imaginative use of existing urban transportation investment and the exercise of some self-discipline in the coordination and efficient use of existing highway facilities, particularly during rush hours. The most important of these facilities are the expressway systems already in existence, or planned, for most metropolitan areas and downtown street space. Nearly every large metropolitan area already has the highway investment needed for a very high performance bus rapid transit system of far greater extent than any rapid transit system currently in place or even contemplated.[11] Activation of such systems requires only that the vehicles using these high performance facilities be monitored and limited to levels that can be expeditiously accommodated; that is, that make full use of the highway capacity and do not overtax and thereby coagulate and actually reduce traffic flow. If monitoring and controlled access of major urban expressways were coupled with priority access schemes for public transit buses, a simple and quite inexpensive form of rapid transit would be quickly available in most American cities. At a minimum, it would be sensible to experiment with these priority access schemes for buses before committing large sums to rail rapid transit installations. The fact that priority access for buses might be put into effect almost immediately, rather than in the five or more years often required to build a rail transit system, only heightens the appeal. Indeed, a good argument might be as an interim measure even if a rail system is to be constructed.

Chapter Sixteen

How to Improve Urban Transportation at Practically No Cost

INTRODUCTION

Urban transport planning and operations in the United States are seriously deficient. In spite of "comprehensive" metropolitan transportation studies in nearly every urban area, much talk of "systems analysis," and frequent references to "balanced" transportation systems, there is little evidence of any meaningful overall analysis of urban transport problems. Rather, analysis and planning in urban transport has meant the design of "rail rapid transit systems," "highway systems," and, even more frequently, "freeway systems."

Even a casual examination of urban travel makes it clear that these "systems" are only components or limited subsystems of the urban transport system. Yet these components are invariably planned, designed, and operated as though they were independent. Different and frequently inconsistent criteria have been used. "Balanced transport planning" has become the planning of redundant investment in each subsystem, rather than a serious effort to determine the appropriate mix of each in terms of overall system optimization. The result has been great waste and gross inefficiency.

To a substantial degree, these partial views of the urban transportation problem are due to existing institutional arrangements which badly fragment the responsibility for providing urban transportation services. State highway departments, city traffic engineers, and local and regional transit authorities all have major responsibilities for the design, construction, or operation of segments of the urban transportation system in metropolitan areas. Typically, these agencies view each other as competitors. At best they ignore one another. At the federal level, modest progress has been made in achieving a more suitable set of institutional arrangements. The Department of Transportation houses most of the agencies concerned with urban transportation. But the maintenance of modal administrations within the department and the preoccupation of UMTA (Urban Mass Transit Administration) with rail rapid transit tends to reinforce the fragmentation of responsibility for urban transportation planning and operation found at the state and local levels. Because of the institutional arrangements and the perspectives they foster, many opportunities for making substantial improvements in the quality of urban transportation at negligible cost are overlooked or ignored.

The most important of these opportunities is the use of existing urban expressways for rapid transit. Freeway rapid transit has the potential of making major improvements in the quality of urban transportation in nearly every U.S. urban area at virtually zero cost. Before considering the freeway rapid transit concept, this paper examines a number of general shortcomings of the urban transit planning process. These fall under three major categories: the premature imposition of constraints, the long range planning syndrome, and the use of inappropriate criteria.

PREMATURE IMPOSITION OF CONSTRAINTS

What might be termed the "premature imposition of constraints" is the most serious shortcoming of the transport planning process. It arises from a misconception about the respective roles of the technician and the policymaker. More than any other factor, it is responsible for the failure of transport planners to consider alternatives that might yield large benefits.

"Premature imposition of constraints" assumes a number of different forms. The most common is that engineers, planners, and other technicians fail to consider promising alternatives because they decide, without analysis, that a particular alternative would not be acceptable to the public or to policymakers. Judgments of this kind imply that there are certain absolutes. Yet it is clear that communities can be educated, that public opinion can be changed, and that politicians are willing to undertake politically difficult actions if they become persuaded that the net benefits are large enough. These judgments also imply that technicians are more capable of determining political feasibility or public acceptability than elected officials and other policymakers. This I regard as both improbable and inappropriate. It should be left to the public and its elected representatives to decide what is and what is not politically feasible or publicly acceptable. Technicians, who are notoriously bad at making these judgments, have the responsibility of providing information on the costs and benefits of alternative actions, not of deciding which alternatives are acceptable. Frequently in complex systems the implications of particular alternative actions are not at all apparent. Thus, it is often impossible to estimate, even crudely, the possible benefits and costs of particular actions until they have been carefully examined and the detailed arithmetic has been done. The arithmetic is difficult to carry out in many instances and can only be roughly approximated in others, but this is no excuse for the "premature imposition of constraints."

The worst aspect of "premature imposition of constraints" is that it frequently leads to a situation in which certain alternatives are no longer considered at all. Constraints acquire the status of immutable laws. More often than not, the original rationale for the constraints no longer exists or has been forgotten. Then it becomes all the more necessary to observe them. Conditions may have changed markedly, but the policy remains in force.

It is not difficult to find examples of the "premature imposition of constraints." An unwillingness to consider peak hour tolls is one of the most obvious. In nearly every city, state, and country I have visited, I have made a point of asking transport planners about the possibility of imposing peak hour tolls on particular facilities as a means of managing the level and composition of traffic, obtaining indications about desirable levels of investment (particularly of expensive peak hour capacity), guiding the location decisions of households, influencing the choice of peak hour travel modes, and affecting the pattern of metropolitan development. With slight variations, the answer has been the same everywhere: "The public would not stand for it." "Tolls are politically impossible." "It is a matter of government policy." "We used to have a toll on that bridge, and the public forced us to take it off."

Further discussion on the subject invariably revealed the following facts. No one had really considered the possibility of using peak hour tolls as a device to manage the use of the road system. No one could begin to suggest the effect of these tolls on the use of road facilities or on the demand for private and public transport. No assessment had been made, or even contemplated, of the costs and benefits of peak hour tolls under any circumstances. Considerable confusion existed in the minds of the technicians, politicians, and public about the purpose and function of peak hour tolls.

Typically tolls are regarded as a means of raising revenue to pay for the construction of a particular facility. Consequently, they are only imposed on newly constructed facilities and are often removed when the facility is paid for.[2] There are substantial objections to using tolls in this way, and technicians, policymakers, and the public are right to reject them. There are far less expensive ways of raising revenue. But more important, the time profile of such tolls is exactly wrong. New facilities almost always have excess capacity. Since the increased use of such underutilized facilities cost no more, it is undesirable and inefficient to impose tolls which limit their use. The irony of this traditional use of tolls is that invariably they are reduced, or removed altogether, at the very time they would begin to be beneficial. Tolls are desirable only when there is excess demand for capacity and increments to capacity are expensive. As a general rule, tolls should be imposed on old rather than new facilities. Also, tolls should be imposed only during peak periods, when the facilities would tend to become congested.

Of course, the ubiquity of highway systems makes it both difficult and expensive to devise operational pricing schemes. The costs of capacity are highly variable, even within a fairly small area, and the large number of intersecting streets makes it impractical to collect tolls by traditional methods. A variety of sophisticated electronic metering systems that would permit the use of extremely detailed pricing systems have been proposed.[3] These systems presumably would allow highway user charges to vary from one block to another, from one street to another, and from one day to another. Although there has been considerable enthusiasm for such schemes, I remain unpersuaded of their practicality. It appears to me that in most applications their costs would exceed their benefits. In addition, I suspect that more primitive controls, including a number that are discussed below, would provide almost all of the benefits of highly sophisticated road pricing systems and at a fraction of their cost.

Rivers and other barriers reduce the ubiquity of highway networks and channel traffic. Thus they increase the possibility of achieving a closer matching between the resource costs of transport facilities and the charges on users. It follows that peak hour tolls on key bridges should be regarded as a charge for the use of the entire road system (or at least the portions that are the most expensive and difficult to provide) rather than as a charge for the use of that particular bridge or facility. Bridges and other convenient barriers should be considered pressure points that can assist in managing road use in order to obtain that level and composition of traffic that provides the greatest benefit to the community.

Development of rational parking policies—that is, decisions on the number of spaces to be provided in a certain area and their price—is another unexploited possibility for increasing the efficiency of urban transportation systems at virtually zero cost. However, reasoned discussion of this alternative is virtually as difficult to achieve as it is for peak hour tolls.

Parking policy should be viewed as another possible means of obtaining a closer matching between the payments of road users for urban highways and the cost of capacity. This would mean that parking charges in central areas would usually have two alternative pricing bases. The first is the cost of providing highway capacity into central areas and should apply to the all-day parker, who generally uses the city streets during peak hours. The second is the cost of providing parking spaces. This should apply to the short term parker, who generally does not use the streets during peak periods. Because there is usually more than ample capacity during the off-peak periods, the cost of highway capacity during these periods should be regarded as zero.

Parking policy in most cities is unbelievably bad. Rates for the all-day (peak hour) parker are frequently lower than for the short term (off-peak) parker. Parking is provided on many streets at no cost or at rates that do not begin to cover the costs of new roads or increments to existing ones. In addition, curbside parking usually reduces the capacity of the street system and seriously affects the performance and cost of transit vehicles. Even when curbside street parking does not reduce street capacity or hamper the performance of transit vehicles, it is often seriously underpriced. This underpricing, of course, encourages peak-hour users to make too much use of the street system.

The major disadvantage of parking policy as a technique for reducing the congestion in high density destination zones, such as the central business district, is that it provides no disincentive for the use of street space by through traffic. Improvements in traffic flow and speed, obtained by discouraging vehicular trips to the area, may simply encourage large numbers of tripmakers with destinations in other zones to route their trips through the central area. The seriousness of this problem will vary greatly depending on the spatial arrangements of jobs and residences and other trip generation activities, the presence of water or other physical barriers to through movement, and the structure of the street systems.

A charge for use of the streets in particular high density zones during all or part of the day, a third kind of primitive road pricing scheme, would produce all of the benefits of increased central area parking charges, while avoiding the problem of attracting traffic that reduces the efficacy of parking charges and policies in some situations. The most common suggestion would involve the sale of special licenses to use central area streets during all or part of the day. A licensing scheme of this type would be inexpensive to administer and police, and should enable the system managers to greatly increase travel speeds and reliability in central areas. The advantages of area licenses as a way of reducing congestion on central area streets are rather clearly demonstrated in a recent study by J. M. Thomson of the probable effects of introducing a daily licensing scheme in central London. Thomson also examined the use of parking policies, but found sizeable advantages from the use of area licenses for the reasons discussed previously.[4]

Admittedly there are formidable problems in analyzing and developing appropriate peak hour tolls, parking policies, or area licensing schemes. Even simple changes may have complex and far-reaching effects. Therefore, careful and detailed analyses of these possibilities should be undertaken before any new policy is adopted. Careful analysis of all of the alternatives might reveal that the existing set of policies is the right one. However, it is crucial that these conclusions be reached after the alternatives are fully evaluated and not on the basis of the "premature imposition of constraints."

In many instances, introduction of these policies might markedly affect the phasing and even the need for major elements of existing highway plans. For example, the existing freeway plan in Hobart, Tasmania (Australia) is predicated heavily on the construction of a second span of the Tasman Bridge over the Derwent River and the vehicle volumes from that span. Introducing a peak hour toll that reflects the great cost of bridging the Derwent might delay for a decade, or possibly forever, the need for a second crossing. Recognition of those possibilities might lead to a vastly different design for the Hobart freeway system. Undoubtedly, the Hobart example has many parallels in U.S. metropolitan areas.

THE LONG RANGE PLANNING SYNDROME

Most current metropolitan transport planning (at least in those instances where there is even a pretense of "comprehensive" urban transport planning) is concerned with conditions and problems 20 or 30 years in the future. While I regard glimpses of the future as useful in decisionmaking, they are only a small part of comprehensive metropolitan transport planning. In fact, it is present and near term conditions that largely determine policy choices in the near future. Most existing transportation studies attempt to optimize future rather than current or existing systems and pay little or no attention to the problems of transition from current conditions to future "optimal" conditions.

This orientation has several implications. It builds a pronounced construction or investment bias into the studies. There is a tendency to concentrate on the preliminary design and feasibility of major capital facilities. For highways, this leads to an emphasis on the design and justification of elaborate freeway systems, with very little consideration of how they should be used. For public transit this focuses the planners' attention on the construction of major rapid transit facilities, typically fixed rail.

This emphasis on systems in the distant future implies that the existing use of facilities is optimal, that there are no choices about their use in the interim, and that these choices have no effect on a future optimum. All of these propositions are false. For several reasons, not the least of which is the discount rate, the greatest potential benefits are those that might be obtained from current decisions about the use of existing facilities or those to be built in the near future.

Still, there is no denying the transport planners' distaste for partial systems. They give great emphasis to the consistency, narrow technical efficiency, and symmetry of the final, complete system. The fact that from the vantage point of current decisions most of the benefits will accrue from partial and uncompleted systems is overlooked entirely. In many instances systems will not be completed, and often this will be the best outcome. Greater benefits may be obtained by several partial systems, although, in terms of engineering "efficiency," they may operate well below the potential of a complete system.

Some of the most difficult and crucial problems of transport planning and analysis arise in the operation and management of the existing transport complex. It might be expected as a result that the most sophisticated tools available would be used to analyze these important questions. Yet transport planning, as it is currently practiced in most metropolitan areas, produces detailed analyses of projected conditions 20 or 30 years in the future, while it virtually ignores the much more certain developments of the immediate future. The crucial decisions about managing the existing system are typically based on primitive data and crude analysis. Systematic quantitative analysis of these management problems is almost unknown.

USE OF INAPPROPRIATE CRITERIA

There has been no attempt to analyze a metropolitan transport system in all of its complexity and detail, on the basis of some overall "operational" criterion. One reason may be that such a criterion would be difficult to devise and even more difficult to use. Yet I suspect the more fundamental explanation is found in the existing institutional arrangements and the limited and partial views of the urban transport problem they encourage.

Because of the complexity of the urban transport system and the need for some decentralization in its administration and management, sub-optimization is probably both necessary and desirable. My objection is not to suboptimization or to the use of low level operational criteria, but rather to inconsistent low level criteria. Developing a more efficient transport system requires that low level operational criteria be derived from consistent higher level criteria. In the existing situation, subsystems based on inconsistent low level criteria are aggregated in some unspecified way to produce an overall transport system.

Many low level operational criteria are so well disguised in the procedural manuals of the professional engineer that it is often difficult to identify them or to evaluate their implications for the efficiency of the overall system. Further difficulties are created by the failure of transport planners to recognize that many so-called technical criteria contain value judgments that are not neutral. Engineers are probably more guilty of this than most other groups, possibly because they have had more opportunities to make these judgments. Their so-called engineering specifications, or technical critera, are loaded with poorly understood benefit-cost evaluations.

The standards used in the design of particular facilities or entire systems are examples of such low level criteria—e.g., the detailed specifications required for the urban interstate system such as minimum grades and curvature of the road itself, and spacing and design of on and off ramps. In some instances these may be useful rules of thumb and even valid examples of suboptimization, but all too often they are applied to situations for which they were never intended or are no longer appropriate. Much of the controversy surrounding the construction of freeways in built-up areas arises from the highway engineers' insistence that these roads be built to the same specifications as rural interstate highways across the sparsely populated great plains. Although it is important to recognize the pervasiveness of these value-laden criteria, my primary interest is in some more fundamental criteria which I believe determine the actions of road builders, traffic engineers, and public transit operators.

It appears that the overriding criterion of highway builders is to provide free and easy access to all portions of the metropolitan area at all times of the day. Their choice of investments and designs are based on existing and projected traffic usage. In this calculus, the existence of congestion is taken as irrefutable evidence of the need for remedial action, which virtually always takes the form of providing additional capacity. Highway engineers never question whether the current or projected levels and composition of traffic are the right ones, and it is inconceivable to them that some level of congestion on particular facilities may be desirable. The existence of congestion, without regard to the conditions which led to it or the costs of benefits of ameliorating it, is the criterion for action. Severity or degree of congestion provides the ranking of competing projects.

The highway builders' criterion implies that current usage of facilities is a valid indication of consumer demand. But it must be emphasized that current usage represents consumer demand for the facilities only under a particular set of circumstances and does not indicate that consumers, if given the choice, would be willing to pay for a higher level of service or the construction of additional capacity. Moreover, such indicators are only valid if we assume that the system is being managed or operated properly. Unless the traffic engineer has optimized use of the facility, current traffic volumes or the level of congestion may mean very little.

Traffic engineers have adopted maximization of vehicular flow, often at some arbitrarily selected speed or performance level, as their principal criterion in the operation and management of highway facilities. This rather simplistic, though reasonably operational, criterion has nice analytical properties; and if vehicles are reasonably homogeneous, no serious capacity restraints exist, and no serious peaking occurs, the criterion may yield reasonably satisfactory results.[5]

The most serious failing of the maximization of vehicular flow criterion is that it disregards the composition or mix of traffic. The "maximization of flow" criterion treats vehicles as though they were homogeneous in terms of the benefits they confer. Yet there are marked differences in the composition of traffic throughout the day and at different locations; in the relative efficiency of the different vehicles; and in the actual and potential benefits associated with each vehicle. These characteristics are especially crucial in dense central areas, where severe limits on peak hour capacity exist and additions to capacity are expensive.

Transit operators, in general, must conform to some profitability criteria. Managers of publicly owned systems usually are required to operate the system in such a way as to break even. In some instances this break even point only includes the covering of operating costs, with capital charges being met from some other source. In other instances, there is some cross-subsidization from freight revenues. Moreover, there is considerable cross-subsidization of less profitable services by more profitable ones. Usually these cross-subsidies are justified as necessary community services and a desirable form of income redistribution. There is far more of this cross-subsidization than is desirable. As a general proposition, system efficiency dictates that where there are unusual community benefits from the provision of uneconomic services, the community should provide a direct subsidy for this purpose. Otherwise cross-subsidization leads to excessive fares, inadequate service, and a consequent underutilization of these more profitable services.

There is considerable scope for systems analysis and operations research in nearly all transit systems. However, with present institutional arrangements, transit managements have virtually no control over the most important variables which influence the speed and reliability of their services. They can change equipment, modify schedules, market their product better, cut out uneconomic services, improve operations, and the like; but they can do very little by themselves to affect the environment in which they operate. Traffic conditions on the roads are the most important variables affecting their efficiency and performance, yet they have very little control over them under existing institutional arrangements. It is somewhat understandable that, given this situation, public transit operators prefer grade-separated rail systems that are solely under their control. The dependence of transit systems on urban highways underlines the importance of providing the traffic engineer with a correct low level criterion.

A simple example may clarify how the use of more appropriate criteria could produce a dramatic improvement in urban transportation. Buses use less street space per passenger than private automobiles at each possible speed of roadway operation.[6] Therefore, the total benefits resulting from a given reduction of bus travel time are much greater than those resulting from a comparable reduction in the travel time for a single automobile traveling during peak hours (or even 1.6 autos, allowing for the difference in street space required by cars and buses).[7] In many instances, total benefits can be increased by proportional increases in bus speeds and proportional decreases in automobile speeds. This suggests that considerable benefits might be achieved by modifying the design and use of urban roads in dense central areas (where there are severe capacity shortages) to reduce total vehicular flow during the peak hour, to increase the proportion of buses in the traffic stream, and to increase substantially both auto and bus speeds. At worst, this might lead to some small delays for automobiles waiting to use the faster moving facilities. However, significant numbers of current auto drivers might shift to the relatively improved bus system. Improved bus speeds might lower costs and permit some reduction in fares, causing still more drivers to shift. It is probable that the resulting system would have larger numbers and larger proportions of peak hour automobile commuters, and higher average travel speeds for both bus users and the remaining auto commuters.

These trade-offs are vividly illustrated by the data in Tables 16–1

Table 16-1.   Vehicle Volumes at Different Performance Speeds and Bus-Auto Mixes: Six-Lane Freeway

| | *Vehicles Per Hour* | | | | | |
| | *30–35 mph* | | *50 mph* | | *60 mph* | |
Buses	*Autos*	*Total*	*Autos*	*Total*	*Autos*	*Total*
0	6,000	6,000	4,800	4,800	2,400	2,400
50	5,920	5,970	4,720	4,770	2,320	2,370
100	5,840	5,940	4,640	4,740	2,240	2,340
200	5,680	5,880	4,480	4,680	2,080	2,280
400	5,360	5,760	4,160	4,560	1,760	2,160
600	5,040	5,640	3,840	4,440	1,440	2,040

Source: Computed from data presented in Vergil G. Stover and John C. Glennon, "A System for Bus Rapid Transit on Urban Freeways," *Traffic Quarterly* (October 1969), table 1, p. 471.

and 16–2 on one way vehicular and passenger volumes on a six lane expressway at different performance speeds and with different bus-auto mixes. In Table 16–1, total vehicular volume is maximized at a speed of 30–35 mph and with no buses. Conditions on the facility at these volumes are characterized by the stop and go (unstable flow) conditions found on existing congested urban expressways.[8] From Table 16–2, it is apparent that the maximum "hypothetical" passenger volume (157,000) is obtained at this performance speed also. The word "hypothetical" in these calculations is crucial, because "actual" volumes will depend on the number of commuters who choose to use transit rather than private automobiles in going to and from work. Although we know less about the demand for transit than would be desirable, all studies agree that the proportion of commuters who use transit in commuting between work and home depends on the relative costs and travel times of the two modes, particularly the latter.[9] Therefore, the "actual," as contrasted with the "hypothetical," number of bus commuters will depend on the performance speed of the facility. For example, if it is assumed that a 30–35 mph performance speed attracts enough transit users to operate 50 buses, the passenger volume would be 10,388 persons per hour. But, if a performance speed of 50 mph attracts enough users to justify 400 buses, the passenger volume would be 19,264 persons per hour, or nearly 2.5 times the number that could be accommodated on the expressway at 30–35 mph in private autos. Even so, this mix includes over two thousand automotive commuters.

It should again be emphasized that the illustrations given are strictly hypothetical. Potential transit patronage would vary from location to location and from facility to facility.[10] It follows that the optimal bus-auto mix and performance speed would vary widely as well. Several possible combinations are

Table 16-2. **Passenger Volumes at Different Performance Speeds and Bus-Auto Mixes: Six-Lane Freeway**

				Passengers Per Hour				
		30–35 mph			*50 mph*		*60 mph*	
Buses	*Bus*[a]	*Auto*[b]	*Total*	*Auto*[b]	*Total*	*Auto*[b]	*Total*
0	0	8,400	8,400	6,720	6,720	3,360	3,360
50	2,100	8,288	10,388	6,608	8,708	3,248	8,708
100	4,200	8,176	12,376	6,496	10,696	3,136	7,336
200	8,400	7,952	16,352	6,272	14,672	2,912	11,312
400	16,800	7,504	24,304	5,824	22,624	2,464	19,264
600	33,600	7,056	40,656	5,376	38,976	2,016	35,616
3,750	157,500	0	157,800	0	126,000[c]	0	63,000[c]

Source: Computed from data in Table 16-1
[a] Assumes 42 passengers per bus
[b] Assumes 1.4 passengers per auto
[c] Assumes 3,000 and 2,400 buses respectively

illustrated by the figures. Almost all congested urban expressways are characterized by the set of figures in the upper left hand corner of Table 16-2 (8,400 passengers at 30–35 mph). Although much research and experimentation would be needed to obtain the optimal mix and performance speed for every urban expressway, one fact is obvious. The present policy is wrong.

The adoption of traffic engineering methods that reflect user benefits and the different efficiency of buses and private automobiles more accurately than the existing ones could have an immense effect on the performance of the overall transport system. Such changes would affect both the level of transport investment over the long run and the ranking of alternatives in the short run. Changing the traffic engineers' criterion from the "maximization of vehicular flow" to the "maximization of vehicle user benefits" simply represents the adoption of a criterion consistent with the development of a transport system that maximizes net benefits to the community. Traffic engineers have been doing a superb technical job; unfortunately it has been the wrong one. If they began to try to solve the right problem, they could quickly and cheaply achieve a great improvement in the performance of the urban transport system.

If these traffic engineering and management innovations were combined with reasonably consistent parking policies and a limited use of peak hour tolls and licenses for the use of a few very expensive facilities, they could revolutionize the urban transport problem within a brief period of time. The urban transport problem in most U.S. cities is not primarily one of too little capacity, but rather one of inefficient use of existing capacity. If existing road systems were optimized in a way that is consistent with benefit-cost maximization of the entire urban transport system, there would be a marked improvement in the quality of transport services and a substantial reduction in user costs.

USING URBAN EXPRESSWAYS FOR RAPID TRANSIT

A revolutionary improvement in the quality and quantity of urban transportation services could be obtained in virtually every U.S. metropolitan area in a relatively short period of time. Moreover, it would require expenditures no larger, and possibly smaller, than those currently programmed. These gains could be achieved by converting existing urban expressways to rapid transit facilities through the addition of electronic surveillance, monitoring and control devices, and the provision of priority access for public transit vehicles.

Comparative cost analyses prepared by John R. Meyer, Martin Wohl, and me indicate that bus rapid transit systems on either their own right of ways or on congestion-free, general use expressways have a commanding cost advantage over rail under most circumstances and can provide higher levels of service.[11] The cost of grade-separated rail transit systems becomes competitive with new bus rapid transit systems only when urban density is extremely high or when rail transit investments have already been made.

Moreover, there are no technical reasons why freeway rapid transit systems should not have peak hour speeds equal to or well in excess of those anticipated from any existing or proposed rail rapid transit system, such as the partially completed BART system currently under construction in the San Francisco Bay area or those proposed for Atlanta, Houston, and Seattle. Express buses are inherently faster than rail transit because their smaller unit size reduces the number of stops they must make to obtain a full load. In addition to having higher potential line haul speeds, freeway express buses have the ability to act as their own residential collectors, saving the time and inconvenience of transferring from feeder buses to the rapid transit line.

Still, these higher potential speeds are less important than the markedly lower capital costs of freeway rapid transit. Because they are able to share costly right of way facilities with other users, such systems can be provided at a fraction of the cost of fixed rail systems. There are no major unsolved technical obstacles. We are prevented from obtaining such systems only by our lack of imagination and our unwillingness to overcome existing political and organizational rigidities. Development of these systems requires a complete integration of highway and transit planning and a willingness to impose certain rational restrictions on the use of high performance urban highway facilities, particularly during peak hours.

Modern limited access highways move huge numbers of vehicles at high speed and with great safety for 20 hours a day. However, for four hours they are allowed to become so badly congested that vehicle capacity, speed, and safety are seriously reduced. This is inexcusable. The design of these facilities makes it relatively simple to meter vehicles onto the expressway and thereby maintain high performance and high speeds even during peak hours.

If transit vehicles were simply given priority access to these uncongested high performance highways, they could achieve higher average speeds than private automobiles during peak hours in congested areas. Current peak hour commuters must choose between a relatively slow and unreliable private automobile system and an even slower and more undependable public transit system. If the proposed system were implemented, the commuter would have the choice of an automobile system that provides service no worse than that presently available and a transit system with vastly improved service. Since the new high performance transit system would be substantially faster and more reliable than existing transit service and would also be considerably cheaper than private automobile commutation for many workers, significant numbers of automobile commuters might shift from private transportation to the transit system. If this occurred, automobile commuters who, because of their origins and destinations, are poorly served by rapid transit or who prefer to drive for other reasons might reduce their travel times.

Even more optimistically, this new high performance alternative might reduce the demand for expensive highway facilities serving central areas and release large amounts of highway funds for use in rapidly growing suburban areas and less urbanized areas, or for other purposes entirely. Similarly, if fewer highways were needed in central areas, the dislocations that have caused so much unrest in recent years would be thus much reduced. These system effects are a major part of the justification for the BART system in San Francisco and for similar rail transit proposals in other cities. However, these rail rapid transit systems are orders of magnitude more costly and provide far less coverage (fewer route miles) than the highway rapid transit systems proposed here.

In addition to having much lower initial cost, express bus systems can be closely tailored to changes in the location, composition, and level of demand. Metropolitan areas are experiencing increases in incomes, changes in job locations, and suburbanization of the population. All of these forces are causing rapid and significant changes in commuting patterns. Fixed rail systems are almost incapable of responding to these shifts. However, an express bus system of the kind described here can adjust rapidly to these changes since it can operate in a variety of ways over any part of the existing or expanded regional highway network. Each new expressway link enriches the rapid transit system and provides penetration of new areas. In addition, such systems can be easily scaled up or down to meet changes in demand levels. If demand declines, there is almost no loss, since there is no unique fixed investment. If employment and population dispersal proceeds far enough or if consumers demand more flexible, costly, and personalized forms of transportation, the proportion of the common right of way devoted to public transit during peak hours can be relinquished to automobiles, trucks, and other vehicles.

A number of metropolitan areas already possess extensive expressway networks linking the downtown area with the entire metropolitan area. Fortunately, the rapid development of these expressways systems has been matched by a steady built-up in the know-how and hardware needed to make an expressway rapid transit system operational. Thus, all that is currently needed to create extensive metropolitan rapid transit systems in a number of metropolitan areas is a limited outlay for instrumentation, some modification of ramp arrangement and design, and, most importantly, a policy decision to keep congestion at very low levels during peak hours and to provide priority access for public transit vehicles.

Instrumentation of the type required is already being evaluated by a number of state highway departments. In general, this is not because they are seriously considering the development of highway rapid transit systems. Rather, it is because installation of such electronics on urban expressways is probably justified under any circumstances. Increases in highway capacity and reliability alone may pay for such instrumented highways, without even considering the very large benefits that would accrue from using such facilities for rapid transit. Still, if these electronic highways are to be used for both rapid transit and private vehicles during peak hours, it would probably be desirable to maintain higher speeds and levels of service than if the facility were to be used for general traffic only. The result of such operating policies would probably be to reduce peak hour vehicular volumes by some small amount and greatly increase passenger volumes.

Obviously, the idea of freeway rapid transit has considerable appeal. Still, some important questions remain. How much modification would be required for existing expressways? How much would such systems cost? Fortunately, answers to these questions are available. In 1967, J. C. Glennon and V. G. Stover completed an important study for the Urban Mass Transportation Administration of the expressway rapid transit concept. The study prepared preliminary designs and detailed cost analysis for four actual freeway corridors, selected so as to pose a variety of engineering and control problems. The expressways analyzed in the study were: (1) the Lodge Freeway in Detroit, (2) the Gulf Freeway in Houston, (3) I–35W in Minneapolis, and (4) the Penn-Lincoln Freeway in Pittsburgh.[12] From analysis of these four test sites, Glennon and Stover determined that "only minor construction modifications plus the installation of a surveillance and control system would be needed to implement service on existing freeways."[13]

As Table 16–3 illustrates, both the capital costs of these modifications and their variation among sites are surprisingly small, ranging from $26,000 to $34,000 per mile for the four facilities despite the wide range of topography and freeway design at the four locations. The annual operating costs for

Table 16-3. Summary of Estimated Additional Capital Cost of Traveled Way and Estimated Annual Operating Cost of Surveillance and Control System for the Bus-Freeway System

Location		Length of Freeway to Be Controlled (Miles)	Capital Costs		Annual Operating Cost for Surveillance and Control
Route	City		Ramp Construction and/or Modification	Surveillance and Control System	
Lodge Freeway	Detroit	16.5	$ 72,000	$492,000	$288,000
Gulf Freeway	Houston	11.7	53,000	341,000	235,000
I-35W	Minneapolis	14.1	64,000	378,000	243,000
Penn-Lincoln	Pittsburgh	14.7	103,000	278,000	226,000

Source: Vergil G. Stover and John C. Glennon, "A System for Bus Rapid Transit on Urban Freeways," *Traffic Quarterly* (October 1969), table V, 474.

surveillance and control varied between $15,000 and $20,000 per mile for the four facilities.

The additional capital outlays required for such a system would differ from one metropolitan area to another, depending principally on the size and complexity of its freeway system. Although obtaining precise cost estimates for individual metropolitan areas would require detailed engineering studies for each, ball park estimates can easily be made from the cost data developed by Stover and Glennon. For example, it appears that a freeway rapid transit system for Detroit would have an incremental capital cost in 1972 of about $7.3 million and a yearly operating cost of about $3.8 million.[14] For this investment, the Detroit metropolitan area would obtain 162 route miles of rapid transit. A smaller metropolitan area, such as Atlanta, could install a system of this kind for an additional capital outlay of about $5.5 million and a yearly operating cost of approximately $3.0 million. Comparable estimates for 20 major U.S. cities are presented in Table 16–4.

In the decade since John Meyer, Martin Wohl, and I prepared our first analysis of bus rapid transit for the White House Panel on Civilian Technology, there has been a growing interest in it and related ideas.[15] This interest has spawned a growing number of studies and demonstration projects using reserved lanes and other kinds of bus priority arrangements. The findings of nearly all of these investigations strongly support the concept.[16] Of greater significance, Minneapolis, Minnesota recently obtained a grant under the urban corridor demonstration program to test an expressway metering and priority access scheme that bears more than an accidental resemblance to the proposal

Table 16–4. Estimated Costs of the Freeway Rapid Transit System in 20 Large Cities (millions of 1972 dollars)

City	Population (1967)	Miles of Freeway[a]	Capital Cost[b]	Yearly Operating Cost of Control System[c]
Atlanta	1,290	124	$ 5.5	$ 3.0
Baltimore	1,967	86	3.8	2.0
Boston	3,243	288	12.9	6.8
Buffalo	1,321	71	3.2	1.7
Chicago	6,780	341	15.3	8.0
Cincinnati	1,362	145	6.6	3.4
Cleveland	2,056	166	7.5	3.9
Dallas	1,412	164	7.4	3.9
Detroit	4,111	162	7.3	3.8
Houston	1,797	163	7.4	3.9
Jacksonville	507	45	2.0	1.1
Los Angeles	6,844	459	2.1	10.9
Miami	1,116	58	2.6	1.4
New York	11,474	899	40.5	21.2
Philadelphia	4,766	242	11.0	5.8
Pittsburgh	2,381	107	4.8	2.5
St. Louis	2,310	156	7.0	3.7
San Francisco	2,991	314	14.1	7.4
Seattle	1,298	109	4.9	2.6
Washington, D.C.	2,697	164	7.4	3.9

[a]Miles of freeway open to traffic, under construction, or in final design stages in 1964. From Automotive Safety Foundation, *Urban Freeway Development in Twenty Major Cities* (Washington, D.C., August 1964), p. 62.

[b]This figure includes the capital cost of the surveillance and control devices needed for the system and necessary modifications to the freeways and ramps. The combined cost of these improvements in 1972 is estimated to be $45,120.24 per mile. This figure is obtained by adjusting the largest of the four figures obtained by Stover and Glennon in any of the four test cities, $34,182, by the increase in the Federal Highway Administration Cost Index between 1968 and 1972. *Construction Review* XVIII (July 1972): 48, Table E–1, "Construction Cost Indexes."

[c]The estimated yearly operating costs of the freeway control system are based on a figure of $23,712.10 per mile. This figure is obtained by adjusting $20,095 per mile, the largest of the four figures obtained by Stover and Glennon in any of the four test cities, for increases in the consumer price index between 1968 and 1972. U.S., Department of Labor, Bureau of Labor Statistics, *The Consumer Price Index* (January 1972), p. 11.

described in this paper.[17] The Minneapolis project, which has an estimated capital cost of $2.68 million, will use traffic detection devices and television cameras to monitor traffic operations. Information on traffic flow provided by this surveillance equipment will be analyzed and used to control bus and auto entry onto I–35W, the urban interstate highway being used for the experiment. The system will include both special bus lanes and park-and-ride and kiss-and-ride facilities.

The Minneapolis project should go a long way toward demonstrating the operational feasibility of expressway metering and priority access for transit vehicles. There is reason to doubt, however, whether it will provide a very good test of the bus rapid transit concept. Minneapolis-St. Paul is a low density metropolitan area with high levels of automobile ownership, relatively low levels of congestion, large amounts of street capacity, dispersed workplaces, and low levels of transit use historically. These characteristics make it unlikely that bus rapid transit will be more than a modest success.[18]

It is inevitable that the success of the system will be measured by the increase in transit use, which in turn will depend on how much transit speed and reliability improve relative to the automobile. Conditions in Minneapolis are such that only a modest improvement is likely, and only modest increases in transit use should be anticipated. This is particularly true if transit services are not dramatically improved in other respects, which apparently is to be the case. As a result, it is likely that the Minneapolis program will provide modest improvements at even more modest cost.

These considerations suggest the need for a more ambitious experiment in an area with a greater latent demand for rapid transit and one where larger relative improvements in transit might be anticipated from implementation of the bus rapid transit concept. A large scale demonstration project of this kind would provide a meaningful test of the bus rapid transit concept as a more meaningful test of consumer acceptance. To encourage state and local decisionmakers to agree to the highway operations policies that are central to the proposal, the Departments of Transportation and Housing and Urban Development should pay all or a major portion of the cost of a demonstration project for the first state or metropolitan area agreeing to implement such a plan on a five year trial basis. In return, state or city officials would agree to limit private auto use of the area expressways during peak hours. To provide a meaningful test of the proposal, it would be desirable to select a metropolitan area that has significant downtown development, a well-developed highway system serving downtown, and fairly high levels of congestion.

The cost data developed by Glennon and Stover suggest that the needed electronics could be installed and the surveillance and control system operated for a five year demonstration period for between $20 and $40 million.[19] However, to fully test the demand for high performance transit systems, it might be desirable to provide operating subsidies for saturation transit services throughout the entire region during all or part of the demonstration. The public's response to fast and frequent services would provide much needed information about the demand for high-performance transit services. It is essential that these high levels of service be provided long enough for potential users to regard them as more or less permanent. Five years should be a sufficiently long period to evaluate the long run impacts of these service improvements on such matters as choice of residence and decisions whether to buy either a first or a second car.

It is difficult to estimate the dollar cost of these operating subsidies prior to choosing a particular city and deciding on the level and duration of subsidized service. However, I would guess that a very significant experiment could be carried out for less than $50 million. This is by no means a trivial amount of money, but it still compares favorably with the $1.5 billion capital cost of the BART experiment.[20]

Chapter Seventeen

Transportation and Poverty

with John R. Meyer

Widespread concern about the problems of poverty and race has led to a proliferation of schemes for reducing the unemployment, increasing the incomes, and generally improving the well-being of disadvantaged groups in our society. Prominent among these are several that would use transportation to increase the employment opportunities of the poor. The concept that inadequate transportation must be numbered among the disadvantages of the poor and that improved mobility, particularly as it improves access to jobs, could increase their self-sufficiency was publicized widely in the aftermath of the Watts riots in 1965. The McCone Commission report on the causes of the riots concluded that "the most serious immediate problem [facing] the Negro in our community is employment. . . ." The commission suggested that, although a serious lack of skill and overt discrimination are major causes of high Negro unemployment, inadequate and costly public transportation also limit Negro employment opportunities:

> Our investigation has brought into clear focus the fact that the inadequate and costly public transportation currently existing throughout the Los Angeles area seriously restricts the residents of the disadvantaged areas such as south central Los Angeles. This lack of adequate transportation handicaps them in seeking and holding jobs, attending schools, shopping and fulfilling other needs.[2]

The McCone Commission, therefore, recommended that public transit services in Los Angeles be expanded and subsidized. (Its report was strangely silent about the possibility of improving access to jobs by reducing segregation in the housing market.) This recommendation attracted considerable public attention, and the federal government, through the Department of Housing and Urban Development, has sponsored some demonstration projects

341

designed to ascertain if better and more extensive transit services between ghettos and employment centers would yield additional jobs for ghetto residents. The entire subject is very fashionable. But it is astonishing how little knowledge lies behind the popular political opinions it provokes.

A NEW PROBLEM?

In light of the new public awareness of the relation between poverty and transportation, it is appropriate to ask whether the problem itself is new. Obviously, poverty is no new problem; nor is it a growing problem. But when the relation between transportation and poverty is examined, it becomes apparent that something *is* new. Postwar changes in urban spatial structure and transportation systems, while conferring significant improvements on the majority, have almost certainly caused a *relative* deterioration in the access to job opportunities enjoyed by a significant fraction of the poor.

To be sure, many, if not most, poor continue to live in centrally located residential areas, and these are reasonably well served by public transit to the central business district, where one usually finds the highest density of job opportunities. But in the past two decades, new job opportunities have grown more swiftly outside this central business district. It is estimated that there may be 100,000 fewer low income jobs in New York City than there are low income workers.[3] A similar pattern has apparently emerged in several other American cities.[4] Living in a neighborhood well served by public transit to the central business district is therefore less of an advantage for lower income groups today than it once was.

THE AUTOMOBILE AND THE POOR

Reflecting these and other changes in the postwar pattern of American urban living, the total number of passenger trips by mass transit has declined in every year since World War II. Much of the early postwar decline must be viewed against the abnormal conditions of wartime, when transit use was artificially swollen by restrictions on automobile use; transit patronage in 1953 was almost the same as in 1940 or 1941. But the deline in transit use has continued well past 1953, and today transit patronage is about two-thirds of what it was in 1940 or 1953, in spite of a considerable growth in urban population during the past decade.

This can be explained by the fact that a growing proportion of the urban population chooses to travel by automobile. To a considerable extent this results from steadily expanding auto ownership. In 1950, six out of every ten United States households owned one or more private automobiles. By 1967, the figure was nearly eight out of every ten. But of family units with incomes between $2,000 and $2,999 before taxes, only 53 percent owned an automobile in 1967. The percentage of those with autos in the below $2,000 bracket is, of course, much lower still.

The low levels of auto ownership among the poor reflect the fact that the automobile, though a near necessity in much of urban America, is a very expensive one. The high initial capital outlay and operating costs of a private automobile are a heavy strain on the budgets of low income households. In general, then, when adequate transit services are available, low income households can and do obtain substantial savings by foregoing auto ownership.

The acquisition of an efficient private automobile (one without exorbitant maintenance costs) requires considerable financing, a chronic difficulty for the poor. Poor people, therefore, even when they own cars, generally own poor cars. Many of these are inadequate for long distance commutation and expressway operation. Often they are also uninsured. Thus, statistics on car ownership among the poor, as adverse as they are, may paint a more favorable picture than is actually justified.

The dependence on public transit by the urban poor therefore continues to be very great. In the New York region, for example, less then 25 percent of the households earning under $1,000 per year in 1963 used private automobiles to reach work; over 75 percent used some form of transit. The proportions using automobiles were 57 percent for those with incomes between $4,000 and $10,000, and 62 percent for those with incomes over $10,000 per year.[5]

Transit managements have made some effort to offset the steady decline in transit use by developing new markets. They have done this mainly by expanding route miles or services offered. The route miles of rapid and grade-separated rail transit service have increased about 2 percent since 1945 and soon will increase further as new rail rapid transit systems under construction are completed. Route miles of all kinds of transit service, bus and rail, have risen nearly 20 percent since 1955. In the same period, however, transit operators have curtailed the vehicle (revenue) miles of services offered by 20 percent in response to decreases in ridership. To some extent this decline in vehicle miles of service has been offset by the use of larger vehicles with more seats. Nevertheless, the overall effect has been a reduction in the frequency and, therefore, the basic quality of the service rendered. In general, reductions in service offerings have been most severe on weekends and other off-peak periods (particularly evenings) and for commuter trains.

TRANSIT TO SUBURBAN JOBS

The effectiveness of the additional route miles, moreover, has been less than it might have been because modern bus transit tends to follow the same routes as the old streetcar lines. This means that a high percentage of services in most cities converge on the central business district. For an individual to make a trip from one point at the periphery of a city to another point at the periphery usually requires taking one radial line into the central business district and then transferring to another line to make the trip out to his destination. This arrangement tends to be costly for both operators and users. Bus lines operating through a central business district encounter congestion, with all that entails for increasing operating costs. For the user wanting to make a trip from one peripheral urban location to another, the radial trip to and from the CBD means a much longer and more time-consuming journey than is geographically necessary. Commuters at all income levels, therefore, tend to use automobiles for such trips. Even the poor tend to do so whenever they can make the necessary arrangements, either by owning an inexpensive car or by joining a car pool.

In general, conventional transit is at a performance disadvantage compared to driving or carpooling when serving thinly traveled, long distance routes between central city residences and suburban workplaces. Even when available, the transit service is often too little and too slow to compete with the automobile. Moreover, such transit service can impose dollars and cents handicaps that go beyond the direct costs in money and time of the commuter's trip itself. For example, conventional transit often adapts to limited demand by providing only peak hour service between the suburban workplaces and centrally located residential areas. The worker must either catch the bus when it leaves, exactly at closing time, or find some other mode of transportation, often at considerable additional expense. This means that the worker who depends on public transit cannot easily accept overtime employment. The unavailability of a worker for overtime work not only denies him a lucrative opportunity, but can involve costs to his employer as well. Limited public transit scheduling, for example, can make it difficult for the employer to stagger shifts or closing hours. (And staggered closing hours can be helpful in solving such other transportation problems as traffic congestion at peak commuter hours.)

It is therefore not surprising that transit operators serving suburban plants report that low income workers frequently use transit only when obtaining their jobs and for the first few days or weeks of employment. Once the workers manage to save enough for the down payment on a car, or become acquainted with some fellow workers living near them, they drive to work or join a car pool. If this is a common pattern, existing transit services may indeed be serving a critical function for low income households, but one whose value is badly gauged by the farebox or by aggregate statistics on transit use.

The basic problem, however, remains: efficient transit requires that large numbers of persons travel between the same two points at approximately the same time. The growing dispersal of workplaces and residences means that this condition is satisfied less frequently than before. As jobs, and particularly blue collar jobs, have shifted from areas that are relatively well served by public transit to areas that are poorly served, employment opportunities for low income households dependent on public transit service have been reduced. Increasingly, low income workers are forced to choose between a higher paying job that is inaccessible by public transit, and thereby pay more for transportation (e.g., by buying and operating an automobile), or a lower paying job that is served by transit. To put it in somewhat different terms, low income households now have at their disposal at most only a bit more, and oftentimes less, transit service than they once did for reaching what is, in effect, a much larger metropolitan region.

THE PROBLEM OF RACE

The dispersal of the job market and the decline of transit systems have created particular difficulties for low income Negroes. If the job of a low income white worker shifts to the suburbs, he is usually able to follow it by moving to a new residence. If not, he may be able to relocate his residence to be near a transit line serving his new suburban workplace reasonably well. The low income Negro worker, however, may not be so fortunate. Regardless of his income or family situation, if his job moves to the suburbs, he may find it difficult to move out of the ghetto. That is, his residence may not easily follow his job to the suburbs. For him, the service characteristics, coverage, and cost of the transportation system can therefore be especially critical.

Unfortunately, conventional transit systems usually do not provide adequate services between the ghetto and suburban workplaces. The black worker, confined to ghetto housing near but not directly at the urban core, cannot readily reach many new suburban job locations by simple reverse commuting on existing transit systems. Existing public transit tends to connect suburban residential locations with the very core of the central business districts; it may not pass through, or even near, new suburban industrial or office parks, just as it may also fail to pass through the ghetto.

If the ghetto resident is able to reach a suburban workplace at all by public transit, the trip may be expensive. If he is lucky, he may be able to join a carpool with a fellow worker and share the considerable expense of a long distance auto trip from the ghetto. Here, too, the limitations on his residential options and the remoteness of most suburban workplaces from the ghetto reduce the possibilities of his making an advantageous arrangement.

THE POLICY QUESTIONS

Despite the public discussion and federally financed experiments that followed publication of the McCone Commission report, virtually nothing has been done so far to establish a factual basis for evaluating the utility of improved transportation in reducing urban poverty and unemployment. In particular, answers must be found to a number of questions. What effects do existing transportation policies have on income distribution? Are they the ones that were anticipated? Can transportation policy be an effective tool for expanding the opportunities and increasing the welfare of the disadvantaged? Should transportation be used this way? If so, what specific policies and programs should be adopted for achieving these purposes?

Jobs and Transportation

Inferior access to new jobs is by no means the only disadvantage of the ghetto resident. Indeed, in terms of his participation in the labor market, it may be much less important than other factors.[6] Thomas Floyd, who was deeply involved in the administration of demonstration projects in Watts and elsewhere, notes: "There is . . . reason to believe that some employers were using the transportation barrier as a convenient excuse for not hiring for other reasons. In addition to racial bias, there may be presumed or actual inadequate job skills or work habits."[7] When the improved transportation services were provided, he observed, the jobs did not always materialize.

If transportation is but one of many factors influencing job opportunities, provision of more or cheaper transportation, by itself, is probably an inefficient method of reducing unemployment or increasing incomes. Effective measures to increase the opportunities, employment, and incomes of the long term unemployed or underemployed must operate simultaneously on several fronts. Training, education, counseling, placement, and transportation programs complement one another. Most or all of these programs should have a role in any well-designed assault on employment problems, and any one of these programs in isolation could well fail because it lacked other essential services. On the other hand, simply putting all these programs into effect simultaneously would not guarantee results either. The different programs must be properly articulated and synthesized.

Income Redistribution and Transportation

Subsidies for urban transportation have long enjoyed wide support on the ground that such subsidies help the poor. In spite of the fact that the poor generally are more reliant on transit than the rich, the truth of this proposition is less than self-evident.[8]

Advocates of public transit subsidies need to be discriminating if the subsidies they support are actually to aid the poor. Many proposed new systems, such as the BART system in San Francisco and the transit extensions in Boston, will provide only nominal benefits for the poor. In fact, it is probable that both systems will have a highly regressive impact. They are to be subsidized out of the property tax, which is heavily regressive and virtually all of the benefits will accrue to high income, long distance commuters traveling between high income suburbs and central employment centers. They will do practically nothing to improve accessibility between centrally located ghettos and suburban employment centers.

In general, users of high speed, long distance rail commuter systems are among the wealthier classes of society. Local bus systems, by contrast frequently serve large numbers of low income users. Paradoxically, these local bus services rarely require large public subsidies. In fact, the available evidence suggests that local bus systems serving low income and dense central city neighborhoods often make a profit, and often subsidize unprofitable long distance commuter systems serving low density, high income neighborhoods.[9]

Another anomalous fact is that a disproportionate number of taxi trips are made by poor persons. The explanation apparently is that many locations are simply inaccessible to carless households except by taxi. For many of the poor, occasional use of taxicabs as a supplement to transit and to walking is relatively economical compared with automobile ownership.

New York provides contrasting figures that illustrate this point. In New York, poor households do not make proportionately more taxi trips than middle income families. The reason is that a smaller proportion of middle and upper income families own automobiles in New York than elsewhere. Moreover, the public transit system is much more extensive in New York than in most other cities and is thus a better substitute for taxicabs. In small cities and towns, however, taxicabs are sometimes the only form of public transit available to the poor. In these instances the poor and infirm may be almost the only users of taxicabs—because everyone else drives.

Thus, the apparently simple question of which income groups use which modes of transportation is a good deal more complex than is commonly imagined. Such hasty generalizations as "taxicabs are a luxury used only by the very rich"; "automobile ownership is limited to the well-to-do"; and "transit is used only by the poor" fail to hold up under scrutiny.

The mobility and transport choices of different income groups could be discussed more cogently if we had better measures of urban mobility.[10] Unfortunately, the usual measure of "trip-making" used in metropolitan transportation studies is poorly suited for defining mobility differences between different income classes. By definition, only vehicle trips (transit, truck, taxi, or automobile) and walk to work trips are counted as trips; walking trips other than those made to and from work are omitted. On average, such noncommuter walking trips are probably of far greater importance in low income than in high income neighborhoods. Poor people more often than higher income people live in high density neighborhoods where shopping, recreation, and employment are located close to home. Many trips that must be made by auto or transit in low density areas can conveniently be made by foot in high density neighborhoods. Whether this means, as some believe, that the poor should be considered less mobile is not entirely clear.

In general, almost no data exist that describe how persons of different life styles, living at different urban densities and income levels, solve their personal transportation problems. Moreover, there is no hard information to demonstrate the existence of large and unfulfilled latent demands for alternative forms of transportation. Information on such matters is crucial for designing programs to improve the mobility of the poor and for evaluating the benefits of such programs as against their costs. Yet, to date, the information simply has not been gathered.

Indirect Costs

Most observers agree that the indirect and secondary costs of major transportation investment, such as urban expressways and rapid transit, have not been given adequate consideration when choosing locations and alignment, designing facilities, and deciding whether construction is justified at all. At least two major kinds of such costs can be identified.

First there are uncompensated costs imposed on individuals—residents, property owners, and businessmen—who are forced to move. These uncompensated costs commonly include not only the direct money outlays for moving but also losses engendered by destruction of cherished friendships, familiar environments, business relationships, and other intangibles.

Second, there are collective costs. These consist of adverse changes in the neighborhood or environment and largely affect those who are not required to move. It is sometimes remarked that the owners whose property is taken by eminent domain are often the lucky ones. Those located nearby, but not within, the right of way frequently suffer disruption and loss of value for which they receive no compensation. There can be no doubt that the building of a major highway or transit line through a residential area causes fundamental changes to the neighborhood. These changes may be either beneficial or harmful; quite often, they are both.

There is some evidence that the disruption may be greater if the highway or transit line is put through a tightly knit working class community as opposed to a middle class area. Some observers have argued that the working class family is more immobile than the middle class family, and more tightly linked to an extended family that typically lives within walking distance.[11] If true, when a decision is made to carry out construction in a working class neighborhood, greater aid may be needed to compensate displaced residents and to assist the reconstruction of their environment.

Unfortunately, few operational tools are available for improving route selection decisions by taking such broader social considerations into account. To do so, several hard questions must be faced. How much community wide benefit from construction of a road should be sacrificed for these neighborhood and individual values? Can cash payments of whatever amount compensate residents for the real character of their loss? If they cannot reconstruct their present environment, would adequate resources allow the displaced to construct a different but equally satisfactory or better environment? Is the problem in question essentially unique, or is it typical of all or most low income communities? If it is typical, the road builders' options are, of course, limited. Almost any alignment would impose comparable costs on the affected communities. The range of choice is then narrowed to whether the road should be built, which remedial actions should be taken to limit the displacement or damage, and how generously the damaged population should be compensated.

Existing compensation formulas and mechanisms, unfortunately, fail to compensate many losers altogether and provide many others with grossly inadequate compensation. These inadequacies are responsible for much of the current resistance to urban transportation construction. A few individuals are often required to bear a disproportionately large share of the costs of urban transportation improvements in order to provide benefits for all. In these circumstances, spontaneous community action to oppose the new construction is hardly surprising.

PROPOSED SOLUTIONS

Perhaps the most ambitious proposal for improving urban transportation services for the poor is to make public transit free, thereby eliminating income as a determinant of transit use. Clearly, though, this is inefficient.[12] A large proportion of transit users are not poor, and free transit would subsidize the affluent as well as the poor. Moreover, the major difficulty facing the poor, and particularly the ghetto poor, is not that transit is too expensive, but that it is all to frequently unavailable in forms and services that are needed. In general, transit use seems far more sensitive to service improvements than to fare reductions, even for the poor. Nor is "free" transit particularly cheap. It has been estimated that, nationwide, the costs of free transit would be approximately $2 billion a year, assuming no increase in service.[13]

Boston can be used to illustrate the comparative costs of free transit and service improvements for the poor. Until very recently, access between Boston's Roxbury ghetto and rapidly expanding suburban employment centers has been nonexistent for all practical purposes. The costs of providing transit services between all Boston's poverty areas (i.e., census tracts with median family incomes below $5,500 per year) and low skill employment centers has been estimated at about $4.3 million annually. This is to be compared with an estimate of $75 million a year for free transit in Boston. The $4.3 million figure is, moreover, a total or gross cost; it would be less if any fare box revenues were realized. Furthermore, the $75 million subsidy for free transit would not provide any significant improvement in transit service between central city poverty areas and suburban employment centers.[14]

An increasingly popular view is that public transit systems, as currently constituted, are incapable of increasing the mobility of the poor.[15] The argument is that the transportation demands involved in serving outlying workplaces from central city residences are too complex to be met adequately by any kind of public transit services at costs that are competitive with private automobiles. At two persons per car, for example, the cost of private automobile operation often is comparable to or lower than bus transportation in serving dispersed workplaces.[16]

If so, it may be cheaper and more effective to provide some form of personal transportation for the poor. One such proposal, which its originator terms "new Volks for poor folks," is to rent, lease, or otherwise finance new or relatively new cars for low income households.[17] Cheap used cars are seldom low cost cars. If the cost of automobile use is to be reduced for low income groups, their cars must be relatively new; if they are to have such new cars, the cost of credit must be lowered. A related proposal is to assist those workers who live in central ghettos and work in the suburbs to sell transportation services to fellow workers.[18] Such sales would help pay the purchase and operating costs of an automobile. In many cities, however, this proposal would encounter a number of institutional and legal barriers.

Of course, new cars for poor people will not help nondrivers, who are now estimated to make up 20 percent of the population over 17 years of age. In fact, any extension of automobile ownership among the able-bodied poor may only serve to further degrade public transit services for nondrivers. To provide mobility for nondrivers, some have advocated the development of so-called demand actuated systems.[19] Different versions of this concept come under a variety of names or acronyms, including Taxi-bus, Dial-a-bus, DART, GENIE, and CARS. In all cases, however, the idea is to provide something approximating the point to point service of taxis, while achieving better utilization levels and load factors than transit vehicles can now achieve on fixed routes and schedules.

In these systems, vehicles intermediate in size between a taxicab and a conventional bus would be used to pick up and deliver passengers at specific origins and destinations. By use of electronic control and scheduling, it is claimed, loads could be assembled with a minimum of delay. Proponents believe these systems usually would have cost characteristics intermediate between the conventional bus and the taxicab. By providing more individualistic door to door service than public transit, these systems might be of particular use for the elderly and the infirm. Furthermore, if such systems have the advantages suggested, they might be a better and more politically acceptable solution to the problems of ghetto access than subsidies to extend ownership of private automobiles, particularly in older cities with high density central residential neighborhoods.

Indeed, were it not for franchise restrictions and prohibitions on group fares, taxicabs could improve their operating efficiency considerably without any technological improvements. Demand-activated systems are functionally identical with taxis, but have more sophisticated scheduling, control devices, and operating policies.

Indeed, many benefits would accrue to the poor if there were fewer restrictions on the provision of taxi and jitney services.[20] A deregulated taxi industry would provide a considerable number of additional jobs for low income workers. It has been calculated that removing entry barriers and other controls might expand the number of taxis by as much as two-and-a-half times in most American cities. In Philadelphia, for example, deregulation could create an additional 7,400 jobs for drivers alone; if these jobs went to the poorest 20 percent of the population, unemployment among these poor would fall by about 3.2 percentage points.[21]

Taxi operation can also be an important income supplement for low income households even where it is not a full-time job. A significant number of Washington's taxi drivers own and operate their own cabs on a part-time basis as a supplement to a regular job. The off-duty cab often doubles as the family car, thus substantially reducing the cost of auto ownership and increasing the mobility of residents of low income neighborhoods.[22]

A much expanded taxi and jitney industry could also provide an appreciable increase in urban mobility, particularly for the poor. Except for restrictive legislation, jitneys and taxicabs might now be providing a significant fraction of passenger service in urban areas. The greater number of taxis per hundred persons in Washington, D.C., an essentially unregulated city, and the sizable capital value of medallions (franchises to operate a cab) in New York, Boston, and several other cities, attest to a substantial latent demand for these services.

In short, simply providing larger subsidies to transit systems is unlikely to be an effective way of increasing the mobility of the poor. New systems seem needed, and there is some agreement on their characteristics. Such systems would normally use a smaller vehicle than conventional transit, would be demand activated rather than on fixed routes and schedules, and would provide point to point service or some close approximation of it. Such systems would most likely have somewhat lower passenger mile costs than do taxicabs (even those operating in unrestricted markets like Washington), but unit costs probably would be somewhat above those of current transit systems. In some instances, such services might merely supplement the more heavily used transit services; in others, they might replace such services altogether.

Ownership of these more ubiquitous systems might vary from place to place and from time to time. Where elaborate control and scheduling are required, a fleet might be necessary. In other instances, the services could be provided by large numbers of owner-operators working either independently or in a cooperative. Another possibility is nothing more complicated than organized car pooling, compensated or uncompensated.

Most such systems require very little long-lived investment. The most extensive capital requirements, of course, would be for the more elaborate, electronically controlled, demand-activated systems. All would require major changes in institutions and regulatory frameworks. Fortunately, however, most also lend themselves to experimentation on a modest scale. Such experimentation could do much to improve our fund of information, which at this point is simply inadequate to support bolder policy initiatives.

Owning and Saving vs. Renting and Consuming

In an analysis of the relative costs of owning and renting a home, Shelton concludes that owning is usually cheaper than renting, as long as the household expects to live at the same location for more than three-and-one-half years.[1] The three-and-one-half year cut-off is obtained by dividing a 2 percent per year annual savings into a nonrecurring transfer cost for owner-occupied units of about 7 percent of their value.

The nonrecurring transfer cost consists of realtor commissions plus an allowance for certain fixed costs. The annual savings from homeownership include tax differences, management costs, vacancy allowances, and savings in annual maintenance expenditures for homeowners (who are able to maintain the same level of quality for about 0.05 percent of market value less per year). For homeowners, the total annual housing costs include maintenance, obsolescence, property taxes, interest on mortgage, opportunity cost of money plus (discounted) transfer cost. For renters, annual rent equals landlord costs plus return on investment, maintenance, obsolescence, property taxes, vacancy allowance, management, interest on mortgage, plus return on investment.

Much of the savings from homeownership results from favorable tax provisions, i.e., from the ability to deduct interest payments and property taxes and especially from the absence of any tax on imputed rent. Therefore, the magnitude of the savings in monthly housing costs varies somewhat according to family circumstances, the size of the. mortgage and the amount amortized, and the assumed opportunity costs of the family's equity.

Shelton develops an example which suggests the magnitude of the yearly savings in housing costs obtained through ownership. This example assumes that a family may choose to buy its dwelling for $20,000 or to rent it for $167 per month. (This represents a gross rent of $2,000 per year, based on a widely used gross rent-value ratio). To purchase the unit, the prospective homeowner invests $4,000 as a downpayment on the house and assumes a 6 percent mortgage.

As compared to the $2,000 yearly rental costs, Shelton estimates that purchase would mean yearly expenses before taxes of $1,590. Property tax and interest payments create tax shields that reduce the true costs of these two items by an amount which depends on the homeowner's tax bracket. He concludes that a conservative estimate of the tax savings created by homeownership would be $200, yielding yearly after-tax costs of ownership of $1,390. This represents a saving of $610 or a 15.2 percent return (after taxes) on the $4,000 invested in homeownership, as compared to an assumed stock market return of 9 percent before taxes. Since stock market earnings are taxable, the comparable before-tax return on homeownership is 18 percent. The relative return on a homeownership investment declines as the mortgage is amortized. The investment return is larger, however, if downpayments are smaller or if the opportunity cost of equity capital is lower. Thus, 18 percent is likely to be a low estimate.

The savings from homeownership can also be expressed as a percentage of the costs of renting. From this viewpoint, a limitation on homeownership would increase housing costs beyond three-and-a-half years by 30 percent, assuming no price appreciation ($610 savings÷$2,000 annual rent). As with the rate of return analysis, the savings are larger if a smaller downpayment or a lower opportunity cost of capital is assumed.

Aaron obtains even larger estimates of the tax subsidy to homeowners. He presents an example, similar to the one just discussed but with a more valuable house ($25,000) and a larger equity ($10,000), which yields a $342 tax saving (as contrasted to the $200 saving computed by Shelton), and an after-tax return on a $10,000 equity of 7.4 percent (as contrasted with a before-tax return of 4 percent on other assets). However, Aaron implicitly assumes that the real price of owner- and renter-occupied housing is the same. Shelton, in contrast, contends that there is an equilibrium price difference, excluding tax differences, favoring owner-occupied housing by 1.4 percent of value. If Shelton's analysis of the comparative costs of homeownership and renting is correct in this respect, the savings to homeownership based on Aaron's example would amount to 28 percent of monthly rent computed as

[$342 + .014 ($25,000 in housing value)] / ($2,500 annual rent).

The substantial divergence in housing costs noted above is in addition to any discriminatory pricing which may exist. Moreover, it must still be regarded as a lower bound estimate of the economic cost of an effective limitation on homeownership during the postwar period, since it fails to incorporate the effects of inflation on housing costs and does not admit to the special position of homeownership in the savings behavior and capital accumulation of low and middle income households.

A spending unit's equity in its home can be divided into three components: the initial equity or downpayment, the amortization of the mortgage (savings), and any appreciation or depreciation of the property as a result of general or particular price changes (capital gains or losses). The last two items form the important link between homeownership and capital accumulation.

Although it is technically correct to view an increase in the value of an owned home as an increase in the household's wealth and to consider the opportunity cost of the equity capital as part of the spending unit's monthly housing costs, there are indications that many households do not view the matter in precisely this way. Out-of-pocket costs appear to be more important considerations for many low and middle income families, and it seems many view the savings in the home as a bonus to homeownership. Thus, it is of more than passing interest to compare the current out-of-pocket costs of a St. Louis family who purchased an $8,000 FHA or VA home on a 20 year mortgage in 1949 with an otherwise identical family who rented throughout the entire period.

Assuming a conservative capital appreciation of 100 percent over the 20 year period, the value of this house in 1969 would be $16,000. Since the mortgage has been paid off, the homeowner has only insurance, real estate taxes, heating and utilities, and maintenance and repairs as out-of-pocket costs. These would total roughly $64 per month for a St. Louis home of this value in 1969. By comparison, a renter would have to pay somewhat more than twice this amount ($133–160 per month) to rent a dwelling unit of this value.

The $64 per month out-of-pocket cost is based on estimated homeownership costs for existing (used) FHA insured homes in St. Louis in 1967. These totaled $58.02 for the median home in 1967 (valued at the difference in median value $14,597 vs. $16,000) plus increases in costs between 1967 and 1969. If the homeowner still itemizes his tax return (less likely without interest payments), he can deduct $26 per month of these expenses. This would produce tax savings of between $5 and $10 per month depending on his tax bracket. These expense data were obtained from U.S. Federal Housing Administration.[2]

The $133 ($160) per month rent is again based on the same widely used rent-to-value ratio 1 to 120 (1 to 100). There is reason to believe the above calculations understate the extent of asset accumulation by the average homeowner. Many homeowners increase the value of their structures by improvements and additions. These outlays, of course, represent further savings and capital accumulation. Others trade up by using their accumulation equity as a downpayment on a larger or better quality house, thus maintaining an even higher savings rate.

The preceding comparisons may help to explain the recent findings of the Survey of Economic Opportunity which indicate that at every level of current income, black families have fewer assets than whites, but that housing equity represents a larger proportion of the net worth of black households than of white households.[3] In fact, limitations on homeownership over several generations may be an important part of the explanation of the smaller quantity of assets owned by Negro households at each income level.

Appendix B

TABLE B-1. Estimated Density Functions, 47 SMSAs, 1960, Alternative Models

	Dummy Variable		Basic Model		Cross Section		Actual S*	
	D_0	D_1	D_0	D_1	D_0	D_1	D_0	D_1
Albany	27.4	0.473	30.0	0.510	27.2	0.468	30.9	0.530
Atlanta	13.0	0.221	13.7	0.237	13.3	0.227	16.3	0.274
Baltimore	22.7	0.223	24.1	0.234	22.9	0.222	25.3	0.185
Birmingham	11.4	0.168	12.8	0.217	12.0	0.175	11.0	0.149
Bridgeport	18.1	0.478	20.2	0.522	17.7	0.472	15.4	0.264
Chattanooga	13.2	0.461	14.5	0.516	13.2	0.456	10.6	0.400
Chicago	20.9	0.069	21.2	0.070	20.9	0.069	26.4	0.102
Cleveland	19.5	0.150	20.1	0.155	19.6	0.151	21.5	0.184
Columbus	16.3	0.344	17.6	0.375	16.3	0.344	12.8	0.264
Dallas	10.7	0.169	11.2	0.183	11.1	0.177	13.5	0.221
Davenport	20.6	0.639	23.9	0.709	20.1	0.628	13.3	0.486
Dayton	15.5	0.349	16.4	0.370	15.3	0.346	13.4	0.328
Denver	14.4	0.254	15.4	0.272	14.6	0.256	13.2	0.277
Des Moines	16.6	0.545	18.6	0.605	16.5	0.940	11.9	0.443
Detroit	16.1	0.076	16.4	0.078	16.4	0.077	16.1	0.108
Fort Worth	10.1	0.244	10.7	0.269	10.4	0.251	11.0	0.314
Grand Rapids	18.3	0.526	20.3	0.577	18.3	0.525	10.3	0.399
Harrisburg	18.6	0.602	20.9	0.657	20.2	0.600	26.6	0.677
Hartford	20.5	0.419	22.0	0.448	18.2	0.415	27.4	0.519
Houston	10.6	0.144	11.0	0.500	10.9	0.150	12.1	0.192
Indianapolis	17.1	0.318	18.1	0.337	17.2	0.319	15.4	0.326
Johnstown	20.0	0.756	21.5	0.855	18.0	0.753	16.7	0.640
Knoxville	12.1	0.425	13.4	0.470	11.9	0.421	10.6	0.418
Los Angeles	13.5	0.056	13.9	0.058	13.0	0.055	11.2	0.053
Memphis	13.7	0.295	14.5	0.317	14.0	0.300	17.7	0.344
Milwaukee	19.3	0.186	20.4	0.199	19.5	0.190	17.6	0.158
Nashville	14.9	0.396	16.2	0.438	14.7	0.393	15.4	0.378
New Haven	25.3	0.554	28.0	0.598	24.8	0.546	29.4	0.624
New Orleans	20.2	0.267	21.5	0.282	20.2	0.266	26.9	0.292
Oklahoma City	10.1	0.251	10.0	0.243	12.4	0.279	10.4	0.270
Peoria	16.0	0.544	18.3	0.619	15.5	0.532	9.5	0.382
Pittsburgh	22.5	0.183	23.2	0.188	22.4	0.182	22.8	0.172
Portland	13.8	0.213	20.9	0.657	14.1	0.218	10.4	0.195
Reading	24.8	0.785	28.9	0.869	24.1	0.769	31.9	0.838
Richmond	16.2	0.428	17.7	0.468	15.9	0.424	18.5	0.470
Rochester	22.9	0.447	24.8	0.475	22.9	0.444	15.3	0.377
Sacramento	10.6	0.292	11.3	0.324	10.4	0.290	3.1	0.173
Salt Lake City	14.6	0.435	15.3	0.468	14.5	0.433	12.8	0.392
San Antonio	12.2	0.261	12.9	0.284	12.4	0.265	12.6	0.260
San Diego	10.6	0.141	11.0	0.151	10.7	0.143	9.9	0.118
Seattle	12.4	0.135	13.0	0.144	13.2	0.144	11.8	0.139
Spokane	13.2	0.436	15.3	0.529	14.9	0.507	9.8	0.364
Syracuse	19.5	0.516	21.4	0.556	19.2	0.510	19.0	0.512
Tacoma	13.6	0.381	14.9	0.421	13.7	0.383	9.2	0.254
Toledo	20.0	0.427	21.9	0.479	20.0	0.426	12.5	0.309
Utica	26.9	0.793	30.0	0.847	26.1	0.780	26.1	0.718
Wichita	10.0	0.274	11.7	0.406	10.8	0.369	11.9	0.379

TABLE B-2. Average Lot Size (square feet) by Structure Type by Time Period, Chicago[a]

			Structure-Type			
Time Period	*One Family Detached*	*One Family Attached Two Family*	*3 to 4 Family*	*5 to 9 Family*	*10 to 19 Family*	*20 or more*
Pre-1879	3,125	1,562	900	445	205	125
1880–89	3,125	1,562	900	445	205	125
1890–99	3,125	1,562	900	445	205	125
1900–09	3,125	1,562	900	445	205	125
1910–19	3,750	1,875	1,070	535	250	150
1920–24	3,750	1,875	1,070	535	250	150
1925–29	3,750	1,875	1,070	535	250	150
1930–34	5,000	2,500	1,430	715	333	200
1935–39	5,625	2,815	1,600	800	375	225
1940–44	5,625	2,815	1,600	800	375	225
1945–49	6,750	3,375	1,930	965	450	270
1950–54	7,425	3,710	2,120	1,060	495	300
1955–60	8,100	4,050	2,315	1,160	540	325

[a]The following city of Chicago documents were used to estimate "typical lots" in each time period: *Master Plan of Residential Land Use of Chicago* (Chicago: The Chicago Plan Commission, 1943); *Planning the Region of Chicago* (Chicago: The Chicago Regional Planning Association, 1956); *The Comprehensive Plan of Chicago* vol. 1, *Analysis of City Systems: Residential Areas, Recreation and Park Land, Education, Public Safety and Health* (Chicago: Department of Development and Planning, 1967). The other source was Homer Hoyt, *One Hundred Years of Land Values in Chicago* (Chicago: The University of Chicago Press, 1933).

The estimates of lot sizes for multifamily units was obtained by dividing the "typical lot" figure by the number of units in the structure type. For example the 715 square feet/unit figure for 5 to 9 units structures in the pre–1879 period was obtained by dividing 5,000 square feet by seven units.

TABLE B-3. Fraction of Units by Structure Type by Time Period, Chicago[a]

Time Period	Total Units Added (in 1000s)	One Family Detached	One Family Attached, Two Family	3 to 4 Family	5 to 9 Family	10 to 19 Family	20 or more
Pre-1879	31	0.16	0.22	0.32	0.18	0.07	0.05
1880–89	78	0.12	0.24	0.33	0.19	0.06	0.06
1890–99	175	0.15	0.26	0.28	0.15	0.07	0.09
1900–09	223	0.18	0.28	0.24	0.15	0.07	0.08
1910–19	252	0.24	0.28	0.19	0.15	0.06	0.08
1920–24	163	0.34	0.19	0.13	0.11	0.07	0.16
1925–29	254	0.33	0.13	0.11	0.10	0.08	0.25
1930–34	32	0.49	0.10	0.10	0.08	0.07	0.16
1935–39	30	0.80	0.06	0.04	0.06	0.02	0.02
1940–44	63	0.75	0.13	0.02	0.05	0.05	0.00
1945–49	102	0.81	0.09	0.04	0.02	0.04	0.00
1950–54	190	0.83	0.06	0.02	0.02	0.00	0.07
1955–60	240	0.82	0.03	0.03	0.05	0.00	0.07

[a]U.S. Bureau of the Census, *Census of Population: 1940* "Characteristics by Structure Type," Illinois Table C–1 (Washington, D.C.: U.S. Government Printing Office, 1945); U.S. Bureau of the Census, *Census of Population: 1950* vol. II, part 2 (Washington, D.C.: U.S. Government Printing Office, 1951); U.S. Bureau of the Census, *Census of Population and Housing: 1960* vol. II, part 2, (Washington, D.C.: U.S. Government Printing Office, 1961).

TABLE B–4. Historical Changes in Utilized Land by Various Uses: Chicago, 1850–1961[a]

		1850	*1870*	*1890*	*1923*	*1941*	*1956*	*1961*
Utilized land	Acres	2,458	12,669	48,008	91,514	104,289	116,736	128,832
	Percent	100	100	100	100	100	100	100
Residential	Acres	465	3,481	11,008	31,004	33,228	41,600	45,184
	Percent	19	28	23	34	32	36	35
Industrial	Acres	185	2,703	10,647	16,577	19,696	19,712	19,712
	Percent	8	21	22	18	19	17	15
Commercial	Acres	33	535	1,722	6,317	6,359	8,704	8,960
	Percent	1	4	4	7	6	7	7
Road and Highway	Acres	1,630	4,725	20,721	29,624	33,852	33,216	34,496
	Percent	66	37	43	32	32	28	27
Other public and semi public	Acres	145	1,235	3,890	7,686	11,154	13,504	20,480
	Percent	6	10	8	9	11	12	16

[a]*Master Plan of Residential Land Use of Chicago* (Chicago: The Chicago Plan Commission, 1943); and John M. Niedercorn and Edward F. R. Hearle *Recent Land Use Trends in Forty-eight Large American Cities* (Santa Monica, Cal.: Rand Corporation, Memorandum, RM–3664–FF, April 1963).

TABLE B–5. Dwelling Units Built Before 1940 and Between 1950–1960 in the City of Chicago (estimates from the 1940, 1950, and 1960 census by distance from the Loop, in 1,000s[a])

| | Pre-1940 Units | | | 1940-50 Units | |
Distance	1940 Census	1950 Census	1960 Census	1950 Census	1960 Census
0–1	35	35	45	0.2	0.6
1–2	141	145	132	1.7	2.5
2–3	236	243	249	2.1	3.9
3–4	252	252	272	2.6	3.8
4–5	192	193	201	9.9	10.5
5–6·	81	81	84	15.7	14.7
6–7	25	26	26	10.8	9.9
7–8	23	24	24	7.9	7.3
City Total	985	999	1,033	50.9	53.2
Suburban Total	291	391	428	130.5	129.6

[a]Same as Table 11–7 and U.S. Bureau of the Census, *Census of Housing: 1940,* "Housing Characteristics by Type of Structure," Illinois, Table B–1, C–1 (Washington, D.C.: U.S. Government Printing Office, 1945).

Notes

Introduction

1. There were very few courses in urban economics offered by the economics departments of leading U.S. colleges and universities before 1958. In a 1968 survey of the 149 university departments that offered a doctorate in economics or business administration, 53 reported they had, or would introduce next year, a program in urban economics as a field of specialization for the doctorate. Of course, many more undergraduate courses in U.S. colleges and universities were initiated during the period. A highly interesting and useful discussion of the growth and development of urban economics as a field of specialization in U.S. colleges and universities is provided by Irving Hoch, *Progress in Urban Economics, 1959–68 and the Development of the Field* (Washington, D.C.: Resources for the Future, 1969).

2. Robert Murray Haig, "Toward an Understanding of the Metropolis," *Quarterly Journal of Economics* XL (May 1926): 402–34.

3. William Alonso, *Location and Land Use* (Cambridge, Mass.: Harvard University Press, 1964).

4. Richard Muth, "The Demand for the Non-Farm Housing", A.C. Harberger, ed., in *The Demand for Durable Goods* (Chicago: University of Chicago Press, 1960).

5. John F. Kain, "The Journey to Work as a Determinant of Residential Location" (Ph.D. dissertation, University of California, Berkeley, 1961).

6. Alonso, *Location and Land Use;* Richard Muth, *Cities and Housing* (Chicago: University of Chicago Press, 1969); Lowdon Wingo *Transportation and Urban Land* (Washington, D.C.: Resources for the Future, 1961); Ira S. Lowry, "Filtering and Housing Standards: A Conceptual Analysis," *Land Economics* 36 (November 1960): 362–70.

7. Francis Bello, "The City and the Car" in The Editors of Fortune, *The Exploding Metropolis* (New York: Doubleday Anchor Books, 1958), p. 57.

8. U.S., Bureau of the Census, *Historical Statistics of the United States, Colonial Times to 1957* (Washington, D.C.: U.S. Government Printing Office, 1960); U.S., Bureau of the Census, *Statistical Abstract of the United States: 1972,* 93rd edition (Washington, D.C.: U.S. Government Printing Office, 1972).

9. U.S., Bureau of the Census, *Statistical Abstract, 1972.*

10. American Transit Association, *Transit Fact Book* (New York: American Transit Association, 1961, 1952, and 1946 editions).

11. Robert Mitchell and Chester Rapkin, *Urban Traffic: A Function of Land Use,* (New York: Columbia University Press, 1954); John R. Meyer and Mahlon R. Straszheim, *Techniques of Transport Planning;* vol. I, *Pricing and Project Evaluation;* (Washington, D.C.: The Brookings Institution, 1971); Richard Zettle and Richard R. Carll, *Summary Review of Major Metropolitan Area Transportation Studies in the United States* (Berkeley: University of California Press, 1962); John F. Kain, "Urban Travel Behavior," in Leo F. Schnore and Henry Fagin, eds., *Urban Research and Policy Planning* (Beverly Hills: Sage Publishers, 1967), pp. 161–92.

12. William Goldner, "The Lowry Model Heritage," *Journal of the American Institute of Planners* XXXVII, no. 2 (March 1971); Ira S. Lowry, "A Model of Metropolis" (The Rand Corporation, Memorandum RM–4035–RC, 1964); Ira S. Lowry, "Seven Models of Urban Development: A Structural Comparison" (The Rand Corporation, Memorandum P–3673, September 1973).

13. Charles River Associates, Inc., *A Disaggregated Behavioral Model of Urban Travel Demand* (Cambridge, Ma.: Charles River Associates, Inc., 1972); Anthony Downs, "Uncompensated Non-Construction Costs which Urban Highways and Urban Renewal Impose upon Residential Households," in Julius Margolis, ed., *The Analysis of Public Output* (New York: National Bureau of Economic Research, 1970); Edgar M. Hoover, "Motor Metropolis: Some Observations on Urban Transportation in America," *The Journal of Industrial Economics* XII, no. 3 (June 1965); Gerald Kraft, "Free Transit Revisited," *Public Policy* XXI, no. 1 (Winter 1973): 79–105; William S. Vickery, "Pricing in Urban and Suburban Transport," *American Economic Review,* May 1963; William S. Vickery, "Congestion Theory and Transport Investment," *American Economic Review,* May 1969; Leon N. Moses and Harold F. Williamson, Jr., "Value of Time, Choice of Mode, and the Subsidy Issue in Urban Transportation," *Journal of Political Economy* 71 (June 1963): 247–64; Herbert Mohring, "Earned Values and the Measurement of Highway Benefits," *Journal of Political Economy* LXIX (June 1961); Wilfred Owen, *Cities in the Motor Age* (New York: The Viking Press, 1959);

Wilfred Owen, *The Metropolitan Transportation Problem,* (Washington, D.C.: The Brookings Institution, 1956).

14. Henry J. Aaron, *Shelter and Subsidies: Who Benefits from Federal Housing Policies?* (Washington, D.C., The Brookings Institution, 1972); Frank de Leeuw et al., *The Market Effects of Housing Policies* (Washington, D.C., The Urban Institute, Paper No. 208–23); Ira S. Lowry, "Housing Assistance for Low-Income Urban Families: A Fresh Approach" (Paper prepared for U.S. House of Representatives, Committee on Banking and Currency, Subcommittee on Housing, 92nd Congress); Peter C. Rydell, "Review of Factors Affecting Maintenance and Operating Costs in Public Housing," *The Regional Science Association Papers,* 27 (1971), pp. 229–47; Frank de Leeuw and Nkanta F. Ekanem, "The Supply of Rental Housing," *The American Economic Review* LXI, no. 5 (December 1971): 806–818; Frank de Leeuw and Nkanta F. Ekanem, "Time Lags in the Rental Housing Market," *Urban Studies* 10, no. 1 (February 1973): 39–68; Gregory K. Ingram, Gary R. Fauth, Eugene Kroch, *TASSIM: A Transportation and Air Shed Simulation Model,* vols. I and II (Final Report to U.S. Department of Transportation under contract DOT–OS–30099, May 1974); *Air Quality and Automobile Emission Control* (Report by the Coordinating Committee on Air Quality Studies of the National Academy of Sciences and the National Academy of Engineering for the Committee on Public Works, U.S. Senate, 93rd Congress, 2nd session, September 1974); Donald Dewees, *Economics and Public Policy: The Automobile Pollution Case* (Cambridge, Mass.: The MIT Press, 1974), Appendix B; Robert J. Anderson, Jr. and Thomas P. Crocker, "Air Pollution and Residential Property Values," *Urban Studies* (October 1971), pp. 171–80; Robert J. Anderson, Jr. and Thomas P. Crocker, "Air Pollution and Property Values: A Reply," *Review of Economics and Statistics* 54, no. 4 (November 1972): 470–73; Robert J. Anderson, Jr. and Thomas P. Crocker, "The Economics of Air Pollution: A Literature Assessment," in P. B. Downing, ed., *Air Pollution and the Social Sciences* (New York: Praeger Publishers, 1971), pp. 133–66; Thomas P. Crocker, "The Measurement of Economic Losses from Uncompensated Externalities," in William R. Walker, ed., *Economics of Air and Water Pollution* (Springfield, Va.: National Technical Information Service, 1969), pp. 180–94; A. Myrick Freeman III, "Distribution of Environmental Quality," in Allen V. Kneese and Blair T. Bower, eds., *Environmental Quality Analysis* (Baltimore: Johns Hopkins Press, 1972), pp. 243–78; Henry D. Jacoby and John D. Steinbruner, *Clearing the Air* (Cambridge, Mass.: Ballinger Publishing Co., 1973); Lester B. Lave, "Air Pollution Damage: Some Difficulties in Estimating the Value of Abatement," in Kneese and Bower, *Environmental Quality Analysis* pp. 213–242; Eugene P. Seskin, "Residential Choice and Air Pollution: A General Equilib-

rium Model," *American Economic Review* 63, no. 5 (December 1973): 960–67; Hugh O. Nourse, "The Effect of Air Pollution on House Values," *Land Economics* (May 1967) pp. 181–9.

15. Alonso, *Location and Land Use;* Muth, *Cities and Housing;* Wingo, *Transportation and Urban Land.*

16. Muth, *Cities and Housing.*

17. Alonso, *Location and Land Use,* Appendix C.

18. For example, Nancy J. Leathers in a 1967 article presents what she views as a replication of the nine equation econometric model presented in Chapter Three. But she uses residence zone aggregates rather than workplace aggregates and replaces the gross price proxy used in Chapter Three with a variable that measures the land value for each sample dwelling unit. Thus, Ms. Leathers appears to have completely overlooked the significance of workplace location in the consumer choice model developed in Chapters One and Two. Nancy J. Leathers, "Residential Location and Mode of Transportation to Work: A Model of Choice," *Transportation Research* 1, no. 2 (1967): 129–55.

19. Gregory K. Ingram, John F. Kain and J. Royce Ginn, *The Detroit Prototype of the NBER Urban Simulation Model* (New York: National Bureau of Economic Research, 1973), Chapter 8 and Appendix A.

20. While the San Francisco-Oakland study considers a wider range of housing attributes than the study included in Chapter Three, it included estimates for single family, two family, and multiple units similar to those in Chapter Three. The analyses revealed that a household whose primary wage earner is employed in the city of San Francisco is about 17 percent less likely to live in a single family unit, 3 percent more likely to live in a two family unit, and 14 percent more likely to live in an apartment than an otherwise identical household whose primary wage earner is employed on the periphery of the region. The values 17, 3, and 14 percent, which are interpreted as the probabilities of choosing a particular type of housing, may assume values between zero and one hundred.

Comparable estimates for Detroit in 1952 can be obtained from the structure type choice equations presented in Chapter Three. The equations presented in Chapter Three indicate that a worker employed in the Detroit central business district is 30 percent less likely to reside in a single family unit, 16 percent more likely to reside in a two family unit, and 14 percent more likely to live in an apartment than a worker employed at a workplace on the periphery of the region. If the Detroit estimates were for all central city workplaces rather than the CBD alone, the estimated probabilities would be quite similar to those obtained for the Bay Area. Ibid., Appendix A.

21. Edgar Hoover and Raymond Vernon, *Anatomy of a Metropolis* (Cambridge, Mass.: Harvard University Press, 1959).

22. John Meyer, John F. Kain and Martin Wohl, *The Urban Transportation Problem* (Cambridge, Mass.: Harvard University Press, 1965).

23. Niedercorn subsequently refined the analysis presented in Chapter Five and extended it to include a number of additional employment categories. See John H. Niedercorn, *An Econometric Model of Metropolitan Employment and Population Growth* (Santa Monica, Cal.: The Rand Corporation, RM–3758–RC, 1963).

24. Hoover and Vernon, *Anatomy of a Metropolis;* Daniel Creamer (assisted by Walter B. Brown), *Manufacturing Employment by Type of Location: An Examination of Recent Trends* (New York: National Industrial Conference Board, 1969); Daniel Creamer (assisted by Walter B. Brown), *Changing Location of Manufacturing Employment, Part I: Changes by Type of Location, 1947–61,* (New York: National Industrial Conference Board, 1963); Coleman Woodbury (assisted by Frank Cliffe), "Industrial Location and Urban Development," in Coleman Woodbury, ed., *The Future of Cities and Urban Redevelopment* (Chicago: University of Chicago Press, 1953).

25. Leon M. Moses and Harold Williamson, "The Location of Economic Activity in Cities," *American Economic Review* 57 (May 1967); Edwin S. Mills, "An Aggregative Model of Resource Allocation in a Metropolitan Area," *American Economic Review* 57 (May 1967): 197–211; R. Fales and L. Moses, "Land-Use Theory and the Spatial Structure of the Nineteenth-Century City" in M. Perlman, C. L. Levin, and B. Chinitz, eds., *Spatial, Regional and Population Economics: Essays in Honor of Edgar M. Hoover* (London: Gordon and Breach, 1973).

26. Benjamin Cohen, "Trends in Negro Employment within Large Metropolitan Areas," *Public Policy* XIX (Fall 1974); Alexander Ganz and Thomas O'Brien, "The City: Sandbox, Reservation or Dynamo? A Reply", *Public Policy* XXI (Winter 1973); Franklin J. James, Jr., "The City: Sandbox, Reservation or Dynamo? A Reply," *Public Policy* XXII (Winter 1974); Roger Noll, "Metropolitan Employment and Population Distribution and the Conditions of the Urban Poor," in John P. Crecine, ed., *Financing the Metropolis,* The Urban Affairs Annual Review, vol. 4 (Beverly Hills: Sage Publications, 1970); Alexander Ganz and Thomas O'Brien, "New Directions for Our Cities in the Seventies," *Technology Review,* June 1974.

27. Raymond J. Struyk (assisted by Sue A. Marshall), *Income and Urban Homeownership* (Washington, D.C.: The Urban Institute, 1973); Daniel R. Fredland, "Residential Mobility and Home Purchase," (Lexington, Mass.: D.C. Heath Co., 1974); J. F. McDonald, "Housing Market Discrimination, Homeownership and Savings Behavior: Comment," *American Economic Review* 64 (March 1974): 225–29; Howard Birnbaum and Rafael Weston, "Home Ownership and the Wealth Position of Black and White Americans," *The Review of Income and Wealth* vol. 20, no. 1 (March 1974): pp. 103–19.

28. Henry Terrell, "Wealth Accumulation of Black and White Families: The

Empirical Evidence" (Paper presented at the American Economic Association — American Finance Association Convention, Detroit, Michigan, December 1970); Birnbaum and Weston, "Home Ownership;" Duran Bell, Jr., "Indebtedness in Black and White Families," *Journal of Urban Economics,* vol. I (1974).

29. John F. Kain, "The Effect of the Ghetto and the Distribution and Level of Non-White Employment in Urban Areas," *American Statistical Association, Proceedings of the Social Statistics Section* (1964), pp. 260–272.; John F. Kain, "Housing Segregation, Negro Employment and Metropolitan Decentralization," *Quarterly Journal of Economics* 82, no. 2 (May 1968): 175–97.

30. Roger Noll, "Metropolitan Employment and Population Distribution and the Conditions of the Urban Poor," in John P. Crecine, ed., *Financing the Metropolis,* The Urban Affairs Annual Review, vol. 4 (Beverly Hills: Sage Publications, 1970), pp. 481–509; Joseph D. Mooney, "Housing Segregation, Negro Employment, and Metropolitan Decentralization: An Alternative Perspective," *Quarterly Journal of Economics* 83 (May 1969); Bennett Harrison, "The Intrametropolitan Distribution of Minority Economic Welfare," *Journal of Regional Science* 12, no. 1 (1972): 23–43; Paul Offner and Daniel H. Saks, "A Note on John Kain's 'Housing Segregation, Negro Employment, and Metropolitan Decentralization'," *Quarterly Journal of Economics* 85, no. 1, (February 1971): pp. 147–160, Stanley H. Masters, "A Note on John Kain's 'Housing Segregation, Negro Employment, and Metropolitan Decentralization'," *Quarterly Journal of Economics* 88, no. 3 (August 1974): 505–12.

31. Mooney, "Housing Segregation," p. 309.

32. Peter Labrie, "Black Central Cities: Dispersal or Rebuilding, Part 1," The *Review of Black Political Economy,* (Fall 1970); Peter Labrie, "Black Central Cities: Dispersal or Rebuilding, Part II", The *Review of Black Political Economy* 1, no. 3 (Winter-Spring, 1971); William K. Tabb, "Marxist Exploitation and Domestic Colonialism: A Reply to Donald J. Harris," The *Review of Black Political Economy* 4, no. 4 (Summer 1974); Donald J. Harris, "The Black Ghetto as an 'Internal Colony': A Theoretical Critique and Alternative Formulation," The *Review of Black Political Economy* 11, no. 4 (Summer 1972); Carolyn Shaw Bell, *The Economics of the Ghetto* (New York: Western, 1970); Arthur I. Blaustein, "What is Community Economic Development?" *Urban Affairs,* September 1970; Theodore Cross, *Black Capitalism: Strategy for Business in the Ghetto* (New York: Atheneum, 1969); William Haddad and Douglas Pugh, eds., *Black Economic Development* (Englewood Cliffs, N.J.: Prentice-Hall, 1969); Daniel Mitchell, "Black Economic Development and Income Drain: The Case of Numbers," The *Review of Black Political Economy,* Autumn 1970; Thaddeus Spratlen, "Ghetto Economic Development: Content and Character of the Literature," The *Review of Black Political Economy,* Summer 1971; Frederick

Sturdivant, ed., *The Ghetto Marketplace* (New York: Free Press, 1969); William Tabb, "Government Incentives to Private Industry to Locate in Urban Poverty Areas," *Land Economics,* November 1969; William Tabb, *The Political Economy of the Black Ghetto* (New York: Norton, 1970); Thomas Vietorisz and Bennett Harrison, *A Proposed Investment Program for the Economic Development of Central Harlem* (New York: Praeger, 1970).

33. Peter Doeringer, "Ghetto Labor Markets—Problems and Programs" (Paper presented at the Conference on Transportation and Poverty, the American Academy of Arts and Sciences, June 7, 1968); Thomas H. Floyd, "Using Transportation to Alleviate Poverty: Progress Report on Experiments under the Mass Transportation Act" (Paper presented at the Conference on Transportation and Poverty, The American Academy of Arts and Sciences, June 7, 1968); Martin Wohl, "Users of Urban Transportation Services and their Income Circumstances" (Paper presented at the Conference on Transportation and Poverty, The American Academy of Arts and Sciences, June 7, 1968); *Report of the National Advisory Commission on Civil Disorders,* Otto Kerner, chairman (Washington, D.C.: U.S. Government Printing Office, 1968).

34. Ingram, Kain and Ginn, *Detroit Prototype.*

35. Steven Dresch in Ibid.; John M. Quigley, "Residential Location with Multiple Work Places and a Heterogeneous Stock" (Ph.D. dissertation, Harvard University, 1972); John M. Quigley, "Housing Demand in the Short Run: An Analysis of Polytomous Choice" (Paper presented at the winter meetings of the Econometric Society, New York City, December 1973); John F. Kain, William C. Apgar, Jr., J. Royce Ginn and Gregory K. Ingram, *First Interim Report on Contract to Improve the NBER Urban Simulation Model and to Use the Improved Model to Analyze Housing Market Dynamics and Abandonment* (New York: National Bureau of Economic Research, 1973).

36. Quigley, "Housing Demand in the Short Run."

37. Meyer, Kain and Wohl, *The Urban Transportation Problem.*

38. M. J. Beckmann, "On the Distribution of Urban Rent and Residential Density," *Journal of Economic Theory* 1, no. 1 (1969): 60–7; M. J. Beckman, "Von Thunen's Model Revisited: A Neoclassical Land Use Model," *Swedish Journal of Economics* 74, no. 1 (March 1972): 1–7; A. Dixit, "The Optimum Factory Town," *The Bell Journal of Economics and Management Science* 4, no. 2 (Autumn 1973): 637–51; J. MacKinnon, "Urban General Equilibrium Models and Simplicial Search Algorithms" (Manuscript); J. Mirrlees, "The Optimum Town," *Swedish Journal of Economics* 74, no. 1 (March 1972): 114–135; A Montesano, "A Restatement of Beckmann's Model on the Distribution of Urban Rent and Residential Density," *Journal of Economic Theory* 4, no. 2 (April 1972): 329–54; Y. Oron, D. Pines, and E. Sheshinski, "Optimum vs. Equilibrium Land

Use Pattern and Congestion Toll," *The Bell Journal of Economics and Management Science* 4, no. 2 (Autumn 1973): 619–36; R. Solow, "Congestion Cost and the Use of Land for Streets," *The Bell Journal of Economics and Management Science* 4, no. 2 (Autumn 1973): 602–18; R. Solow, "Congestion, Density and the Use of Land in Transportation," *Swedish Journal of Economics* 74, no. 1 (March 1972): 161–73; R. Solow, "On Equilibrium Models of Urban Location," in J. M. Parkin, ed., *Essays in Modern Economics* (London: Longmans, 1973); R. Solow and W. Vickery, "Land Use in a Long Narrow City," *Journal of Economic Theory* 3, no. 4 (December 1971): 430–47.

39. E. S. Mills and J. Mackinnon, "Notes on the New Urban Economics," *The Journal of Economics and Management Science,* vol. 4, no. 2 (Autumn 1973); R. Solow, "Congestion, Density and the Use of Land in Transportation"; R. Solow, "On Equilibrium Models of Urban Location"; R. Solow and W. Vickery "Land Use in a Long Narrow City."

40. Charles River Associates, Inc., *A Disaggregated Behavioral Model;* Thomas King, "Land Values and the Demand for Housing" (Ph.D. dissertation, Yale University, 1972); John M. Quigley, "Racial Discrimination and the Housing Consumption of Black Households," in George M. Von Furstenberg, ed., *Patterns of Racial Discrimination,* vol. 1 *Housing* (Lexington, Mass.: D.C. Heath, 1974); J. Quigley, "Housing Demand in the Short Run: An Analysis of Polytomous Choice"; Mahlon Straszheim, "Estimation of the Demand for Urban Housing Services from Household Interview Data," *Review of Economics and Statistics* LV, no. 1 (February 1973); Mahlon Straszheim, "Urban Housing Market Discrimination and Black Housing Consumption," *Quarterly Journal of Economics* 88, no. 1 (February 1974): 19–74; M. Straszheim, *An Econometric Analysis of the Urban Housing Market* (New York: National Bureau of Economic Research, 1972); Robert Leone, *Location of Manufacturing Activity in the New York Metropolitan Area* (New York: National Bureau of Economic Research, 1971); Robert Leone, "The Role of Data Availability in the Intrametropolitan Workplace Location Studies," *Annals of Economic and Social Measurement* 1, no. 2 (April 1972); R. W. Schmenner, "City Taxes and Industry Location" (Ph.D. dissertation, Yale University, 1973); P. Kemper, "The Location Decisions of Manufacturing Firms Within the New York Metropolitan Area" (Ph.D. dissertation, Yale University, 1973); P. Kemper and R. Schmenner, "The Density Gradient for Manufacturing Industry," *Journal of Urban Economics* 1 (1974); R. J. Struyk, "Spatial Concentration of Manufacturing Employment in Metropolitan Area: Some Empirical Evidence," *Economic Geography* 48, no. 2 (April 1972); R. J. Struyk and F. James, Jr., *Discussion of Recent Trends in Industrial Composition and Location in Four cities* (New York: Na-

tional Bureau of Economic Research, 1971); F. James, Jr., "The City: Sandbox, Reservation or Dynamo? A Reply" *Public Policy* Vol. 22 (Winter, 1974); A Ganz and T. O'Brien, "The City: Sandbox Reservation or Dynamo?" *Public Policy* Vol. 21 (Winter 1973).

41. H. James Brown, J. Royce Ginn, Franklin J. James, John F. Kain, and Mahlon Straszheim, *Empirical Models of Urban Land Use: Suggestions on Research Objectives and Organization* (New York: National Bureau of Economic Research, 1972); Goldner, "The Lowry Model Heritage"; Lowry, "A Model of Metropolis"; Lowry, "Seven Models of Urban Development"; James C. Ohls and Peter Hutchinson, "Models in Urban Development," in *A Guide to Models in Governmental Planning and Operations* (Washington, D.C.: Office of Research and Development, Environmental Protection Agency, August 1974).

42. John F. Kain and John R. Meyer, "Computer Simulations, Physio-Economic Systems and Intra-Regional Models," *American Economic Review, Papers and Proceedings* 63, no. 2 (May 1968); Gregory K. Ingram, "Review of Urban Dynamics," *Journal of the American Institute of Planners,* May 1970; Ira S. Lowry, "Seven Models of Urban Development"; H. James Brown, "Empirical Models of Urban Land Use"; Gary D. Brewer, *Politicians, Bureaucrats, and the Consultant: A Critique of Urban Problem Solving* (New York: Basic Books, Inc., 1973).

43. Edwin S. Mills, "Markets and Efficient Resource Allocation in Urban Areas," *Swedish Economic Journal,* June 1972; John M. Hartwick and Philip G. Hartwick, "Durable Structures and Efficiency in the Development of an Urban Area," October 1972 (processed); Frank de Leeuw and Raymond Struyk, "The Urban Institute Housing Model"; Ingram, Kain, and Ginn, *Detroit Prototype.*

Chapter One

The Journey to Work as a Determinant of Residential Location

1. See, for example, Edgar M. Hoover and Raymond Vernon, *Anatomy of a Metropolis* (Cambridge, Mass.: Harvard University Press, 1959); William Alonso, "A Theory of the Urban Land Market," in *Papers and Proceedings of the Regional Science Association* (Philadelphia, Pa.: University of Pennsylvania, 1960); John D. Herbert and Benjamin H. Stevens, "A Model for the Distribution of Residential Activity in Urban Areas," *Journal of Regional Science* 2, no. 2 (Fall 1960); Lowdon Wingo, Jr., *Transportation and Urban Land* (Washington, D.C.: Resources for the Future, 1961); Ira South Lowry,

"Residential Location in Urban Areas" (Ph.D. dissertation, Department of Economics, University of California, 1960).

2. Alonso, *Urban Land Markets;* Wingo, *Transportation and Urban Land.*

Chapter Two

Commuting and Residential Decisions of Central Business District Workers

1. .See, for example, Edgar M. Hoover and Raymond Vernon, *Anatomy of a Metropolis* (Cambridge, Mass.: Harvard University Press, 1959); William Alonso, "A Theory of the Urban Land Market," in *Papers and Proceedings of the Regional Science Association* (Philadelphia, Pa.: University of Pennsylvania, 1960); John D. Herbert and Benjamin H. Stevens, "A Model for the Distribution of Residential Activity in Urban Areas," *Journal Regional Science* 2, no. 2 (Fall 1960); Lowdon Wingo, Jr., *Transportation and Urban Land* (Washington, D.C.: Resources for the Future, 1961); Ira South Lowry, "Residential Location in Urban Areas" (Ph.D. dissertation, University of California, 1960).

2. See, for example, Alonso, "Urban Land Markets," and Wingo, *Transportation and Urban Land.*

Chapter Three

An Econometric Model of Urban Residential and Travel Behavior

1. U.S., Bureau of the Census, "Characteristics of the Population; Part 22: Michigan," *U.S. Census of Population: 1950,* vol. II (Washington, D.C.: 1952), Table 78.

2. These assumptions about the shape of the location rent surface are obtained from premises about the determinants of the surface, which state that location rents result from the competition for nearby residential space among workers employed in the same general area. A number of theoretical works, including those by Alonso and Wingo (William Alonso, "A Theory of the Urban Land Market," *Papers and Proceedings of the Regional Science Association* (Philadelphia, Pa.: University of Pennsylvania, 1960); and Lowdon Wingo, Jr., *Transportation and Urban Land,* (Washington, D.C.: Resources for the Future, 1961), have obtained site rent or location rent surfaces in an urban area assuming positive transportation costs and utility maximization by households.

3. Transit service is the second variable included in the model as an exogenous variable that the author would like to include as an endogenous variable in a more complete model. It is hoped in future work to explicitly include in the model a transit service equation expressing the functional relationships between transit service levels and transit usage, workplace and residence densities, incomes, family size, automobile ownership, and other determinants of transit service levels.

Chapter Four

The Distribution and Movement of Jobs and Industry

1. These studies include: Raymond Vernon, *The Changing Economic Function of the Central City* (New York: Area Development Committee of the Committee for Economic Development, January 1959); Edgar M. Hoover and Raymond Vernon, *Anatomy of a Metropolis* (Cambridge, Mass.: Harvard University Press, 1959); Chapter 5 of this book; John H. Niedercorn and John F. Kain, "Suburbanization of Employment and Population, 1948–1975," *Proceedings of the Highway Research Board, Highway Research Record No. 38, Travel Forecasting & Reports*, 1963; John R. Meyer, John F. Kain and Martin Wohl, *The Urban Transportation Problem* (Cambridge, Mass.: Harvard University Press, 1965).
2. Coleman Woodbury, (assisted by Frank Cliffe), "Industrial Location and Urban Redevelopment," in Coleman Woodbury, ed., *The Future of Cities and Urban Redevelopment* (Chicago: The University of Chicago Press, 1953), pp. 103–286; and Daniel Creamer, *Changing Location of Manufacturing Employment*, Part I: "Changes by Type of Location, 1947–1961" (New York: National Industrial Conference Board, 1963).
3. Creamer, *Changing Location,* pp. 37–38.
4. Surplus Property Administration, *The Liquidation of War Surpluses, Quarterly Progress Report to the Congress,* Fourth Quarter, (Washington: GPO, 1945), p. 18.
5. U.S., Department of Commerce, *Construction Statistics 1915–1964: A Supplement to Construction Review,* (Washington, D.C.: U.S. Government P.O., January 1966).
6. Niedercorn and Hearle determined that industry used only 9 percent of all land within 48 large American cities and only 11 percent of all developed land. These data were obtained from land use surveys conducted at various dates since 1945 within the 48 cities. By comparison, residential uses account for 30 percent of developed land. Even following the postwar expansion, central cities contained

substantial amounts of vacant land. The Niedercorn-Hearle survey reports that 21 percent of all land in the 48 cities included in their survey was vacant. John H. Niedercorn and Edward F. R. Hearle, *Recent Land Use Trends in Forty-Eight Central Cities* (Santa Monica, Ca.: Rand Corporation, Memorandum RM–3663–FF, June 1963), p. 4.

7. If true, the author's own earlier studies would understate the effect of employment redistribution in causing population suburbanization. Meyer, Kain, and Wohl, *The Urban Transportation Problem;* Chapter 5 of this book; Niedercorn and Kain, "Suburbanization and Population, 1948–1975"; Vernon, *The Changing Economic Function.*

8. The analyses of postwar trends in the location of employment and population presented in this section rely heavily on analyses presented in Chapter 3 of Meyer, Kain, and Wohl, *The Urban Transportation Problem,* pp. 25–56. In fact, they might be viewed as an updating and extension of the analyses presented there.

    Analyses of postwar changes in spatial distributions of employment are seriously handicapped by the lack of consistent and comprehensive data. The best overall view of recent changes in employment locations is found in the Census of Business and Manufactures. However, these data are available for only a limited number of years, are not always consistent, provide very little information on changes within large and heterogeneous central cities, and account for only about 60 percent of all metropolitan employment. Still, they are the best data we have. The 1948, 1954, 1958, and 1963 Censuses of Business present data on total employment in retailing, selected services, and wholesaling for central cities and standard metropolitan statistical areas (SMSAs). Figures on total employment in manufacturing in SMSAs and central cities are available from the 1947, 1954, and 1958 Censuses of Manufactures and for a limited number of cities from the 1963 Census of Manufactures. Suburban ring employment may be obtained by subtracting central city employment from SMSA employment. This geographic division of metropolitan areas is crude, but it provides at least somewhat meaningful descriptions of postwar trends in urban development.

    Most of the analyses of postwar changes in the spatial distribution of employment and population that appear in this chapter are based on the experience of the 40 largest metropolitan areas. (The 40 largest SMSAs are: Akron, Atlanta, Baltimore, Boston, Buffalo, Chicago, Cincinnati, Cleveland, Columbus, Dallas, Dayton, Denver, Detroit, Fort Worth, Houston, Indianapolis, Jersey City, Kansas City, Los Angeles–Long Beach, Louisville, Memphis, Miami, Milwaukee, Minneapolis–St. Paul, New Orleans, New York, Newark, Oklahoma City, Philadelphia, Phoenix, Pittsburgh, Portland, Rochester, St. Louis, San Antonio, San Diego, San Francisco–Oakland,

Seattle, Tampa–St. Petersburg, and Washington, D.C.) Most of the trends observable in the central cities in these larger metropolitan areas have been occurring in smaller centers as well. However, because the central cities of these smaller areas more often have room for expansion inside their political boundaries or can more often annex outlying areas (are less often hemmed in by existing political subdivisions), these redistributions of employment are harder to identify from published data.

9. Statistics presented in Tables 4–3 to 4–8 and 4–10 were calculated from published data obtained from the following publications of the U.S. Department of Commerce, Bureau of the Census: *Census of Manufactures: 1947, vol. III, Area Statistics; Census of Manufactures: 1954, vol. III, Area Statistics; Census of Manufactures: 1958, vol. III, Area Statistics; Census of Manufactures: 1963, vol. III, Area Statistics; Census of Business: 1948, vol. III, Retail Trade–Area Statistics; Census of Business: 1948, vol. V, Wholesale Trade–Area Statistics; Census of Business: 1948, vol. VII, Selected Services–Area Statistics; Census of Business: 1954, vol. II, Retail Trade–Area Statistics; Census of Business: 1954, vol. IV, Wholesale Trade–Area Statistics; Census of Business: 1954, vol. VI, Selected Services–Area Statistics; Census of Business: 1958, vol. II, Retail Trade–Area Statistics; Census of Business: 1958, vol. IV, Wholesale Trade–Area Statistics; Census of Business: 1958, vol. VI, Selected Services–Area Statistics; Census of Business: 1963, vol. II, Retail Trade–Area Statistics; Census of Business: 1963, vol. V, Wholesale Trade–Area Statistics; Census of Business: 1963, vol. VII, Selected Services–Area Statistics; Census of Population: 1940, vol. II, Characteristics of the Population; Census of Population: 1950, vol. II, Characteristics of the Population; Census of Population: 1960, vol. I, Characteristics of the Population; Current Population Reports* Series P–25, no. 371, "Estimates of the Population of Standard Metropolitan Statistical Areas: July 1, 1965."

10. The 1960 Census of Population provides the 1960 population within the central city boundaries of 1950; data on population annexations by the 40 central cities are obtainable from the Municipal Year Books 1949–1965 (Chicago: The International City Managers Association, *The Municipal Year Book* 1949–1965).

Table 4–4 lists the mean annual percentage changes in population and in manufacturing, wholesaling, retailing, and selected services employment in the central cities and metropolitan rings of these same 40 SMSAs during three postwar periods, 1948(1947)–1954, 1954–1958, and 1958–1963. Employment and population data in Table 4–4 are corrected for annexations to the central city. Use of uncorrected data systematically, and on occasion hugely, overstate central city growth. No information is available on the amount of employment annexed to central cities. Thus, employment data used in this paper are corrected for annexations by assuming that the percentage of employment annexed in each category was the same as the percentage of population annexed. It is believed this yields a conservative estimate of employment annexations. [Meyer, Kain, and Wohl, *The Urban Transportation Problem*, p. 27.] The annexation corrections for 1958–1963 are somewhat different from those used for 1948(1947)–1954 and 1954–1958 because of differences in data availability.

It is contended that for most analytical purposes, estimates of employment and population change within constant areas are more useful than ones that are not "corrected" for annexations. This is particularly true for those aspects of public policy that are related to the pattern of urban development. The emphasis of this paper is on attempting to describe, explain, and project changes in urban form or structure. However, there are some uses—for example, questions of central city finance—for which employment and population within legal boundaries may be the crucial variables. Obviously central city declines would be fewer and on average smaller if legal boundaries were used.

11. The 13 SMSAs with the highest percentage rate of population growth for 1950–1960 were Atlanta, Columbus, Dallas, Denver, Fort Worth, Houston, Los Angeles–Long Beach, Miami, Phoenix, San Antonio, San Diego, Tampa–St. Petersburg, and Washington, D.C. The 13 SMSAs with the second highest percentage change were Baltimore, Dayton, Detroit, Indianapolis, Kansas City, Louisville, Memphis, Milwaukee, Minneapolis–St. Paul, New Orleans, Oklahoma City, San Francisco–Oakland, and Seattle. The 14 SMSAs with the lowest percentage change were Akron, Boston, Buffalo, Chicago, Cincinnati, Cleveland, Jersey City, New York, Newark, Philadelphia, Pittsburgh, Portland, Rochester, and St. Louis.

12. For a summary of some of these data, see Meyer, Kain, and Wohl, *The Urban Transportation Problem*, pp. 35–39.

13. There are numerous problems associated with these data. The most serious is significant variations in coverage by industry. In the Chicago SMSA an estimated 77 percent of all wage and salaried workers were covered by unemployment insurance in March 1954. However, the percentage of workers varies considerably as between manufacturing and nonmanufacturing, being nearly 100 percent in the former, but only 64.9 percent in the latter. No government employees are covered. Even so, if the ratio of covered to noncovered workers remained relatively constant as between areas, analysis of changes in covered employment would provide a reasonably accurate index of changes in the distribution of total employment over time. An assumption of stability seems plausible for relatively short time periods. Also, because coverage tends to increase over time, these data, if anything, would probably understate employment declines.

14. Delaware Valley Regional Planning Commission, *1985 Regional Projections for the Delaware Valley*, DVRPC Planning Report no. 1, 1967, p. 3.

15. *Ibid.,* p. 3.
16. Some time series data on "education, institutions, and communications" and "office" employment can be obtained from the U.S. Bureau of the Census, *U.S. Census of Governments: 1957,* vol. II, no. 3, "Local Government in Standard Metropolitan Areas" G.P.O., 1958 and *U.S. Census of Governments: 1962,* vol. V, "Local Government in Metropolitan Areas," G.P.O. 1963. In 1962, the Census of Government accounted for over 45,000 full-time jobs in education and 46,000 "other" government jobs in the Philadelphia metropolitan area. The experiences of these two categories differ significantly. Between 1957 and 1962 education employment in the central city grew by 990 jobs, nearly 10 percent a year, while education employment in the suburbs grew by 3,120 jobs, 22 percent a year. "Other" government employment in the central city declined by 426 jobs, 1.3 percent a year, while suburban "other" government employment grew by 100 jobs, only 0.6 of 1 percent a year. These limited historical data on education and other government employment, which represent 26.9 percent and 17.6 percent of the 1960 employment in "office" and "education, institution, and communications" categories, do not present a markedly different picture from employment data for the four census categories.
17. Because the city of Philadelphia is coextensive with Philadelphia County, additional historical data from *County Business Patterns,* Pennsylvania, 1946, 1947, 1948, 1949, 1950, 1951, 1953, 1956, 1959, 1962, 1964, 1965, and 1966, (U.S. Bureau of Census, Washington: GPO) provide some further insights about postwar changes in the location of covered employment in the metropolitan area. Despite the probable definitional growth of the central city labor force, resulting from increased social security coverage and more complete assignment of employment to counties, covered employment in the city of Philadelphia declined from 774,000 in 1951, to 744,000 in 1956, to 732,000 in 1962, to a low of 708,000 in 1964, before it rose to 724,000 in 1965. Even so the decline in "covered" employment between 1951 and 1965 was 50,000. The overall decrease in covered employment masks a complex pattern of growth and decline. Between the initial (1951) and terminal year (1965) manufacturing employment declined by 90,000 jobs; transportation and public utilities, by over 10,000 jobs; retailing, by nearly 15,000 jobs; and wholesaling, by nearly 4,000 jobs. Partially offsetting these declines were increases in finance, real estate, and insurance of 8,000 jobs and increases in services of 69,000 jobs. Closer examination of these changes suggest that much of the increases in central city "covered" employment, especially services, are probably due to extension in coverage. These statistics for additional categories of employment, as those for government and education, do not depict a significantly different pattern of historical changes in central city employment from that indicated by the four census categories.

18. See Real Estate Research Corporation, *Economic Survey and Market Analysis of Downtown Denver,* (prepared for the Downtown Denver Master Plan Committee, Denver, Colorado, September 1962), pp. 77–83. The Denver projections, which are based on a single year's information, predict an increase of 26,000 jobs between 1962 and 1974, 54 percent in the central business district, with 93 percent of this increase accounted for by office employment. In 1962 only 9.5 percent of the SMSAs office employment was located in the CBD. These optimistic employment projections for Denver's CBD assume the proportion will increase to 16.1 for the period 1962–1968 and to 18.9 for the period of 1968–1974.

19. In this study, addresses published in the *1960 Dun and Bradstreet Million Dollar Directory* were matched with listings in the *1950 MacRae's Blue Book* and the *1950 Standard and Poor's Directory.* About 6,000 firms were located in both years, of which 2,000 had different street addresses in 1960. These 6,000 sample firms and 2,000 movers were coded by 1950 and 1960 locations. For a more detailed discussion of this study see, Meyer, Kain, and Wohl, *The Urban Transportation Problem,* pp. 40 and 41.

20. James Q. Wilson, ed., *The Metropolitan Enigma,* (Cambridge, Mass.: Harvard University Press, 1968).

21. Benjamin Cohen, "Trends in Negro Employment within Large Metropolitan Areas," *Public Policy* XIX, No. 4 (Fall 1971); Roger Noll, "Metropolitan Employment and Population Distribution and the Conditions of the Urban Poor," in John P. Crecine, ed., *Financing the Metropolis,* (Beverly Hills: Sage Publications, 1970); Alexander Ganz and Thomas O'Brien, "The City: Sandbox, Reservation or Dynamo?" *Public Policy* XXI (Winter 1973); Franklin James, Jr., "The City: Sandbox, Reservation or Dynamo? A Reply", *Public Policy* XXII (Winter 1974); Charlotte Freeman, "The Occupational Patterns in Urban Employment Change, 1965–67" (Washington, D.C.: The Urban Institute Paper, URI No. 70000, August 1970); Dorothy K. Newman, "The Decentralization of Jobs," *Monthly Labor Review,* May 1967.

22. Benjamin I. Cohen and Roger G. Noll, "Employment Trends in Central Cities" (Pasadena, California: California Institute of Technology, 1968, Social Science Discussion Paper No. 69-1, p. 4); Cohen, "Trends in Negro Employment", and Noll, "Metropolitan Employment."

23. Noll, "Metropolitan Employment."

24. Cohen, "Trends in Negro Employment."

25. Ganz and O'Brien, "The City."

26. James, "The City: A Reply."

27. For an analysis that provides some indication that housing segregation may affect Negro employment, see Chapter 8 of this book.

28. See John F. Kain, "The Big Cities' Big Problem," *Challenge* 15, no. 1 (September-October 1966): 4–8, and Chapter 10 of this book.

Chapter Five

An Econometric Model
of Metropolitan Development

1. These areas are Akron, Atlanta, Baltimore, Boston, Buffalo, Chicago, Cincinnati, Cleveland, Columbus, Dallas, Dayton, Denver, Detroit, Ft. Worth, Houston, Indianapolis, Jersey City, Kansas City, Los Angeles–Long Beach, Louisville, Memphis, Miami, Milwaukee, Minneapolis–St. Paul, Newark, New Orleans, Oklahoma City, Philadelphia, Phoenix, Pittsburgh, Portland, Rochester, St. Louis, San Antonio, San Diego, San Francisco–Oakland, Seattle, Tampa–St. Petersburg, and Washington, D.C. New York has been excluded from the sample because of its size and other special characteristics.
2. *The Municipal Year Book,* 1949–59, (Chicago: The International City Managers' Association).
3. For evidence of this contention in the Chicago SMSA see, Department of City Planning, City of Chicago, *Industrial Movements and Expansion, 1947–57, City of Chicago and Chicago Metropolitan Area,* Economic Base Study Series, Study No. 3, Jan. 1961, especially Map 6, "Metropolitan Location of Manufacturing Establishments which Relocated from the City of Chicago, 1947–57", p. 31.
4. Total United States manufacturing employment grew at the annual rate of 0.15 percent between 1954 and 1962, but declined at the rate of 0.56 percent during the period 1954–1958. For an average SMSA with 169,000 manufacturing workers (the mean of the 39 areas), the first growth rate implies an annual increase of 254 employees and the second a decline of 950. The algebraic difference of these two numbers is 1204. Adding this difference to the constance term of Equation (5.18) gives a constant term of +559 or +0.559 measured in thousands.
5. See John F. Kain and John H. Niedercorn "Suburbanization of Employment and Population, 1948–1975," *Highway Research Record, No. 38: Travel Forecasting & Reports, 1963,* pp. 25–40.
6. For example, M. S. Gordon, *Employment Expansion and Population Growth, The California Experience, 1900–1950* (Berkeley and Los Angeles: University of California Press, 1954).

Chapter Six

Theories of Residential Location and
Realities of Race

1. Davis McEntire, *Residence and Race: Final and Comprehensive Report to the Commission on Race and Housing* (Berkeley: University of

California Press, 1960); Gary S. Becker, *The Economics of Discrimination* (Chicigo: The University of Chicago Press, 1957); Beverly Duncan and Philip M. Hauser, *Housing a Metropolis–Chicago* (Glencoe: The Free Press, 1960); Otis D. Duncan and Beverly Duncan, *The Negro Population of Chicago–A Study in Residential Succession* (Chicago: The University of Chicago Press, 1957); Martin J. Bailey, "Effects of Race and Other Demographic Factors on the Values of Single-Family Homes," *Land Economics* XLII, no. 12 (May 1966): 215–220; Martin J. Bailey, "Note on the Economics of Residential Zoning and Urban Renewal," *Land Economics* 35 (August 1959): 288–90; Richard F. Muth, "The Variation of Population Density and Its Components in South Chicago," *Papers and Proceedings of the Regional Science Association,* vol. II (1964).

2. U.S., Bureau of the Census, *U.S. Census of Population: 1960. 1960 Selected Area Reports. Standard Metropolitan Statistical Areas.* Final Report PC (3)–1D (Washington, D.C.: U.S. Government Printing Office, 1963), Table 1.

3. Karl E. and Alma F. Taeuber, *Negroes in Cities: Residential Segregation and Neighborhood Change* (Chicago: Aldine Publishing Co., 1965).

4. Taeuber and Taeuber, *Negroes in Cities;* A. H. Pascal, "The Economics of Housing Segregation," Memorandum, RM–5510–RC (Santa Monica: The Rand Corporation, November 1967); John R. Meyer, John F. Kain, and Martin Wohl, *The Urban Transportation Problem* (Cambridge, Mass.: Harvard University Press, 1965), Chapter 7; McEntire, *Residence and Race.*

5. The most comprehensive comparative study of the segregation of Negroes and other ethnic groups is by Stanley Lieberson, *Ethnic Patterns in American Cities* (Glencoe: The Free Press, 1963). Similar findings are reported in: Otis Dudley Duncan and Stanley Lieberson, "Ethnic Segregation and Assimilation," *American Journal of Sociology* LXIV, no. 4 (January 1959): 364–374; and Karl E. Taeuber and Alma F. Taeuber, "The Negro as an Immigrant Group," *American Journal of Sociology* LXIX, no. 4 (January 1964).

6. William Brink and Louis Harris, *Black and White* (New York: Simon and Schuster, 1967), pp. 232–233.

7. McEntire, *Residence and Race,* Charles Abrams, *Forbidden Neighbors: A Study of Prejudice in Housing* (New York: Harper and Brothers, 1955); Robert Thompson, Hylan Lewis, and Davis McEntire, "Atlanta and Birmingham: A Comparative Study in Negro Housing" in Nathan Glazer and Davis McEntire, eds., *Studies in Housing and Minority Groups* (Berkeley: University of California Press, 1960).

8. Chester Rapkin, "Price Discrimination Against Negroes in Rental Housing Market," *Essays in Urban Land Economics* (Los Angeles: University of California, 1966); Ronald G. Ridker and John A. Henning, "The Determinants of Residential Property Values with Special Reference to Air Pollution," *The Review of Economics and Statistics* XLIV, no. 2 (May 1967); Chester Rapkin and William Grigsby, *The*

Demand for Housing in Racially Mixed Areas (Berkeley: University of California Press, 1960); Luigi Laurenti, *Property Values and Race: Studies in Seven Cities* (Berkeley: University of California, 1960); Duncan and Duncan, *Negro Population of Chicago;* Duncan and Hauser, *Housing A Metropolis;* McEntire, *Residence and Race;* Muth, "The Variation of Population Density"; Bailey, "Effects of Race and Other Demographic Factors."

9. Becker, *The Economics of Discrimination.*

10. For example, the tendency for the ghetto to expand through Jewish neighborhoods has been noted by a number of observers. Ernest W. Burgess commented on this question in an early paper and remarked that "No instance has been noted ... where a Negro invasion succeeded in displacing the Irish in possession of a community. Yet, frequently ... Negroes have pushed forward in the wake of retreating Jews ..." Ernest W. Burgess, "Residential Segregation in American Cities," *Annals of the American Academy of Political and Social Science* CXL (November 1928), p. 112.

11. For example, see William M. Ladd, "The Effect of Integration on Property Values," *American Economic Review,* September 1962; and Laurenti, *Property Values and Race.*

12. The most detailed analysis of ghetto expansion is found in Duncan and Duncan, *Negro Population of Chicago.*

13. U.S., Bureau of the Census, Current Population Reports, Series, P–23, Special Studies (formerly Technical Studies), no. 27, "Trends in Social and Economic Conditions in Metropolitan Areas" (Washington, D.C.; U.S. Government Printing Office, 1969), p. 2.

Chapter Seven

Housing Market Discrimination, Homeownership and Savings Behavior

1. See B. Duncan and P. Hauser, *Housing a Metropolis–Chicago* (Glenco, Ill: The Free Press, 1960); R. A. Haugen and A. J. Heins, "A Market Separation Theory of Rent Differentials in Metropolitan Areas," *Quarterly Journal of Economics 83, (November 1963); 660–72;* D. McEntire, *Residence and Race* (Berkeley, Cal.: University of California Press, 1960), chapter 11; Richard Muth, *Cities and Housing: The Spatial Pattern of Urban Residential Land Use* (Chicago, University of Chicago Press, 1969); C. Rapkin, "Price Discrimination Against Negroes in the Rental Housing Market," in *Essays in Urban Land Economics,* edited by University of California at Los Angeles, Real Estate (Los Angeles: 1966); pp. 333–45; C. Rapkin and W. Gugsby, *The Demand for Housing in Racially Mixed Areas* (Berkeley, Cal: University of California Press, 1960); Ronald Ridker and

John Henning "The Determinants of Residential Property Values with Special Reference to Air Pollution," *Review of Economics and Statistics* 49 (May 1967): 246–47; M. Stengel, "Price Discrimination in the Urban Rental Housing Market" (Doctoral dissertation, Harvard University, May 1970).

2. See Martin Bailey, "Note on the Economics of Residential Zoning and Urban Renewal," *Land Economics* 33 (August 1959): 288–92, and "Effects of Race and Other Demographic Factors on the Values of Single Family Homes," *Land Economics* 40 (May 1966): 215–20.

3. See James L. Hecht, *Because It's Right: Integration in Housing* (Boston: Little Brown & Co., 1970); D. McEntire, *Residence and Race;* K. and A. Taeuber, *Negroes in Cities* (Chicago: Aldine Publishing Co. 1965).

4. See Martin David, *Family Composition and Consumption* (Amsterdam: North Holland Publishing Co. 1962); John Lansing and L. Kish, "Family Life Cycle as an Independent Variable," *American Sociological Review* 22 (1957): 512–19; Sherman Maisel, "Rates of Ownership, Mobility and Purchase," in *Essays in Urban Land Economics* (Los Angeles: 1966), pp. 76–108; J. N. Morgan, "Factors Related to Consumer Savings When it is Defined as a Net-Worth Concept", in L. R. Klein, ed., *Contributions of Survey Methods to Economics* (New York: Columbia University Press, 1954).

5. The generalized least squares regression estimates are obtained by weighing each observation by $[1/P(1-P)]^1$ where P is the value of the probability predicted by ordinary least squares. It can be shown that this procedure provides more efficient estimates of a linear probability function.

6. D. Fredland, "Residential Mobility and Choice of Tenure" (Doctoral dissertation, Harvard University, 1970).

7. See R. Ramanathan, "Measuring the Permanent Income of a Household: An Experiment in Methodology," *Journal of Political Economy* 79 (January 1971): 177–85.

8. This technique was suggested by the anonymous referee. We report it, in spite of strong statistical and theoretical reservations.

9. The housing expenditure models reported in Table 7–2 use housing value ÷ 100 as an estimate of homeowners' monthly expenditure (see R. F. Muth, *Cities and Housing*). This gross rent multiplier, as well as the 1-to-120 rule (see John Shelton, "The Cost of Rental Versus Owning a Home," *Land Economics* 42 (February 1968): 59–72), is widely used in housing market analysis to make market value roughly commensurate with monthly rent. In addition to the results reported, we estimated equations using gross rent multipliers of 1/185 and 1/164. These ratios were derived by regressing monthly rent and value upon a detailed set of the individual characteristics of rental and owner-occupied units and thus deriving estimates of the equivalent value of the average rental unit (164 x rent) and the average rental fee for the characteristics of owner-occupied units

(value/185). The race coefficients were indistinguishable from those presented.

10. Muth, *Cities and Housing.*

11. As a further test of the influence of housing market discrimination, separate Negro and white equations of the same form as equation (7.4) were estimated; a covariance test indicated no statistically significant difference between them (F = 1.32). In addition, separate models for equation (7.4) were estimated for each of four household types described above: single persons, couples; female-headed families; and male-headed families. In each case, the coefficient of the race variable was highly significant and varied in magnitude between −0.13 and −0.16. When similar analyses were performed for the probability of home purchase, the sample sizes became uncomfortably small for some subgroups.

12. Household expectations about moving frequency may be the only important excluded taste variable. (As will be discussed subsequently, mobility also affects the economics of homeownership.) However, a fairly extensive analysis of the mobility rates of the households in this sample indicates no important differences in the frequency of moves between white and Negro households after accounting for other socioeconomic factors.

13. For example, recent Survey of Economic Opportunity tabulation indicates that for lower middle income ($5,000–$7,000 per annum) families, housing equity alone represents 40 percent of the net worth of white households and an even larger proportion of the net worth of black households. See Appendix A for further details.

14. Price markups were estimated for owner- and renter-occupied structures using the St. Louis sample for three alternative specifications (see Chapter 12). Of the three specifications, two indicate a smaller percentage markup in the owner market. Even if the markup were smaller for rental than for owner-occupied properties, it would require an extremely large price-elasticity-of-choice to reduce the probability of black ownership by 10 percentage points.

15. The 18 SMSAs consisted of all those for which the data on black and white ownership rates by income and family size classes were published. The expected black ownership rate was obtained by applying the ownership proportions for white households by income and family size for each SMSA to the income and family size distribution of black households (see U.S., Bureau of the Census, *U.S. Census of Housing, 1960, vol. II, Metropolitan Housing* (Washington, D.C.: U.S. Government PO, 1963), and summing.

16. The percent of single family housing in the central city for SMSA was obtained from *U.S. Census of Housing: 1960, vol. II.* The percent of SMSA blacks residing in the central city was obtained from U.S., Bureau of the Census, *U.S. Census of Population: 1960, vol. I, Characteristics of Population* (Washington, D.C.: U.S. Government PO, 1963).

17. At the minimum, it would take a peculiar spatial distribution of tastes for homeownership of asset differences to explain these findings.

18. See Henry Aaron, "Income Taxes and Housing," *American Economics Review* 60 (December 1970): 89–806 and J. P. Shelton, "The Cost of Rental Housing..."

19. U.S., Federal Housing Administration, *FHA Homes, 1967; Data for States and Selected Areas on Characteristics of FHA Operations under Section 203* (Washington, D.C.: U.S. Government PO, 1967).

20. *Ibid.* Our sample suggests an annual rate of increase in value of white-owned properties of 4.7 percent during the 5 to 10 year period prior to 1966.

21. Henry Terrell, "Wealth Accumulation of Black and White Families: The Empirical Evidence" (Paper presented before a joint session of the American Economic Association and the American Finance Association, Detroit, Michigan, December 28, 1970), mimeographed.

22. See D. S. Projector et al., "Survey of Changes in Family Finances," Federal Reserve Technical Paper, Washington, D.C., 1968.

23. As long ago as 1953, James Duesenberry argued persuasively that levels of savings and asset accumulation are heavily dependent upon the form in which savings is maintained. Citing specifically the high proportion of savings invested in assets associated with the reason for saving (e.g., housing equity, pension and insurance reserves, and investment in unincorporated businesses), he suggests a close connection between the motives for saving and the form which the saving takes. Thus, although we cannot deduce that because people invested in some particular asset, they would not have saved if that type of asset had not been available, there appears to be a strong association.

    If Duesenberry's insight is valid, then even if capital markets were perfect in every sense of the word, we would expect to find substantially fewer assets for households denied certain forms of saving (i.e., those forms associated with the reason for saving) such as homeownership, pension and insurance investment, and unincorporated business investment. See James Duesenberry, "The Determinants of Savings Behavior: A Summary" in W. W. Heller, F. M. Boddy and C. L. Nelson, eds., *Savings in the Modern Economy* (Minneapolis: Univ. of Minnesota Press, 1953).

Chapter Eight

Housing Market Discrimination and Negro Employment

1. The terms Negro and nonwhite are used interchangeably. Since Negroes are 99 percent of all Chicago nonwhites in 1960 and 97 percent of all Detroit nonwhites in 1960, the distinction has little practical significance.

2. Detroit Area Traffic Study, *Report on the Detroit Metropolitan Area Traffic Study:* Part 1–*Data Summary of Interpretation* (Lansing, Mich.: July 1955); *Chicago Area Transportation Study,* vol. 1 (Chicago: 1959).

3. Chicago city (block) segregation indexes are: 1940, 95.0; 1950, 92.1, and 1960, 92.6. The metropolitan (tract) indexes are 1950, 88.1 and 1960, 89.7. Detroit city segregation indexes (block) are 89.9 in 1940, 88.8 in 1950, and 84.5 in 1960, and the metropolitan area indexes (tract) are 83.3 in 1950 and 86.7 in 1960. Karl E. Taeuber and Alma F. Taeuber, *Negroes in Cities: Residential Segregation and Neighborhood Change* (Chicago: Aldine Publishing Co., 1965).

4. By comparison with other U.S. metropolitan areas, Detroit and Chicago have a large number of relatively large outlying Negro residential areas. Detroit possesses three and Chicago possesses two of the 30 suburban communities with 1,000 or more nonwhite households. Only the metropolitan areas of New York and San Francisco–Oakland have a larger number. Moreover, nonwhites are highly segregated within these suburbs; the 1960 indexes for Chicago are: Evanston, 87.2 and Joliet, 90.2. Those for Detroit suburbs are: Highland Park, 77.4; Inkster, 95.0; Pontiac, 90.5. Taeuber and Taeuber, *Negroes in Cities: Residential Segregation and Neighborhood Change* (Chicago: Aldine Publishing Co., 1965).

5. Otis and Beverly Duncan conclude that the spatial outline of the Negro community in Chicago had been established by 1920, if not by 1910; that further expansion of the Negro community occurred within areas which already had been accommodating a nucleus of Negro residents in 1920; and that what expansion there has been of the Negro residential areas has consisted of adding areas contiguous to existing Negro concentrations. O.D. Duncan and Beverly Duncan, *The Negro Population of Chicago* (Chicago: University of Chicago Press, 1957), p. 87–107.

6. Labor mobility studies show that few jobs are located from newspaper advertisements, employment offices, and the like. Workers most frequently learn of jobs from friends, by passing the place of work and seeing help wanted signs, and by other casual associations. Since nonwhites have few associations with white areas distant from the ghetto and since few of their friends and neighbors are employed there or make frequent trips there, the chances of their learning of distant job opportunities may be significantly lessened.

7. Meyer, Kain, and Wohl, *The Urban Transportation Problem,* (Cambridge, Mass.: Harvard University Press, 1965), chapter 7; John F. Kain, "The Big Cities' Big Problem," *Challenge* 15 (September-October 1966): 5–8.

8. The simple correlation coefficients between distance from the major ghetto and distance from the nearest ghetto are $R = 0.91$ for Chicago and $R = 0.75$ for Detroit.

9. It should be noted that the variance of the dependent variable is considerably smaller in Detroit.

10. This is not to deny the possible importance of other differences between the two cities, such as the nondiscriminatory behavior of the United Auto Workers in Detroit and the importance of the auto industry there.

11. Findings published elsewhere indicate that the location of Negro employment does affect the location of Negro residences within the constraints imposed by housing market segregation. However, the location decisions of Negroes appear irrational and inconsistent, if the hypothesis of significant restriction on their choice of residences is not accepted. Meyer, Kain, and Wohl, *The Urban Transportation Problem,* pp. 144–77.

12. These data are based upon a 1 and 30 sampling rate. Thus, for some occupations and industries with either relatively few workers or relatively low nonwhite proportions the number of nonwhite workers is very small. The sample included only 211 nonwhites employed in wholesale trade: 671 employed in finance, insurance, and real estate; and only 740 employed in public administration. Even fewer nonwhites were sampled within several occupation groups. There were only 170 nonwhite sales workers; 316 nonwhite private household workers; 287 nonwhite managers, officials, and proprietors; and 370 nonwhite professional, technical, and kindred workers.

13. A much poorer fit was obtained for private household workers. That equation (not reported above) explains only 15 percent of the total variance. The poor statistical fit obtained for domestics is hardly surprising. Private household workers include an especially small number of workers and thus the sampling variability is especially great. Moreover, because of "living in" their behavior would be expected to be much different than hypothesized by the above model.

14. In interpreting the data in Table 8–2 on the number of analysis areas or workplace zones having no nonwhite workers, it should be remembered that these data are based on a 1 and 30 sample. Thus, the number of analysis zones having no nonwhite workers in a given industry or occupation group will generally be smaller than the number of areas having no sampled workers in a given occupation or industry group. Moreover, 11 analysis areas have no sampled nonwhite workers whatsoever and this thereby is a lower bound for any given occupation or industry group.

15. These estimates for Chicago are lower than those reported in an earlier paper by the author (see "The Effect of the Ghetto on the Distribution and Level of Nonwhite Employment in Urban Area," *American Statistical Association, Proceedings of the Social Statistics Section* (1969) pp. 260–72.). These differences are due to a data correction that affected the estimates obtained in Equations (8.1) through (8.3).

16. U.S., Bureau of Census, *1960 Census of Population,* vol. I, *Characteristics of the Population,* part I, *U.S. Summary* (Washington, D.C.: U.S. Government Printing Office).

17. The central cities of 24 of the 40 largest metropolitan areas lost manufacturing employment in the 1947–58 period using constant 1950 boundaries. Retailing employment declined in 30 and wholesaling employment in 13 of these central cities during the 1947–58 decade. If anything these trends appear to have accelerated during the period 1958–63. See chapter 4.

18. U.S., Commission on Civil Rights, *Racial Isolation in the Public Schools,* vol. 1 (Washington, D.C.: U.S. Government Printing Office 1967), p. 11.

19. In addition, significant annexations to central cities have occurred in every decade. These annexed populations invariably have been white.

20. U.S., Bureau of the Census, *Census of Population, 1960. Standard Metropolitan Areas,* PC (3)–11), Washington, D.C.: U.S. Gov. Printing Office, 1962.

21. Chapter Four of this book.

22. This problem may be less visible in cities other than Chicago, but it may be potentially as serious in metropolitan areas having large and growing ghettoized Negro populations. Suburbanization of federal offices apparently has caused problems for Negroes employed in or seeking federal jobs. *The New York Times* reported a speech by President Johnson concerning the housing problems of Negroes holding or seeking federal jobs. The article quoted informed sources as stating that "sometimes Negroes were unable to find adequate housing near federal installations and did not want to commute long distances to work. Therefore, they turn down federal jobs at those installations." The article adds that the problem, according to officials, "is becoming increasingly acute as more federal offices move from central cities into outlying areas." John D. Pomfret, "Johnson Asks Aid on Negro Housing," *The New York Times,* March 18, 1966.

23. Quoted in a feature article by William Schaub, "County 'Miracle' Makes Workers of Reliefers," *Chicago's American,* February 11, 1965.

24. James Ridgeway, "Poor Chicago, Down and Out with Mayor Daley," *The New Republic,* May 15, 1965.

25. The manufacturing employment estimates were obtained by interpolation and extrapolation of employment data contained in Northeast Illinois Planning Commission, *Metropolitan Planning Guidelines, Phase One: Background Documents* (Chicago: 1965); Center for Urban Studies, *Mid-Chicago Economic Development Study, vol. III: Technical Supplement, Economic Development of Mid–Chicago* (Chicago: University of Chicago, 1956); Illinois State Employment Service, *Employed Workers Covered by the Illinois Unemployment Compensation Act, 1955–1964* (Chicago: 1965); and U.S., Bureau of Census, *Census of Manufactures,* vol. III, *Area Statistics,* 1954,

1958, 1963, Washington G.P.O., 1957, 1960, 1966. A detailed discussion of the way in which these estimates were prepared is available on request from the author.

26. John F. Kain, "The Effects of the Ghetto on Distribution and Level of Non-White Employment in Urban Areas," *American Statistical Association, Proceedings of the Social Statistics Section* (1964) pp. 260–72; "Housing Segreation, Negro Employment and Metropolitan Decentralization", *The Quarterly Journal of Economics*, Vol. LXXXII, No. 2, (May 1968), pp. 1-23.

27. Roger Noll, "Metropolitan Employment and Population Distribution and the Conditions of the Urban Poor," in John P. Crecine, ed., *Financing the Metropolis,* The Urban Affairs Annual Review, vol. 4, (Beverly Hills, Cal.: Sage Publications, 1970), pp. 481–509; Joseph D. Mooney, "Housing Segregation, Negro Employment, and Metropolitan Decentralization," *Quarterly Journal of Economics* LXXXIII (May 1969); Bennett Harrison, "The Intrametropolitan Distribution of Minority Economic Welfare," *Journal of Regional Science* 12, no. 1 (1972); 23–43; Paul Offner and Daniel H. Saks, "A Note on John Kain's Housing Segregation, Negro Employment, and Metropolitan Decentralization," *Quarterly Journal of Economics* LXXXV (February 1971); Stanley H. Masters, "A Note on John Kain's 'Housing Segregation, Negro Employment, and Metropolitan Decentralization'" *Quarterly Journal of Economics* (August, 1974).

28. Noll, "Metropolitan Employment," p. 501. The notions of primary and secondary labor markets are of some relevance in this context. Doeringer, Piore, and others have pointed out that job vacancies and unemployment rates may be rather misleading indicators of conditions in secondary labor markets, which are characterized by low wages, poor working conditions, high rates of turnover, job instability, and the like. Peter B. Doeringer and Michael J. Piore, *Internal Labor Markets and Manpower Analysis* (Lexington, Mass.: Lexington Books, 1972).

29. I am mindful of the fact that these black welfare losses may be reflected more in the housing market than the labor market. Even so, it would be surprising if these effects were not evident in the labor market at all. See chapter seven.

30. Meyer, Kain, and Wohl, *The Urban Transportation Problem.*

31. Joseph D. Mooney, "Housing Segregation, Negro Employment and Metropolitan Decentralization," *Quarterly Journal of Economics* Vol. LXXXIII (May 1969).

32. Mooney, "Housing Segregation..." p. 308. Beta coefficients measure the change in the dependent variable from its mean measured in standard deviations, that would occur as a result of a change in the independent variable from its mean by one standard deviation.

34. Masters, "A Note on John Kain's 'Housing Segregation'," p. 6.

35. Harrison, "Intrametropolitan Distribution."

36. William Alonso, *Location and Land Use* (Cambridge, Mass.: Harvard University Press, 1964); Richard Muth, *Cities and Housing* (Chicago: University of Chicago Press, 1969); chapter three of this book.
37. Masters', "A Note on John Kain's 'Housing Segregation'," footnote 20.
38. Offner and Saks, "A Note on John Kain's 'Housing Segregation'."
39. Ibid., p. 180. Equation 8.1 implies an estimated job gain of approximately 22,000, while Equation 8.24 implies a job loss of nearly 40,000.

Chapter Nine

Alternatives to the
Gilded Ghetto

1. Chapter 8.
2. U.S., Commission on Civil Rights, *Racial Isolation in the Public Schools* (Washington, D.C.: U.S. Government Printing Office, 1967), vol. 1, p. 13.
3. Of the one-quarter million public housing units constructed by all city authorities, only 76, and these in only one metropolitan area, have been built outside central cities. Ibid, p. 24.
4. Casual empirical evidence on this point is provided in an article in the *Washington Post* (February 16, 1968): "Job Scheme Backfires in Detroit," In response to a job creation program for the hardcore unemployed, the Detroit Urban League reported out-of-city job seekers using their employment facilities were up 9 to 12 percent over 1966.

Chapter Ten

The NBER Urban Simulation
Model as a Theory of
Urban Spatial Structure

1. William Alonso, *Location and Land Use* (Cambridge, Mass.: Harvard University Press, 1964); Martin J. Beckman, "On the Distribution of Urban Rent and Density," *Journal of Economic Theory* 1 (1969): 60–67; Chapter One of this book; Edwin S. Mills, "An Aggregative Model of Resource Allocation in a Metropolitan Area," *American Economic Review, Papers and Proceedings* 57 (May 1967): 197–210; Aldo Montesano, "A Restatement of Beckman's Model on the Distribution of Urban Rent and Residential Density," *Journal of Economic Theory* 4 (1972): 329–54; Richard F. Muth, *Cities and Housing* (Chicago: University of Chicago Press, 1969); Robert M. Solow, "Congestion, Density, and the Use of Land in Transportation," *Swedish Journal of Economics,* 74, no. 1 (1972): pp. 161–73; Low-

don Wingo, Jr., *Transportation and Urban Land* (Washington, D.C.: Resources for the Future, 1961).

2. For a critique of several such models, see H. James Brown et al., *Empirical Models of Urban Land Use: Suggestions on Research Objectives and Organization*, Exploratory Report no. 6 (New York: National Bureau of Economic Research, 1972). An even less reserved assessment is presented in Douglas B. Lee, Jr., "Requiem for Large Scale Models," Institute of Urban and Regional Development, University of California, Berkeley, April 1972 (mimeo). See also Ira S. Lowry, *Seven Models of Urban Development: A Structural Comparison* P–3673 (Santa Monica, Cal.: The Rand Corporation, 1967); John F. Kain and John R. Meyer, "Computer Simulation, Physio-Economic Systems, and Intra-Regional Models," *American Economic Review, Papers and Proceedings* 57 (May 1967): pp. 223–34.

3. The effort to develop the NBER urban simulation model is one of three major components of the NBER urban studies program. The other two are a series of econometric analyses of urban housing markets and a series of studies of industry location. Findings from several of these studies have been published or are nearing publication. These include: (1) a study of the St. Louis housing market in Chapters 8 and 12 of this book and in John F. Kain and John M. Quigley, *Housing Markets and Racial Discrimination: A Microeconomic Analysis.* (New York: National Bureau of Economic Research, 1975); (2) a study of the San Francisco-Oakland Housing market, Mahlon Straszheim, *An Econometric Analysis of the Urban Housing Market* (New York: National Bureau of Economic Research, 1975); (3) a study of the residential location decisions of Milwaukee households, Stephen K. Mayo, "An Econometric Model of Residential Location" (Ph.D. dissertation, Department of Economics, Harvard University, 1971); (4) a study of moving behavior by Philadelphia households, Daniel Fredland, "Residential Mobility and Choice of Tenure" (Ph.D. dissertation, Harvard University, 1970); (5) a study of housing demand and the residential location decisions of Pittsburgh households, John M. Quigley, "Residential Location: Multiple Workplaces and a Heterogeneous Housing Stock" (Ph.D. dissertation, Department of Economics, Harvard University, 1972); (6) a study of decisions to move by San Francisco-Oakland households, H. James Brown and John F. Kain, "Moving Behavior of San Francisco Households," 1970 (processed); and H. James Brown, "Changes in Workplace and Residential Location," May 1972 (processed); (7) a study of industry location in New York, Robert A. Leone, *Location of Manufacturing Activity in the New York Metropolitan Area* (New York: National Bureau of Economic Research, forthcoming); (8) Raymond Struyk and Franklin James, *Intrametropolitan Industrial Location: The Pattern of Process and Change in Four*

Metropolitan Areas (New York: National Bureau of Economic Research, forthcoming); (9) a study of the effects of location taxation on industry location by Roger Schmenner.

4. Gregory K. Ingram, John F. Kain, and J. Royce Ginn, with contributions by H. James Brown and Stephen P. Dresch, *The Detroit Prototype of the NBER Urban Simulation Model* (New York: National Bureau of Economic Research, 1972).

5. The model of the individual consumer and the geometric analysis follow closely a similar analysis presented in Chapter One. The principal difference is that the analysis in the earlier paper is carried out in terms of a single housing attribute, that is, the quantity of residential space, rather than in terms of housing bundles.

6. T. C. Koopmans and M. J. Beckman. "Assignment Problems and the Location of Economic Activities," *Econometrica* 25 (January 1957), 53–76.

7. Byran Ellickson, "Jurisdictional Fragmentation and Residential Choice," *American Economic Review, Papers and Proceedings* 61, no. 2 (May 1971): 334–40; Byran Ellickson, "Metropolitan Residential Location and the Local Public Sector," Institute of Government and Public Affairs, University of California, Los Angeles, Memorandum 137, January 1970; Wallace E. Oates, "The Effects of Property Taxes and Local Public Spending on Property Values: An Empirical Study of Tax Capitalization and the Tiebout Hypothesis," *Journal of Political Economy* 77 (November 1969): 957–71; Charles M. Tiebout, "A Pure Theory of Local Expenditures," *Journal of Political Economy* 24 (October 1956): 416–24; Jerome Rothenberg, "Strategic Interaction and Resource Allocation in Metropolitan Intergovernmental Relations," *American Economic Review, Papers and Proceedings* 59 (May 1969): 494–503.

8. Ingram, Kain, and Ginn, *Detroit Prototype.*

9. Gregory K. Ingram, "A Simulation Model of an Urban Housing Market" (Ph.D. dissertation, Department of Economics, Harvard University, 1971).

10. Kain and Quigley, "Discrimination and a Heterogeneous Housing Stock"; Straszheim, "An Econometric Analysis."

Chapter Eleven

Cumulative Urban Growth and Urban Density Functions

1. Colin Clark, "Urban Population Densities," *Journal of Royal Statistical Society* ser. A, 114, 375–386 (1951).

2. William Alonso, *Location and Land Use* (Cambridge, Mass.: Harvard University Press, 1964); Martin Beckman, "On the Distribution of Urban Rent and Residential Density," *Journal of Economic*

Theory 1 (1969): 60–67; Aldo Montesano, "A Restatement of Beckman's Model on the Distribution of Urban Rent and Residential Density," *Journal of Economic Theory* 4 (1972): 329–354; Chapter One of this book. Edwin S. Mills, "An Aggregative Model of Resource Allocation in a Metropolitan Area," *American Economic Review* (1967): 197–211; Edwin S. Mills, "Urban Density Functions," *Urban Studies* vol. 7, no. 1 (February 1970); Richard Muth, *Cities and Housing* (Chicago: The University of Chicago Press, 1969); Robert M. Solow, "Congestion, Density and the Use of Land in Transportation," *Swedish Journal of Economics* (1972), pp. 161–73; Lowden Wingo, Jr., *Transportation and Urban Land* (Washington, D.C.: Resources for the Future, 1961).

3. This model was developed in an earlier paper. See David Harrison, Jr. and John F. Kain, "An Historical Model of Urban Form," Harvard Program on Regional and Urban Economics, Discussion Paper no. 63, November 1970.

4. Although Muth does not consider historical development patterns in the theoretical model he presents in *Cities and Housing*, he does recognize the probable importance of history in the development of real cities. Therefore, he includes the proportion of dwelling units built prior to 1920 as an independent variable in two of his statistical analyses of urban density gradients. First, he includes the variable in his regression analysis of interurban variations in density function parameters as a taste variable to test the hypothesis that households have an aversion to living in the central city because of the age of its dwelling units (pp. 151–56). Then Muth uses the same variable to explain intraurban variations in density in his analysis of the determinants of gross density in six selected cities (pp. 192–95). While this second use of the proportion built prior to 1920 is in the spirit of our analysis, a single cross-sectional measure of age cannot reflect the complicated timing of urban growth which has characterized the physical development of large U.S. metropolitan areas. Therefore, it should come as no surprise that this part of his statistical analysis yields rather disappointing results. Neither of these ad hoc approaches provides a satisfactory representation of the effects of timing on urban spatial structure.

5. The 1960 U.S. Census of Housing report on the components of inventory change, 1950–59, reported that merged units accounted for only 1.3 percent and converted units 3.0 percent of the 1959 SMSA housing inventory. In contrast, units added by new construction during the 10 year period accounted for 28.0 percent of the 1959 stock. Moreover, the number of units added by conversion almost exactly cancelled out the number of units subtracted by merger, leaving the net effect of merger and conversion a relatively insignificant aspect of inventory change.

Demolition of existing units and their replacement at the same site or elsewhere by units of more suitable density have been more important ways of modifying the density of urban development, although only 3.8 percent of the 1950 SMSA housing inventory was reported as demolished in 1959. The effect of demolitions on incremental density has likely changed over time. In the first part of the century most demolition probably involved razing lower density structures to permit their replacement by higher density ones. Since World War II, the record of demolition has been more mixed. In some cases lower density structures have been replaced by higher density ones. On net, however, postwar demolition has probably worked to reduce average net residential densities in most urban areas, as high to medium structures in central cities were typically "replaced" by much lower density structures in the suburbs. Thus, in the decade from 1950 to 1959, only 38.0 percent of the units demolished in SMSAs were single family structures, compared to 80.3 percent single family for the units constructed during the period.

See U.S. Bureau of the Census, *U.S. Census of Housing, 1960* vol. IV, *Components of Inventory Change*, part 1A, no. 1 (Washington, D.C.: U.S. Government Printing Office, 1962).

6. There are two major difficulties involved in using S^* to characterize net residential density. First, the measure fails to consider the structure type composition of the remaining dwelling units. Two metropolitan areas might have the same value of S^* in a given time period (or a single metropolitan area might have the same percentage in two time periods), yet the residential density of the two increments might differ as a result of differences in the mix of multiunit structures. For example, in one city the remaining units might consist primarily of apartment houses, and in another they might be primarily duplexes and three family structures. S^* will be biased to the extent that differences in density over time and among different metropolitan areas are accounted for by differences in composition among the remaining structure types.

The second major bias results from variations in average lot size for each structure type over time and among metropolitan areas. By using S^* we assume that the amount of residential land per dwelling unit is constant over time and between metropolitan areas for single family detached and other structures. While lot size per unit probably does not vary much for multiple units, there is evidence that the lot size of single family units differs significantly between different metropolitan areas at the same point in time and over time within the same metropolitan areas. S^* is therefore additionally biased to the extent that differences in density are accounted for by differences in the average lot size of single family dwelling units.

7. Of course, these variables vary among metropolitan areas as well; but this cross sectional variation is relatively small compared to the changes in their magnitudes over time.

8. Because most new development occurs on vacant land, the price of vacant

land rather than occupied land is of primary importance in influencing the density of new development. The theoretical link between city size and land rents was developed to explain developed land rents. However, undeveloped land prices are likely to be closely correlated to developed land prices because of greater speculative demand in large cities.

9. Our earlier study, "An Historical Model of Urban Form," presents a more detailed discussion of these alternative formulations. That study also reported the results of our efforts to use data on per capita income and per capita automobile registration to replace the time period proxy. Since these formulations are not used in this study as data for estimating density functions, the results are not discussed here.

10. For example, Sherman Maisel determined that in San Francisco–Oakland Bay area average lot size has tended to increase in the postwar period, and he suggested that this trend might accelerate in the future. Sherman Maisel, "Background Information on Costs of Land for Single Family Housing," *Report on Housing in California* (San Francisco: April 1963), Appendix pp. 221–82.

11. The choice of 100,000 dwelling units is completely arbitrary. Only the intercepts of the graphs are affected by the level of the city size variable.

12. In addition to the inflection point corresponding to the introduction of the automobile and the postwar topping out, Figure 11–2 illustrates a number of other historical phenomena that are discussed in our earlier study. For example, the effects of controls during World War II are clearly evident from the sharp decline in S^* during 1940–1944.

13. This "concentric circle" model of urban growth is hardly novel, having been suggested by Burgess many years ago. Robert E. Park and Ernest W. Burgess, eds., *The City* (Chicago: University of Chicago Press, 1925).

14. The parameters were estimated by ordinary least squares using the natural log of gross density as the dependent variable, following Muth's estimation procedure.

15. These other density function estimates were obtained from the following sources: Muth, *Cities and Housing*, p. 142; Mills, "Urban Density Functions," p. 10; and James Barr, "Transportation Costs, Rent, and Intraurban Location" (Working paper, Washington University, St. Louis, November 10, 1970), pp. 44–5. We wish to thank James Barr for making his unpublished estimates available to us.

    None of these three other estimates of metropolitan density functions can be considered "correct" in any final sense. Muth's and Barr's estimates are based on samples of 25 central city census tracts. The technique used by Mills to estimate density functions is ingenious, but it is based on two sample points for each city.

16. The parameters of this function were estimated omitting the pre–1880 period observation, and thus are based on three observations. The

pre–1879 observation is somewhat suspect in young cities such as Denver which had relatively little development by 1880. Inclusion of this earliest observation has almost no effect on the 1960 estimates (the estimated gradient only changes from –0.25 to –0.26). But the 1910 function is probably more accurately estimated with the early observation omitted.

17. We wish to thank Edwin Mills for providing us with the data he used to estimate his Denver density functions.

18. See *Denver Municipal Facts*, vol. IV. no. 9, March 2, 1912, p. 8–9. (Denver, Co.: the City of Denver, Co., 1912).

19. See East Denver Park District, *Information Concerning the Issue of Bonds of the City and County of Denver*, 1912 (Denver, Co.; the City of Denver, 1912).

20. Actually Muth's analysis for Denver seems to confirm our estimates; his 1950 estimate is virtually identical to our estimate for 1950. Unfortunately, Barr did not include Denver in his analysis. Therefore, we have no 1960 estimate using the Muth technique.

21. This percentage suffers from several inadequacies as a measure of urban spatial structure. The measure is not very useful in comparing various urban areas since it depends so heavily on the happenstance of central city boundaries. For one city, the measure may be misleading as a reflection of differences over time because of "suburban style" areas within the central city and concentrated employment "city" areas in the suburbs. Still, the percent of the total urban population living outside the central city is a useful indication of changes over time in the relative numerical importance of central city and suburban districts.

22. Studies prepared by Chicago planning agencies, particularly the 1943 "Master Plan of Residential Land Use of Chicago," are the major references for our estimates. Homer Hoyt's 1933 study, *One Hundred Years of Land Values in Chicago*, was an additional reference for early development. (Chicago: University of Chicago Press, 1933).

23. Estimates of average lot sizes in each time period were derived from data on lot sizes by structure types obtained from a number of local Chicago sources (Appendix B Table B–2), while the mix of units by structure type in each time period was derived from the 1940, 1950, and 1960 censuses of housing (Appendix B Table B–3).

24. Time series land use data for the city of Chicago indicates that residential development accounted for a smaller fraction of developed land in 1900 than for land developed after 1900. (See Appendix B Table B–4) Since 1923, however, the share of developed land devoted to residential purposes in Chicago has been quite constant, ranging from 32 percent in 1941 to 36 percent in 1936. The relatively low share of developed land accounted for by residential use in the early surveys reflects the large share of developed land devoted to roads and highways during these periods. Of course, these land use figures

exclude vacant land and indicate nothing about the density of development in suburban areas.

25. In some instances, data for a number of census tracts had to be combined to make the data comparable for all three census years.

26. E. F. R. Hearle and J. H. Niedercorn, *The Impact of Urban Renewal on Land Use* (The Rand Corporation, RM–4186–RC, June 1964).

Chapter Twelve

Measuring the Value of Housing Quality

1. Chester Rapkin, "Price Discrimination Against Negroes in the Rental Housing Market," in *Essays in Urban Land Economics* (Los Angeles: Real Estate Research Program, University of California, 1966) pp. 333–45.

2. John F. Kain, "Effect of Housing Market Segregation on Urban Development," *1969 Conference Proceedings* (Chicago: United States Savings and Loan League, May 1969), pp. 7–9; Richard Muth, "The Variation of Population Density and its Components in South Chicago," *Papers and Proceedings of the Regional Science Association* 15 (1965): 173–83; Hugh O. Nourse, "The Effect of Air Pollution on House Values," *Land Economics* 43 (1967): 181–9; Wallace E. Oates, "The Effects of Property Taxes and Property Values: An Empirical Study of Tax Capitalization and the Tiebout Hypothesis," *Journal of Political Economy* 77 (1969): 957–71; W. C. Pendleton, "The Value of Highway Accessibility" (Ph.D. dissertation, Department of Economics, University of Chicago, 1962).

3. John F. Kain and John M. Quigley, "Evaluating the Quality of the Residential Environment," *Environment and Planning* 2 (1969).

4. Martin J. Bailey and Richard F. Muth, "A Regression Method for Real Estate Price Index Construction," *Journal of the American Statistical Association* 58 (1963): 933–42; Zvi Griliches, "Hedonic Price Indexes Revisisted: Some Notes on the State of the Art," *1967 Business and Economics Statistics Section Proceedings of the American Statistical Association* 1967.

5. John C. Musgrave, "The Measurement of Price Changes in Construction," *Journal of the American Statistical Association* 64 (1969): 771–86.

6. The sample consisted of 1,526 household addresses selected randomly within the city. Of the sample, 205 units were vacant; nonresponses and refusals further reduced the sample size to 1,103. The sample design and selected tabulations of the raw data are discussed in Ronald G. Ridker and John A. Henning, "The Determinants of Residential Property Values with Special References to Air Pollution," *The Review of Economics and Statistics* 49 (1967): 246–57.

7. In designing the survey we considered and rejected the technique developed

by the Committee on the Hygiene of Housing of the American Public Health Association. The APHA technique, used in many cities, involves a field survey of individual dwelling units. Many items are recorded for each dwelling and penalty scores are assigned to each item which falls below a certain standard. These penalty points are then summed to obtain a "dwelling score," which represents the overall quality of the dwelling. (See American Public Health Association Committee on the Hygiene of Housing, *An Appraisal Method for Measuring The Quality of Housing*, part 1 [New York: 1945]).

8. Each sample was located within the appropriate public school district, and the average eighth grade math achievement score for the public school servicing that district was recorded. This exam, given to all public school students in the eighth grade, measures student performance in school year equivalents.

   The police department in the city of St. Louis maintains crime statistics for small geographical areas of approximately equal size. Sample dwelling units were matched with these areas, known as "Pauley Blocks," and the number of major crimes (felonies) reported for each was used as the index of criminal activity.

9. Richard F. Muth, *Cities and Housing* (Chicago: University of Chicago Press, 1969); George Sternlieb, *The Tenement Landlord* (New Brunswick, N.J.: Urban Studies Center, Rutgers University, 1966).

10. Robert A. Haugen and Jones A. Heins, "A Market Separation Theory of Rent Differentials in Metropolitan Areas," *Quarterly Journal of Economics*, November 1969, pp. 660–72; Muth, *Cities and Housing*; Muth, "The Variation of Population Density"; Rapkin, "Price Discrimination Against Negroes"; Ridker and Henning, "The Determinant of Residential Property Values."

11. Kain, "Effect of Housing Market Segregation."

12. Chapter Seven of this book.

13. An employment accessibility index (based on auto driving times), obtained from the East-West Gateway Transportation Study, was also used with no better results.

14. William Alonso, *Location and Land Use* (Cambridge, Mass.: Harvard University Press, 1964); R. N. S. Harris, G. S. Tolley and C. Harrell, "The Residence Site Choice," *Review of Economics and Statistics*, 50 (1968) 241–7. Edgar M. Hoover and Raymond Vernon, *Anatomy of a Metropolis* (Cambridge, Mass.: Harvard University Press, 1959); Chapter One of this book; Edwin S. Mills, "An Aggregative Model of Resource Allocation in a Metropolitan Area," *American Economic Review* May 1967, pp. 197–211; Muth, *Cities and Housing;* Muth, "Economic Change and Rural-Urban Conversions," *Econometrica* 29 (1961): 1–23; Lowdon Wingo, Jr., *Transportation and Urban Land* (Washington, D.C.: Resources for the Future, 1961).

15. Oates, "Effects of Property Taxes."

16. Eric A. Hanushek and John F. Kain, "On the Value of Equality of

Educational Opportunity as a Guide to Public Policy," in Frederick Mosteller and Daniel P. Moynihan, eds., *On Equality of Educational Opportunity* (New York: Random House, 1970).

17. As in the previous models, several auto accessibility indexes were tested with results no better than those reported above.

18. Further analysis and discussion of this interrelationship is contained in Kain and Quigley, "Evaluating the Quality of the Residential Environment."

Chapter Thirteen

A Sample Model of Housing Production

1. Perhaps the most unguarded statement of this view is contained in a paper by Edgar O. Olsen entitled "A Competitive Theory of the Housing Market," *The American Economic Review* LIX, no. 4, part 1 (September 1969): 612–22. This approach is also followed in Richard Muth, *Cities and Housing* (Chicago: University of Chicago Press, 1969).

2. John F. Kain and John M. Quigley, *Housing Markets and Racial Discrimination: A Microeconomic Analysis* (New York: National Bureau of Economic Research 1975); Mahlon Straszheim, *An Econometric Analysis of the Urban Housing Market* (New York: National Bureau of Economic Research, 1972); John M. Quigley, "Residential Location: Multiple Workplaces and a Heterogeneous Housing Stock" (Ph.D. dissertation, Harvard University, 1972); Gregory K. Ingram, John F. Kain, and J. Royce Ginn, *The Detroit Prototype of the NBER Urban Simulation Model* (New York: The National Bureau of Economic Research, 1972), chapter 8; William Apgar and John F. Kain, "Neighborhood Attributes and the Residential Price Geography of Urban Areas" (Paper presented at the winter meetings of the Econometric Society, Toronto, Canada, December 1972).

3. Fuller discussions of these questions are presented in Chapter 10 and in Kain and Quigley, *Discrimination and a Heterogeneous Housing Stock*.

4. Neighborhood attributes, though associated with a particular location, are treated as part of the definition of housing bundles. Location in the sense used here refers to pure location or accessibility considerations.

5. To simplify the analysis, we consider only two kinds of structure outputs of the same generic type: outputs that can be ordered in terms of larger or smaller quantities of structure services. In fact, our view of housing markets emphasizes that, in general, structure services cannot be ordered in this way. Individual housing consumers can

always provide a unique ordering of their preferences for all kinds of structure services within neighborhoods or for all housing bundles, but these preferences cannot be combined to produce a unique aggregate ordering. Similarly, the production relationships employed assume that each quantity of structure services can be produced using either type of specific structure capital available at the beginning of the period. In real housing markets this condition will often not hold, except in the sense that any structure output can be produced from any kind of structure capital and current outlays by demolishing the original structure and replacing it with a structure that is suitable for the production of the specific type of structure output.

6. Equation (13.2) defines an expression that is of immense importance to analyses of housing and market behavior and the production of housing services. It states the elementary result that the value of a piece of specific housing capital depends on the discounted present value of the difference in anticipated revenues and cost. Yet a surprising number of analyses of the abandonment problem appear to employ book values of the specific structure or even carrying charges in their analysis of landlord behavior.

7. For a discussion of the relations between individual decisions and aggregate outcomes, see Thomas C. Schelling, "On the Ecology of Micromotives," *The Public Interest,* no. 25 (Fall 1971); Idem "Models of Segregation," (Santa Monica, Cal.: The Rand Corporation, Memorandum RM–6014–RC, May 1969); "A Process of Residential Segregation: Neighborhood," in Anthony H. Pascal, ed., *Racial Discrimination in Economic Life,* (Lexington, Mass.: Lexington Books, 1972).

8. For example, rehabilitation could be represented as an increase in the stock of physical capital in a structure and/or as a change in structure type. The productive functions could be altered to require minimum stocks of physical capital for the production of certain structure service levels.

Chapter Fourteen

What Should America's Housing Policies Be?

1. Henry Aaron estimated that the subsidy to homeowners was at least $7 billion in 1966, with only 8 percent of this subsidy accruing to households with incomes below $5,000 a year. *Shelter and Subsidies: Who Benefits From Federal Housing Policy* (Washington, D.C.: The Brookings Institution, 1972). The report of the National Housing Policy Review concluded that the full cost of federal

intervention in the housing market in 1972 was at least $14 to $15 billion. *Housing in the Seventies*, (U.S. Department of Housing and Urban Development, Washington, D.C.: U.S. Government Printing Office, 1973). Of this total only $2.5 billion was for direct housing subsidy programs. Of the remainder, $6.2 billion was homeowners income deductions, $3 to 4 billion was for other taxes foregone, particularly capital gains on home sales, and $2.6 billion was federal welfare assistance payments for housing.

2. This impression is supported by the president's October 1973 message on housing in which he stated, "our principal efforts should be directed toward determining whether a policy of direct cost assistance—with first priority on the elderly poor—can be put into practical operation," (U.S. National Archives and Record Service, Federal Register Office, *The Weekly Compilation of Presidential Documents*, vol. 9, no. 38, p. 1148, September 1973). "The President's Message to the Congress on Housing Policy" September 19, 1973.

3. See Robert F. Gillingham, "Place to Place Rent Comparisons Using Hedonic Quality Adjustment Techniques," research discussion paper no. 7, March 1973 (Washington, D.C.: U.S. Bureau of Labor Statistics, Research Division, Office of Prices and Living Conditions, 1973); Victoria Lapham, "Do Blacks Pay More for Housing?" *Journal of Political Economy* 81, no. 3 (May-June 1973): 590–607; Chester Rapkin and William G. Grigsby, *The Demand for Housing in Racially Mixed Areas* (Berkeley, Cal.: University of California Press, 1960); Chester Rapkin and William G. Grigsby, "Price Discrimination Against Negroes in the Rental Housing Market," in *Essays in Urban Land Economics* edited by University of California at Los Angeles, Real Estate Research Program (Los Angeles: University of California, 1966); M. Stengel, "Price Discrimination in the Urban Rental Housing Market" (Ph.D. dissertation, Harvard University, May 1970); Chapter Seven of this book.

4. See Robert A. Haugen and A. Jones Heins, "A Market Separation Theory of Rent Differentials in Metropolitan Areas," *Quarterly Journal of Economics* LXXXIII (November 1969): 660–672; and Ann Schnare, "An Empirical Analysis of the Dimensions of Neighborhood Quality" (Ph.D. dissertation, Harvard University, May 1974).

5. See Mahlon Strasheim, *An Econometric Analysis of the Urban Housing Market* (New York: National Bureau of Economic Research, 1975 processed); William J. Apgar, Jr. and John F. Kain, "Neighborhood Attributes and the Residential Price Geography of Urban Areas" (Paper presented at the winter meetings of The Econometric Society, Toronto, Ontario, Canada, December 28–30, 1972); John F. Kain and John M. Quigley, *Housing Markets and Racial Discrimination: A Microeconomic Analysis* (New York: National Bureau of Economic Research, 1975).

6. See Chapter Twelve.

7. John F. Kain and John M. Quigley, *Housing Markets and Racial Discrimination.*

8. Ibid.

9. See Chapter Seven.

10. See U.S., Commission on Civil Rights, *Racial Isolation in the Public Schools*, vol. 1 (Washington, D.C.: U.S. Government Printing Office, 1967); and Eric Hanushek. *Education and Race An Analysis of the Educational Production Process* (Lexington, Mass.: Lexington Books, 1972).

11. William Holshouser, Keith Moore, Richard Santner, and Robert Schafer, *Spatial Variations in the Operating Costs of Rental Housing Within the Boston Metropolitan Area* (Cambridge, Mass.: Harvard University Press, 1972).

12. Such a policy may raise some significant constitutional issues. The evidence of the effects of discrimination on black homeownership and black housing consumption, however, might justify a remedial program of this kind.

13. See David H. Karlen, *Racial Integration and Property Values in Chicago*, Urban Economics Report no. 7 (Chicago: University of Chicago, 1968 processed); Donald Phares, "Racial Change and Housing Values: Transition in an Inner Suburb," *Social Science Quarterly*, December 1971; Jospeh P. McKenna and Herbert D. Werner, "The Housing Market in Integrating Areas," *The Annals of Regional Science* IV, no. 2 (December 1970).

14. See Paul B. Sheatsley, "White Attitudes Toward the Negro," in John F. Kain, ed. *Race and Poverty: The Economics of Discrimination*. (Englewood Cliffs, N.J.: Prentice-Hall, 1969).

Chapter Fifteen

Comparative Costs of Alternative Urban Transport Technologies

1. For a detailed discussion of the costing procedures and assumptions, see Meyer, Kain, and Wohl, *The Urban Transportation Problem*, Cambridge, Mass.: (Harvard University Press, 1965), chapter 8, "Costing Procedures and Assumptions," pp. 171–196.

2. Ibid, chapter 9, "Line-Haul Systems," pp. 196–250. Costs for the high density area are based on a gradient of average net residential density by distance from the CBD for Chicago. The medium density area costs are based on a net residential density gradient for Pittsburgh.

3. It is in a sense unfair to include parking charges in line haul cost comparisons between automobiles and transit systems. Parking charges incorporate some of the costs that would be associated with downtown collection and distribution, and such costs have not been included in the public transit system line haul analysis.

4. Hyman Joseph, "Construction Costs of Urban Expressways," *CATS Research News* 4, no. 1 (December 19, 1960) for a more complete

discussion of these problems see Meyer, Kain, and Woh., *The Urban Transportation Problem* pp. 200–208.

5. The base and paving costs are assumed to be $86,000 per lane mile. For a discussion of sources and assumptions, see Ibid., p. 204.

6. For a discussion of sources and methods used in deriving these percentages, see Ibid., pp. 204–207.

7. For a detailed discussion of the derivation of Equation (15.6), see Ibid., pp. 210–211.

8. Obtaining service equivalence for the alternative residential collection modes is even more difficult than for line haul modes. Both feeder buses and automobiles operate on the residential street system. Under these conditions buses cannot match the average trip speed of automobiles on the residential collection portion of the trip, and therefore cannot provide services of equal quality. To establish a modicum of service equivalence between feeder bus and automobile in the cost models, it is assumed that seats are provided for all passengers, bus stops are located so that passengers have to walk no more than two blocks, and feeder bus headways are no more than ten minutes. See Ibid., chapter 10, "Residential Collection and Distribution," pp. 250–269.

9. For a more complete discussion of the methods of estimating downtown distribution costs and the principal findings, see Ibid., chapter 11, "Downtown Distribution," pp. 269–309.

10. The number of downtown stations greatly affects the costs of the rail, and to an even greater extent bus, subway modes because station costs are very high. See Ibid., pp. 283–285.

11. The San Francisco Bay area is an excellent example. BART is a 75 mile system paralleling almost exactly parts of the existing expressway network. The system had a capital cost in excess of $2 billion, yet it serves only three of the nine bay area counties. A bus rapid transit system using existing freeways could provide rapid transit services to all nine counties.

Chapter Sixteen

How to Improve Urban Transportation at Practically No Cost

1. This chapter is adapted from testimony presented to the hearings of the Joint Economic Committee Subcommittee on Economy in Government, U.S. Congress, May 6th, 1970. The author is grateful to the editors of *Public Policy*, in which this study first appeared, for their encouragement and suggestions in revising and extending that testimony; Gary Fauth for his many helpful suggestions, and to the Office of Economic Research of the Economic Development

Administration, Department of Commerce, for its research support.

2. Even when they are retained to help pay for new projects, tolls are almost never increased. Therefore, inflation produces large decreases in real price over the life of the facility.

3. Ministry of Transport, *Road Pricing: The Economics and Technical Possibilities* (London: Her Majesty's Stationery Office, 1964); William Vickrey, "Pricing as a Tool in Coordination of Local Transportation," in *Transportation Economics* (New York: National Bureau of Economic Research, 1965), pp. 275–279.

4. J. M. Thomson, "An Evaluation of Two Proposals for Traffic Restraint in Central London," *Journal of the Royal Statistical Society* CXXX, series A, part 3 (1967): 327–367.

5. Unfortunately, none of these conditions are satisfied by urban street and road systems. Even under these restricted conditions, it is possible to think of other criteria that would give different results for example "minimum travel time on a particularly facility," or "minimum door to door travel time," These alternative criteria appear at first glance equally plausible, as tractable analytically, and no less arbitrary.

6. This discussion deals with passenger travel only. In actual practice, consideration would have to be given to the use of urban highways by trucks and other noncommuting vehicles. Since this discussion is concerned primarily with peak hour conditions, when passenger travel represents the overwhelming share of all highway use, this important complication can be ignored for the purposes of this discussion.

7. This assumes that the benefits from making a particular trip at a particular time and the benefits from travel time savings are not too dissimilar between car and bus passengers.

8. Actually, because of the instability of traffic flow at volumes near "capacity," volumes on congested expressways may be much lower than those consistent with higher speeds. Highway engineers have devoted a great deal of attention to the avoidance of this instability. Their object, however, is always to maximize vehicles' capacity.

9. Good summaries of the evidence are presented in Robert G. McGillivary, "Demand and Choice Models of Modal Split," *Journal of Transport Economics and Policy* IV (May 1970): 192–207; and in D. A. Quarmby, "Choice of Travel Mode for the Journey to Work," *Journal of Transport Economics and Policy* (September 1967): 273–314.

10. A somewhat more elaborate analysis of these trade-offs and their relation to modal choice is presented in C. H. Sharp, "The Choice between Cars and Buses on Urban Roads," *Journal of Transport Economics and Policy* I (January 1967): 104–111.

11. John R. Meyer, John F. Kain, and Martin Wohl, *The Urban Transportation Problem* (Cambridge, Mass.: Harvard University Press, 1965).

12. John C. Glennon and Vergil G. Stover, "A System to Facilitate Bus Rapid

Transit on Urban Freeways" (Final Report on Contract No. H–807, Urban Mass Transportation Administration, U.S. Department of Transportation, December 1968).

13. Vergil G. Stover and John C. Glennon, "A System for Bus Rapid Transit on Urban Freeways," *Traffic Quarterly* (October 1969), p. 474.

14. It should be emphasized that these estimates are for "bare" systems. They include the cost of installing and operating the needed freeway surveillance and control equipment and making necessary modifications to the expressway, but include no provision for stations or terminals. Although these extras are not essential to the concept, some capital outlays for these purposes might be desirable. It should also be pointed out, however, that not all the benefits of the system accrue to transit users. Indeed it appears that the system would be justified in many urban areas even if no express buses used the facility.

15. John R. Meyer, John F. Kain, and Martin Wohl, *Technology and Urban Transportation* (Washington, D.C.: Executive Office of the President, Office of Science and Technology, June 1962).

16. An excellent survey of these studies and projects is presented in Alan M. Voorhees and Assoc., Inc., et al., *An Analysis of Urban Highway Public Transportation Facility Needs* (prepared for the Federal Highway Administration, Department of Transportation, Washington, D.C.: November 1971), vols. I and II.

17. Ibid., vol. I, pp. 51, 52.

18. It should be emphasized that a large number of U.S. cities would provide a more fertile ground for a test of the expressway rapid transit concept than Minneapolis. Only two or three of the list of 20 cities shown in Table 16–4 would be less promising.

19. This would permit full instrumentation and control of up to 250 miles of urban expressway for a five year period. Only the Boston, Chicago, Los Angeles, New York and San Francisco–Oakland metropolitan area would cost approximately 55 million dollars. The cost estimates for the Minneapolis project suggest that the Glennon and Stover cost estimates may be somewhat low. but not seriously so.

20. The comparison is still more favorable, since this $50 million buys a system with two to three times as many rapid transit route miles as the BART system.

Chapter Seventeen

Transportation and Poverty

1. This chapter summarizes a conference on transportation and poverty, Held June 7, 1968 which was organized and chaired by the authors. The conference was sponsored by the American Academy of Arts and Sciences, and financed by the Department of Housing and Urban

Development and by the Bureau of Public Roads of the Department of Transportation.

2. California Governor's Commission on the Los Angeles Riots, *Violence in the City—An End or a Beginning?* (Los Angeles: 1965), p. 65.

3. Harold Kassoff and Harold Deutschman, "People, Jobs, and Transportation: A Profile of Low Income Households in the Tri-State Regions" (Paper presented at the Conference on Transportation and Poverty, American Academy of Arts and Sciences, June 7, 1968).

4. William F. Hamilton, "Transportation Innovations and Job Accessibility" (Paper presented at the Conference on Transportation and Poverty, American Academy of Arts and Sciences, June 7, 1968).

5. Harold Kassoff and Harold Deutschman, "People, Jobs, and Transportation."

6. Peter B. Doeringer, "Ghetto Labor Markets—Problems and Programs" (Paper presented at the Conference on Transportation and Poverty, American Academy of Arts and Sciences, June 7, 1968).

7. Thomas H. Floyd, "Using Transportation to Alleviate Poverty: Progress Report on Experiments under the Mass Transportation Act" (Paper presented at the Conference on Transportation and Poverty, June 7, 1968), p. 17.

8. Martin Wohl, "Users of Urban Transportation Services and Their Income Circumstances" (Paper presented at the Conference on Transportation and Poverty, American Academy of Arts and Sciences, June 7, 1968).

9. Ibid.

10. Phillip B. Herr and Aaron Fleisher, "The Mobility of the Poor" (Paper presented at the Conference on Transportation and Poverty, American Academy of Arts and Sciences, June 7, 1968).

11. Gordon Fellman and Roger Rosenblatt, "The Social Costs of an Urban Highway: Cambridge and the Inner Belt" (Paper presented at the Conference on Transportation and Poverty, American Academy of Arts and Sciences, June 7, 1968).

12. Gerald Kraft and Thomas A. Domencich, "Free Transit" (Paper presented at the Conference on Transportation and Poverty, June 7, 1968).

13. Ibid.

14. Ibid.

15. Hamilton, "Transportation Innovations"; Herr and Fleisher, "Mobility of the Poor"; Sumner Myers, "Personal Transportation for the Poor" (Paper presented at the Conference on Transportation and Poverty, American Academy of Arts and Sciences, June 7, 1968).

16. Myers, "Personal Transportation."

17. Ibid.

18. Ibid.

19. Floyd, "Using Transportation"; and Myers, "Personal Transportation."

20. Sandra Rosenbloom, "Taxis, Jitneys and Poverty" (Paper presented at the Conference on Transportation and Poverty, American Academy of Arts and Sciences, June 7, 1968).

21. Ibid.
22. Ibid.

Appendix A

1. J. P. Shelton, "The Cost of Renting Versus Owning a Home."
2. U.S. Federal Housing Administration, *FHA Homes, 1967, Data for States and Selected Areas on Characteristics of FHA Operations Under Section 203.* (Washington, D.C.: F.H.A., Division of Research and Statistics, Statistics Section, 1967).
3. Recent tabulations from the Survey of Economic Opportunity on the asset and liability position of Negro and white families by income group show that home equities account for an even greater share of Negro than white wealth. For example, these data indicate that white families with incomes between $5,000 and $7,499 have a net worth of $12,556 as compared with a net worth of $3,636 for Negro families in the same income class. Despite the fact that Negroes at each income level are less likely to be homeowners, housing equity represents 67 percent of this smaller Negro net worth as compared to 40 percent of that of white families.

Although the mean housing equity of Negro homeowners is smaller than that of white homeowners, $7,344 vs. $11,753, the difference in Negro net worth is not to any significant degree attributable to this difference. Rather, it results from the fact that at each income level a smaller proportion of Negroes than whites are homeowners and even more importantly from the fact that the discrepancy in Negro and white ownership of other assets is even larger than the discrepancy in homeownership. Thus, if the Survey of Economic Opportunity data on assets are to be believed, Negroes in the income class $5,000–$7,499 have net worth in nonhousing assets equal to only 16 percent of that of white households in the same income level, and all Negroes have net worth in nonhousing assets equal to only 9 percent of that of all whites. Of course, these results can be considered as suggestive only. The weaknesses of savings and wealth data are notorious, and the interpretation of these differences, if real, would require a complete theory of Negro and white savings behavior, which encompasses the manner in which discrimination or lack of opportunity in the various markets affects the savings behavior of Negro households. The authors wish to thank Andrew Brimmer and Henry S. Terrell for making these unpublished tabulations available to them.

Index

Aaron, 354
abandonment: concept of, 288
Alonso, William, 2, 6; model pioneer, 25; residential space, 31
Atlanta: rapid transit, 5
automobile: and move from CBD, 80; ownership trend, 3' range of and consumer choices, 10; role in Detroit residence/workspace model, 68, 69; travel system, 310; and urban spatial structure, 239

Barr, James, 245–248
BART, 5, 334, 335
BBURG (Boston Banks Urban Renewal Group), 301
Becker, Gary, 141
blacks: employment data, 184–189; employment dispersal, 157; ghetto unemployment, 113; homeownership, 213; housing market, 15; job access, 341; migration, 206; mortgage loan program, 300; neighborhood entry, 142; patterns of homeownership, 167; price of racism, 294; self segregation, 136; in suburbs, 194; welfare, 291
Boston: free transportation, 349; population, 91; rapid transit, 4; urban form, 235
Brown, H. James, 11

capital depreciation, 281
CBD (Central Business District): and commuters, 57; jobs beyond, 342; and location rents, 9; and residence rings, 46; traffic policy, 327; trends, 13; and work trips, 37
central city: and employment analyzed by

industry, 88; construction trend, 84; decay, 79; ghetto expansion, 200; government as employer, 105; growth, 93; in model, 120; Philadelphia forecasts, 100; poverty and ghettos, 155; residential services, 159; social cost of ghetto, 302; tax base and population density, 113; trend development, 13; vacant land absorption, 127
Chicago, 12; black employment, 17; CBD, 146; density and choice, 60–62; density functions, 256; ghetto housing supply, 169; highway construction, 313; homeownership rate, 172; overview of poverty and blacks, 155; population, 91; racial segregation, 144; rapid transit, 4; segregation overview, 176; workspace and location, 54–57
Clark, Colin, 233
Cleveland: rapid transit, 5
Cohen, B., 106; –and Roger Noll, 105
Commission on Civil Rights, 203
commuters: bus transit system, 334, 335; cost from racism, 297; cost/rent ratio, 7; and density, 242; discrimination and blacks, 149; high income whites, 194; time valuation, 55
construction: and displacement, 348; dwelling density, 257; housing production, 284; housing supply, 139; Los Angelos, 235; nonresidential urban renewal, 114; and price ceiling, 144; and profit maximization, 229; quality, 264; rail and highway, 314, 315; suburbanization trend, 82, 83
consumers: housing pricing, 278; role of in theories, 20; in simulation model, 215

Creamer, D., 81; and Woodbury, C., 13

Dallas, 91
decisionmaking: transportation planners,
  328; worker components, 66
Delaware Valley Planning Commission,
  92–102
deLeeuw, F., 26
density: in Alonso, Muth, Wingo theories,
  8; function by Mills for Denver, 251;
  incremental residential, 236; in Kain
  and Harrison, 22; and location rent, 138;
  and transportation, 58; and urban
  spatial structure, 21, 234
Denver: density function, 251; rapid
  transit, 5
Detroit: CBD, 146; data and methodology,
  68; location rents and CBD, 51; occupation and residence, 39; proposed freeway rapid transit, 337; residential
  location, 36; segregation, 144, 175; workspace and commuters, 54–56
discrimination: black purchase probability,
  166–168; costs, 294; government priority,
  5; and homeownership, 163; housing
  quality, 269; market imperfection, 51;
  markup, 141; in NBER model, 231;
  overview, 133
downgrading: concept, 55
Dresch, S., 11

education, 204
employment: analyzed by Ganz and
  O'Brien, 110; black distribution, 176;
  black workplace zones, 184; dispersal
  data, 84, 186; distribution projection,
  98; effect of housing segregation, 201;
  equilibrium, 124; geographic location
  data, 12; location and industry, 86–89;
  redistribution, 130; and space consumption pattern, 47; trend in CBD, 94

family: life cycle and homeownership, 162
Federal Housing Authority, 146
federal income tax, 172; homeownership,
  296
"filtering," concept of, 292
Floyd, Thomas, 346
Fredland, Daniel, 164
freeways, 329, 336

Ganz, Alex and O'Brien, T., 105, 108
ghetto: black workplace zones, 181; discount and services, concept of, 154;
  economic development, 18; "gilding,"
  205, 209; as government priority, 5;

growth in Chicago, 96; heavy commuting cost, 136; location rent, 140;
  price discrimination, 161; pricing in
  Quigley and Kain, 295; public services,
  272; schools, 204; "suburbs," concept
  of, 155
Glennon, J.C. and Stover, V.G., 336
government: central city decay, 79; and
  construction trend, 82, 83; employment in central city, 105; housing policy,
  297; low income subsidy, 292; Minneapolis grant, 337; minority mortgage loan
  program, 300; open occupancy laws,
  137; policy paper, 190; priorities, 5;
  transportation experiments, 18

Haig, Robert Murray, 2
Harrison, Bennett, 18, 194, 195
Harrison, David, 21
Hartwick, J.M. and P.G., 26
Hearle, Edward and Niedercorn, John,
  258
Henning, J.A., 261
highways: construction cost, 313; residential collection, 321; system development,
  4
Hilliard, Raymond, 187
homeownership: analysis, 162; black
  access, 296; rates, 16; in Shelton, 353;
  and tax structure, 173
Hoover, E. and Vernon, R., 12
housing: allowance program, 299; concept of "abandonment," 283; cost
  location, 8; discrimination, 16; durability, 153; effect of subsidy, 293;
  extent of racial discrimination, 291; low
  income, 203; market discrimination, 133,
  168, 191; market price, 219; output
  factors, 277; production in Kain and
  Ingram, 22; production and NBER
  model, 225, 226; quality, 261; quantity/
  quality index, 276; role of family size,
  74; and services, 49; simulation model,
  215; tenure, 164; and travel behavior, 54
Houston, 91, 155; homeownership rate,
  172

income: and black concentration, 135;
  distribution and transportation policy,
  346; guaranteed, 206; and home ownership, 163; residential and location, 7;
  role in choice, 74; and substitution
  effect, 49; and urban mobility, 347
Ingram, G.K., 221, 230

James, Franklin, Jr., 26, 111

Joseph, Hyman, 313

Kain, J.F., 11; transportation decentralization/suboptimization, 329
Kemper, P., 26
Kerner Commission, 19
King, A.T., 26

labor force: composition, 180
land use: planning methodology, 4; quantity and quality index, 275
Leone, R., 26
line haul: and rail transit, 321
London, 327
Los Angelos, 155; homeownership rate, 172; transit, 341; urban form, 235
Lowry, I.S., 3

McCone Commission, 341
McFadden, D., 26
manufacturing: black employment, 189; and raw material location, 121; and urban structure, 115
Masters, Stanley, 18, 193
methodology: demand analysis, 220; and density choice, 65; incremental residential density, 236; linear programming and NBER model, 228; measurement, 270; production function, 278; race variable and ownership analysis, 166; time series information, 103; for urban growth analysis, 118
Meyer, J.R., 11, 23; Wohl, M. and Kain, J.F., 330, 334
Mills, E., 12, 25; density functions, 245–248, 260; Denver development, 252; and Richard Muth, 233; optimization model, 26
model: consumer choice, 10; density functions, 260; for Detroit and Chicago, 178; elasticity, 73; Kain compared to Muth and Mills, 244; layering process, 233; metropolitan growth, 116, 120; partial equilibrium, 20; for racial discrimination, 138; residential collection, 316, 317; residential location and transportation cost, 29; role of, 25; role in economic analysis, 25, 26; simulation, 213; workplace and choice, 65
Mooney, Joseph, 18, 191, 192
Moses, L., 12
Musgrave, John C., 262
Muth, Richard, 2, 6, 261; density functions, 245–248; model pioneer, 25

National Housing Policy Review, 291

National Rural Electric Cooperative Association, 207
NBER (National Burueau of Economic Research) model, 214; and disequilibrium, 224; market clearing and price determination, 228; theory of demand, 219
Negro American. *See* Blacks.
neighborhoods, 141; black entry, 301; in Pittsburgh, 230; quality, 268, 278; structure services, 198; white mobility, 191
Newark: in Ganz and O'Brien, 108
New York City: population, 91; rapid transit, 4
Niedercorn, J.: and Kain, F.F., 12
Noll, Roger, 18, 191; role of central city, 107

Oates, W.E., 261
occupation: and resident location, 38–43
Offner, Paul and Saks, D.H., 18, 195

Pendleton, W.C., 261
Persky, J.: and Kain, J.F., 19
Philadelphia: Delaware Valley Planning Commission, 12; in work of Fredland, 164; land use forecast, 99; population, 91
Pittsburgh: and NBER model, 230; in work of Quigley, 20
policy: access provision, 303; black residential choice, 158; highway operations, 339; and trend reversal, 112; and use of models, 213
population: density gradient, 242, 243; density and travel system, 311; dispersal, 85; ghetto dispersal strategy, 209; in major cities, 91; and manufacturing employment, 127
poverty: and ghetto, 155; social disorganization, 202; and substandard housing, 293; and transportation, 341; and workplace transit, 345
production: model, 277

Quigley, J.M., 20, 26

rapid transit: bus system, 331; bus system in work of Meyer, Wohl, and Kain, 334, 337; and density, 58; and residential collection concept, 320; situation overview, 24
rent, 279; bundle and interdependence, 286; location, 54; structure life, 282
residential location: assumptions, 32; black

supply restrictions, 167; and choice
components, 67; and density, 241; and
empirical analysis, 72, 73; empirical
testing, 35; and housing segregation,
152–156; individual and housing consumers, 221; integration and employment, 195; and occupation, 39; priority,
7; quality, 262; theory of, 9, 137; within
ghetto, 143
retailing, 116; in central city, 128
Ridgeway, James, 187
Ridker, R.G., 261

St. Louis: in Ganz and O'Brien, 108;
homeownership, 162; housing market
value, 168; in work of Kain and Quigley,
22; methodology, 262; supply restrictions, 170
San Diego, 91, 155
Schmenner, R., 26
Schnare, Ann, 26
"scrapping," concept of, 283, 289
Seattle: rapid transit, 5
segregation: and black unemployment,
25; effect on education opportunities,
296; extent, 133; housing and spatial
patterns, 146–152; residential in Kain,
195; and residential location model,
38; role, 15
service: advantage and travel mode, 318;
redistribution, 129; residential, 49, 270
Shelton, J.P., 353
Solow, R., 25
Straszheim, M., 26
Struy, R., 26
subsidy: federal transit, 4; and ghetto
housing, 201; to homeowner in tax
benefit, 354; production, 298; public
transit, 79; and social class, 291; transit
service, 339; urban transit, 346
suburbs: attraction, 46; and blacks, 134;
bussing, 205; and employment dispersal,
187; and employment dispersal by industry, 86–90; and employment redistribution, 130; growth in Denver, 254;
housing quality, 265; manufacturing, in,
97; move to decentralize, 80; move to
by New York City and Philadelphia
firms, 104; as a phenomenon, 2; population spurt, 156; residential collection,
37; supply restrictions, 170; transit to
jobs, 342; and workplace location, 17

Taeuber, Karl and Alma, 134
taxicabs, 350, 351
technology: and commuter overview, 23;
NBER model, 227; transportation, 309
tenants: and housing quality, 269
theory: assumption of workplace, 7;
central city manufacturing employment,
123; in Kain and Harrison, 21; place
of employment and population, 11;
of simulation model, 214
Thomson, J.M., 327
tolls, 326
traffic: innovations, 333; maximization
of flow concept, 330
transportation: bus system, 312; cost
analyses, 314, 316; cost of and workplace,
177; family size in Detroit, 52; intraurban, 239; line haul systems, 308,
309; and location rent function, 32, 33;
and low density housing, 152; overview,
23; in simulation model, 217; tolls, 325;
travel cost substitutions, 76; in urban
spatial structure theory, 8

UMTA (Urban Mass Transit Administration), 324
unemployment: and central city, 107;
government priority, 5; in Mooney, 193
upgrading: concept of, 55
urban spatial structure: and black housing,
146; and black ownership rate, 170, 171;
and central city, 94; competition, 229;
determinants, 5; family size and residence, 43; individual behavior, 224;
industry location, 12; organized by
industry, 89; and rapid transit, 62–
64; residential space, 31; in work
of Muth, 249

Washington, D.C.: rapid transit, 5
wholesaling, 116; gain in central city, 129
Wingo, L., 3, 6; model pioneer, 25;
residential space, 31
Wohl, M., 23
Woodbury, C., 81
workplace: dispersal and transit, 344; and
market disequilibrium, 54; role in residential location, 33–35; and space
preference, 44, 45; and transportation,
179; travel to in model, 69

About the Authors

John F. Kain is Professor of Economics at Harvard University and a member of the senior staff of the National Bureau of Economic Research, where he has primary responsibility for the development of the NBER Urban Simulation Model. His previous books include *The Urban Transportation Problem* (Harvard University Press, Cambridge, Mass., 1965) coauthored with John R. Meyer and Martin Wohl, *Race and Poverty: The Economics of Discrimination* (Prentice-Hall, Inc., Englewood Cliffs, N. J., 1969), and *The Detroit Prototype of the NBER Urban Simulation Model* (Columbia University Press, New York 1972) coauthored with Gregory K. Ingram and J. Royce Ginn.

John R. Meyer is 1907 Professor in Transportation, Logistics, and Distribution at Harvard University and President of the National Bureau of Economic Research. Professor Meyer is co-author with John F. Kain and Martin Wohl of *The Urban Transportation Problem* (Harvard University, Cambridge, Mass., 1965), co-author with M. J. Peck, J. Stenason, and C. J. Zwick of the *Economics of Competition in the Transportation Industry* (Harvard University Press, Cambridge, Mass., 1959), and numerous other books and articles.

David Harrison, Jr. is Assistant Professor of City Planning at Harvard University, where he teaches courses in applied economics and economics of the environment. Professor Harrison, who received his Ph.D. in Economics from Harvard University in 1974, is author of *Who Pays for Clean Air: The Cost and Benefit Distribution of Federal Automobile Emmission Standards* (Ballinger Publishing Company, Cambridge, Mass. 1975).

John M. Quigley is an Associate Professor of Economics at Yale University. He is co-author with John F. Kain of *Housing Markets and Racial Discrimination: A Microeconomic Analysis* to be published this spring by the

411

National Bureau of Economic Research as well as several articles on urban housing markets.

John H. Niedercorn is Professor of Economics at the University of Southern California. Before accepting his present position, Professor Niedercorn taught at California State University and was employed as a research economist for the RAND Corporation. He is author of several published papers on gravity models and the optimal distribution of income.

Joseph J. Persky is Associate Professor of Economics at the Chicago Circle Campus of the University of Illinois. Before accepting his present position in 1974, he taught at Fisk University and at the Birmingham Campus of the University of Alabama. He is author of several articles on southern economic development and migration.

Gregory K. Ingram is Associate Professor of Economics at Harvard University where he teaches courses in urban economics, transportation economics, and micro-analytic modeling. He is co-author with John F. Kain and J. Royce Ginn of *The Detroit Prototype of the NBER Urban Simulation Model* (New York: Columbia University Press, 1972). More recently he has been engaged in research on the relationships between transportation, urban development, and air quality. He was a principal author of the National Academy of Sciences report to the Senate Public Works Committee, *Air Quality and Automobile Emmission Control, Vol. 4: The Costs and Benefits of Automobile Emmission Control* and served as staff director of the study.